Core Concepts in
AMERICAN GOVERNMENT

Core Concepts in AMERICAN GOVERNMENT

Jeanne Zaino

Boston Columbus Indianapolis New York San Francisco Upper Saddle River
Amsterdam Cape Town Dubai London Madrid Milan Munich Paris Montreal Toronto
Delhi Mexico City Sao Paulo Sydney Hong Kong Seoul Singapore Taipei Tokyo

Executive Editor: Reid Hester
Director of Development: Eileen Calabro
Senior Development Editor: Lisa Sussman
Executive Marketing Manager: Wendy Gordon
Executive Digital Producer: Stefanie Snajder
Senior Digital Editor: Paul DeLuca
Digital Project Manager: Janell Lantana
Supplements Editor: Beverly Fong
Senior Media Producer: Paul DeLuca
Production Manager: Eric Jorgensen
Project Coordination, Text Design, and Electronic Page Makeup: PreMediaGlobal
Cover Designer/Manager: Wendy Ann Fredericks
Senior Manufacturing Buyer: Roy L. Pickering, Jr.
Printer/Binder: RR Donnelley & Sons / Crawfordsville
Cover Printer: Lehigh-Phoenix Color / Hagerstown

Credits and acknowledgments borrowed from other sources and reproduced, with permission, in this textbook appear on the appropriate page within text [or on page 315].

Library of Congress Cataloging-in-Publication Data

CIP information is on file with the Library of Congress.

10 9 8 7 6 5 4 3 2 1—DOC—14 13 12 11

www.pearsonhighered.com

Student ISBN 10: 0-136-04074-8
Student ISBN 13: 978-0-136-04074-3

Table of Contents

Chapter 2 Federalism 27

Chapter 11 American Public Policy 240

Preface

In "The Lure of the List," Lindsay Waters begins by asking "[w]ho doesn't find lists irresistible?" If the amount of "lists" we are inundated with is any indication, the answer is clear—very few.[1] From David Letterman's Top Ten to the FBI's Ten Most Wanted List, the American Film Institute's list of the Top 100 Films, the *New York Times* weekly rundown of best-selling books, Ryan Seacrest's Weekly Top 40, and historian's rankings of the Best and Worst American Presidents, we are flooded with lists and rankings on almost every topic imaginable. Much to the chagrin of some scholars, even the journal *Foreign Policy* jumped on the "list" bandwagon not long ago when it offered up its list of the world's top 100 public intellectuals.[2]

This book uses this fascination—and frustration—with lists as a means of teaching introductory students about the basics of American government and politics. To this end, we begin with the deceptively simple question: What are the most important things students should know about American government?

We posed this question to scholars working in various subfields of the discipline, and several took up the challenge and produced lists of the top ten concepts they think students should know about each topic area. They did this bravely, knowing that like all lists, theirs would be subject to discussion, criticism, and debate. Readers may disagree with what is included on the list, what is left off, the order of concepts, the presentation of material, and so on.

The notion of encouraging readers, particularly introductory students, to disagree with and question material in an introductory book is unconventional. It is also what makes this approach to teaching American government and this book as a whole unique: Students and faculty are invited to, indeed encouraged to, engage in the lists and then critique them and offer their own ideas. We may have missed something in the eyes of the reader or provided a ranking that is subject to wide debate. To that extent, unlike many introductory textbooks, this one is designed to be used as a starting point for discussion in the classroom and beyond. It is designed to encourage critical thinking among introductory students who we hope will not only be engaged by the approach but by the material and all the fascinating aspects of government and politics that have long attracted scholars, politicians, and casual observers alike.

NOTE TO THE INSTRUCTOR

I have used this somewhat unconventional approach to teach American government for years. I initially started using a top-ten approach as a result of my frustration in three areas. First, like many faculty I initially used large, hardcover introductory textbooks,

[1]Lindsay Waters, "The Lure of the List," *The Chronicle of Higher Education: The Chronicle Review*, May 26, 2006.

[2]"Top 100 Public Intellectuals," *Foreign Policy*, May 15, 2008, available online at: http://www.foreignpolicy.com/articles/2008/05/14/top_100_public_intellectuals (accessed June 26, 2011).

which were not only extremely expensive but became dated quickly. By asking students to spend the money, it was difficult to justify either (a) not using the book in its entirety or (b) asking them to buy additional texts, the ones I really wanted to assign and the ones I knew would engage them more than any text. If I had been able to forgo the expensive introductory text for the other, more engaging texts, I would have done it.

But like many faculty I was faced with a dilemma—abandoning textbooks often also means failing to provide students with basic information that is essential to understanding the more advanced concepts and engaging in the more challenging and difficult questions confronting students of American government today. This dilemma, the second source of my frustration, made it difficult to justify abandoning the expensive hardcover texts.

The third source of my frustration was the sense I had from students that when introductory books served as the major text in the course it made the substance of American government and politics less engaging and interesting to them. Despite rumors to the contrary, most students of this generation come to class excited to learn about politics and government, particularly current events and issues that impact their lives and the lives of their family and friends—the war in Afghanistan, the upcoming presidential election, the possibility of a draft, potential changes to student loan policies, the tensions between the judiciary and executive branches, the prospect of gay marriage, and the list goes on. Although students are interested in learning about current issues, however, most faculty agree students often lack the knowledge and background necessary to put this information into context.

When I couldn't locate a text or approach that served to address these problems, I began searching for a way to accomplish these goals on my own. After experimenting with different approaches, I stumbled on the method that forms the basis of this book: Present each major topic in the American government course as a series of "Top 10's" (e.g., the "Top 10 Most Important Things You Should Know About … the U.S. Congress, the presidency, the judiciary, political parties, elections, mass media, policymaking, etc.…).

Normally, I begin each topic by asking the students what they think are the two or three most important things people need to understand about, for example, the U.S. Congress or presidency. Then I compare their list to the one I compiled. In this way, we are able to cover the basics of any given topic fairly quickly and without resorting to long, expensive texts. Most importantly, this approach also leaves us the time to foster their interest in the topic by focusing on current issues and events.

While this approach began as a quick, easy, and low-cost (both monetarily and time-wise) way to provide students with basic information so that we could move on to more engaging discussions and advanced readings, over the years it has developed into something more. In my experience, the benefits of this approach include the following: It is a simple, straightforward, but still innovative way of presenting material; it engages students in a format they are familiar with in their daily lives; it enables students to grasp a great deal of information fairly quickly; it leaves me time to focus on interesting topics and issues; and it works regardless of what other materials I assign (textbooks, novels, journal articles, etc.…).

Most importantly, however, because this approach is not staid, by nature it invites and encourages students to be critical, to think and express their opinions, to discuss and debate, and to evaluate American government, rather than simply memorize facts. Given the nature of the political world we live in today, there is no more important gift we can give our students than the opportunity to cast a critical eye on experts and to challenge the assumptions of those who presume to tell them how the world is.

NOTE TO THE STUDENT

This text is one my students have been asking for and that I have been promising to deliver to them for years. I understood and shared their frustration with other texts, but their requests were not easily met. They wanted an introductory book that was at once less expensive than traditional hardcover government textbooks but which contained the same basic information in a format that is familiar, easy to understand, and accessible. In honor of all my students, both past and present, and those of the contributors to this text, I am hopeful we have met these demands.

We have written a book that invites debate, critique, criticism, and discussion. Unlike traditional texts, this is a book that we hope you will not only engage in but at points disagree with. After experimenting with teaching American government in this way for years, I invited experts and scholars in a variety of subfields to contribute their lists of the top 10 most important things you, as a student of American government, should know. They did this knowing that lists are meant to be argued with and constructed and deconstructed just as quickly. That is your role, as both a reader and student, to understand what they've presented here. And then, if you are so inclined, to disagree with what they've suggested and to explain both your reasoning and how you would remedy the problem.

My students have found this approach engaging because politics is not just for scholars and experts. It is something we all know and experience daily, intimately, whether we are cognizant of it or not. We should all be engaged in the study and examination of the political world, and we should all be given the basic information necessary to do this. That is, without question, the primary goal of this text: to give you the basics to engage in politics and to voice your thoughtful opinions, whether they run contrary to the ideas of experts or not.

FEATURES

This text includes several features designed to maximize the utility of the top-10 approach, engage students, and encourage students to think critically about American politics and government.

Top Ten List. Every chapter opens with a list of the top ten things students should know about the given chapter topic. The lists serve to draw students into the topic and to help them learn more about what many scholars agree are the key aspects of American government. These lists then serve as the headings within each chapter, providing students with a framework for critically examining each element on the list.

Your List. Included at the start of each chapter, this feature assesses baseline knowledge by asking students to develop their own top-ten lists. At the end of each chapter, students are asked to revisit these lists and to compare them more thoroughly against the chapter lists developed by the author.

Their List: An Insider's View. This boxed feature gives students a chance to see what people who actually work in government and politics think are the most important things to know about each chapter topic. For instance, the campaigns and elections chapter contains an interview with a campaign manager, the civil liberties and civil rights chapter includes an interview with a lawyer and judge, and the presidency chapter includes an interview with a former presidential candidate from one of the major parties. In each instance, these insiders were asked the same deceptively simple question as the authors: What are the most important things you think a student of American government should know about campaigns and elections or civil liberties and civil rights, or the presidency...? The juxtaposition of what a practitioner thinks is important for students of politics to know versus what an academic/scholar thinks is most important can be startling and insightful, and serve as the basis of a fascinating discussion about American government.

Your List Revisited. This feature appears at the end of each chapter and encourages students to revisit the lists they developed at the start of the chapter, to compare their lists with the chapter lists developed by the author, and to use their critical thinking skills to critique the content and order of the lists.

Chapter Review Questions. These ten questions appear at the end of each chapter and directly correspond to the top-ten chapter list. They ask students to recall and, in many cases, think critically about the most important information covered in each section.

Top-Ten Suggested Readings, Films, and Websites. The purpose of these pedagogical elements is to reinforce the top-ten approach and provide students with additional avenues of exploration that will further spark their interest in the material addressed in each chapter.

Marginal Glossary. A marginal glossary clearly defines key terms where they appear in the text to reinforce the most important ideas and make reviewing key concepts easier.

SUPPLEMENTS

Instructor's Manual/Test Bank: Available for download at www.pearsonhighered.com/irc, the Instructor's Manual contains the following tools for each chapter in the book: a summary, learning objectives, a chapter outline, a lecture outline, and critical thinking exercises. The Test Bank offers hundreds of multiple-choice, true/false, and essay questions covering factual, conceptual, and applied information from the text. (ISBN 0-136-04075-6)

MyTest Test Bank: This flexible, online test-generating software includes all the questions found in the Test Bank section of the Instructor's Manual/Test Bank. Available at www.pearsonmytest.com (access code required). (ISBN 0-136-04077-2)

ACKNOWLEDGEMENTS

I would like to acknowledge a number of people who helped see this book through from its inception to publication, including: Reid Hester, Lisa Sussman, Eric Stano, Dickson Musslewhite, Naomi Friedman, Eileen Calabro, Meg Botteon, Daryl Fox, Donna Garnier, Elizabeth Alimena, Nesin Osman, and Eric Jorgensen.

I would also like to thank the many reviewers whose feedback has proven invaluable, including:

Matthew Mark Caverly, *University of North Florida*
Ellen Creagar, *Eastern Wyoming College*
Chris Farnung, *Wake Technical Community College*
Frederick Gordon, *California State University, Los Angeles*
Rick Groper, *California State University, Los Angeles*
Peter Heller, *Manhattan College*
Terri R. Jett, *Butler University*
Stephen Ma, *California State University, Los Angeles*
John Maynor, *Middle Tennessee State University*
Chris Mobley, *Chattanooga State Community College*
William Wallis, *California State University, Northridge*

This book would not have been possible without the willingness of the scholars from around the world who bravely agreed to put together their lists of the most important things they think students should know about the topic they have committed their lives to examining. It is brave not only because they are aware they may be called to task but because the process of putting together lists like these is without question a harrowing endeavor for any academic. For these reasons, their collegiality, and friendship, I am indebted to: Lawrence Becker, Michele DeMary, Jerold Duquette, Tom Hogen-Esch, Daniel McCarthy, Kristy E.H. Michaud, Jerome Mileur, Henrik P. Minassians, Tricia Mulligan, Brian Nickerson, Paul Petterson, and Jordan Wishy.

I reserve final acknowledgment for those to whom I am most indebted: my students and my family. If it wasn't for the students of Iona College who I have had the privilege to work with this idea might never have come to fruition. And if it wasn't for the love and support of my family, my husband Jeff and our two sons, Maxim and Logan, I might never have been able to see it to completion.

Contributors

Lawrence Becker, Ph.D. (Congress and The Bureaucracy)
Chair and Professor, Political Science, California State University, Northridge

Michele DeMary, Ph.D. (The Judiciary)
Associate Professor, Political Science, Pre-Law Advisor, Susquehanna University, PA

Jerold Duquette, Ph.D. (Political Participation, Socialization, Public Opinion, and the Media)
Associate Professor, Political Science, Central Connecticut State University

Tom Hogen-Esch, Ph.D. (Federalism)
Professor, Political Science, California State University, Northridge

Daniel McCarthy, Ph.D. (Civil Liberties and Civil Rights)
Professor, Political Science, College of New Rochelle

Kristy E.H. Michaud, Ph.D. (The Foundations of American Government)
Assistant Professor, Political Science, California State University, Northridge

Jerome Mileur, Ph.D. (Political Parties and Interest Groups)
Professor Emeritus, Department of Political Science, University of Massachusetts, Amherst

Henrik P. Minassians, Ph.D. (The Bureaucracy)
Director of Public Sector Degree Programs at the Tseng College, California State University, Northridge

Tricia Mulligan, Ph.D. (Foreign Policy)
Chair & Associate Professor, Political Science, Iona College, New Rochelle

Brian Nickerson, Ph.D. (American Public Policy)
Dean, School of Arts & Science, Iona College, New Rochelle

Paul Petterson, Ph.D. (The Presidency)
Chair and Professor Political Science, Central Connecticut State University

Jordan Wishy, Ph.D. (American Public Policy)
Research Associate, University of Albany

Jeanne Zaino, Ph.D. (Campaigns and Elections)
Director of Honors Program, Professor, Political Science, Iona College, New Rochelle

Core Concepts in
AMERICAN GOVERNMENT

Chapter 1

THE FOUNDATIONS OF AMERICAN GOVERNMENT

Top Ten List

10 Governments maintain order and provide public services.

9 The United States is the first established modern democracy, but there are other forms of government, including autocracies, oligarchies, and theocracies.

8 The American colonists' experience as British subjects influenced the form of government they adopted after they declared independence from Great Britain.

7 The American experiment with a confederal form of government failed because the national government lacked the power it needed to function effectively.

6 The U.S. Constitution is a result of compromise.

5 The U.S. Constitution created a system of government in which power is limited and divided.

4 The Bill of Rights clarifies the limits of the national government and the rights reserved to the states.

3 Amending the Constitution is not meant to be easy.

2 The Constitution establishes majority rule but allows for the protection of minority rights.

1 The Constitution is ambiguous, which leaves it open to multiple interpretations.

WE the People of the States of New-Hampſhire, Maſſachuſetts, Rhode-Iſland and Providence Plantations, Connecticut, New-York, New-Jerſey, Pennſylvania, Delaware, Maryland, Virginia, North-Carolina, South-Carolina, and Georgia, do ordain, declare and eſtabliſh the following Conſtitution for the Government of Ourſelves and our Poſterity.

ARTICLE I.

The ſtile of this Government ſhall be, "The United States of America."

II.

The Government ſhall conſiſt of ſupreme legiſlative, executive and judicial powers.

III.

The legiſlative power ſhall be veſted in a Congreſs, to conſiſt of two ſeparate and diſtinct bodies of men, a Houſe of Repreſentatives, and a Senate; ~~each of which ſhall, in all caſes, have a negative on the other. The Legiſlature ſhall meet on the firſt Monday in December in every year.~~

IV.

Sect. 1. The Members of the Houſe of Repreſentatives ſhall be choſen every ſecond year, by the people of the ſeveral States comprehended within this Union. The qualifications of the electors ſhall be the ſame, from time to time, as thoſe of the electors in the ſeveral States, of the moſt numerous branch of their own legiſlatures.

Sect. 2. Every Member of the Houſe of Repreſentatives ſhall be of the age of twenty-five years at leaſt; ſhall have been a citizen in the United States for at leaſt [illegible] years before his election; and ſhall be, at the time of his election, [illegible] of the State in which he ſhall be choſen.

Sect. 3. The Houſe of Repreſentatives ſhall, at its firſt formation, and until the number of citizens and inhabitants ſhall be taken in the manner herein after deſcribed, conſiſt of ſixty-five Members, of whom three ſhall be choſen in New-Hampſhire, eight in Maſſachuſetts, one in Rhode-Iſland and Providence Plantations, five in Connecticut, ſix in New-York, four in New-Jerſey, eight in Pennſylvania, one in Delaware, ſix in Maryland, ten in Virginia, five in North-Carolina, five in South-Carolina, and three in Georgia.

Sect. 4. As the proportions of numbers in the different States will alter from time to time; as ſome of the States may hereafter be divided; as others may be enlarged by addition of territory; as two or more States may be united; as

Shown here is the first page of a draft of the U.S. Constitution that includes George Washington's annotations. The Constitution embodies many principles that have shaped our political system. But it also reflects the many compromises of the founders over power and representation. Would the nation's founders be pleased with the way the political system has evolved? Where have we succeeded, and how can we do better?

YOUR LIST

Before you read this chapter, take a few moments to think about what you might include on a list of the Top 10 Most Important Things to Know About the Foundations of American Government. At the end of the chapter you will be asked to compare and contrast your list with the one supplied in this chapter.

INTRODUCTION

How would the founding fathers feel about the way the United States has turned out? If you're like most Americans, you don't think the men who signed the Declaration of Independence over 230 years ago would be pleased. According to a 2008 CNN public opinion poll of Americans, nearly seven out of ten people (69 percent) said that the founding fathers would be disappointed by the way the nation has turned out.[1] What is it about the country today that Americans think the founders would disapprove of? Just how far off is our system of government today from the one envisioned by the founders? Even if the founders would be disappointed, what do you think of what Americans have achieved over the past 200+ years?[2]

As you evaluate our current political system over the course of this chapter, bear in mind that it is the product of a second attempt at governing—after an initial failure. It is also rooted in many principles, republicanism, federalism, the separation of powers, and checks and balances—worthy principles that are not easy to achieve. Each of these principles and the document that embodies them are the product of years of conflict and compromise. As we examine these principles and how they are implemented in practice, we may ask ourselves whether the result is the best we can do. How have we worked to improve our political system? And how can we do better?

Governments maintain order and provide public services.

Government An organization with the authority to exercise control over human behavior.

Throughout history, cities, states, and empires have established many different forms of **government**, organizations with the authority to exercise control over human behavior. Governments serve a number of important purposes. A primary purpose of government is to maintain order. In the American tradition, maintaining order means protecting the lives and property of citizens. From traffic laws to laws against theft of personal property or acts of violence against others, the government is constantly trying to maintain order by controlling human behavior. Democratic governments around the world struggle with preserving individual freedoms while protecting the lives and property of citizens.

A second purpose of government is to provide public services. Military protection against foreign invasion and police protection of the lives and property of citizens represent services provided by the government to its citizens. Many governments are also involved—either directly or indirectly—in the provision of other basic services, such as building or maintaining the infrastructure that delivers water or electricity. Although everyone expects some basic services, the range and scope of services that people believe their government should provide vary greatly from place to place. In many nations, including the United States, people have demanded more services over time. Today, we expect much more from our government than we did in the past. For example, many Americans expect the government to retrain workers if they lose their job, provide pensions to the elderly, and regulate industries to protect citizens from potentially harmful products.

The United States is the first established modern democracy, but there are other forms of government, including autocracies, oligarchies, and theocracies.

Governments differ in many ways, but one of the central distinctions is related to how governments maintain order, the first purpose of government discussed above. We can place various governments on a continuum, such as the one in Figure 1.1, based on the degree to which they exercise power and preserve individual liberties.

Totalitarianism A form of government in which the government exercises total power and is involved in nearly every facet of people's lives.

Anarchism A situation in which government is not involved in any way with maintaining order or providing public services. Anarchy has generally only existed for short periods of time after the fall of a state.

At one extreme is **totalitarianism**, a type of government that exercises total authority. This is a government, such as the one in Germany under Hitler, that is involved in nearly every facet of people's lives, including social, political, economic, and cultural aspects. As the name suggests, these governments exercise total power, and citizens living under them enjoy very few liberties, if any.

At the other extreme is **anarchism**, in which the government is almost nonexistent to the extent that it exercises little authority, maintains no order, and provides no public services. While people living in an anarchy have full liberties (freedom from government authority), their rights can be violated by others living in the community. Anarchy has generally only existed for short periods during times of great upheaval, such as following the revolutions in France in the late eighteenth century and Russia in the early twentieth century.

Figure 1.1 **Continuum of Power by Political System Type**

Governments differ in terms of the amount of power they exercise—totalitarian governments exercise almost 'total' power over the people, while anarchies are devoid of power. Constitutional democracies, such as the United States, fall somewhere in the middle of the continuum of power.

Constitutional democracies Types of governments that arose largely in the eighteenth and nineteenth centuries and that were inspired by the liberal philosophies of great theorists such as John Locke and Jean-Jacques Rousseau.

Liberalism A philosophy reflected in many constitutional democracies that every individual has natural rights that the government should respect and protect. This philosophy is rooted in the strong belief in individual freedom.

Autocracy A form of government in which power is concentrated in the hands of one person, such as a monarch.

Oligarchy A form of government in which power is concentrated in the hands of a few members from an elite segment of society, such as the military.

Theocracy A form of government in which power resides in the hands of the religious leadership.

In between these two extremes we find **constitutional democracies**. These types of governments arose largely in the eighteenth and nineteenth centuries, inspired by the liberal philosophies of great theorists such as John Locke and Jean-Jacques Rousseau. The premise of **liberalism** is that every individual has natural rights that the government should respect and protect. The American Declaration of Independence specifies that "among these rights are life, liberty, and the pursuit of happiness." The Constitution translates this language into specific rights defined within the Bill of Rights, as we will see later. Whether they are based on written constitutions like that of the United States or unwritten constitutions such as Great Britain's, these forms of governments fall perfectly in the middle of the continuum because their governments try to maintain a balance between the exercise of power and respect for citizens' liberties. It is not a balance that is easy to maintain. Following the terrorist attacks against the United States on September 11, 2001, for instance, the United States confronted a dilemma that is common in these types of systems: How do you ensure against future attacks while at the same time not unduly stomping on the liberties of citizens?[3]

Governments can also be categorized by how much citizen involvement they allow. Again, we can think in terms of a continuum (see Figure 1.2). At one extreme is **autocracy**, in which power is concentrated in the hands of one person, such as a monarch. A modern example of an autocracy is North Korea under the rule of Kim Jong-il. In an **oligarchy**, on the other hand, power is concentrated in the hands of a few members from an elite segment of society, such as those with the most wealth, military strength, or political influence. South Africa in the twentieth century, for instance, is often cited as an example of an oligarchy. In a **theocracy**, by contrast, power resides in the hands of the religious leadership. Iran is led by Muslim clerics whose leader, the Ayatollah Ali Khamenei, controls the army and

Figure 1.2 Continuum of Citizen Involvement by Government Type

Governments differ in terms of how involved their citizens are in the governing process. Citizens in a direct democracy are, as the name indicates, 'directly' involved in the governing process, while citizens in an autocracy have very little, if any, say in their government.

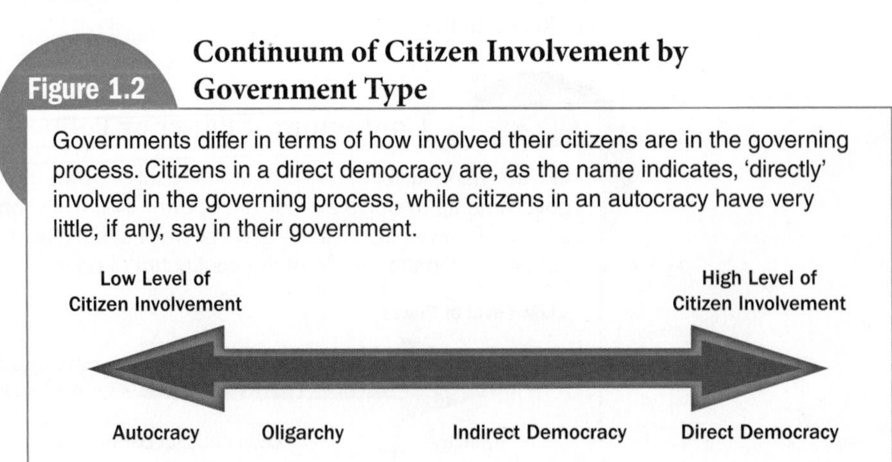

the media, decides who can run for president, and has the power to dismiss the elected president.

At the other end of the continuum are forms of government established under liberal principles. In addition to natural rights, another premise of liberalism is that individuals are inherently reasonable and should be allowed to govern themselves. **Democracy** is a system of government that allows the people to rule, either directly or indirectly. In a direct democracy, the people themselves, rather than elected officials, make the political decisions. Direct democracies existed in the city-state of Athens in Ancient Greece. Although the Athenian model inspired the founders, direct democracies often resulted in the rise of powerful autocrats, and the founders associated it with the rule of the mob. As a result, the founders established a **representative democracy**, also called a democratic **republic** (or a republican government). This is a type of democracy in which the people elect representatives to act on their behalf and make the political decisions.

Democracy A form of government that allows for the people to rule, either directly or indirectly.

Representative democracy A form of democratic government in which the people elect representatives to act on their behalf; also known as a republican government.

Republic A form of democratic government in which the people elect representatives to act on their behalf; also known as a representative government.

When the founders authored the Constitution, they determined who would participate in elections and how decisions should be made. Originally, the vote was limited to free white men. Today, however, the United States practices universal suffrage, in which all citizens have the right to vote.

Democracy in America represents an accidental experiment. The founders were skeptical of the principle of democracy because at the time it was associated with mob rule. Although they intended to create a political system in which the people governed, the founders put in place barriers to direct rule. Over 200 years later, most of those barriers remain in place, but the experiment with democracy continues, and we each play a part in it.[4]

8 The American colonists' experience as British subjects influenced the form of government they adopted after they declared independence from Great Britain.

Although the rallying cry of "no taxation without representation" is remembered in American history books for helping to inspire a revolt against British rule, the American colonists actually had quite a bit of freedom compared to other people in the world at the time. While the king and the British legislature controlled America's foreign affairs and overseas trade, the colonies were free to govern themselves on all other issues. As Table 1.1 shows, this peaceful compromise ended in 1765 when Britain began taxing the colonists in order to pay for the cost of administering the colonies and providing them with military protection.[5]

The Crown viewed taxation as a reasonable exchange for services rendered by the British government, but the colonists viewed it as a form of oppression because

Table 1.1 **10 Key Events Leading to War: 1763–1775** *[6]

1763:	King George signs "Proclamation of 1763"
1764:	Sugar Act
1764:	James Otis publishes "The Rights of the British Colonies Asserted and Proved"
1765:	Stamp Act
1767:	Townsend Duties
1770:	Boston Massacre
1773:	Tea Act
1773:	The Boston Tea Party
1774:	First Continental Congress meets
1775:	Patrick Henry delivers speech: "Give me liberty or give me death!"

*For more information on these key events, visit: http://www.historyplace.com/unitedstates/revolution/rev-prel.htm.

they were not allowed representation in the British legislature. Britain's imposition of a series of taxes was met with immediate resistance. Tensions spiked in 1773, when a group of colonists opposed a British tax on tea by dumping shipments of tea into Boston Harbor. The Boston Tea Party, as it came to be known, led the British Parliament to institute the Coercive (or Intolerable) Acts, which essentially established martial law in Massachusetts. The colonial legislature was dissolved, the port was closed, and soldiers were dispatched and quartered (housed) in the homes of colonists.

First Continental Congress In 1774, delegates from twelve of the thirteen American colonies (Georgia was absent) met in Philadelphia with the goal of reconciling with Britain.

These actions by the British government did not, however, prevent the colonists from seeking to govern themselves. In 1774, in violation of British law, the **First Continental Congress** was formed. Delegates from twelve of the thirteen colonies (Georgia was absent) met in Philadelphia with the goal of reconciling with Britain. By the end of the meeting, the delegates adopted a statement of their rights, established a boycott of British goods, and called for a second meeting of the Continental Congress in May 1775.

Second Continental Congress A meeting of delegates in May 1775, some of whom wanted to work toward reestablishing harmony between Britain and the American colonies, and others who wanted to break all ties with the Crown and form an independent nation.

By the time the **Second Continental Congress** met, colonial rebellion against British oppression had escalated to the point of revolution. The delegates were divided on the action that should be taken. Some wanted to work toward reestablishing harmony between Britain and the American colonies, while others wanted to break all ties with the Crown and form an independent country.

On June 7, 1776, with the strong support of John Adams of Massachusetts, the Virginia delegation introduced a resolution to absolve allegiance to the Crown and dissolve all political connections to Britain. The resolution was hotly debated, since a declaration of independence would constitute a crime against the Crown punishable by death. Although the delegates did not immediately adopt the resolution, they did agree to organize a committee responsible for drafting a declaration of independence and a statement of reasons for absolving allegiance to the Crown in case the resolution was adopted.

Declaration of Independence Drafted in 1776 by Thomas Jefferson of Virginia, this document summarized the purpose of government and the political rights of citizens.

The **Declaration of Independence** was drafted in 1776 by Thomas Jefferson of Virginia, who eloquently expressed the ideals of individual liberty shared by the delegates to the Constitutional Convention and the American colonists. His document summarized the purpose of government and the political rights of citizens. It also listed the many acts of the Crown that violated the rights of man and constituted tyranny rather than legitimate rule.

The principles embodied by the Declaration of Independence—that government is established by the people to protect their life, liberty, and happiness, and is to be replaced when it no longer does that—were rooted in the political ideas of English philosopher John Locke. At the time of his writing in the seventeenth century, Locke argued that people have natural rights that cannot be taken away by government. Furthermore, the legitimacy of government to exist is based on the consent of the governed and on its ability to preserve the natural rights of man. In the case of government denying the people their God-given rights, the people had the right to overthrow it.

On July 4, 1776, the Declaration of Independence was approved by the Second Continental Congress (see Table 1.2). The motion was carried unanimously by the

Table 1.2 **10 Key Events during the American Revolution: 1775–1783*[7]**

1775:	Paul Revere's ride
1775:	Battles of Lexington and Concord
1775:	Second Continental Congress meets
1775:	Battle of Bunker Hill
1776:	Thomas Paine publishes *Common Sense*
1776:	Declaration of Independence
1777:	Articles of Confederation and Perpetual Union
1780:	British capture Charleston
1781:	British surrender at Yorktown
1783:	Treaty of Paris signed by United States and Great Britain

*For more information on these key events, visit: http://www.historyplace.com/unitedstates/revolution/revwar-75.htm; http://www.historyplace.com/unitedstates/revolution/revwar-77.htm.

eleven voting states. (The Rhode Island delegation was not present, and the New York delegation withheld its vote until July 15 while it awaited instructions). By the end of the summer, the Declaration had been signed by fifty-five revolutionaries who pledged "our lives, our fortunes and our sacred honor" to the cause of freedom from Great Britain. If the American states had lost the Revolutionary War, each signing member could have been tried for treason, an act punishable by hanging and drawing and quartering. Fortunately for the signers, America defeated the British in October 1781, after a six-and-a-half-year battle that resulted in the loss of thousands of lives.

The American experiment with a confederal form of government failed because the national government lacked the power it needed to function effectively.

Once they dissolved all connections to Great Britain, the American colonists were left without a national government that could preserve the unalienable rights of citizens and protect order. Within a week of declaring independence from Great Britain, the Continental Congress declared America a republic and began to consider a proposal to establish a **confederation** of states united under a national government. The decision to establish a republic was reached quickly. The proposal to establish a confederation of states was not; debate over the proposal by the Continental Congress lasted for more than a year.

Confederation An alliance of sovereign states united for common objectives.

Articles of Confederation Adopted in 1777, this governing document reflected the founders' fears of a powerful national government. The thirteen states retained supreme powers within their borders, while the national government was given very little power.

Under the proposal, which came to be known as the **Articles of Confederation**, each of the thirteen states would retain supreme power within its borders, while the national government—made up of a single-chamber legislature in which each state had a single vote—would be given very little power. Fearful that vesting power in a single executive would lead to tyranny, the Articles did not establish an executive branch of government. The national government was given the authority to organize the actions of the states, but it was not granted any power to control the actions of the states or to enforce its decisions. The weak national government proposed by the Articles of Confederation reflected the founders' fears of a powerful national government that might resemble the British rule they had just rejected.[8]

After a year of debate, the Continental Congress adopted the Articles of Confederation in November 1777. The Articles were ratified by each of the thirteen states and took effect more than three years later, in March 1781. Americans finally had their own **constitution** (a set of rules and principles that establish a system of government) and national government. Unfortunately, the government established under the Articles was largely powerless and did not last long.

Constitution A set of rules and principles that establish a system of government.

By limiting the power of the national government out of fear of reproducing something similar to British rule, the founders created a government that lacked the economic and military power to govern effectively. This became painfully clear once the Revolutionary War ended and economic disparity continued to spread throughout each of the states, causing civil unrest. Farmers were particularly distressed because many could not pay their debts or state taxes and were forced into bankruptcy. In 1786, their discontent was mobilized by Daniel Shays, a Revolutionary War veteran and a farmer, who led an armed uprising in Western Massachusetts known as **Shays' Rebellion**.

Shays' Rebellion In 1786, Daniel Shays, a Revolutionary War veteran, led a group of discontented farmers in Western Massachusetts in uprisings over debt. The national government was unable to muster the power needed to put down the uprisings, reflecting the weaknesses of the Articles of Confederation.

Shays, like many other farmers, found himself in court for nonpayment of debts. Facing foreclosure on his farm, he organized a march on the courthouse with the intention of closing it to prevent court-ordered foreclosures of farms. Over the next year, Shays and his supporters continued their rebellion against the established order. When Massachusetts appealed to the national government for help quelling the domestic upheaval, the state legislature approved funding to establish a national army. However, only one state (Virginia) agreed to the request for money, and the national government did not have the power to compel the other states to comply. In the end, the Massachusetts militia was able to restore order without the help of the confederation.

Shays' Rebellion made it clear that the national government lacked the power it needed to function effectively, particularly in times of crisis. The failure of the Articles of Confederation to establish an effective government can be attributed to several factors. First, the national government was not granted the power to generate revenue or regulate trade between states and with foreign nations. Without the ability to generate revenue, the government had no way to repay the national debt (the Revolutionary War had cost millions of dollars that the new government had borrowed from foreign nations and domestic creditors) or to raise an army that could serve to maintain order.

In addition, the government's lack of power to regulate commerce made trade with foreign nations and between states complicated. Each state wanted the benefit of trading with foreign nations, so foreign nations attempting to forge a treaty with America often found themselves negotiating with each of the thirteen states in addition to Congress. Trading between states was not much easier; each state could make its own currency and establish its own rules for exporting goods across state lines, such as charging tolls and fees.

Second, the Articles of Confederation could not be amended without the approval of all thirteen states. This meant that each state had the power to veto any proposed changes to the Articles, and states did not hesitate to exercise this power. When Congress proposed an amendment to the Articles that would allow it to collect taxes to support General Washington's troops during the Revolutionary War, it was vetoed by Rhode Island, which represented less than 2 percent of the nation's population. The unanimous consent requirement resulted in a constitution that was inflexible and gave the minority too much power.

Monarchy A form of government in which all political power rests with a single individual; it is usually passed down through heredity.

Third, there was no executive leader who could direct government. The founders intentionally omitted this position because they were fearful of recreating a **monarchy** (a form of government in which all political power rests with a single individual; it is usually passed down through heredity). However, it left the nation without a leader who could guide the affairs of government and see the country through times of crisis. Each of these problems left the national government largely powerless under the Articles of Confederation. In their dedicated attempt to limit the power of government, the founders had created a government that was unable to maintain domestic order.

6 The U.S. Constitution is a result of compromise.

Constitutional Convention Meeting of delegates from twelve of the thirteen states in 1787 to encourage uncensored debate and discussion about changing the structure of government created by the Articles of Confederation.

By 1787, the shortcomings of the first constitution were evident. As a result, delegates from twelve of the thirteen states (Rhode Island was again absent) met at a **Constitutional Convention** in Philadelphia to discuss revisions to the existing document. In total, there were fifty-five delegates present in Philadelphia during that hot summer. All were white, property-owning males who had been elected to represent their states. Among the most well known of the delegates were Alexander Hamilton, James Madison, and George Washington. Washington was elected to serve as president of the convention.[9]

All of the delegates in attendance believed that changes to the Articles were needed, but the agreement ended there. Much of what we know about the convention comes from James Madison's journal. Madison, who would go on to become president of the United States, wrote in the preface to *Notes of Debates in the Federal Convention of 1787* that he purposefully sat up front so he could record the proceeding:

> in pursuance of the task I had assumed I chose a seat in front of the presiding member. . . . In this favorable position for hearing all that passed, I noted in terms legible & in abbreviations & marks intelligible to myself what was read from the Chair or spoken by the members; and losing not a moment unnecessarily between the adjournment & reassembling of the Convention I was enabled to write out my daily notes.[10]

In accordance with his wishes, Madison's *Notes* were not published until 1840 after the death of all convention attendees (as well as his own death). John P. Kaminski, the director of the Center for the American Constitution, notes the importance of Madison's notes:

> It would be hard to imagine any other historical work that has been so important as Madison's notes of the convention. It was a gift—a legacy left by Madison to his country. . . . More than any other source, Madison's notes of the debates have remained for over 160 years the standard authority for what happened in the Constitutional Convention. It has allowed historians to look back at the founding and see the genesis of our Constitution. It was an incredible gift.[11]

 The U.S. Constitution is a result of compromise.

Madison's notes indicate that much of the Constitutional Convention was spent debating two key issues: representation and power. Three debates involving representation emerged: majority rule versus minority rights, small states versus large states, and slave states versus nonslave states. In addition, the founders were still fearful of a tyrannical national government and therefore debated the balance of power between the legislative branch and the executive branch, as well as between the national government and the state and local governments. Fortunately, conflict regarding these issues was met with compromise, which eventually resulted in the creation of the U.S. Constitution in existence today.

Within a week of convening, delegates began debating a proposal to replace the Articles of Confederation with an entirely new constitution that would establish a more powerful national government. The proposal, which became known as the **Virginia Plan**, was introduced by Edmund Randolph of Virginia and consisted of a list of changes suggested by fellow Virginian James Madison (who later became known as the "Father of the Constitution" for his contributions). The plan recommended a government composed of three separate branches—legislative, executive, and judicial—that would be granted specific powers and responsibilities that could not be exceeded.

Virginia Plan Proposal introduced at the Constitutional Convention that recommended a more powerful government to replace the Articles of Confederation.

In addition to changes to the structure of the national government, the Virginia Plan also proposed changes related to the basis for representation and the system of selecting representatives. Though limited in its power, the proposed government would have increased authority over the states and the people. Debate about the proposal was largely focused on three issues related to power and representation: the basis for representation in the legislature, the structure and powers of the executive branch, and the system of choosing representatives.

As debate continued, division arose between the large states, which would be granted greater representation in the legislature according to the plan, and the small states, which feared that they would be underrepresented by the new government. In response, a coalition of small states introduced an alternative proposal, known as the **New Jersey Plan**. The intent of the New Jersey Plan was to amend rather than replace the Articles of Confederation. The proposal sought to maintain the power that the states had under the Articles and to guarantee equal representation for each state, regardless of its population size. The proposal made very few changes to the structure of the government established under the Articles, but it did include a provision for a multiperson executive branch to be elected by Congress. Although the New Jersey Plan was defeated by a vote of 7 to 3, the small states had succeeded in gaining enough support to force negotiation on the issue of representation.

New Jersey Plan Proposal introduced at the Constitutional Convention that would have amended rather than replaced the Articles of Confederation.

The question of representation for both small and large states was answered with the **Great Compromise** (sometimes known as the Connecticut Compromise because it was developed with the help of the Connecticut delegation). The compromise involved incorporating equal and proportional representation into a two-chamber legislature. The number of legislators in the House of Representatives would

Great Compromise Compromise at the Constitutional Convention that involved incorporating equal and proportional representation into a two-chamber legislature.

be apportioned according to the population of each state. The number of legislators in the Senate, on the other hand, would be equal in all states, regardless of population size. This compromise pleased small states, who wanted equal representation, and the large states, who wanted proportional representation. Because all legislation had to be approved by both houses of Congress, there was little threat of legislative dominance by large or small states.

When the conflict between small and large states on the issue of representation had been resolved, the conflict between slave states (primarily in the South) and nonslave states (primarily in the North) began. Those opposed to slavery and from nonslave northern states generally favored counting only free people for purposes of representation. Those from slave-holding states in the South, however, were generally in favor of counting slaves as part of the population so they could increase their numbers in the House of Representatives and the Electoral College. As difficult as it is for us to imagine today, even though there were delegates who opposed the institution of slavery, the debate at the convention was largely one over power in government, rather than morality.

The proposed solution to this impasse that satisfied both northern and southern states, but that hardly seems satisfactory by any modern measure, is known as the **Three-fifths Compromise**. According to this plan, for the purpose of apportioning seats in the House of Representatives, each state's population was to be calculated using a formula that counted five slaves as three people. It is quite possible that without the Three-Fifths Compromise, the southern states might have unanimously rejected the Constitution.

Three-Fifths Compromise A compromise at the Constitutional Convention that determined, for the purpose of apportioning seats in the House of Representatives, each state's population was to be calculated using a formula that counted five slaves as three people.

With the issue of legislative presentation resolved, the founders moved on to address the executive branch. The delegates first opposed an executive branch composed of a single person out of fear that it would result in a monarchy. When they finally agreed on a single executive with clearly outlined limitations, the next point of debate centered on how the executive would be elected. Distrustful of the people's judgment, the delegates rejected the idea of a directly elected executive. However, delegates from small states also feared that if the legislature elected the executive, then large states would control the branch.

The delegates reached a compromise that satisfied both concerns. They developed an indirect presidential election system in which a group of individuals (known as electors) selected by each state legislature would cast votes for the president and vice president. To address the concern of small states that they would have little influence in presidential elections, the system required that each state be granted a number of electors equal to the number of representatives it had in Congress (both the House and the Senate). The proposed indirect election system (today known as the Electoral College) eliminated the fear of a popularly elected president and guaranteed that small states would have some impact on the selection of the executive.

In the end, the delegates were able to compromise on a system of government that looked quite different from the one established by the Articles of Confederation (see Table 1.3). Rather than the loose alliance of sovereign states and weak national

Table 1.3 **Major Differences Between the Articles of Confederation and the Constitution**

Element	Articles of Confederation	Constitution
Legislature	Unicameral congress	Bicameral congress divided into the House of Representatives and the Senate
Apportionment of members of Congress	No fewer than two and no more than seven delegates per state	Representatives apportioned according to state population size; two senators per state
Selection of members of Congress	Appointed by state legislatures	Representatives elected by popular vote; senators appointed by state legislatures (*Note: senators are now elected by popular vote according to the Seventeenth Amendment ratified in 1913*)
Voting in Congress	One vote per state	One vote per representative; one vote per senator
Term of legislative office	One year	Two years for representatives; six years for senators
Source of congressional pay	States	National government
Executive	None	President
Judiciary	No federal court system	Supreme Court; Congress authorized to establish federal court system
Body authorized to settle disputes between states	Congress	Supreme Court
Proportion of states required to amend document	All	Three-fourths
Power to coin money	National government and the states	National government only
Taxes	Collected by the states; apportioned by Congress	Collected and apportioned by Congress

Sources: The Articles of Confederation; the U.S. Constitution.

government produced by the Articles, the Constitution created a republic of states under a strong national government. The Constitution that formed this government structure was the product of years of experiences with monarchy, revolution, and a failed government. The document that emerged from the Constitutional Convention was brief—only about 4,500 words—but it clearly conveyed the principles that the founders believed were essential to an effective and stable national government. Central to the Constitution are the principles of separation of powers, checks and balances, and federalism.

The U.S. Constitution created a system of government in which power is limited and divided.

Separation of powers The Constitution established a legislative branch with the power to make laws, an executive branch with the power to enforce laws, and a judicial branch with the power to interpret laws.

In an effort to limit the power of the national government, the founders established three distinct branches of government with specific powers and responsibilities that cannot be exceeded. Under this principle, known as **separation of powers**, they established a legislative branch assigned to make laws, an executive branch assigned to enforce laws, and a judicial branch assigned to interpret laws. The principle was part of what Madison called a "double security" that would protect the rights of the people. As Madison explains in *Federalist No. 51*, any power that people surrender to the national government is then divided up between distinct and separate branches that, in theory, cannot exercise the powers of the other branches. This separation prevents any one branch from becoming too powerful.

Legislative supremacy Fearful of a monarchy, the founders of the Constitution sought to establish a government in which the legislative branch was more powerful than the executive.

The powers of each of the three branches are outlined in the first three Articles of the Constitution. They reflect the compromise the founders reached regarding the balance of power between the legislative and executive branches. Fearful of a monarchy, they sought to establish **legislative supremacy** rather than executive supremacy in their new government. Article I, establishing the legislative branch, is the longest of all of the Articles; it contains a detailed account of the responsibilities and powers of the House of Representatives and the Senate. The executive is granted far fewer responsibilities in Article II of the Constitution. The judiciary, created by Article III, establishes a Supreme Court and authorizes Congress to create a federal court system.

Checks and balances Principle reflected in the Constitution that grants each of the three branches (legislative, executive, and judicial) some control and scrutiny over one another.

As a further limit on the power that any single person or branch may possess, the founders integrated **checks and balances** into each of the first three Articles of the Constitution. This principle grants each of the three branches some control and scrutiny over the other two branches. By dividing the responsibilities of government among three branches and then granting each branch some control over the others, Madison argued that the rights of the people would be protected because the power of each branch would be checked by the other branches. For instance, while Congress is explicitly granted the power to make laws, both the executive and the judicial branches are given some responsibility in the legislative process. The president may veto legislation passed by Congress, and the judiciary may review legislative acts to ensure that they are constitutional. Table 1.4 highlights some of the responsibilities assigned to each of the branches according to the principle of separation of powers and how each branch's power is checked by the other branches.

The founders faced a challenge when it came to creating a system in which the national government had enough authority to be effective while at the same time leaving most of the power to the states. There was general agreement that the

Table 1.4

Some of the Powers and Checks and Balances of the Three Branches of Government

	Powers of the Legislature	Powers of the Executive	Powers of the Judiciary
Checks on the Legislature	**Make laws** Power of purse	Veto legislation Call Congress into special session Recommend legislation	Review legislative acts
Checks on the Executive	Override executive veto with a 2/3 majority Impeach Confirm executive appointments (Senate) Reject foreign treaties (Senate) Power to fund (or not) executive actions	**Enforce laws**	Review executive acts Issue injunctions
Checks on the Judiciary	Create or eliminate courts Impeach Power to fund (or not) judiciary	Grant pardons Nominate judges	**Interpret laws**

national government had been too weak under the Articles of Confederation, but states were not eager to sacrifice any of the power they possessed under the system. The conflict over the balance of power between the national and state governments was addressed by the principle of **federalism**. According to this principle, government is divided into two levels—national and state—that must share power and responsibilities with one another.

Federalism A situation in which government is divided into two levels—national and state—that must share power and responsibilities with one another.

Under a federal system, the states would be required to forfeit to the national government some of the powers they held under the Articles, but the Constitution would place specific limits on the power of the national government. To satisfy those fearful of empowering the national government at the expense of the states, the Constitution lists exactly what powers belong to the national government. Any power that is not granted to the national government or denied to the states by the Constitution is left to the states and the people.

Instituting federalism as a governing principle was a bold move—no other nation had ever adopted such a system before. Without a model to follow, the founders were left to negotiate the details in a way that would please those who favored a stronger national government and those who favored stronger state governments. These details were among several that needed to be negotiated before at least nine states would agree to ratify the Constitution (see Table 1.5). Moreover, **ratification** (officially approving of the Constitution) did not end the debate about the proper balance of power between the national and state governments. Not only has the debate continued over time but the two levels of government have regularly challenged each other for power.

Ratification An act that gives official sanction or approval to a formal document such as a treaty or constitution.

Table 1.5 Ratification of the Constitution by the States

State	Date Ratified	Vote of Approval by the States	
		Yes	**No**
Delaware	December 7, 1787	30	0
Pennsylvania	December 12, 1787	46	23
New Jersey	December 18, 1787	38	0
Georgia	January 2, 1788	26	0
Connecticut	January 8, 1788	128	40
Massachusetts	February 6, 1788	187	168
Maryland	April 28, 1788	63	11
South Carolina	May 23, 1788	149	73
New Hampshire	June 21, 1788	57	47
Virginia	June 26, 1788	89	79
New York	July 26, 1788	30	27
North Carolina	November 21, 1789	195	77
Rhode Island	May 29, 1790	34	32

Sources: Jensen, Merrill, John Kaminski, and Gaspare Saladino, eds. *The Documentary History of the Ratification of the Constitution and the Bill of Rights, 1787–1791.* Madison, WI: *State* Historical Society of Wisconsin, 1976; The Avalon Project, *American History: A Documentary Record, 18th Century Documents*. Available at http://avalon.law.yale.edu/subject_menus/chrono.asp (accessed 6/15/2009).

4 The Bill of Rights clarifies the limits of the national government and the rights reserved to the states.

In the months following the Constitutional Convention, debate raged between those who supported the Constitution and those who opposed it. In the end, compromise again overcame conflict, and the Constitution was ratified. The compromise took the form of the first ten amendments to the Constitution.

Although the Constitution does not refer to political parties, the differing viewpoints on the appropriate strength and scope of the national government held by those who supported and opposed the Constitution laid the foundation for the first American political parties. **Federalists** supported the Constitution and the strong national government it created. **Anti-Federalists** opposed the Constitution and favored a decentralized national government that left more power to the state governments. In response to the Anti-Federalists' concerns about the Constitution, supporters of the document and the government it created wrote a series of essays that were printed as newspaper articles during the ratification battle. Known as the *Federalist Papers*, and penned primarily by James Madison and Alexander Hamilton, they are still used today by those who seek to understand the meaning of the Constitution and its founders' intentions.[12]

Federalists Those who supported the Constitution and the strong government it created.

Anti-Federalists Those who opposed the Constitution and favored a decentralized national government that left more power to the state governments.

The Anti-Federalists responded with essays of their own—penned under the names Brutus and Federal Farmer—that expressed their views on the dangers of centralizing power in a national government. They argued that a strong national government would undermine the states and violate the rights of citizens as expressed in the Declaration of Independence. Most of the state constitutions written in the years after the declaration of independence from Great Britain included a list of the basic freedoms guaranteed to citizens. As such, many Americans—including Thomas Jefferson, who supported the Constitution—wanted to see the same guarantees in the Constitution.[13]

Madison and Hamilton thought the reason for excluding such a list was obvious. The Constitution lists only those things that the government *may* do. To begin listing all of the things that government *may not* do would mean that the government may assume that anything not on the list is within its power.

Finally, Washington suggested that such guarantees be added to the Constitution once it was ratified through the amendment process. The states proposed over one hundred amendments that would protect the basic freedoms of citizens. From this list, Congress approved and sent twelve to the states for ratification. Of those sent to the states, ten were ratified and added to the Constitution in 1791. These ten amendments are the first changes made to the ratified Constitution and are collectively known as the **Bill of Rights**.

Bill of Rights The first ten amendments to the Constitution.

The amendments placed clearer and tighter boundaries on each of the three branches. For instance, the First Amendment clarifies the powers of Congress, while the Second, Third, and Fourth Amendments clarify the powers of the executive branch. The Fifth, Sixth, Seventh, and Eighth Amendments provide safeguards against the exercise of governmental power by defining the judicial branch more clearly. The Ninth and Tenth Amendments place limits on the national government as a whole by making it clear that any powers not granted to the national government or denied to the states by the Constitution are reserved to the people and the states. Among other things, the Bill of Rights guarantees that citizens may participate in the political process and that personal beliefs and personal privacy are to be respected.

The Bill of Rights represents yet another compromise that arose out of conflict. This compromise, along with the others made during the period between revolution and ratification, produced a new and independent nation. The governmental framework established by the Constitution has endured for more than two hundred years, and in that time, only minor changes have been made to the structure of the three institutions created. However, each of the twenty-seven amendments to the Constitution has made a lasting impact on the American political landscape.

3 Amending the Constitution is not meant to be easy.

The Bill of Rights illustrates the influence of the founders' historical experience: Unlike the Articles of Confederation, which could not be easily improved because it required that any changes be approved by all states, the Constitution included realistic measures that allowed for change if necessary. Though possible, change to the Constitution was not meant to be easy. Since the Bill of Rights was added in 1791, the Constitution has only been amended seventeen times, for a total of twenty-seven amendments.

It was important to the founders to have an amendment process that would allow for changes if faults were found with the Constitution but that would not be so easy as to render the Constitution victim to every whim of the people that might arise throughout time. Accordingly, the founders designed a two-stage amendment process that is outlined in Article V. In the first stage, amendments are proposed by one of two methods. They can be proposed by a two-thirds vote in both the House and the Senate or by a national convention called by Congress in response to petitions by two-thirds of the states. Of these two methods of proposal, only the first has ever been employed.

The second stage in the amendment process involves ratification, which can also be done using one of two methods. A proposed amendment has been ratified when it has been approved by the legislatures of three-fourths of the states or by ratification conventions in three-fourths of the states. Of these two methods of ratification, the second has only been used once (it was used to ratify the Twenty-First Amendment, which repealed the Eighteenth Amendment).

In short, the most commonly used method of amending the Constitution involves proposal by a two-thirds vote in both houses of Congress and ratification by three-fourths of the state legislatures. Since 1787, tens of thousands of amendments have been introduced in Congress, but only thirty-three have made it through the proposal process. Of the thirty-three approved by Congress, twenty-seven have been ratified. As this illustrates, once an amendment has been formally proposed by Congress, it faces a good chance of ratification. The founders intended for the proposal and ratification processes to be difficult so that only the most important changes to the Constitution would be made. They also limited the actors in the formal process to the legislative branch and the states; presidential approval is not required to amend the Constitution.

Since the Bill of Rights was added in 1791, the Constitution has been amended seventeen more times. Amendments 11 through 27 range in their scope and purpose, from clarifying the structures and processes established by the original document, to expanding citizenship, suffrage, and representation, to expanding or limiting the power of the national or state governments. The Eighteenth Amendment, which prohibited the manufacture, sale, and transportation of alcoholic beverages, was the only attempt to constitutionally limit the freedoms of citizens and make public policy. The attempt failed miserably; the Amendment did not curb drinking and was soon repealed by the Twenty-First Amendment.

The Constitution establishes majority rule but allows for the protection of minority rights.

The founders were concerned that in a system where the majority decided the outcome of elections, the rights of the minority had the potential to be violated. When we think about minorities today we tend to think about racial or ethnic minorities, but the founders were worried about a very different type of minority: economic and regional interests. The founders themselves were among the minority of wealthy Americans, and they feared that the poor majority would treat them unfairly given the chance. Similarly, those from the southern agricultural states feared that the merchants from the northern states would seek to benefit themselves at the expense of the southerners, and vice versa.

Factions Groups of people motivated by selfish interests. In today's terms, a faction can be thought of as an interest group or a political party.

Madison referred to these groups of people motivated by selfish interests as **factions**. In today's terms, a faction can be thought of as an interest group or a political party. Though the founders were generally fearful of factions of any kind because of the potential for conflict, they were particularly anxious about tyranny by a faction that represented a majority of the population. While a minority faction could simply be voted out of office by the majority in the next election, if a ruling majority faction could not be voted out of office by the minority and continued to rule, then tyranny similar to the kind the Americans had escaped through the Revolutionary War posed a real threat.

According to Madison, the Constitution contained several protections against both the tyranny of the majority and of the threat of small but powerful factions, which he explains in the *Federalist No. 10* and *Federalist No. 51*. A federal republic, in which power is divided between the national and state governments and people control the national government indirectly through their elected representatives, would prevent the tyranny of the majority by limiting the amount of control that the people have over the government. This system would also prevent the violence of faction by diversifying the interests that have to compete with one another for control of the government. According to Madison, the larger the republic, the more difficult it would be for a large majority faction to form. In essence, a large republic would place a check on the power of any single faction because it would be forced to compete with many other factions to gain control of the federal government.

The rights of the minority are again protected from the tyranny of the majority by the separation of powers, which divides power within the national government among three branches, and checks and balances, which give each branch of the national government some control and scrutiny over the others. In the end, the founders—who were likely motivated in part by their desire to establish a government that could maintain order enough to protect their property and their families—crafted a system that they believed would prevent tyranny but would not deny the rights of the minority.

1 The Constitution is ambiguous, which leaves it open to multiple interpretations.

The Constitution's brevity is remarkable—it contains only about 4,500 words, which is about the length of a fifteen-page term paper. Yet in those few words, the Constitution establishes a framework for government that has functioned for over two hundred years. In that time, the understood meaning and intent of the Constitution has changed, in part because the document is ambiguous enough that it is able to evolve along with the changing social and political contexts. Although Congress and the president have played a role in deciphering the meaning of the powers granted to them, the judicial branch is ultimately responsible for defining the boundaries of constitutional interpretation. In interpreting the Constitution, the courts often give it new meaning.

The founders left the Constitution vague in part so that it would remain relevant for generations to come, and in part out of necessity. While the founders were very specific about certain powers that could be exercised by each of the three branches (these powers are known as expressed or enumerated powers), they were vague about many others. Over time, Congress, the president, and even the Supreme Court have claimed implied powers—those powers that they feel are necessary to execute their expressed powers.

In some cases, wording was left vague simply because it was the only wording that could be agreed upon by the delegates to the Constitutional Convention. Certain phrases in particular are written in such indeterminate language that they have allowed the Constitution a certain degree of flexibility over time. Among the most ambiguous sections are the commerce clause, the necessary and proper clause (also known as the elastic clause), and the executive clause.

The commerce clause and the necessary and proper clause are found in Article I, which establishes the legislative branch and its powers. The **commerce clause** grants Congress the power "to regulate commerce with foreign nations, and among the several states, and with the Indian Tribes." The **necessary and proper clause** grants Congress the power "to make all laws which shall be necessary and proper for carrying into execution the foregoing powers." Both clauses are rife with undefined words that leave their meaning open to interpretation by Congress and the courts. The necessary and proper clause is also vague enough to allow for multiple interpretations. This clause gives Congress the practically unrestricted power to enact laws that are related to the powers it is expressly granted in the Constitution. Congress is largely responsible for deciding what is necessary and proper, though the courts are able to check that Congress does not exceed its constitutional boundaries.

Commerce clause This clause in the Constitution grants Congress the power "to regulate commerce with foreign nations, and among the several states, and with the Indian Tribes."

Necessary and proper clause This clause in the Constitution grants Congress the power "to make all laws which shall be necessary and proper for carrying into execution the foregoing powers."

A third key section of the Constitution that is vaguely worded is the **executive clause**, which is found in Article II and states that "The executive powers shall be vested in a president of the United States of America." It does not, however, define what executive powers are. As such, presidents have used this clause to justify taking broad liberties, such as issuing executive orders, claiming executive privilege, or forming executive agreements with foreign nations. This section is particularly vague in part because the founders could not agree on what the powers of the executive should be, and in part because they did not want to restrict the executive's ability to lead in times of crisis.

Executive clause This clause in the Constitution states that "executive powers shall be vested in a president."

Article II also requires that the president take an oath of office in which he affirms to "preserve, protect, and defend the Constitution of the United States." Presidents have also used this phrase to justify taking certain actions that they claim are necessary to protect the Constitution, such as engaging in military action abroad without a formal declaration of war by Congress. While presidents have expanded the definition of executive power over time, they must still act within the constitutional boundaries determined by the courts.

CONCLUSION

The Constitution embodies several principles that characterize the American political system. Among them are republicanism, federalism, the separation of powers, and checks and balances. Each of these principles and others that the founders valued grew out of the American historical experience and was the product of conflict and compromise.

Was the conflict worth it? Have the compromises worked? We began this chapter with a question: What would the founders think of our country today? Have we

THEIR LIST

An Insider's View

JANE FITZGERALD

Archivist, National Archives

Anyone who has ever visited the National Archives on Pennsylvania Avenue in Washington, D.C. (or watched the 2004 film *National Treasure*, for that matter) knows that the handwritten Declaration of Independence, U.S. Constitution, and Bill of Rights sit proudly on public display under the Rotunda for the Charters of Freedom. Only archivist Jane Fitzgerald and three agency archivists, however, are allowed full access to the rest of our nation's founding documents. For residing deep within the secure and climate-controlled vaults of the National Archives are the records of the Continental and Confederation congresses and the Constitutional Convention. These records tell the story of our founding from the perspective of the founders themselves, and Jane has come to learn this story well during her 20 years at the National Archives and Records Administration.

Jane studied history as an undergraduate and went on to earn a Master of Arts degree in American history. She then began working as an archives technician at the National Archives. After completing a 3-year archivist program, Jane eventually began managing records from the Continental and Confederation congresses and the Constitutional Convention, as well as all public laws, presidential proclamations, executive orders, and treaties. This is no small task. On a day-to-day basis, Jane handles reference requests for these historical jewels from the general public, federal, state and local government agencies, authors, publishers, production companies, as well as from the agency's exhibit staff. In addition, she also works with the agency's document conservation and digital imaging labs to treat and scan many of these records. All of this involves getting to know the documents and the history that surrounds them well. Even after 20 years on the job, Jane still learns something new every day.

So what does someone who sees our nation's historical records on a daily basis think everyone should know about the time of our founding? First, the importance of compromise cannot be understated. Nearly all of the official documents and journals from both the Continental and Confederation congresses and the Constitutional Convention show signs of intense conflict between the delegates so great that it is a wonder that the thirteen states were able to join in confederation or union in the first place.

lived up to their expectations? Does the nation embody the principles they held dear? In short, at more than two hundred years old, how are we doing?

The founders rejected the notion of direct democracy in favor of a republican or representative democracy. Thinking about our modern system, how well are we living up to this principle of republicanism? Many people who are eligible do not even vote and those that do often report unhappiness with the candidates. By the same token, the founders placed enormous value on liberty—freedom from governmental power. How well are we doing in the twenty-first century living up to this value? After all, we live in a system in which you have to take your shoes off before you board a plane, wear a seatbelt, and be subject to metal detectors and bag searches before you enter many buildings. These requirements have been found necessary to maintain our overall public safety, health, and well-being, but at the same time do they give us pause to think about what the founders might say?

Second, compromise was possible in part because of the committee structure that was set up in both the congresses and the convention. Though we tend to attribute independence and union to a few well-known founders, in reality the Declaration of Independence and the Constitution were born out of committees of compromising men who were elected by their states to act as representatives on their behalf. These committees allowed the workload to be divided up so that goals could be met more quickly and efficiently. (Keep in mind that the entire Constitution was written in only one summer—and without the help of mass communication or the Internet!) These committees also allowed streamlined negotiations to take place, since the number involved in the initial bargaining was smaller, and when items went to the full delegation for a vote, a coalition of supporters already existed.

There are also a number of commonly held misconceptions that Jane would like to see cleared up. When convened, the First Continental Congress was not a lawmaking body, as the Congress in existence today is. In fact, you'll recall that it was not even a lawful assembly according to Britain's Coercive Acts. This first congress initially served and functioned as an advisory council for the colonies to voice their grievances against Great Britain. In addition, the presidents of the Continental and Confederation congresses were selected by fellow delegates and had no executive powers—quite different from the Office of the President as ultimately established by the Constitution. Finally, although he served as a delegate from Virginia in the First and Second Continental Congresses, George Washington was not involved in the writing of the Declaration of Independence—he was busy leading the Continental Army at the time it was written.

Washington did, however, have a hand in writing the Constitution, as his handwritten notes in the margins of the very first printed draft of the Constitution illustrate (see the chapter-opening image). This record is among the most appreciated by Jane, who views it as a symbol of the compromises that ultimately led to the U.S. Constitution that continues to structure our government and embody American ideals today. That she is able to turn the pages of this magnificent document is only one of the many reasons Jane Fitzgerald loves her job.[14]

The principles of republicanism and liberty are but two of the many values embodied in the U.S. Constitution. As we move through the text, you should consistently ask yourself what the founders would think about where we are and who we've become today. Would they even recognize the system of government they created?

YOUR LIST REVISITED

At the beginning of the chapter you were asked to think about what you might include on your own list of the Top 10 Most Important Things to Know about the Foundations of American Government. Now that you have read the chapter, take a moment to revisit your list. What, if anything, would you change about your list? Do you agree or disagree with the chapter list constructed by the author? What might you add or delete? Why?

KEY TERMS

Anarchism 3
Anti-Federalists 17
Articles of Confederation 8
Autocracy 4
Bill of Rights 17
Checks and balances 14
Commerce clause 21
Confederation 8
Constitution 8
Constitutional Convention 10
Constitutional democracies 4
Declaration of Independence 7
Democracy 5
Executive clause 21
Factions 19
Federalism 15
Federalists 17
First Continental Congress 6
Government 2
Great Compromise 11
Legislative supremacy 14
Liberalism 4
Monarchy 9
Necessary and proper clause 21
New Jersey Plan 11
Oligarchy 4
Ratification 15
Representative democracy 5
Republic 5
Second Continental Congress 6
Separation of powers 14
Shays' Rebellion 9
Theocracy 4
Three-Fifths Compromise 12
Totalitarianism 3
Virginia Plan 11

CHAPTER REVIEW QUESTIONS

10 What are the two primary purposes of government? Are there ever times when these purposes may conflict?

9 In what ways does a republic differ from an autocracy, oligarchy, and theocracy?

8 Explain three of the most significant events that led to the Declaration of Independence.

7 What are three reasons why the Articles of Confederation failed?

6 In what ways was the U.S. Constitution a result of compromise?

5 How did the founders limit the power of the national government? What did Madison mean by "double security"?

4 Why did some of the founders fear that the Bill of Rights would actually limit individual freedom?

3 Why did the founders make it difficult for the Constitution to be amended?

2 How does a system that allows many factions to exist reduce the danger of factions?

1 What role has the Supreme Court played in changing the meaning of the Constitution over time?

SUGGESTED READINGS

- Breyer, Stephen. *Active Liberty: Interpreting our Democratic Constitution.* New York: Knopf, 2005.
- Chernow, Ron. "The Founding Fathers versus the Tea Party." *New York Times*, September 24, 2010, p. 29.
- Dahl, Robert. *How Democratic Is the American Constitution?* New Haven, CT: Yale University Press, 2001.
- Derthick, Martha. *Keeping the Compound Republic: Essays on American Federalism.* Washington, DC: Brookings Institution, 2001.

- Jensen, Merrill. *The Articles of Confederation: An Interpretation of the Social-Constitutional History of the American Revolution, 1774–1781.* Madison, WI: University of Wisconsin Press, 1959.
- Madison, James, Alexander Hamilton, and John Jay. *The Federalist Papers.* New York, NY: Penguin Classics, 1987.
- Madison, James, Alexander Hamilton, and John Jay. *The Federalist Papers,* 1787–1788. Available online at: http://thomas.loc.gov/home/histdox/fedpapers.html.
- Paine, Thomas. *Common Sense and Other Writings: A Norton Critical Edition.* J.M. Opal (Ed.) New York, NY: WW. Norton, 2011.
- Posner, Richard. *Not a Suicide Pact: The Constitution in a Time of National Emergency.* New York: Oxford University Press, 2006.
- Riker, William. *The Strategy of Rhetoric: Campaigning for the American Constitution.* New Haven, CT: Yale University Press, 1996.
- Storing, Herbert, ed. *The Complete Anti-Federalist.* Chicago: University of Chicago Press, 1981.

SUGGESTED FILMS

- *Johnny Tremain* (1957)
- *1776* (1972)
- *Chinatown* (1974)
- *Lord of the Flies* (1990)
- *Liberty! The American Revolution* (1997)
- *The Patriot* (2000)
- *National Treasure* (2004)
- *When the Levees Broke: A Requiem in Four Acts* (2006)
- *American Outrage* (2007)
- *John Adams* (2008)

SUGGESTED WEBSITES

- **Constitution Timeline:** http://www.constitutioncenter.org/timeline/flash/cw.html
- **National Constitutions:** http://confinder.richmond.edu/
- **State Constitutions:** http://www.law.cornell.edu/statutes.html
- **The Avalon Project:** http://avalon.law.yale.edu/subject_menus/debcont.asp
- **The Federalist Papers:** http://thomas.loc.gov/home/histdox/fedpapers.html
- **The Founders' Constitution:** http://press-pubs.uchicago.edu/founders/tocs/toc.html
- **The National Archives:** http://www.archives.gov/exhibits/charters/charters.html
- **The National Conference of State Legislatures:** http://www.ncsl.org/StateFederalCommittees/tabid/773/Default.aspx
- **The National Governors Association:** http://www.nga.org/portal/site/nga/menuitem.b14a675ba7f89cf9e8ebb856a11010a0
- **The U.S. Conference of Mayors:** http://usmayors.org/

ENDNOTES

[1]"CNN poll: Most say Founding Fathers wouldn't be impressed," July 4, 2008, accessible on-line at: http://www.cnn.com/2008/US/07/04/us.poll/index.html.

[2]An an interesting discussion of what the founders would have said regarding politics today, see: Ron Chernow, "The Founding Fathers versus the Tea Party," *New York Times*, September 24, 2010, p. 29.

[3]For more on the Constitution in times of crisis, see Richard Posner, *Not a Suicide Pact: The Constitution in a Time of National Emergency* (New York: Oxford University Press, 2006).

[4]Robert Dahl is one of the prominent thinkers who has written about how democratic the United States Constitution is, see: Robert Dahl, *How Democratic is the American Constitution?* (New Haven, CT: Yale University Press, 2001).

[5]You can read more about the history of the United States in Samuel Eliott Morison's *The Oxford History of the United States, 1783–1917*. (Oxford, UK: Oxford University Press, 1927).

[6]For a more complete timeline, see "The History Place: American Revolution—Prelude to American Revolution," available at: http://www.historyplace.com/unitedstates/revolution/index.html.

[7]For a more complete timeline, see "The History Place: American Revolution—The War for Independence," available at: http://www.historyplace.com/unitedstates/revolution/index.html.

[8]The Articles of Confederation. 1787, available online at: http://www.ourdocuments.gov/doc.php?flash=false&doc=3. Max Farrand, ed. *The Records of the Federal Convention of 1787*. (New Haven: Yale University Press, 1911). Madison's *Notes* are also available online at: http://avalon.law.yale.edu/subject_menus/debcont.asp.

[9]You can learn more about the delegates to the Constitutional Convention by reading Gordon Lloyd's "Individual Biographies of the Delegates to the Constitutional Convention," *Teachingamericanhistory.org*. http://www.teachingamericanhistory.org/convention/delegates/ (accessed June 2, 2011).

[10]John P. Kaminski, "Madison's Gift," *Common-Place*, v. 2, no. 4 (July 2002), http://www.common-place.org/vol-02/no-04/reviews/kaminski.shtml (accessed June 2, 2011).

[11]Merrill Jensen, John Kaminski, and Gaspare Saladino, eds., *The Documentary History of the Ratification of the Constitution and the Bill of Rights, 1787–1791*. (Madison, WI: State Historical Society of Wisconsin, 1976).

[12]James Madison, Alexander Hamilton, and John Jay. The Federalist Papers, 1787–1788, available online at: http://thomas.loc.gov/home/histdox/fedpapers.html.

[13]For more on the Anti-Federalists' contributions to constitutional development, see Herbert J. Storing, *What the Anti-federalists Were For?: The Political Thought of the Opponents of the Constitution*. (Chicago: The University of Chicago Press, 1981).

[14] You can read even more about Jane and the records she thumbs through daily in Michael E. Ruane's article "Preserving America's Paper Trail," which appeared in the *Washington Post* (Metro, p. B03) on December 5, 2006.

Chapter 2

FEDERALISM

Top Ten List

10 Federalism differs significantly from confederate and unitary forms of government.

9 Federalism allows states to become laboratories of democracy and lends itself to governing geographically large and culturally diverse nations.

8 The *Federalist Papers* were a sales pitch for federalism.

7 From 1789 to 1900, federalism evolved into dual federalism.

6 From 1900 to 1930, the federal government began to actively regulate the economy.

5 From 1930 to 1980, the New Deal and Great Society programs expanded the national government even further, reflecting a period of cooperative federalism.

4 From 1980 to 2008, the Reagan Revolution ushered in a "new federalism."

3 Federalism remains contested terrain during the Obama presidency.

2 Federalism looks different from the "bottom up."

1 The No Child Left Behind Act shows the complexities, challenges, and opportunities of American federalism.

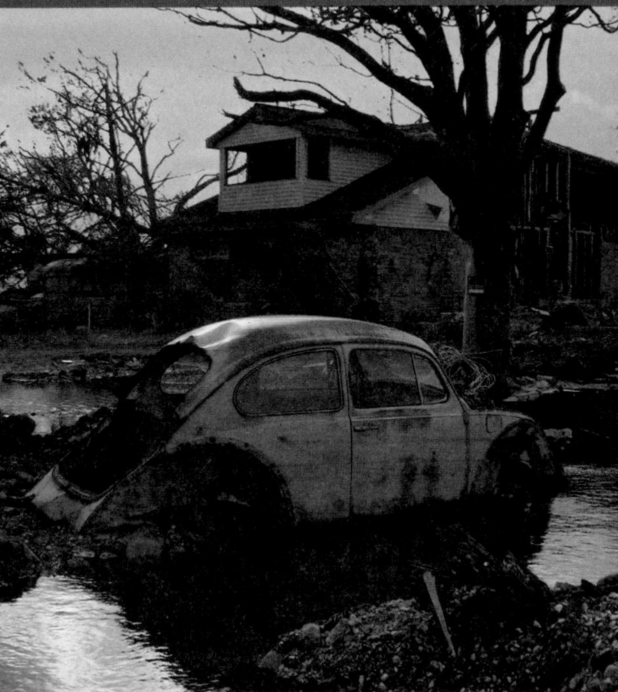

Three months after Hurricane Katrina, water continued to leak from the New Orleans Levee Breach, 100 ft. from the 17th Street Canal. Many observers saw the government's ineffective response to Hurricane Katrina as a downside of the political structure known as federalism. The case of Hurricane Katrina shows that issues of governmental structures are more than just the subject of mundane academic debate—they have very real consequences for the lives of everyday citizens.

YOUR LIST

Before you read this chapter, take a few moments to think about what you might include on a list of the Top 10 Most Important Things to Know About Federalism. At the end of the chapter you will be asked to compare and contrast your list with the one supplied in this chapter.

INTRODUCTION

In August of 2005, one of the strongest hurricanes ever to make landfall in the United States slammed into the Gulf Coast. By the time the storm dissipated, Hurricane Katrina had left a wake of destruction throughout the southern Gulf states of Florida, Mississippi, Louisiana, and Alabama. Some of Katrina's most devastating impacts were felt in the city of New Orleans, where a system of levees designed by the federal government's Army Corps of Engineers failed spectacularly. When the storm hit, huge swaths of New Orleans—especially the city's 9th ward—were inundated by as much as 15 feet of water. Although most of the area's residents had already evacuated, many of the city's poorest residents who lacked transportation—particularly those from primarily African American areas—were left to fend for themselves.[1] Over the next few days, Americans saw images of their fellow citizens stranded and waving from their rooftops for help. Many were saved in daring rescues by private volunteers, the U.S. Coast Guard, and various other officials of national, state, and local governments. But many of the stranded never received any help at all. In total, it is estimated that nearly 2,000 people perished from the effects of the storm, most of those in Louisiana, and many of them elderly.[2]

Federalism A political structure that divides political power between a national government and one or more subnational governments.

Many observers saw the government's ineffective response to Hurricane Katrina as a downside of the political structure known as **federalism**, which divides political power between a national government and one or more subnational governments. During the crisis, national, state, and local agencies struggled to communicate with one another in the absence of functioning land and cell phone lines. New Orleans Mayor Ray Nagin, who had ordered a mandatory evacuation of the city, argued that his city simply lacked the resources to take the lead in responding to a disaster of such magnitude.

In the days after the storm hit, the Louisiana Superdome became the site of particular human suffering, as thousands of residents crowded into the stadium seeking shelter and awaiting food, water, medical, and other assistance. Meanwhile, Louisiana Governor Kathleen Blanco called out the Louisiana National Guard and, in a letter, appealed for federal disaster assistance, arguing that Louisiana too lacked sufficient resources and manpower to deal effectively with the crisis. But that assistance either never came or came too late. At the federal level, officials such as Federal Emergency Management Agency (FEMA) Director Michael Brown later testified to Congress that the national government lacked the constitutional authority to intervene in geographic areas not specifically listed in the Louisiana governor's formal request for assistance to the state.

Critics noted that FEMA, a formerly independent agency that had been merged with the Department of Homeland Security created after the 9/11 terrorist attacks, was no longer able to independently respond to natural disasters. Instead, some argued that the agency was hamstrung by the new chain of command. Others claimed the agency had shifted too much of its focus from preventing natural disasters to preventing terrorist attacks. Many believe that President George W. Bush's seemingly tepid response dealt a severe blow to his image as a competent manager, leading to steep declines in his popularity rating. In the end, almost everyone agreed that the lack of communication between and failure of leadership at the national, state, and local levels were signature causes of the extensive human suffering resulting from the storm.

The case of Hurricane Katrina raises a number of questions about governmental responsibility for a natural disaster under a structure of government known as "federalism." Throughout this chapter, we will examine questions such as: What is federalism, and how is it different from other types of government? What are the advantages and disadvantages of federalism? How has federalism operated and evolved over time in the United States? Then we will look at federalism from the bottom up, from the perspective of state and local governments. Finally, we will end with an examination of how federalism impacts the governance of American K–12 public education. The case of Hurricane Katrina shows that issues of governmental structures are more than just the subject of mundane academic debate—they have very real consequences for the lives of everyday citizens.

10 Federalism differs significantly from confederate and unitary forms of government.

Our first constitution, the Articles of Confederation (1777–1787), was a **confederation**, in which ultimate authority or **sovereignty** is vested in each of the state (or subnational) governments, and the national government has virtually no power. The Articles of Confederation established an extremely loose political alliance among the various newly established American states, and many of them began to equip their own armies and navies, establish separate currencies, and forge their own diplomatic relations with foreign countries. Although these nations (called New York, Massachusetts, Virginia, etc.) had come together to defeat mighty Great Britain as the colonial overlord, in the aftermath of the American Revolution it was not clear what the unifying factors for the new nation would be.

Confederation Ultimate authority or sovereignty is vested in subnational governments, and the national government has virtually no power.

Sovereignty Supreme power or authority, especially over a political or governmental body.

Today, many consider the European Union to be an example of a quasi-confederation, with each of the member states maintaining independent sovereignty over most issues. The European Union maintains a single currency, known as the euro, but individual member states still maintain national sovereignty over most internal matters and most diplomatic relations with other nations. The American Confederacy during the Civil War serves as another classic example of a confederation. Under the Confederacy, based in Richmond, Virginia, all eleven southern states that seceded from the Union were effectively separate nations.

Unitary government Ultimate power is vested in a single national government.

Unitary governments, in contrast, occupy territory on the other end of the continuum of power (see Figure 2.1). In unitary forms of government, power is vested in a single national government. Regional and local governments exist in unitary systems, but they are not sovereign. Instead, they largely function to implement policies developed at the national level. Since policies can be coordinated by a single

Figure 2.1 Continuum of Power

Governments differ in terms of the degree to which power is centralized. In a unitary government, power is centralized in the national government, while in a confederation power is decentralized, and the national government has very little power. In federal systems, both the national and subnational (local, state) governments share power.

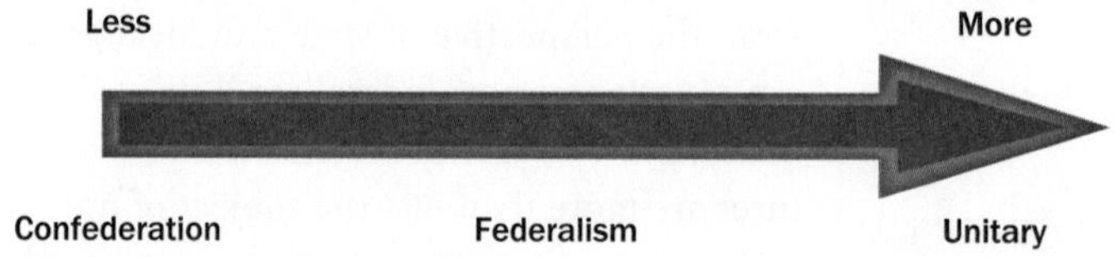

entity, there is far less opportunity or need for duplication of programs, agencies, or governments themselves. There is also clearer accountability for the success or failure of policies. Today, classic examples of unitary governments include Japan, Denmark, England, and France.

9 Federalism allows states to become laboratories of democracy and lends itself to governing geographically large and culturally diverse nations.

Federalism allows individual states to become, in Supreme Court Justice Louis D. Brandeis's famous phrase, "laboratories of democracy" where experiments with new and innovative policy approaches can be tailored to the needs of a particular state. For example, California has its own Environmental Protection Agency—independent of the federal EPA—that allows California to fashion additional environmental policies to fit the state's unique climate and geography. With federalism, if a state's problem-solving approach appears successful, other states may choose to adopt it as a model. If they are unsuccessful, the program's failure will have not been forced upon the state by the national government.

International relations scholars also note that federalism lends itself well to the governing of territories that are either large geographically or diverse ethnically or culturally. By allowing remote regions of geographically large nations (like the United States) a sense of self-determination or autonomy, federalism can head off some of the disconnection, isolation, and resentment that citizens in far-flung regions often feel toward decisions made by a distant national government (see Figure 2.2).[3]

Figure 2.2 Selected Countries Using the Federalist System, 2011

This map highlights several countries around the world that have a federal system of government. Federalism lends itself well to the governing of territories that are either large geographically, or diverse ethnically or culturally.

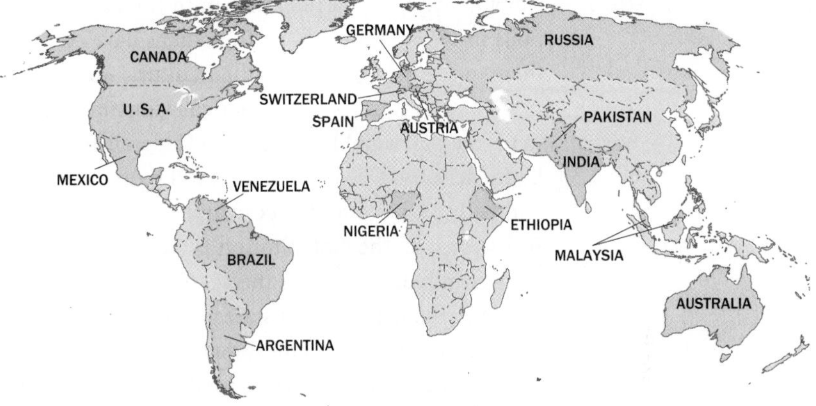

Nation	Population*	Geographic Size, sq km
Argentina	41,343,200	2,780,400
Australia	21,515,754	7,741,220
Austria	8,214,160	83,871
Brazil	201,103,330	8,514,877
Canada	33,759,742	9,984,670
Ethiopia	88,013,491	1,104,300
Germany	82,282,988	357,022
India	1,173,108,018	3,287,263
Malaysia	28,274,729	329,874
Mexico	112,468,855	1,964,375
Nigeria	152,217,341	923,768
Pakistan	184,404,791	796,095
Russia	139,390,205	17,098,242
Spain**	45,505,963	505,370
Switzerland	7,623,438	41,277
United States	310,232,863	9,826,675
Venezuela	27,223,228	912,050

*CIA 2010 estimate.
**Spain is considered "quasi-federal."

Source: The CIA World Fact Book, 2011.

In ethnically diverse nations such as Spain, Canada, and India, subnational governments such as states, provinces, and territories are given a significant amount of self-government over language and other cultural issues. In the province of Québec, Canada, French speakers have long been the majority, and relations with Anglo-Canadians have not always been amicable. In fact, during the 1960s and 1970s, and again in the 1990s, a movement emerged to create a nation separate from the rest of Canada. Although a referendum in the province of Québec narrowly failed at the polls in 1995, Francophone Canadians have continued to pursue policies that allow them to retain and promote their cultural identity.[4]

The effort to rewrite America's Constitution in 1787 was in large part an effort to try out a new political structure, federalism, to fit the political needs of the society. Ultimately, the U.S. Constitution did more than just list civil rights and civil liberties and define a system of checks and balances among three branches of government. At its essence, the Constitution is a document that attempts to define the basics of American federalism and the age-old question of how much sovereignty should be vested in the national and state governments. But the reality is that the Constitution is at best ambiguous on most questions of federal power, which in part explains why the balance of power between national and state governments has come to define much of American political conflict.

8 The *Federalist Papers* were a sales pitch for federalism.

Although it's easy to look back and believe that the United States was somehow destined to successfully adopt federalism as the nation's defining political structure, such an interpretation misses the important role that political theory, smart politics, and perhaps even luck played in the evolution of the country's governmental system. Published as a series of 84 newspaper articles coinciding with the Philadelphia Constitutional Convention (1787–1789), the ***Federalist Papers***, as they became known, were critical in persuading Americans to adopt a system of shared sovereignty between national and state government, a system that had never before been tried on such a large scale.

Federalist Papers Written by three influential authors and proponents of stronger national government, they were published as a series of 84 newspaper articles and critical in persuading Americans to adopt a system of federalism.

The *Federalist Papers* were written by three influential authors and proponents of stronger national government—Alexander Hamilton, James Madison, and John Jay—although their identities were kept secret until after passage of the new constitution. Each of the 84 articles makes the case for a stronger national government, but scholars consider certain of the articles to be classics. *Federalist No. 10* is probably the most widely read and purest expression of the political philosophy contained in the *Federalist Papers*.

In *Federalist No. 10*, James Madison attempts to address the concerns of many who feared the emergence of an all-powerful, perhaps monarchical, central government. Turning conventional wisdom on its head, Madison argued that creating a stronger national government would help prevent powerful interest groups—in Madison's terminology, "factions"—from dominating the nation's politics. Unlike in the states, where powerful factions, southern plantation owners or northern manufacturing interests, for example, could go unchallenged, Madison argued that in a new and pluralistic national legislative body, no single faction could amass sufficient political power to threaten individual liberty. For Madison, only a national political body could effectively dilute the influence of any single powerful faction.

In a sense, you can think of the argument for federalism as another dimension of the larger argument about the need for checks and balances in the new constitution. Above all, Americans were afraid of the reemergence of an aristocracy. Advocates of the new constitution could argue that not only would power be restrained by three competing branches of government but power would also be curtailed by a political system that required competition for power between the national and state governments.

Keep in mind, however, that the *Federalist Papers* were not uniformly well received. In particular, opposition to the idea of a stronger national government came from individuals who became known as Anti-Federalists. Primarily southerners concerned about protecting the economic and social institution of slavery, Anti-Federalists scrambled to write their own competing treaties defending the existing political order of state sovereignty, but they were unable to match the authors of the *Federalist Papers* point for point. Many historians consider the *Federalist Papers* to be as significant a contribution as any writings of American political theory.

The debate between the Federalists and Anti-Federalists about the role of government has formed the essence of American ideological conflict between the two major political parties for nearly all of American history. Even today, it is easy to trace the philosophical lineage of the modern Democratic Party, which since the 1930s has supported an active and robust national government, to the authors of the *Federalist Papers*. Conversely, in many ways, the modern Republican Party can trace its ideological heritage to the states' rights philosophy of the Anti-Federalists.

7 From 1789 to 1900, federalism evolved into dual federalism.

One cannot understand the dynamics of American politics—particularly our current debates about the role of the national government—without understanding the ways that American federalism has evolved over time. The relationship between the federal and state governments in the United States has changed a great deal since the founding.[5]

Dual federalism Legal theory in operation in the United States until 1900 that promoted the idea of separate spheres of authority for national and state governments.

The first period of American federalism (from 1789 to 1900) is known as **dual federalism**. Often characterized as a **layer cake**, this theory promotes the idea of distinct and separate spheres of authority for national and state governments.

Layer cake A metaphor for American federalism as three more or less independent spheres of policymaking among national, state, and local governments.

In short, it is a system of government in which both the national and state governments are supreme within their own sphere and responsible for specific types of policies. For example, during the period of dual federalism, the national government was responsible for foreign policy and military engagement and a limited number of domestic policies. It did little more than print money, deliver the mail, engage in international diplomacy, and help move the country westward through military and other means. In contrast, state governments were responsible for policies that had a more direct role in the daily lives of people, such as local law enforcement, building and maintaining roads, and education. As a result, during this early period, the national government had limited power.

This minimal role for the national government initially was not surprising given that the United States began as an alliance of thirteen independent and sovereign states, which reluctantly *gave up* portions of their sovereignty to a newly created national government. Contrast that to the experience of other federal systems like Canada's where the national government *breathed life into* the subnational governments. Understanding how our federal system formed helps us understand the trajectory of the expansion of the national government during the twentieth century. It also explains some of the intensity of our debates about the role of government in American politics.

The American Civil War (1861–1865) marked the beginning of the end of dual federalism. Following the war, the national government began to play a role in areas previously reserved for state action alone. For instance, the national government began slowly to exert itself in areas such as civil rights and the rights of citizens. One key example is the passage of the "Civil War Amendments," the Fourteenth, Fifteenth, and Sixteenth Amendments, which themselves dealt a major blow to the notion of a rigid dual citizenship. In particular, the Fourteenth Amendment set out to explicitly create the concept of a unified national citizenship whose privileges could not be abridged by state and local government.[6] In addition, the federal government also began to take a more active role in the regulation of the economy and business.

6 From 1900 to 1930, the federal government began to actively regulate the economy.

For most of the seventeenth, eighteenth, and nineteenth centuries, the United States was predominantly an agricultural nation. Blessed with a temperate climate and a seemingly endless supply of arable land, navigable rivers, and easy access to overseas markets, the United States emerged on the world stage as an agricultural powerhouse. While the United States was becoming a global supplier of food and other raw materials, most industrial activity to refine those raw materials into commercial products was taking place in major European cities. But this dynamic shifted in the late nineteenth century with the development of new industrial technologies and production systems in cities such as New York, Boston, and Chicago. The era heralded the arrival of American industry and the emergence of powerful economic sectors such as steel, railroads, meatpacking, oil, and coal.[7]

Simultaneously, powerful new players in American politics known as corporations also emerged. These corporations, and in particular their leaders, began to amass economic power in ways that distorted previous market relations. Of primary concern to most Americans was the emergence of powerful corporate monopolies. Some of you may have played the classic board game "Monopoly," which (not surprisingly) appeared early in the twentieth century. Originally known as "The Landlord's Game," the genesis for the game was essentially political: to reveal to Americans the negative impacts of real estate monopolies. The game "Monopoly" usually ends up with one individual in a dominant market position, controlling coveted properties such as Boardwalk and Park Place and all four railroads with virtually everyone else ending up flat broke!

Capitalism Economic system based upon the free exchange of privately owned property between individuals.

Oligopolies Economic markets or sectors that are controlled by a small number of owners.

Trusts A nineteenth-century name for monopolies; power and wealth are concentrated in corporations.

Essentially, the game is a metaphor for late-nineteenth-century American **capitalism**. As envisioned by the Scottish economist Adam Smith (1723–1790), capitalism is an economic system based upon the free exchange of privately owned property between individuals. By the late nineteenth century, monopolies, or at the very least **oligopolies** (economic markets or sectors controlled by a small number of owners), had emerged, artificially driving prices up and competition out of most sectors of the American economy.

Because of their ability to concentrate economic and political power in fewer and fewer hands, monopolies, then commonly known as **trusts**, were seen as both a threat to free-market capitalism as well as to democracy itself. The result was public pressure for federal regulation of monopolies. The classic case is John D. Rockefeller's Standard Oil, which by 1900 had begun to corner the oil and refined gasoline market in the United States. Ultimately, the administration of President Theodore Roosevelt, backed by the U.S. Supreme Court, forced the breakup of Standard Oil into numerous smaller corporations.[8]

During the late nineteenth and early twentieth centuries, the American economy was characterized by pronounced "boom and bust" cycles, resulting in numerous financial "panics" between 1870 and 1910. Indeed, in the aftermath of the Banker's Panic of 1907, political momentum gathered for the creation of a Federal Reserve Bank. Established in 1913, the Federal Reserve Bank was charged with helping to stabilize the American economy through the use of such tools as interest rates and the ability to issue credit to struggling banks.

The late nineteenth and twentieth centuries also witnessed a growth in the national government's role in regulating food and drugs. Prior to the creation of the Food and Drug Administration there was little or no government oversight (federal or otherwise) over the food supply. Probably more than any other factor prompting government action was the publication of Upton Sinclair's novel *The Jungle* (1903). Sinclair's novel contained graphic depictions of horrific conditions in American meat processing plants. Revelations contained in the book were so salacious that it became an immediate bestseller. After reading the novel, President Roosevelt ordered the creation of a special commission to examine the allegations contained in the book. After its investigation, the commission produced a report that largely corroborated the descriptions found in *The Jungle* and ultimately led to passage of the Food and Drug Act and the creation of what we today know as the Food and Drug Administration.

Progressivism A political movement that saw a greater need for government intervention in American economic and social relations.

The role of the national government in regulating food, drugs, and other aspects of society coincided with a political movement known as **Progressivism**, which saw a need for greater government intervention in American economic and social relations. And although the Progressive movement petered out during the 1920s, the governing philosophy behind it would soon make a spectacular comeback.

5 From 1930 to 1980, the New Deal and Great Society programs expanded the national government even further, reflecting a period of cooperative federalism.

By the mid-1920s, the pendulum of federalism had begun to swing back in favor of advocates of less government. The Progressive movement achieved a great measure of success, only to run out of steam. During the Roaring 20s, the American stock and real estate markets soared to unprecedented heights, and the potential for broad societal prosperity seemed limitless. Then came the crash. On October 28, 1929, forever known as Black Monday, the American stock market and other major world markets tumbled, and a psychology of fear gripped the nation. Over the ensuing months and years, banks failed, properties were foreclosed, and millions of Americans of all social classes were plunged into poverty. The Great Depression, as it became known, was the most serious crisis to face the nation since the Civil War.

As the Depression lingered into 1932, Democratic presidential candidate Franklin Delano Roosevelt began to articulate a vision for a far more involved national government. Relying on the theories of British economist John Maynard Keynes, who believed that national governments could correct for failing markets by deficit spending during severe economic downturns, Roosevelt's **New Deal** laid out an entirely new vision for the role of the national government in American society.

New Deal The name given to the programs laid out by President Franklin Delano Roosevelt to create a social safety net as well as ensure federal oversight of financial markets.

Social Security New Deal-era program created to provide direct financial assistance to elderly and disabled persons.

Roosevelt made the case that the national government should both create a new social safety net as well as take on greater responsibility to ensure federal oversight of financial markets. On the social side of the ledger emerged programs that became known as **Social Security** and Unemployment, which sought to provide financial "security" to those who had been unable to find work or were past their productive working years. Another program, Aid to Families with Dependent Children, sought to provide general relief in the form of cash payments to those in poverty who had children. On the financial side, Roosevelt signed legislation that led to the creation of agencies such as the Federal Deposit Insurance Corporation (FDIC), the Securities and Exchange Commission (SEC), as well as a host of banking and other regulations intended to regain the confidence of Americans and reverse the downward spiral of the American economy.

Cooperative federalism An era in which the national government assisted the states in addressing the nation's economic and social crises.

Marble cake View of federalism, which holds that policies are made and implemented by multiple levels of government simultaneously rather than independently.

Roosevelt's New Deal marked a watershed moment in the history of American federalism and the realization of what some scholars call **cooperative federalism**, an era in which the national government assisted the states to address the nation's social and economic crises. In contrast to the layered cake analogy used to describe dual federalism, cooperative federalism reflected a **marble cake**—one in which the power and policy responsibilities of the national and state governments overlapped. Instead of operating in distinct spheres, the governments now shared not only power but also the costs and potential blame for programs that did not work as intended.

In one sense, the New Deal extended the impulse of the Progressive movement in furthering a regulatory framework for the American economy. But by extending the national government's responsibility to directly provide for the economic security of individual Americans, the New Deal represented a quantum leap toward the creation of what many conservatives derisively call a "welfare state" that they believe encourages dependence on government rather than old-fashioned self-reliance. Indeed, many contemporary critics attempted to undercut popular support for Roosevelt's programs by referring to his programs as "socialism" and "communism." However, the depths of the crisis and human suffering helped to blunt the political effect of these charges. At the bottom of the Depression, unemployment in many cities approached a staggering 40 percent (compare that to the roughly 10 percent average unemployment rate for 2008–2011).

It is hard to overstate the impact of the Great Depression on the debate about the proper role of the national government. Even Republican presidents began to accept the new paradigm and add to the New Deal legacy. President Dwight D. Eisenhower signed the 1956 Federal-Aid Highway Act—at the time the largest public works project in American history—to construct the world's first network of highways, helping to economically and socially integrate the nation. And President Richard Nixon (1968–1973) signed legislation creating the Environmental Protection Agency.

But by far the greatest extension of national authority in the post–New Deal era took place during the presidency of Democrat Lyndon Baines Johnson (1963–1968). As during the Progressive era and the New Deal, major crises helped prompt federal action during the 1960s. However, unlike previous crises, the problems of the early 1960s were more social than economic. Although African Americans had been granted full citizenship on paper, in practice they remained second-class citizens throughout many sections of the country, particularly the South. In the decades following the Civil War, many southern states passed what were known as Jim Crow laws that, in essence, created a system of cradle-to-grave racial segregation. African Americans across the country were frequently born in segregated hospitals, lived in segregated housing, went to segregated schools, and rode on segregated public transportation. In many parts of the country, states permitted employers and private citizens to discriminate against minority citizens in the workplace and to erect barriers to voting.

Pressured by the civil rights movement, the political system responded with federal laws to ban the discriminatory practices. Most prominently, the Civil Rights Acts of 1964, 1965, and 1968 specifically targeted discrimination in jobs, voting, and housing, respectively. By expanding the reach of the national government into private social and economic relations and healthcare with the 1965 creation of Medicare and Medicaid, and through numerous other programs directed toward addressing poverty in American cities, Johnson's vision of a **Great Society** represented yet another dramatic expansion of national authority.

Great Society President Johnson's program during the 1960s that expanded the reach of the national government into private social and economic relations.

During the 1960s, Americans faced crises in other areas as well. Although the American economy had become the envy of the world, the nation's vast economic engine had also begun to produce industrial-scale pollution, threatening air and water quality throughout the nation. The 1962 publication of Rachel Carson's best-selling book *Silent Spring* helped spur public awareness of petrochemicals and other industrial pollutants in the American food, water, and air supply.[9] And nationally televised environmental crises in 1969, such as a fire in Cleveland's Cuyahoga River and an oil spill in Santa Barbara, helped transform nascent public awareness of environmental degradation into a full-fledged political movement. As a result of pressure from interest groups such as the Sierra Club, the political system responded in 1970 with the creation of the Environmental Protection Agency (EPA), designed primarily to implement the 1963 Clean Air Act and 1967 Water Quality Act.

Johnson characterized his take on federalism as **creative federalism**, in which the national government would assume new responsibilities in assisting both state and local governments, as well as helping private organizations and individuals to overcome social and economic inequality in American society.[10] Others, however, refer to the period between 1964 and 1980 as **centralized federalism**, in which the national government transitioned from a supportive role to more direct and sometimes coercive relations with state and local governments.

Creative federalism President Johnson's vision of federalism in which the national government would take on new responsibilities in assisting state and local governments as well as private organizations and individuals in overcoming social and economic inequality.

Centralized federalism The period of time between 1964 and 1980 when the relationship between the national government and the state and local governments transitioned from being supportive to being more direct and sometimes coercive.

Seen in retrospect, the tremendous expansion of the role of the national government into new economic and social spheres between 1932 and 1980 may perhaps seem unremarkable. Indeed, it is hard to imagine much political support today for repealing federal laws banning racial and gender discrimination or doing away with the clean air and water laws. And yet, by the 1970s many Americans had begun to question the national government's rapid expansion into new areas of their lives. Brewing underneath the surface was a growing discontent. All that was needed was someone to tap into it. That someone was Ronald Reagan.

From 1980 to 2008, the Reagan Revolution ushered in a "new federalism."

Ronald Reagan was something of an unlikely salesman for revolutionary economic policies. During the 1940s and 1950s, Reagan had been a Hollywood actor, president of the Screen Actors Guild union, and an ardent supporter of Roosevelt's New Deal. During the 1950s, however, Reagan became host of a new television program, *General Electric Theater*, which promoted new General Electric products such as vacuum cleaners, refrigerators, and televisions to a growing American consumer market. Reagan's biographers describe this period as critical in his political conversion from a New Deal Democrat to a free-market conservative.[11]

After serving two terms as California governor, Reagan continued to embrace free-market capitalism. Like many conservatives, Reagan believed that the expansion of the national government since 1932 had stifled personal and economic freedom with high taxes and excessive regulation. University of Chicago economist Milton Friedman, an influential proponent of free-market ideals, is said to have had a particular impact on Reagan's evolving political outlook. After securing the Republican nomination for president in 1979, Reagan took his message of returning power to the states, lowering taxes, and deregulation of business to the national stage against Democratic presidential incumbent Jimmy Carter, winning in a landslide.

New federalism A process of deregulation in which the national government reduced aid grants to state and local governments.

President Carter had actually begun the process of deregulation, most prominently in the airline industry. But Reagan took the approach, known as **new federalism**, to new levels. Under Reagan, the federal government reduced aid grants to state and local governments, consolidated many grant programs while limiting others, and attempted to return more responsibility to the states.[12] In his 1980 inaugural address, Reagan famously charted a new course for the nation's sputtering economy, announcing: "In this present crisis, government is not the solution to the problem, government *is* the problem." In one of his first major initiatives, Reagan worked with the Democratically controlled Congress to significantly lower taxes, particularly on the nation's top earners. The philosophy became known as **trickle- down economics**, the idea that freeing up capital for the nation's wealthy would spur investment and ultimately create jobs for everyone.

Trickle-down economics The idea that freeing up capital for the nation's wealthy would spur investment and ultimately create jobs for everyone.

And yet, one of the strange ironies of Reagan's legacy is that government didn't actually get smaller. Instead, parts of the national government got smaller, in particular those devoted to regulation of business and the enforcement of civil rights and environmental laws. In other areas, such as military spending, however, the government operations grew dramatically. By the end of the 1980s, the combination of increased government spending and decreased revenue had caused the United States to amass record budget deficits. Since the American economy also grew, Reagan was rewarded with both a second term and a revered status among conservatives. The policies of his vice president and eventual successor, George H. W. Bush, generally carried on the Reagan Revolution.

Even Democratic President Bill Clinton, who tried and failed to pass national healthcare reform in 1993, came to embrace Reagan-style free markets and smaller government. In his 1996 State of the Union address, Clinton announced: "the era of big government is over." With significant Republican support in Congress, President Clinton went on to put this philosophy into practice, signing the **1996 Welfare Reform Act**, which placed limits on how many years a person could receive welfare. Clinton also signed the 1996 Telecommunications Act, which rolled back New Deal-era regulations on media ownership. And in 1999, amid little fanfare, Clinton signed legislation overturning the 1933 Glass-Steagall Act, which had created a wall of separation between investment banks and traditional depository banks. Many critics believe this reform allowed banks to pursue riskier and riskier investments, contributing to the 2008 financial crisis.

1996 Welfare Reform Act Signed by President Clinton, this program placed limits on how many years a person can receive welfare.

To a great extent, the presidency of George W. Bush (2000–2008) also followed Reagan's revolutionary script. In one of his first initiatives, Bush signed legislation reducing taxes for all income earners, though heavily weighted in favor of top earners. Bush then proposed partially privatizing Social Security, an idea that failed to gain traction. And although Bush was an ardent proponent of returning power to the states, his presidency, like Reagan's, led to an unprecedented expansion of national government power.

Following the 2001 terrorist attacks in New York City and Washington, D.C., Bush consolidated the nation's fragmented national security apparatus into a new federal agency, the Department of Homeland Security. In 2002, Bush signed the **No Child Left Behind Act (NCLB)**, vastly expanding the national government's power in the area of public education. Then, in 2003, Bush signed legislation enacting an expensive prescription drug benefit to help senior citizens on Medicare pay for rising healthcare costs. And, of course, the wars in Afghanistan and Iraq have led to tremendous increases in military spending, more than $3 trillion by some estimates.[13] Bush justified many of his expansions of national authority under a controversial theory of presidential power known as the **unitary executive theory**, which essentially argues that the president's wartime constitutional power as commander-in-chief supersedes the authority of other branches of government.

No Child Left Behind Act (NCLB) Signed by President Bush in 2002, this law mandates annual standardized testing for students in grades 3 through 8 and greater accountability for teachers, among other reforms.

Unitary executive theory A theory that argues the president's wartime constitutional power as commander-in-chief supersedes the authority of other branches of government.

In October of 2008, a severe financial crisis shook American and world financial markets. Not unlike reactions during the Great Depression, both political leaders and average Americans were gripped by fear and uncertainty about the fundamental health of the American and global economy. With his presidency in its waning months, Bush instructed his Treasury Secretary, Hank Paulson, to rescue the nation's failing banks. Known as the **Troubled Asset Relief Fund**, or TARP, the program injected roughly $700 billion into the American financial system to address the unfolding subprime mortgage crisis.

Troubled Asset Relief Fund (TARP) A program that passed in 2008 in the waning months of President George W. Bush's administration, which injected roughly $700 billion into the American financial system to address the unfolding subprime mortgage crisis.

In short, just as the New Deal had infused the thinking of mainstream Republicans during the 1950s and 1960s, so did free-market capitalism become the dominant paradigm during the 1980s, 1990s, and beyond. The presidencies of both

Franklin Roosevelt and Ronald Reagan stand out in our understanding of American federalism because both so clearly articulated and embodied the ideological divisions at the heart of American politics.

3 Federalism remains contested terrain during the Obama presidency.

The election in 2008 of the nation's first black president, Barack Obama, represented a huge symbolic leap forward in American politics and race relations. But the vast scope of the many challenges facing the new president quickly eclipsed the historical significance of the moment: two wars, a near-collapse of the financial industry, record housing foreclosures, and a serious economic downturn that became known as the Great Recession.

During his run for the presidency, Obama had campaigned on the somewhat vague themes of "hope" and "change." Early on, Obama had cast himself in the mold of President Abraham Lincoln, someone with the personal charisma and coalition-building skills that could help bridge Washington's deep ideological divisions and bring the country together to face multiple crises. But many believed the nature of the crises called out for more obvious comparisons to the Great Depression and the presidency of Franklin Roosevelt.

On its November 24, 2008 cover, *Time* magazine showed an image of Obama hearkening back to what is perhaps the most famous photograph taken of Franklin Roosevelt. The headline asked, "The New, New Deal?" In his cover story Peter Beinart stated: "the coalition that carried Obama to victory is every bit as sturdy as America's last two dominant political coalitions: the ones that elected Franklin Roosevelt and Ronald Reagan. And the Obama majority is sturdy for one overriding reason: liberalism, which average Americans once associated with upheaval, now promises stability instead."[14] Have we witnessed a "new, New Deal" under President Obama?

American Recovery and Reinvestment Act Signed in 2009 by President Barack Obama, this was a nearly $1 trillion stimulus package to help get the economy moving again after the recession that began in 2008.

In some ways, yes. In 2009, President Obama signed the **American Recovery and Reinvestment Act**, a nearly $1 trillion stimulus package that included programs such as "cash for clunkers" to help convince Americans to trade in their old cars for newer, less polluting models. The stimulus also helped cover budget shortfalls in numerous states, temporarily saving thousands of public-sector jobs. The nonpartisan Congressional Budget Office estimated, in 2010, that the president's stimulus program saved or created 3 million jobs.[15] Obama also instructed the national government to assume majority ownership to save the struggling car company General Motors, an act which drew particular ire from conservatives.

In 2010, President Obama also signed The Patient Protection and Affordable Care Act, achieving something that presidents since the New Deal could not: near-universal healthcare coverage for Americans, including provisions that protect Americans with preexisting conditions, remove insurance industry lifetime monetary caps on coverage, and require all Americans without health insurance to pay a tax penalty. In addition, Obama signed the Wall Street Reform and Consumer Protection Act in 2010, to allow regulatory agencies such as the SEC, FDIC, and the Department of Treasury to more tightly regulate America's financial industry. That legislation created a new federal agency, the Bureau of Consumer Financial Protection, to serve as a public watchdog over potentially predatory financial practices. In order to stimulate the fledgling economy, Obama also took a page out of the Reagan playbook in signing legislation to lower Americans' taxes, even extending the Bush tax cuts on the very wealthy through 2012.

Yet, in expanding the role of the federal government in the areas of healthcare and the economy, Obama witnessed a withering political backlash to his plans. Known as the **Tea Party movement**, this effort first emerged in 2009 to galvanize political opposition to Obama's healthcare reform proposal. Amid charges of "government-run" healthcare and the specter of government "death panels," Tea Party supporters objected to what they viewed as creeping socialism under Obama. Adopting slogans of the American Revolutionary War, the Tea Party garnered a huge following and has chartered an alternate path for the nation along the core tenants of American conservatism: low taxes, small government, and less regulation. In large part due to Tea Party mobilization, the Democrats lost control of the House of Representatives in the 2010 midterm elections. In one of their first legislative initiatives in 2011, Republicans in the House voted to overturn Obama's healthcare law and proposed unprecedented cuts to federal spending.

Tea Party movement A movement that first emerged in 2009 in opposition to the national healthcare reform proposal and that has chartered an alternate path for the nation along the core tenants of American conservatism: low taxes, small government, and less regulation.

2 Federalism looks different from the "bottom up."

As noted earlier, for many years the classic metaphor for understanding American federalism (and dual federalism in particular) had been the layer cake. Among academics, many if not most thought about American federalism as three more or less independent spheres of policymaking among national, state, and local governments. This view was challenged in a 1960 report by Morton Grodzins, who argued that "a far more accurate image is the rainbow or marble cake, characterized by an inseparable mingling of differently colored ingredients, the colors appearing in vertical and diagonal strands and unexpected whirls. As colors are mixed in the marble cake, so functions are mixed in the American federal system."[16] Grodzin's article represented a new way of thinking about American federalism in which policies are made and implemented by multiple levels of government simultaneously, rather than independently.

Although there is a tendency to focus on the national government in debates about American federalism, the national government is only one of roughly 89,000 governments in the United States—along with 50 state governments, the rest are various types of local government.[17] Looking at American federalism from the perspective of state and local government—from the "bottom up"—gives us an entirely new way of looking at the conflict and cooperation that takes place between all levels of government under federalism.

For most of American history, local governments were the workhorses of American society, performing such critical functions as road and other infrastructure construction, electricity, safe drinking water, social services for the poor, schools, public safety, and tax collection. According to federalism scholar Martha Derthick, "at the opening of the 20th century, American local governments were raising more revenue and doing more spending than the federal and state governments combined."[18] It really wasn't until the middle of the twentieth century that states and the national government began to take on a much greater role as service providers.

Counties Divisions of American states. There are 3,000 counties in the United States that carry out state and federal programs, particularly in areas of health and welfare.

Local governments can be divided into four major categories (see Figure 2.3). Except for tiny Rhode Island and Connecticut, all American states are divided into **counties**, though they are referred to as parishes in Louisiana and boroughs in Alaska. The nation's 3,000 counties are said to be "administrative agencies of state government," and much of what counties do is carry out state and federal programs,

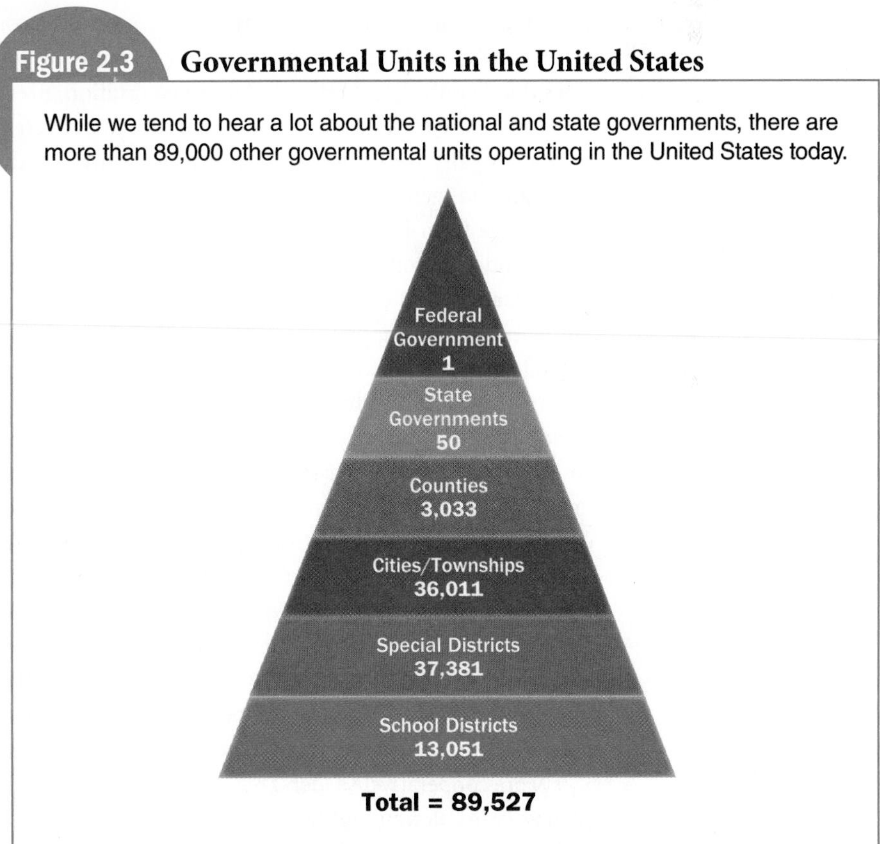

Source: 2007 US Census of Governments.

particularly in the areas of health and welfare. In areas that are rural and unincorporated, counties often serve as the primary local government, providing basic services such as police and fire protection, jails, record-keeping, and healthcare and welfare services. Counties also are responsible for land-use planning in unincorporated areas and usually run parks and library systems as well.

Municipalities Cities that are created out of county territory. They provide land-use planning and other important services.

Incorporation The process of creating a new municipality out of county territory.

School districts More than 13,000 local districts run public schools in many parts of the country.

Special districts Local governmental units that typically provide a single service, ranging from flood control, cemeteries, transportation, fire, and air quality.

Dillon's Rule A theory of state and local relations, which holds that state constitutions breathe life into all local governments, and that theoretically states can abolish all of their local governments.

As of 2007, there were more than 19,000 **municipalities**, or cities, and 16,500 townships in the United States. Municipalities are created out of county territory through the process of **incorporation**. Like counties, cities also provide land-use planning and other important services such as police and fire protection, trash pickup, and road construction and maintenance; in some parts of the country they govern education and provide health and welfare services. In many places, public schools are operated by yet another layer of local government, the more than 13,000 independent **school districts**. The impulse to insulate school governance from the rough-and-tumble of city politics is traced to the Progressive movement, which sought to curtail the power of political parties and leave governing to trained experts, known as civil servants. Finally, the most common, yet least well-known, type of local government is **special districts**. Around the country, these 37,000 governments are "special" in the sense that they typically provide a single service, ranging from flood control, to cemeteries, to transportation, fire, and air quality.

Unlike the states, local governments are not sovereign in the American federal system. Legally speaking, local governments are "creatures" of their state government, an arrangement known as **Dillon's Rule**, so named for the nineteenth-century Iowa judge John F. Dillon who first articulated this theory of state and local relations. Under Dillon, state constitutions breathe life into all local governments and, theoretically, states can abolish all of their local governments. And yet, both the tradition of strong local governments as well as the realities of implementing state and federal policies make it unlikely that a state would unilaterally abolish a local government. In fact, despite their legally dependent status, American local governments wield a level of authority—over land use and, in some places, education in particular—that is rare or nonexistent in other parts of the industrialized world.

Although the U.S. Constitution makes no direct mention of local government, examples of interactions between these levels of government abound. Federal courts have frequently intervened in local affairs to apply national standards to actions by state and local governments. For instance, civil rights laws mandating access for the disabled, banning discrimination in public places, and outlawing school segregation and housing discrimination were all direct actions by the national government. National environmental laws, developed since the 1970s, establish requirements for air, water, and land use that state and local governments must adhere to.

More cooperatively, federal policies to stimulate the growth of American suburbs, such as constructing highways and guaranteeing and subsidizing home mortgages, had a major impact on the way that American urban areas have developed. Particularly from the 1930s through the 1970s, the federal government played an important

Grants-in-aid Money given by the national government to state or local governments to address specific policy goals; assistance often comes with specific requirements for how the money is to be spent.

Block grants Money given by the national government to state or local governments to address general policy needs and goals; these grants allow spending flexibility in meeting general goals.

Home-rule charter A municipal "constitution" that allows cities to carve out autonomy from state requirements.

role in delivering **grants-in-aid** to local governments to pay for congressionally designated projects such as libraries, airports, and other infrastructure. Local governments have also received **block grants** from the national government, which allow a greater degree of local discretion in terms of spending. But in recent decades, under the approach known as new federalism, funding for local government programs—particularly federally funded social programs—has been dramatically cut. And more recent policies, such as Temporary Assistance for Needy Families (TANF), which limits lifetime welfare benefits, have resulted in greater stress on local governments.

Relations between state and local government are often far more contentious than federal–local relations. Although Dillon's Rule clearly establishes local governments' legally dependent status, power struggles between cities and states are quite common. In particular, cities that use **home rule charters** (a kind of municipal constitution) often are able to carve out additional autonomy from state requirements in such areas as their governmental structure, public financing of elections, and other so-called municipal affairs. And yet, as with sovereignty conflicts between national and state governments, whether an issue such as education or housing policy is a municipal or statewide affair is frequently ambiguous and often acrimonious. And as with the U.S. Supreme Court, state supreme courts are frequently called upon to decide such sovereignty disputes between local and state governments.[19]

Although American federalism becomes increasingly fragmented as you move down its layers, the study of intergovernmental relations tells us that the power distributions in the marble cake are not permanent or static. Rather, relations among the three layers of government are fluid, constantly morphing and reshaping to fit the politics of the time.

The No Child Left Behind Act shows the complexities, challenges, and opportunities of American federalism.

In his book *Collision Course* (2011), education expert Paul Manna describes the ongoing federalism conflicts of national, state, and local government with respect to American K–12 public education. In particular, Manna examines implementation of the requirements of the 2002 No Child Left Behind Act (NCLB) for greater accountability of American schools to national education standards.[20] Although there are many policy areas that could serve as a case study of how federalism works, few are as critical to the future of the nation as education.

Unlike most other advanced industrialized nations—where the governance of the schools is ultimately a national responsibility—education in the United States has long been a local and state responsibility. In fact, our system of federalism makes it impossible to even speak of an "American school system." Instead, the governance of schools in the United States is extraordinarily fragmented. In all, there are roughly 14,000 public school districts in the United States, though the number of districts and the way that they are governed varies widely from state to state. In Hawaii, there is only one state-run school district, and in Florida, schools are operated by each of the state's 67 county governments. In contrast, California has a whopping 1,000 independently run school districts. Today, all school districts are overseen to one degree or another by state government, and most receive a substantial portion of their funding from the state. Since the 1960s, the federal government has accounted for only about 10 percent of a typical school district budget, and before that even less. Most are governed by elected school boards run by concerned citizens rather than professional politicians. School board members tend to serve part-time, and their primary function is to lay out a general policy direction for the district. Day-to-day management is left to appointed superintendents and other professional education managers.

Although the idea of public education is taken for granted today, it is important to remember that in the early years of the American republic little or no thought was given to the government's role in education policy. In fact, the idea of universal public access to education would have been a fairly strange concept to early Americans. Education was viewed as a private good available only to individuals, mostly boys, whose families could afford private school tuition. However, American political theorists such as Thomas Jefferson realized that their experiment with mass democracy would ultimately fail unless the population had at least a basic formal education. In fact, Jefferson was one of the early proponents of free public education for all Virginians.[21] And in Massachusetts, Horace Mann, considered by many educational historians to be the father of American public education, spearheaded the creation of "common schools," which served as a model for other states' public education systems during the nineteenth century.[22]

By the middle of the twentieth century, the idea of a free public education had become as entrenched a democratic value as any in the American political system. And although most states had adopted constitutional provisions to guarantee free public education, as a practical matter, education remained almost entirely under the purview of local school districts.[23] Prior to World War II, schools were almost entirely funded by local property taxes. As the nation suburbanized during the 1950s and 1960s, wide disparities in school district funding emerged between economically depressed and mostly minority central city districts and wealthier whiter suburban districts, an outcome sanctioned by government-supported racial segregation policies. Still today, funding public schools is heavily dependent on local sources. Only a handful of states, such as California and Hawaii, have attempted to equalize school funding among school districts, with varying degrees of success.[24]

Passage of the 1965 Elementary and Secondary Education Act (ESEA) represented a notable expansion of national authority over education policy. Part of President Johnson's War on Poverty, the ESEA attempted to direct more funds to schools in poor districts, including creating Head Start, a program that provides free preschool to children in poverty. But education policy experts generally trace the national government's more robust interest in education to the 1983 publication of *A Nation at Risk*. Prepared by the Bell Commission, the report identified serious inadequacies in American K–12 public education and warned of dire consequences for the nation's global economic competitiveness if reforms were not made.[25] *A Nation at Risk* was a major turning point in efforts to reform American public education. However, despite the national attention, most major reform initiatives during the 1980s and 1990s remained at the state and local levels.

In fact, most previous attempts by the national government to impose itself on state and local education policy pale in comparison to the 2002 No Child Left Behind Act (NCLB). The law, which is a reauthorization of the 1965 Elementary and Secondary Education Act, mandates annual standardized testing for students in grades 3 through 8 and greater accountability for teachers, among other reforms. All public schools are required to have "highly qualified teachers" and make "adequate yearly progress" (AYP) toward the goal of having 100 percent of their students academically proficient in reading, science, and math by the 2013–2014 school year. If adequate progress is not made, schools can be subjected to a variety of consequences, including the potential closing of a school altogether. The law is consistent with current trends in education reform that attempt to adopt businesslike practices, focusing on setting standards and measuring student and teacher performance through standardized testing. With its power to require adherence to standards and punish districts and teachers who fail to meet them, NCLB represents a quantum leap in the national government's role in American public education.

Many states and school districts have criticized NCLB as an expensive, unnecessary, and counterproductive intrusion into local affairs. First, critics say that most states already had their own testing procedures in place to assess student performance. Second, opponents object to the fact that if a school fails to perform to standards, federal money may be taken away from that school, possibly compounding rather than fixing the problem. Many teachers also cite increased pressure to "teach to the test," which may increase test scores through rote memorization, but at the expense of developing more important skills such as creativity and critical thinking. States and local school districts also view NCLB as another federal "unfunded mandate," which they say requires significantly more money to implement than the federal government currently provides.

Education expert Paul Manna believes that federalism significantly complicates implementation and assessment of NCLB. He argues that although accountability and consequences form the essence of the law, the power to oversee the implementation lies with state and local officials who may try to comply with the letter of the law while frustrating its implementation in practice. For example, Manna argues that by allowing states to set their own standards for educational proficiency and teacher effectiveness, many states simply choose to lower the bar for excellence, making it easier to comply with NCLB's requirements. In Manna's assessment, "the bulk of the evidence shows that there [are] major gaps between what the law's theories proposed would happen and how implementation unfolded at federal, state, and local levels."[26]

However, Manna and other education policy experts credit NCLB for forcing state and local bureaucracies to improve collection of educational data, providing greater transparency to the educational process, and helping to focus public attention on the topic of education reform. For the most part, President Obama and his Education Secretary, Arnie Duncan, have been strong supporters of NCLB. The Obama administration has even advocated strengthening NCLB by proposing that all schools adhere to uniform federal "common core" standards rather than allowing states to set their own. However, bowing to political realities, in 2011 Duncan announced that waivers would be offered to school districts unable to meet all of the requirements of NCLB, provided that those districts adopt additional measures to improve school accountability.[27]

Charter schools Public schools that are freed from some bureaucratic requirements and that encourage innovation in curriculum and spending.

Although the jury is still out on its effectiveness, NCLB represents one of the most significant education policy reforms in decades. Along with the **charter schools** movement, which seeks to free some public schools from bureaucratic requirements and encourage innovation in curriculum and spending, together they represent the vanguard of efforts to reform American public education. Education policy, and in particular NCLB, provides a useful case study of the complexities, challenges, and opportunities of American federalism. Going forward, the trick for reformers will be in striking the right balance between top-down federal mandates and incentives and long-standing traditions of local and state education governance.

CONCLUSION

When asked to discuss the significance of the U.S. Constitution, most Americans would probably emphasize its system of checks and balances or perhaps the Bill of Rights, which lays out the framework for protecting our liberties. But at least as important is the structure of government known as federalism that the Constitution sets forth. As we have seen, federalism is a complicated arrangement whereby two or more levels of government attempt to share power. Federalism emerged from a practical need to compromise between the Articles of Confederation and a unitary form of government. It is important to remember that federalism was essentially an experiment, one that has arguably served the country well over the course of our history.

Federalism evolved in the United States from a relatively minimalist role for the national government for most of the nineteenth century to an incredibly powerful force in the nation's economic and social life by the 1970s. Beginning in the 1980s, the Reagan Revolution emerged to turn the clock back on the scope of the national government, at least to some degree. And later, when the nation faced two serious crises, the 9/11 terrorist attacks and a recession in 2008, the response again hinged on the central question of American politics: whether the crisis should be met with greater or less national government intervention.

We also saw that there are good reasons to look at the structure of federalism from the "bottom up." With roughly 89,000 governmental units in the United States, the vast majority provide basic services like water, power, trash service, and schools at the local level. At various times, each of these local governments finds itself both in cooperation as well as in conflict with their state and national governments, making the study of intergovernmental relations in the United States as interesting as it is complex.

THEIR LIST

An Insider's View

SHAUNA CLARK

City Manager of the City of La Habra Heights, California

Shauna Clark's career in national, state, and local government has spanned more than 30 years. Since 2007 she has served as the city manager of the City of La Habra Heights, California, an affluent community 25 miles southeast of downtown Los Angeles. From 1978 until 1990, Ms. Clark served as the elected city clerk for the City of San Bernardino, California, and from 1990 until 1997, she was the appointed city manager of San Bernardino, overseeing a budget of more than $148 million, 16 major city departments, and more than 1,100 city employees. Ms. Clark has also worked as a private consultant for a variety of state and local governments and private agencies, as well as for the United States Army Research Laboratory to devise ways to improve state and local decision making in disaster and emergency situations.

Based on her experience in government, we asked Ms. Clark to provide her take on the advantages and disadvantages of our system of federalism. "I wouldn't say that federalism is necessarily the ideal model. In some ways it's a utopian concept that's rather hard to make work in practice." Ms. Clark cited the example of the 1996 federal welfare reform law. "Devolution of responsibility to state and local government sounds good in theory, but what it does in reality is put a much greater financial burden on states and localities."

Ms. Clark went on to describe some of the challenges she has faced as city manager of La Habra Heights in negotiating our federal system. In 2005, Hacienda Rd. collapsed following a series of storms that brought heavy rain. The city fronted the money for the repairs and then applied for $2.6 million in Federal Highway Administration funds to cover some of the costs of the damage to the road, a major thoroughfare connecting to La Habra Heights. According to Ms. Clark, "One of the hardest parts of being a city manager is negotiating all of the different procedures. For example, the federal government may have one type of application or series of steps to follow, while the state government sets up a completely different process." In the case of the Hacienda Rd. collapse, Ms. Clark said that, more than 5 years later, the city is still waiting to be reimbursed by the Federal Highway Administration. "Local governments are essentially at the mercy of these intergovernmental relationships. Ultimately, we have very little control."

However, Ms. Clark also cited several advantages to operating in a federal system of government. "Our city is really able to tailor services quite nicely to fit the needs of our residents. This could never be done in a 'one-size-fits-all' system." She also mentioned several benefits of the expanded role for the national government during the twentieth century. "By and large I think actions by the federal government have been well intentioned and positive on the whole. I mean, how much devolution do we want? Do we want to go back to when states have their own separate currencies or when state and local governments could set their own civil rights standards? You can imagine the kinds of discrimination that could emerge."

Ms. Clark summed up her take on federalism this way: "Federalism made a lot more sense when we had only 13 states and a small population. Now, with 50 states and a huge, diverse population, things have become incredibly complex. It's a system that has been in constant negotiation for more than 200 years, and that negotiation is ongoing."

In our federalist system, education evolved from a largely private good in the early years of the country to a public good by the middle of the twentieth century. During most of this time, the national government played little, if any, direct role. It is really only since the 1960s, and in a more direct way, since the 2002 passage of the No Child Left Behind Act that the national government has attempted to directly impose itself on American education policy. And whether you are a supporter or critic of the law, it is clear that the success of NCLB hinges greatly upon how it is implemented by state and local governments.

YOUR LIST REVISITED

At the beginning of the chapter, you were asked to think about what you might include on your own list of the Top 10 Most Important Things to Know About Federalism. Now that you have read the chapter, take a moment to revisit your list. What, if anything, would you change about your list? Do you agree or disagree with the chapter list constructed by the author? What might you add or delete? Why?

KEY TERMS

American Recovery and Reinvestment Act 41
Block grants 45
Capitalism 35
Charter schools 48
Centralized federalism 38
Confederation 29
Cooperative federalism 37
Counties 43
Creative federalism 38
Dillon's Rule 44
Dual federalism 33
Federalism 28
Federalist Papers 32
Grants-in-aid 45
Great Society 38
Home-rule charter 45
Incorporation 44
Layer cake 34
Marble cake 37
Municipalities 44
New Deal 36
New federalism 39
No Child Left Behind Act (NCLB) 40
Oligopolies 35
Progressivism 36
School districts 44
Social Security 36
Sovereignty 29
Special districts 44
Tea Party movement 42
Trickle-down economics 39
Troubled Asset Relief Fund (TARP) 40
Trusts 35
Unitary executive theory 40
Unitary government 29
1996 Welfare Reform Act 40

CHAPTER REVIEW QUESTIONS

10 How does federalism compare to other forms of government such as confederations and unitary structures?

9 In what ways can states be considered "laboratories of democracy"?

8 What did the *Federalist Papers* indicate were the advantages of a federal system of government? Are there any disadvantages?

7 What is dual federalism? How did it influence the lives of Americans during most of the nineteenth century?

6 Why did the federal government begin to actively regulate the economy during the early part of the twentieth century?

5 In what specific ways did Franklin Roosevelt's New Deal and Lyndon Johnson's Great Society expand the role of the national government?

4 What is meant by the Reagan Revolution? In what ways did "new federalism" impact businesses and state and local governments?

3 Have we witnessed a "new, New Deal" under President Obama? Why or why not?

2 Why is the marble cake metaphor thought to be a more accurate depiction of American federalism than the three-layer-cake metaphor?

1 How does the No Child Left Behind Act illustrate the challenges and opportunities of American federalism?

SUGGESTED READINGS

- Bowen, Catherine D. *Miracle at Philadelphia: The Story of the Constitutional Convention, May to September, 1787.* Boston: Little, Brown, 1986.
- Christensen, Terry, and Tom Hogen-Esch. *Local Politics: A Practical Guide to Governing at the Grassroots.* Armonk, NY: M. E. Sharpe, Inc., 2006.
- Elazar, Daniel J. *American Federalism: The View from the States.* New York: HarperCollins Press, 1984.
- Hamilton, Alexander, Madison, James, Jay, John. *The Federalist Papers,* Clinton Rossiter (ed). New York, NY: Penguin, 2003.
- LaCroix, Allison L. *The Ideological Origins of American Federalism.* Cambridge, MA: Harvard University Press, 2010.
- Manna, Paul. *Collision Course: Federal Education Policy Meets State and Local Realities.* Washington, DC: CQ Press, 2011.
- Nagel, Robert F. *The Implosion of American Federalism.* Washington, DC: Oxford University Press, 2001.
- Ostrom, Vincent. *The Meaning of American Federalism.* Washington, DC: ICS Press, 1999.
- O'Toole, Lawrence J., ed. *American Intergovernmental Relations: Foundations, Perspectives, and Issues.* Washington, DC: CQ Press, 2007.
- Skowronek, Stephen. *Building a New American State: The Expansion of National Administrative Capacities, 1877–1920.* Cambridge, UK: Cambridge University Press, 1982.

SUGGESTED FILMS

- *The Life and Times of Harvey Milk* (1984)
- *Eyes on the Prize: America's Civil Rights Years* (1987)
- *Commanding Heights* (2002)
- *Street Fight* (2005)
- *Can Mr. Smith Get to Washington Anymore?* (2006)
- *When the Levees Broke* (2006)
- *The Garden* (2008)
- *Gasland* (2010)
- *Inside Job* (2010)
- *Proposition 8* (2010)

SUGGESTED WEBSITES

- **Council of State Governments:** http://www.csg.org
- **Governing Magazine:** http://www.governing.com
- **International City/County Management Association:** http://icma.org/en/icma/home
- **National Association of Counties:** http://www.naco.org
- **National League of Cities:** http://www.nlc.org
- **StateScape Policy Analysis:** http://www.statescape.com/
- **The Brookings Institution:** http://www.brookings.edu
- **The Cato Institute:** http://www.cato.org
- **The Federalist Society:** http://www.fed-soc.org/
- **U.S. Supreme Court:** http://www.supremecourt.gov/

ENDNOTES

[1]Since Hurricane Katrina, there has been a good deal of discussion regarding the role class and race played in the disaster. See, for instance, Michael A. Fletcher, "Katrina Pushes Issues of Race and Class at Bush," *Washington Post*, September 12, 2005, available at: http://www.washingtonpost.com/wp-dyn/content/article/2005/09/11/AR2005091101131.html (accessed June 1, 2011); "Hurricane Exposes Issues of Race and Class," *USA Today*, September 1, 2005, available at: http://www.usatoday.com/news/opinion/editorials/2005-09-01-katrina-class-race_x.htm (accessed June 1, 2011).

[2]Joby Warrick and Spencer S. Hu, "Levees Construction Faulted in New Orleans Flood Inquiry," *Washington Post*, November 3, 2005, available at: http://www.washingtonpost.com/wp-dyn/content/article/2005/11/02/AR2005110202775.html (accessed August 8, 2011).

[3]Ralph R Premdas, *Secessionist Movements in Comparative Perspective* (New York: St. Martin's Press, 1990).

[4]The Québec secession referendum failed, 50.6% to 49.4%. See also Allan E. Buchanan, *The Morality of Political Divorce from Ft. Sumter to Lithuania and Quebec* (Boulder, Co.: Westview Press, 1991).

[5]For a brief introduction to the history and development of federalism in the United States, see Eugene Boyd, "American Federalism, 1776 to 1997: Significant Events," available online at: http://www.cas.umt.edu/polsci/faculty/greene/federalismhistory.htm#dual (accessed June 2, 2011).

[6]See Stephen Skowronek, *Building a New American State: the Expansion of National Administrative Capacities, 1977–1920* (Cambridge, UK: Cambridge University Press, 1982).

[7]See Alan Trachtenberg, *The Incorporation of America: Culture and Society in the Gilded Age* (New York: Hill and Wang, 2007).

[8]See Robert Wiebe, *The Search for Order, 1877–1920* (New York: Hill and Wang, 1966).

[9]Rachel Carson, *Silent Spring* (New York: Mariner Books, 2007).

[10]Lawrence J. O'Toole, "American Intergovernmental Relations: An Overview," in *American Intergovernmental Relations: Foundations, Perspectives, and Issues*, Lawrence J. O'Toole, ed. (Washington, DC: CQ Press, 2007).

[11]Lou Cannon, *President Reagan: The Role of a Lifetime* (New York: Public Affairs, 2000).

[12]See Dennis L. Dresang and James J. Gosling, *Politics and Policy in American States and Communities*, 7th edition (New York: Pearson, 2010).

[13]Linda J. Bilmes and Joseph E. Stiglitz, "The Iraq War Will Cost Us $3 Trillion, and Much More," *The Washington Post*, March 9, 2008, available at: http://www.washingtonpost.com/wp-dyn/content/article/2008/03/07/AR2008030702846.html (accessed August 8, 2011).

[14]Peter Beinart, "The New Liberal Order," *Time Magazine*, November 13, 2008, available at: http://www.time.com/time/magazine/article/0,9171,1858873,00.html (accessed August 8, 2011).

[15]Congressional Budget Office, *Estimated Impact of the American Recovery and Reinvestment Act on Employment and Economic Output from July 2010 Through September 2010* (Washington, DC: November 2010).

[16]Morton Grodzins, "The Federal System," in *American Intergovernmental Relations: Foundations, Perspectives, and Issues*, Lawrence J. O'Toole, ed. (Washington, DC: CQ Press, 2007).

[17]Lawrence J. O'Toole, "American Intergovernmental Relations: an Overview," in *American Intergovernmental Relations: Foundations, Perspectives, and Issues*, Lawrence J. O'Toole, ed. (Washington, DC: CQ Press, 2007).

[18]Martha Derthick, "The Paradox of the Middle Tier," in *American Intergovernmental Relations: Foundations, Perspectives, and Issues*, Lawrence J. O'Toole, ed. (Washington, DC: CQ Press, 2007).

[19]Terry Christensen and Tom Hogen-Esch, *Local Politics: A Practical Guide to Governing at the Grassroots* (Armonk, NY: M. E. Sharpe, Inc. 2006).

[20]Paul Manna, *Collision Course: Federal Education Policy Meets State and Local Realities* (Washington, DC: CQ Press, 2011).

[21]Keep in mind that America's oldest and elite universities, such as Harvard, Yale, and Princeton, were mostly private institutions. In 1718, Jefferson went on to found the University of Virginia, one of the nation's first public universities.

[22]Mark Groen, "The Whig Party and the Rise of Common Schools, 1837–1854," *American Educational History Journal*, Vol. 35 (Spring/Summer 2008), 251–260.

[23]A major exception to this pattern were state-level efforts during the early twentieth century to consolidate adjacent school districts in order to take advantage of economies of scale in service provision. During this period, the number of school districts dropped dramatically, from roughly 100,000 to approximately 15,000 today. See Dennis L. Dresang and James J. Gosling, *Politics and Policy in American States and Communities*, 7th edition (New York: Pearson, 2010).

[24]In 1971, the California Supreme Court case *Serrano v. Priest* ruled that unequal funding between school districts violated the state constitution, setting off a wave of similar lawsuits around the nation.

[25]United States Department of Education, *A Nation at Risk: The Imperative for Educational Reform: A Report to the Nation and the Secretary of Education*, (Washington, DC: The National Commission on Excellence in Education, 1983).

[26]Manna, *Collision Course*, 156.

[27]Sam Dillon, "Obama to Wave Parts of No Child Left Behind" *New York Times*, September 22, 2011 http://www.nytimes.com/2011/09/23/education/23educ.html

Chapter 3

CONGRESS

Top Ten List

10 Congress was designed to be the most powerful of the three branches of government.

9 The U.S. House and Senate differ in their responsibilities, representation, and rules.

8 Congress's great weakness is its collective action problems.

7 Staff and staff agencies play a major role in running Congress.

6 Most work done in Congress is carried out by committees.

5 Over the past few decades, the power of party leaders in Congress has increased.

4 Members of Congress can represent their constituencies as delegates or as trustees.

3 The legislative process is long and complicated, so most bills never become laws.

2 Electoral incentives drive members of Congress, and most congressional elections are not competitive.

1 Policymaking in Congress reflects public opinion on most issues.

As a result of the 2010 midterm elections, Republicans took control of the House of Representatives with the largest majority since the 1947–1949 session, and Republican John Boehner (shown here) was sworn in as the 53rd Speaker of the House. To understand the complex workings of Congress, it is essential to understand how members of Congress behave, how the institutions of Congress work, and the types of policy outputs Congress is likely to produce as a result.

YOUR LIST

Before you read this chapter, take a few moments to think about what you might include on a list of the Top 10 Most Important Things to Know About Congress. At the end of the chapter you will be asked to compare and contrast your list with the one supplied in this chapter.

INTRODUCTION

In 2001, President George W. Bush and Congress enacted a massive tax cut with several provisions that provided tax deductions to those financing their undergraduate and graduate education with student loans. The 2001 law eliminated a 60-month time limit on the deductibility of student loan interest and raised the income threshold for married couples seeking to take advantage of the full deduction from $60,000 in 2001 to $115,000 in 2008.[1] But these provisions were set to expire on December 31, 2010 because of an odd quirk in how the U.S. Senate works.

When the law passed in 2001, there were exactly 50 Republicans and 50 Democrats in the Senate. Under Senate rules, a minority of just 40 senators can block most legislation, and most Democrats wanted to block the Bush tax cut bill because, among other things, they felt it disproportionately benefited the wealthy. Knowing this, Senate Republicans enacted the tax cut under an unusual procedure known as reconciliation, which offers at least one key advantage: It cannot be blocked by a filibuster—the delaying tactic Democrats were counting on to block the Bush tax cut bill. Reconciliation has a downside too, however. Any tax provision enacted through reconciliation expires in 10 years. As a result, nearly 10 years later, in December 2010, congressional Democrats and Republicans found themselves trying to cut a last-minute deal to extend a wide variety of popular tax provisions like the student loan deductions described above.

In enacting this legislation, did Congress act in your best interests or in what you believe to be the best interests of the country? If not, in whose interests did Congress act? How does Congress arrive at its decisions? To answer these questions and to understand the sometimes convoluted workings of Congress, we will examine how the institutions of Congress work, how members of Congress behave and what explains their behavior, and what kinds of policy outputs Congress is likely to produce.

10 Congress was designed to be the most powerful of the three branches of government.

In *Federalist No. 51*, James Madison famously asserted that "In republican government, the legislative authority necessarily predominates." Madison's logic was that, among the functions of government, the power to make law in the first place is greatest. But Madison also believed that the Congress would be the most powerful branch of government because it is "the people's branch." Of all the officers of the three branches of the national government, members of Congress are the only ones to be directly elected by the people.[2] Neither the president nor members of the U.S. judiciary are directly chosen by the people.[3] In addition, each House member represents a geographically discrete district within a state, and each senator represents a single state. As representatives of local areas and regions, members of Congress have a closer link to the constituents they represent and, therefore, a stronger claim to

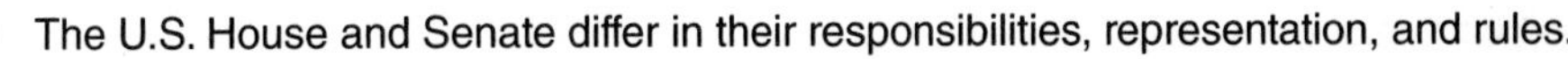

represent the "will" of the people. Finally, the structure and powers of the Congress are not only laid out first within the Constitution, but Article I is, by far, the longest of the seven articles of the Constitution.

The argument that Congress was intended to be the strongest branch of government is not just a matter of symbolic placement or length. Article I places most of the important coercive powers of government in the hands of the members of the House and the Senate. Congress has the power to tax, the power to spend money, the power to borrow money, the power to regulate commerce among the states and with foreign nations, the power to regulate the currency, the power to raise armies and navies, and the power to declare war. As if that were not enough, the last clause of Article I, section 8, gives Congress the power "To make all Laws which shall be necessary and proper for carrying into Execution the foregoing Powers, and all other Powers vested by this Constitution in the Government of the United States, or in any Department or Officer thereof." Known as the **necessary and proper clause**, this clause provides Congress with broad latitude to expand its powers beyond the already-significant array of powers explicitly granted to the Congress elsewhere in Article I, section 8. As Congress has stretched the interpretation of the necessary and proper clause further and further over the years, it has also come to be known as the **elastic clause**.

Necessary and proper clause The clause in Article I, section 8, of the Constitution, also known as the elastic clause, which provides Congress with broad latitude to expand its powers beyond the powers already explicitly granted to it in the Constitution.

Elastic clause The alternate name given to the necessary and proper clause because Congress has stretched the clause's interpretation over the years.

The strength of the elastic clause was demonstrated as early as 1819 in the landmark Supreme Court case of *McCulloch v. Maryland*. In this case, Congress had established a national bank with a branch in the state of Maryland. Because Maryland did not believe the U.S. Congress was empowered to create a national bank, the state imposed a tax on the local branch of the national bank within its borders. In its decision in *McCulloch v. Maryland* (1819), the U.S. Supreme Court ruled that even though Article I, section 8, did not explicitly grant power to Congress to establish a national bank, Congress was authorized to do so because establishing a national bank may be seen as a "necessary and proper" part of both regulating the currency and regulating commerce among the states.

9 The U.S. House and Senate differ in their responsibilities, representation, and rules.

In *Federalist No. 51*, James Madison argues for the predominance of legislative authority. However, to keep Congress from overpowering the other branches, the Constitution divides legislative power in two to create what is known as a **bicameral legislature**, a legislative body made up of two chambers. Today, legislative power is thus divided between two institutions, the Senate and the House of Representatives.

Bicameral legislature A legislative body made up of two chambers. In the United States, Congress is divided into a House of Representatives and a Senate

This division of power is not arbitrary; it is functional. The House is meant to be the body closer to the people and their immediate policy preferences, while the Senate is meant to be more deliberative, more focused on the long-term, and to wield more oversight power over the executive branch of government. Because the House is closer to the people, it has the sole power to be the originator of any legislation that

Impeach The power to charge an executive or judicial officer with misconduct or wrongdoing.

raises taxes[4] and to **impeach** (the power to charge an executive or judicial officer with misconduct or wrongdoing), while the Senate retains the power to remove executive or judicial officers (including the president) from their position. The Senate also retains a number of quasi-executive powers, including the sole power to ratify treaties and the power to confirm presidential nominees for judicial and executive offices.

This functional division of power is based on the different ways the two institutions represent the people. House members are more numerous (435 members), have shorter terms of office (2 years), and come from generally smaller, more homogenous legislative districts than members of the Senate.[5] Each House member represents more than 700,000 citizens of a particular district within their state. Representation in the Senate is very different. Each state has two U.S. Senators, which means the Senate has 100 members in total. As a result, the more than 37 million residents of the state of California are represented by the same number of senators as the less than 600,000 residents of the state of Wyoming. Not only is equal representation among states guaranteed in the Constitution, it is effectively the only unchangeable aspect of the Constitution, as the last clause of Article 5 of the Constitution asserts that "no State, without its consent, shall be deprived of its equal suffrage in the Senate." Senators also have much longer terms (6 years) than House members.

The greater qualifications for senators (see Table 3.1), the longer terms for senators, and the fact that the Senate is a smaller body create important differences between the chambers in both their mode of operation and in the kinds of policy outputs they produce. Because it has so many members, the House delegates much more power to the majority party leadership to determine when and if **bills** (proposed laws) come to the floor, how much time will be allowed for debate, and how many amendments may be allowed. With 435 members, it is easy to see how the absence of this kind of organizational leadership would lead to legislative chaos. As a result, the majority party in the House (even if it is a slim majority) has the ability to control the flow of legislative action on the floor.

Bills Proposed laws

On the other hand, the floor of the Senate generally operates under **unanimous consent agreements**. Individual floor leaders will ask for unanimous consent to bring a bill to the floor under particular conditions. Any senator, even the most junior member from the minority party in the chamber, can object. If that happens, action in the Senate can grind to a halt as a result of a number of procedural delaying tactics available to individual senators.

Unanimous consent agreements Agreements that guide operation of the floor of the Senate. Floor leaders ask for consent, and if any Senator objects, action in the Senate can grind to a halt.

Table 3.1 Qualifications for Congress

A Representative in the House must be	A Senator must be
25 years old	35 years old
a citizen of the United States for 7 years	A citizen of the United States for 9 years
a resident of the state in which he/she is chosen	A resident of the state in which he/she is chosen

Filibuster A delaying tactic employed to tie up the Senate until the majority decides to pull a bill from consideration on the Senate floor.

The most well-known of these tactics is the **filibuster**—a delaying tactic employed to tie up the Senate until the majority decides to pull the bill from consideration on the Senate floor and move on to other business. Historically, senators have launched filibusters by taking to the floor and talking on and on, sometimes reading poetry or cookbooks. But today, the more common delaying tactic is for senators either to simply threaten a filibuster or to offer a dizzying array of amendments, each of which must potentially be considered by the full Senate. The issue of the filibuster was brought to center stage in 2005 when then Senate Majority Leader Bill Frist (R-TN) threatened a procedural maneuver that would have effectively barred filibusters of judicial nominations. Frist instigated this initiative because Democrats had been using the filibuster to block numerous judicial nominations from the Bush administration. At the last moment, a group of seven Republicans and seven Democrats (known as the "Gang of 14") came to an agreement to allow some of the previously blocked nominations to go forward, to oppose any effort by Frist to eliminate the filibuster, and to pledge to use the filibuster only in extraordinary cases.[6]

Individual senators may also place a hold on a nomination or a bill that would otherwise come before the Senate. In a hold, individual senators will ask party leaders not to bring a matter before the Senate, and these holds are usually granted to see if the individual senator's concerns can be accommodated.

Cloture A vote in the Senate that brings an end to debate. Senate rules require three-fifths of the Senate (60 members) to invoke cloture.

Initially, Senate rules did not have any provision for ending debate, so debate and amendments in the Senate would continue until all senators had had enough. In 1917, the Senate adopted Rule XXII, which allows for **cloture**—a vote to end debate. Today, Rule XXII requires three-fifths of the Senate (60 members), not just a majority, to invoke cloture and bring the Senate to a vote on any controversial piece of legislation. This occurred in February 2009 on President Obama's first major legislative initiative—a $787 billion economic stimulus bill that was tied up in the Senate despite support from 58 Democratic senators. To move the bill out of the Senate, Democrats still needed the votes of a few of the Republicans in the chamber. The key vote came on February 9 when 3 Republicans joined all of the Democrats to invoke cloture by a 61–36 vote.[7]

Incumbent Elected government official currently holding an office.

The differing qualifications and modes of election for House members and senators also lead them to produce different kinds of policy outputs. The Senate was expected to generally take a longer-term and more national view of policy problems than the more short-term and more provincial House. The 6-year terms for senators afford them greater freedom to cast votes that may be out of step with public opinion in their state, whereas House members must always be thinking about how a challenger will use the vote a member casts on the House floor to assert that the **incumbent**, the member currently holding office, is out of step with the home constituency.

The differing policy outputs of the House and the Senate are also a function of the fact that House districts are apportioned by population, whereas the Senate gives equal representation to states. In the Senate, states with smaller populations, like Wyoming, Alaska, and Vermont, are given equal representation compared to

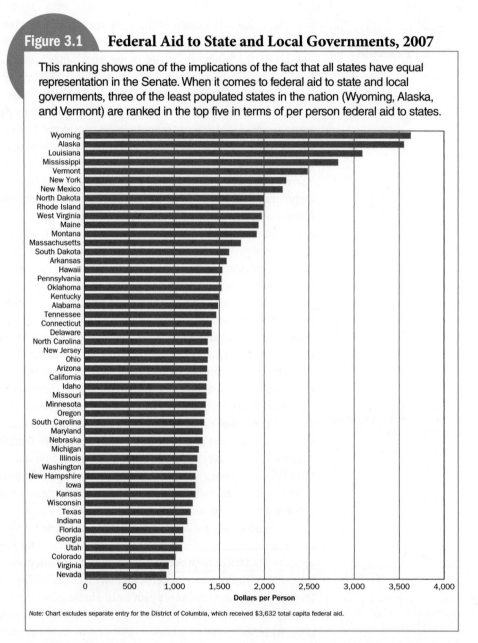

Figure 3.1 Federal Aid to State and Local Governments, 2007

This ranking shows one of the implications of the fact that all states have equal representation in the Senate. When it comes to federal aid to state and local governments, three of the least populated states in the nation (Wyoming, Alaska, and Vermont) are ranked in the top five in terms of per person federal aid to states.

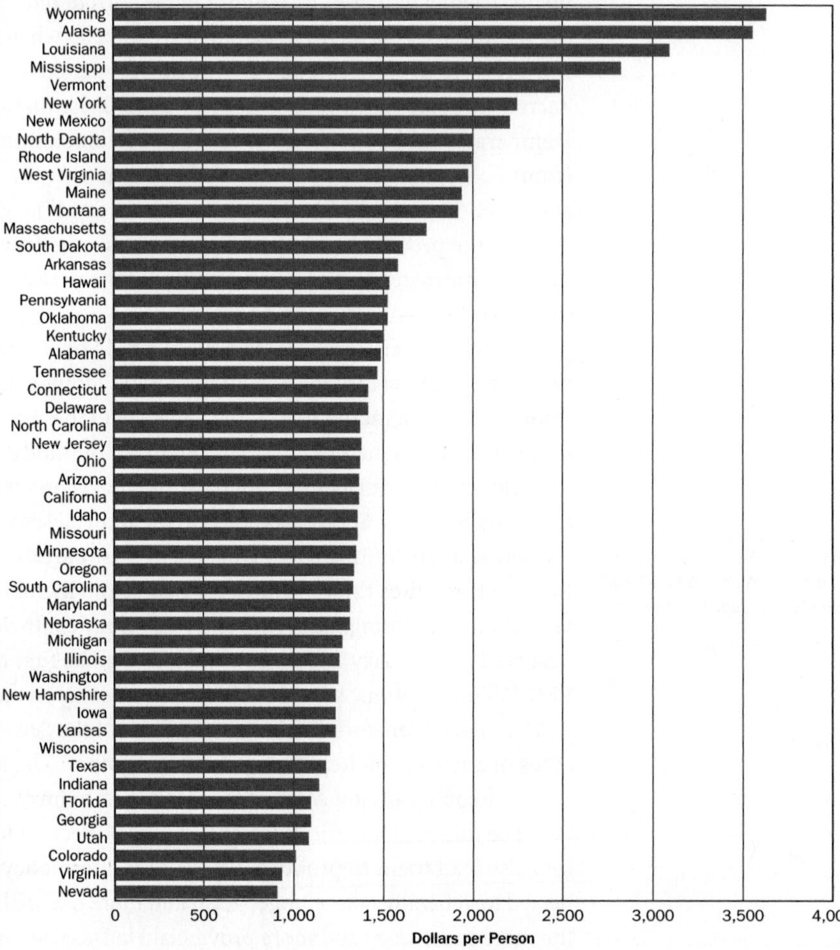

Note: Chart excludes separate entry for the District of Columbia, which received $3,632 total capita federal aid.

Source: U.S. Census Bureau.

states with very large populations, like California and Texas. As a result, the interests of citizens in smaller states are effectively "overrepresented" in the U.S. Senate. As shown in Figure 3.1, three of the least populated states in the nation ranked in the top five in terms of per capita federal aid to states (Wyoming, Alaska, and Vermont).

Congress's great weakness is its collective action problems.

Collective action problems Situations in which individually rational behavior leads to a collectively irrational outcome.

Congress's great institutional difficulty is in getting 535 members and thousands of staff to work together. It is beset by **collective action problems**, situations in which individually rational behavior leads to a collectively irrational outcome. As individuals, we all experience collective action problems in our everyday lives. How often have you been stuck in a traffic jam on the freeway because people well in front of you are slowing down to look at a car that was in an accident and has been moved to the side of the road? Those at the front of the traffic jam have an individual incentive to take a look because they get the benefit of looking without paying the cost of the additional delay it causes other travelers like you behind them. While these drivers are behaving rationally from their own individual perspective, the outcome is collectively irrational because everyone is significantly delayed.

Congress's collective action problems impact its ability to create policy. If the president engages in an action that is opposed by a majority of congressional members, Congress may nevertheless be unable to respond because a majority of members cannot agree on a particular response. When Democrats gained majority control of both houses of Congress in January 2007 for the first time in 12 years, most members of Congress wanted to scale back or end the American military presence in Iraq. President Bush, on the other hand, not only shot down proposals for a particular timetable for withdrawal of American forces, he dramatically increased the number of American troops in Iraq in a policy initiative known as "the surge." Although most members of Congress opposed "the surge," this majority could not come to an agreement on the appropriate response to the president's action. As each member engaged in a futile effort to pursue his or her own individual view of good public policy, the Congress as a whole failed to act, and the ultimate policy decision was therefore one that was different from what most members of Congress wanted.

Pork-barrel spending The incentive each individual member of Congress has to fight for federal dollars that will lead to projects and create jobs in their state.

The example of a collective action problem most frequently associated with Congress is **pork-barrel spending**. Each individual member of Congress has an incentive to fight for federal dollars for construction projects in their district or state, such as roads, dams, and bridges. These projects create jobs, as local workers are employed in construction in the short term, and projects may lead to further regional economic development in the longer term. But, as nearly every member of Congress fights for federal dollars, there is a tendency to overspend on these local projects because no individual member has an incentive to guard the federal treasury.

Similarly, over the years, each member of Congress has sought to locate and construct new military bases in their district. Many military leaders complain that military procurement has too local an orientation and the functions of the armed forces are hindered because of the large number and geographical spread of our military bases. Thus, the collective action problem not only interferes with Congress's ability to be financially responsible and to oppose presidential initiatives, it can also affect important policy outputs like national security.

Staff and staff agencies play a major role in running Congress.

To fulfill its role, Congress needs access to objective expertise and information independent of the executive branch. Congress has developed an extensive set of rules and procedures, has hired thousands of staff members, and has created and staffed its own policy analysis, research, and audit agencies. These institutions empower members of Congress, allowing them to be involved in a wider array of policy areas.

All members of Congress have a personal staff, some based in the home district and some based in their Capitol Hill offices. Hill staffers focus primarily on the member's Washington agenda, including drafting legislation, briefing the member on pending legislation both in committee and on the floor, representing the member in meetings the member cannot attend, and working with federal agencies on matters of interest to **constituents** (the people members of Congress represent).

Constituents The people a member of Congress represents.

District staffers focus on the member's relationship with individuals, organizations, and groups in the home district. Their most important tasks include fielding calls from constituents seeking assistance with federal agencies or legislation, scheduling the member's appearances in the district, and representing the member in the district when the member cannot be present. In addition, members of Congress also have separate staff members who work on the member's reelection efforts. While congressional staff based in the district are paid by the federal government and are not explicitly working to advance the member's electoral efforts, they are effectively doing so by serving constituents and groups in the district who, if satisfied with the member's actions, will be more inclined to support the member in the next election. Finally, Congress also hires committee staffers who work on legislation and hearings within the jurisdictional policy area the committee covers.

Congress has also created internal research, policy analysis, and audit agencies to provide objective, nonpartisan information to the institution and its members. The Congressional Research Service (CRS) was established in 1914 to provide nonpartisan analysis of legislation and legislative options. The Government Accountability Office (GAO) was established in 1921 as an auditing arm of Congress. Specifically, GAO examines how taxpayer dollars are spent and assesses the effectiveness of government programs and policies. The **Congressional Budget Office (CBO)** was established in 1974 to provide members of Congress with budgetary and economic analyses independent of those offered by the executive branch. These staff agencies play more than an informational role. They frequently help determine whether a policy proposal is politically feasible or not.

Congressional Budget Office (CBO) Congressional agency established in 1974 to provide members of Congress with budgetary and economic analyses independent of those offered by the executive branch.

For instance, during the March 2010 debate over the Obama administration's healthcare reform plan, the CBO estimated the cost at $938 billion over 10 years. Republican opponents of the plan objected to the fact that these estimates did not include related administrative costs and spending. A few months after the bill was passed, the CBO revised its estimates and released data suggesting that the new healthcare law might add at least $115 billion more to government healthcare spending over 10 years. If accurate, this would push the total cost of the healthcare overhaul to over $1 trillion.[8] This example underscores why CBO's "scoring" of legislation and its estimates of the costs and benefits of proposed legislation are so important.

Most work done in Congress is carried out by committees.

Since the very first Congress, committees have served to satisfy members' desire for influence over public policy, to manage the increasing workload of the institution, and to allow for the development of expertise in particular policy areas. There are many different types of committees, and they are made up of subsets of the overall membership of Congress.

Standing committees Semipermanent bodies made up of members from both parties; each committee has its own policy jurisdiction.

Ways and Means Committee One of the most powerful committees in the House of Representatives that deals with tax and entitlement laws.

Standing committees are semipermanent bodies established by law or by rule in the chamber and made up of members from both parties. But, the chairperson and the majority of members on each standing committee come from the majority party. Each standing committee has its own policy jurisdiction. For example, the **Ways and Means Committee** in the House covers tax and entitlement laws. In 2004, President Bush proposed an overhaul of Social Security that would have allowed younger workers to divert some of the money they contribute to Social Security to a private investment account. On the long road to enactment, this proposal had to be reported out by the House Ways and Means Committee, and the refusal of members of the committee to support the bill in any form meant it went nowhere.[9]

Most standing committees also have several subcommittees. The Appropriations committees in each chamber are responsible for all spending bills, and the House and Senate Appropriations committees both have thirteen separate subcommittees, each of which is responsible for reporting out one of the thirteen yearly appropriations bills that fund the operations of the federal government every year.

Select committees Ad hoc bodies created to deal with a particular issue or even a single piece of legislation.

Joint committees Committees made up of members of both chambers that usually perform some specialized function.

Conference committees Ad hoc committees created to reconcile differing versions of a single piece of legislation that has been passed on the floor of each chamber.

In addition to standing committees, Congress also has select committees, joint committees, and conference committees. **Select committees** are ad hoc bodies created to deal with a particular issue or even a single piece of legislation. **Joint committees** are committees made up of members of both chambers that usually perform some specialized function. **Conference committees** are ad hoc committees created to reconcile differing versions of a single piece of legislation that has been passed on the floor of each chamber.

Committees serve a variety of functions in the legislative process. First, committees help to manage the significant workload of the institution. In a given Congress, legislators introduce thousands of bills, and there would be no way to read, digest, assess, amend, and vote on every one of them acting as a committee of the whole. Committees allow subsets of members to divide the labor and work on many bills all at once.

Second, committees allow members to specialize and develop expertise in particular policy areas. Once on a committee, members have incentives to stay on the committee for a long time, if not their entire career. Over time, they develop expertise in the policy area that is the jurisdictional turf of that committee. With all members sharing information, the institution as a whole benefits from an informational logroll, trading of favors, or a quid pro quo.

Third, committees allow legislators opportunities to legitimately claim credit for legislative accomplishments. All members need to be able to convince their constituents that they have accomplished something before the next election, and, in an institution as large as Congress, it would be difficult for any member to claim credit for the enactment of any single piece of legislation. Because committees have specific jurisdictional turf, members can legitimately claim credit for the critical role they may have played within their small subset of all members of Congress.

Not all committees provide the same opportunities for influence for ambitious legislators. Some, like the appropriations and tax-writing committees are more desirable than others. Once on a committee, members are generally allowed to stay, but new members and those seeking to change their committee assignments submit their preferences to special committees for each party in each chamber tasked with making these difficult choices. There is a great deal of politicking surrounding committee assignments, and party leaders generally use the process as a source of "carrots and sticks" to reward those who have been good team players and punish those who have not. In 2010, for instance, when Alaska Senator Lisa Murkowski (R) decided to mount a write-in bid to hold her seat after losing the Republican primary, Senate Republicans indicated that she would likely lose her spot on the Energy Committee. Later, however, party officials recanted, and Murkowski went on to win the election and retained her seat on the Energy Committee.[10]

Seniority An important criterion in selecting committee leadership; the longer members of Congress have been in office, the more senior they are, and the greater likelihood that they will be selected to chair a committee.

The most important criterion in selecting committee leadership is **seniority**. The longer members of Congress have been in office, the more senior they are, and the more likely they are to be selected to chair a committee. However, party leaders have been more willing to violate the norm of seniority in recent decades. In one of the more notable cases, when Republicans gained majority control of both chambers in 1995, the new Speaker of the House, Newt Gingrich (R-GA), passed over three more senior Republicans on the powerful House Appropriations Committee to install Robert Livingston (R-LA) as the new chair. And, when Democrats took control of both chambers back from Republicans in 2007, Nancy Pelosi (D-CA), chose the third most senior Democrat on the House Select Committee on Intelligence, Silvestre Reyes (D-TX), as chair instead of the most senior Democrat on the panel, Jane Harman (D-CA), with whom Pelosi had had a difficult relationship. More recently, when he was elected as the new Speaker of the House in late 2010, John Boehner (R-OH) also decided to bypass seniority norms in assigning new members to committees.[11] As a result, two freshman lawmakers were named to the important Ways and Means Committee, four were named to the Appropriations Committee, and seven were named to the Energy and Commerce Committee.

"Congress by committee" has some negative effects as well. Dividing up the work of Congress into semiautonomous subunits decentralizes the work and leads to a lack of coordination in policymaking. It is very easy to see how a Congress organized in this way can enact uncoordinated and even contradictory policies, such as subsidizing tobacco farmers at the same time as funding antismoking education campaigns. Taken to the extreme, Congress by committee can facilitate the formation of "subgovernments" or **iron triangles**—cozy, policymaking relationships among small numbers of players not at all representative of the wider variety of stakeholders who might want to influence policymaking.

Iron triangles Cozy policymaking relationships among small numbers of players that are not at all representative of the wider variety of stakeholders who might want to influence policymaking.

Over the past few decades, the power of party leaders in Congress has increased.

During the post–World War II era, committees dominated policymaking in Congress, and both the benefits and costs of policymaking in this structure were clearly evident. During the 1950s and 1960s, however, rank-and-file members of Congress became increasingly frustrated with the seniority-dominated committee leadership system.[12] At the same time, many members of Congress wanted to improve the institution's ability to compete with the increasingly powerful contemporary presidency. As a result, during the late 1960s and into the 1970s and 1980s, power shifted from committee chairs to party leaders and party institutions.

The foundation of party power in Congress resides with the **party conferences** (House Democrats call theirs a **caucus**). Every member of Congress (even those identified as Independents) is a member of either the Democratic or Republican conference in their chamber. Perhaps the most significant decision these conferences make is to select party leaders for each party in each chamber. In choosing their leader, the majority party in the House is also effectively choosing a person to be **Speaker of the House**. In 2011, the new Republican majority in the House chose John Boehner (R-OH) as the Speaker, taking the gavel from Nancy Pelosi (D-CA), who had been Speaker since Democrats took majority control of the House in 2007. The Speaker is the most recognized and most powerful member of the House of Representatives with a broad array of powers to preside over

Party conferences Every member of Congress is a member of either the Democratic or Republican conference in their chamber. House Democrats call theirs a caucus.

Caucus The House Democrat's party conference.

Speaker of the House The leader of the majority party in the House of Representatives. He or she is the most recognized and most powerful member of the House.

Rules Committee The committee in the House of Representatives that helps determine the conditions under which bills will come to the floor. The committee is headed by the Speaker of the House.

Minority Leader Represents the minority party in the House of Representatives; also refers to the person who represents the minority party in the Senate.

Majority Leader In the Senate, this person has the formal power to bring bills to the floor (or not).

the chamber's debates, rule on procedural matters, and refer legislation to committees. The Speaker's more important role, however, is as leader of the majority party in the House. The Speaker has control over the **Rules Committee**, which helps to determine the conditions under which bills will come to the floor, and has the most influence on committee assignments and committee leadership selection. The **Minority Leader** represents the minority party in the House. With just a minority of votes supporting his or her efforts in the House, however, the Minority Leader's power is mostly informal.

Beneath the Speaker and the Minority Leader is an elaborate network of other party leaders. The majority party has a Majority Leader, a Majority Whip, Assistant Whips, a Campaign Chairman, and members of a Steering and Policy Committee. The minority party has a similar leadership structure. The main purpose of these party leadership networks is to facilitate coordination on party messages and to facilitate communication from leadership down to the rank-and-file and from the rank-and-file up to the leadership.

In the Senate, party leadership structures are similar in most ways with two key differences. First, the presiding officer in the Senate is the vice president. In practice, the vice president rarely comes to the Senate to preside over floor action mainly because the presiding officer lacks significant authority over the calendar or rules of debate in the Senate. Second, because the Senate is a smaller body where members are more collegial, less power is delegated even to the leaders of the two party conferences, the **Majority Leader** and the Minority Leader. The main formal power of the Majority Leader in the Senate is the power to bring bills to the floor or not. Because the power of the minority to tie up the Senate in debate is significant, the Majority Leader usually consults with the Minority Leader in scheduling Senate business and at least tries to accommodate the concerns of the minority party.

Party leaders in Congress ultimately have two distinct constituencies: the people they represent from their congressional district and, because of their leadership role, their party conference. In serving this second constituency, party leaders have to nurture the brand name of the party by shielding members from tough votes they may not want to have to cast and by advancing party messages most likely to enhance the value of the party label. In this role, the party leadership's work extends well beyond the confines of the halls of Congress and beyond their own district's or state's boundaries. They need to recruit challengers to run against incumbents from the other party and help all the party's candidates raise funds and conduct successful campaigns. Party leadership positions are always attractive posts to hold, but they are much more attractive when one's party is in the majority. It may rightly be said that the main job of the Speaker of the House and the Majority Leader in the Senate is to build on the majority's numbers, while the main job of the House and Senate Minority Leaders is to work their way back to majority status.

In committee and on the floor of each chamber, where bills ultimately become law, the party conferences provide the foundation for the voting coalitions necessary

Figure 3.2 House and Senate: Party Means on Liberal-Conservative Dimension

Since the mid-1970s, congressional leaders have accumulated an increasing amount of power. As a result, the parties have started to act more as "teams" with members voting increasingly more liberal (Democrats) or conservative (Republicans).

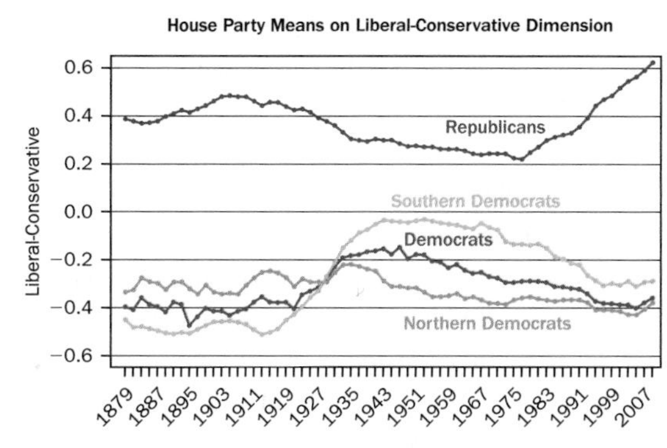

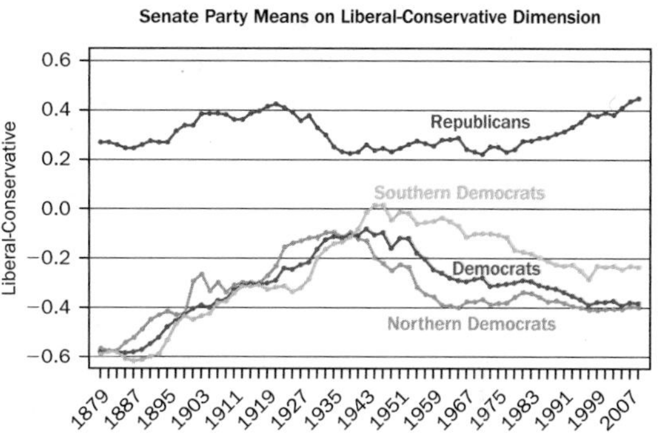

Source: VoteView.com, http://www.voteview.com/polarized_america.htm

to govern in a majoritarian legislative institution. Figure 3.2 shows that as more and more power has been delegated to party leaders over the last few decades, members of the two parties have behaved more and more like cohesive "teams," taking different positions on bills and voting against one another.

The increasing strength of congressional parties has both costs and benefits. Increasing partisan polarization may lead to more conflict in the legislative process and more gridlock, particularly in the Senate where the minority is empowered to block legislation it strongly opposes. On the other hand, stronger congressional parties encourage greater accountability as the parties' records and messages become more clearly distinct and defined for voters. For better or worse, stronger congressional parties empower Congress as an institution in its struggle for influence with the president and the executive branch.

4 Members of Congress can represent their constituencies as delegates or as trustees.

Members of Congress serve in two roles that are sometimes compatible but also sometimes conflicting. On the one hand, they are representatives of the people in the home state or district where they are elected. This means not only seeking to represent the interests of important industries and groups back home but working as a

Delegate The role members of Congress serve in representing the interests and policy preferences of their constituents.

Trustee The role members of Congress serve in acting on behalf of the interests of the home constituents and nation regardless of whether constituents would immediately approve of the members' decisions.

sort of casework liaison between people in the district and the various agencies of the federal government. In this role, members serve as **delegates**, hewing as closely as possible to the interests and policy preferences of their constituents.

On the other hand, members of Congress are national lawmakers seeking not only to forge compromises among the many competing interests from across the country on various issues but to cast votes on behalf of their own vision of the national interest, even when it might conflict with local interests back home. In this role, members serve as **trustees**, acting on behalf of the interests of the home constituents and the nation regardless of whether these constituents would immediately approve of members' decisions.

Finding the right balance in representation between serving as a delegate or a trustee is difficult and frequently is a function of how electorally safe or vulnerable a particular legislator perceives him or herself to be. In general, because of their more frequent elections, House members tend to behave more like delegates, while senators, with their 6-year terms, are freer to act like trustees.

In one famous example of a legislator trying, unsuccessfully as it turned out, to find this balance, President Clinton called on a freshman House member, Marjorie Margolies-Mezvinsky (D-PA), to support his deficit reduction package in 1993. The package included some tax increases, and Mezvinsky, as the first Democrat to be elected in her Republican-leaning House district in 76 years, had pledged to vote against it just a day earlier. Clinton called Mezvinsky at the last moment to tell her that the bill was going to come down to her one vote and he needed her support. As supportive Democratic leaders told Mezvinsky to "Just do what's right," and combative Republicans chanted, "Goodbye Marjorie," Mezvinsky cast her vote in support of the bill much to the dismay of many of her constituents.[13] A little more than a year later, Mezvinsky was defeated by Jon Fox.

3 The legislative process is long and complicated, so most bills never become laws.

The main function of Congress is lawmaking. The process by which bills become law, however, is long and complex, and every bill must overcome many obstacles. We can briefly characterize the legislative process in Congress as consisting of five stages: bill introduction, in committee, on the floor, reconciling different versions, and presidential approval.

Bill Introduction: The first step is that a bill must be drafted and introduced. Most anyone can draft legislation—legislators, legislative staff, interest groups, executive branch officials and agencies, and even concerned citizens—but only a member of Congress can officially introduce a bill in Congress. Particularly in the case of high-profile or controversial legislation, members seek out other members to serve as cosponsors as an indication of bipartisan or broad support for an idea.

Once a bill is introduced, it is usually referred to a standing committee. Technically, the Speaker of the House and the presiding officer in the Senate have the power to refer bills to committees but, in practice, most bills are referred to committees by the parliamentarian of the chamber—a staff person responsible for providing nonpartisan advice on procedural matters to Congress—based on the jurisdiction of the various committees and the name and substance of the bill introduced.

Markup The process of amending or changing a bill.

Discharge petition The power to pull a bill from a recalcitrant committee; this is not used frequently in practice.

In Committee: Once a bill has been referred to a committee, it is up to that committee to hold hearings (or not), to amend the bill (or not), and to report the bill out positively (or not). Most bills do not even receive a hearing and, among the bills that are reported out of committee, many are frequently changed significantly in what is known as **markup**, or the process of amending and changing the bill. Much of the power associated with serving as a committee chair lies in the chair's ability to decide what bills get a hearing, when they are discussed, and what questions will be considered by the committee. The power to decide whether to even discuss the bill in committee is particularly important. Members of Congress do have the power to pull a bill from a recalcitrant committee through the use of a **discharge petition**, but this does not happen very frequently in practice.

On the Floor: Once a bill has been reported from committee, it needs to make its way onto the floor. Once there, it takes a simple majority of members in each chamber for a bill to move to the next stage. As described above, however, the Speaker of the House and the Senate Majority Leader effectively control a bill's access to the floor. Once on the floor, the power of the House Speaker and the Senate Majority Leader differ substantially. With effective control over the House Rules Committee, the Speaker can usually dictate the terms of the debate (how much time, number of amendments allowed, etc.) on the House floor. In contrast, the Senate Majority Leader cannot limit debate or the number of amendments offered by even the most junior senator from the minority party. Instead, debate may only be limited through a unanimous consent agreement or a cloture vote. In effect, 41 senators can block action on any piece of legislation, so long as they stick together.

Reconciling Different Versions: When a bill passes on the floor of each chamber, there is usually at least some difference (and often very significant differences) between the two versions of the bill. In order to become law, it must be approved by a majority of each chamber in exactly the same form. One method of reconciling the differences is for the version passed in one chamber to be taken up by the other and enacted. Alternatively, chambers may make changes and bounce the bill back and forth until it passes each chamber in the same form. But, on more complicated bills or bills where the differences are very great, the bill may be referred to a conference committee made up of a delegation from each chamber. The job of the conference committee is to reconcile the differences between the bills and report the new version back to the two floors, where, advocates hope the bill will be enacted in the same form. In conference, the bill may change substantially, or it even may die if conferees fail to come to an agreement. Assuming the differences can be ironed out and the bill is finally passed on both floors, the bill is presented to the president for his approval.

Presidential Approval: The president can allow a bill to become law without his signature, or he can sign the bill making it a law. However, he also has the power to **veto** a bill. Presidential vetoes are usually upheld, as it requires two-thirds of both chambers to override the veto.

Veto (presidential veto) The power of a president to prevent a bill passed by both houses of Congress from becoming law. Presidential vetoes can only be overridden by a two-thirds vote of both chambers, which is rare.

As described above, there are many, many points at which a bill may be blocked and fail to become law. Failure at any one of these points—in a House committee, on the Senate floor, or a presidential veto—means the bill does not become law. It is a wonder, therefore, that any bill ever becomes law in this long, complicated process that can be characterized as exhibiting "multiple veto points."

So what kinds of practices allow members of Congress to overcome these multiple veto points? One answer is that members of Congress engage in **logrolling**—a bargaining strategy in which one member agrees to support another member's bill in exchange for his or her support on some other piece of legislation. To refer to an earlier example, when Marjorie Margolies-Mezvinsky voted to support President Clinton's deficit reduction package in 1993, she explained her reversal of position by indicating that President Clinton had promised to convene a conference on entitlement spending in her district in return for her vote.[14] There was also much speculation that President Clinton had promised to raise money and campaign for Mezvinsky's next election. Sometimes, legislative support can be secured by including pork-barrel benefits in the bill, like funding for a transportation project in a member's district. In still other cases, support may be secured by utilizing a voice vote instead of a roll-call vote, making it easier for members to obscure the connection between their vote and the negative policy effects of a bill.[15]

Logrolling A bargaining strategy in which one member of Congress agrees to support another member's bill in exchange for their support on some other piece of legislation.

Electoral incentives drive members of Congress, and most congressional elections are not competitive.

Members of Congress are the only federal officials directly elected by the people, and they are not limited to a specified number of terms. Therefore, as soon as members are elected, they have to begin to think about their prospects for reelection. Even for those members with other goals in mind, like making good public policy for instance, reelection must be an important consideration because it is generally difficult to achieve all of one's policy goals in just one term of office.

The electoral motivation of members of Congress can rightly be described as the most important driving force behind member behavior, institutional organization, and congressional policy outputs. We discussed earlier how the time spent at home in the district and the amount of effort members expend on casework for constituents is driven by the electoral motivation. We also described above how institutional structures like committee and party leadership positions were created with electoral motivations in mind, such as providing venues for the distribution of pork-barrel benefits and incentivizing some members to work to protect the value of the party brand name. Finally, we have also seen how the policy outputs of Congress are a reflection of members' electoral needs.

So, if members behave, organize the institution, and produce policy benefits in ways that are geared towards serving their electoral needs, are they successful? The answer is an emphatic yes. Members of Congress who run for reelection are reelected at remarkably high rates. In a normal congressional election year, more than 90 percent of House members are reelected as are more than 80 percent of the senators up for reelection.

Gerrymandered Refers to the way House districts across the country are drawn in such a way that a disproportionate number of voters in the district are registered voters in the incumbent's party.

Senators do not perform quite as well as House members for a couple of important reasons. First, senators tend to attract stronger challengers because a Senate seat is generally more desirable. Second, many House districts across the country are "**gerrymandered**," meaning the district boundaries have been drawn in such a way that a disproportionate number of voters in the district are registered voters in the incumbent's party. In fact, despite the relative parity between the parties in national registration, remarkably few districts across the country are actually "swing" districts in which there is a relatively even number of Democrats and Republicans. Most districts are either solidly Republican or solidly Democratic. Since senators represent entire states, however, Senate districts cannot be gerrymandered. So, as a percentage of all seats in the chamber, there are far more swing states than there are swing districts.

While the vast majority of members of the House and Senate who run for reelection are reelected, in some years, such as 2010 for example, the advantages of incumbency are not as great. In the 2010 congressional elections, Republicans posted a net gain of 63 seats in the House of Representatives and a net gain of 6 Senate seats. However, this actually understates the turnover in Congress. Added to the significant number of incumbents who chose not to run for reelection for various reasons, there were actually 94 new members of the House and 13 new members of the Senate when the 112th Congress was sworn in.

One final note about electoral motivation seems in order. The fact that members of Congress are primarily interested in reelection might strike some as a rather depressing thought. Shouldn't members of Congress be primarily interested in pursuing the public good? For James Madison and many others at the Constitutional Convention, these two goals were not seen as mutually exclusive. In Madison's view, members of Congress would serve as good representatives of the people they represent and pursue good public policy precisely because they would be motivated by electoral concerns.[16]

Policymaking in Congress reflects public opinion on most issues.

Since Congress was designed as "the people's branch," the expectation was that Congress would likely be the most popular branch of government. But today, the institution receives the lowest approval ratings of the three branches of government. Most individual members of Congress remain quite popular in their own districts or states, but most citizens disapprove of the job the institution does as a whole.

What explains these low approval ratings? People believe partisan bickering has prevented Congress from doing a good job of solving the nation's problems. In his aptly named book *Why Americans Hate Politics*, E. J. Dionne, Jr., argues:

> On issue after issue, there is consensus on where the country should move or at least on what we should be arguing about; liberalism and conservatism make it impossible for that consensus to express itself.[17]

The problem with this argument is that it assumes a consensus exists among citizens regarding what ought to be done about most or even very many of the problems the country faces. For example, we all recognize that there is a problem with homelessness in America. Some of us argue for more direct public involvement in the issue, while others argue for more market-based mechanisms. Some argue that we cannot combat homelessness without tackling the issues of mental health coverage or drug abuse. Still others argue for rent control, while some argue against it. The point is that although almost all Americans would like to see the problem of homelessness solved, there is widespread disagreement about the causes of the problem, the extent of the problem, and most certainly, about the proper policy solution. On this issue and many others, Congress may be said to be quite accurately reflecting the dissensus that exists in society. And expecting a majoritarian institution like Congress to manufacture that consensus for us may be expecting a bit too much.

CONCLUSION

If Congress is restrained by its collective action problems and by the dissensus within our society, how can it possibly enact legislation in the best interest of the country in general? The answer lies in the complex procedures and institutions that we have examined throughout this chapter, which ensure that some sort of compromise is reached. When Congress enacts tax deductions for student loan interest, sets troop levels in Iraq, or raises taxes to reduce the deficit, members of Congress and their staff study the problem and then negotiate a solution—a solution that will always be a compromise, as it is unlikely that over 300 million citizens will ever come to a complete agreement.

THEIR LIST

An Insider's View

ROGER LAU

Congressional Staffer

Roger Lau served as a staff member to both Rep. Martin Meehan (D-MA) and Sen. John Kerry (D-MA) and has worked on several congressional campaigns, including serving as campaign manager for John Kerry's 2008 Senate reelection campaign. He started his work in politics when still a college student with an internship in one of Sen. Kerry's local state offices. We asked Mr. Lau what he thought were the most important things to know about Congress, and he identified two things in particular he thought students should know:

First, Mr. Lau said that seniority is even more significant in the Congress than most people imagine. Having a chairmanship is critical to a member who wants to advance a legislative agenda, and seniority is the most frequent path to a chairmanship. But Mr. Lau argues that being the most senior member of one's state delegation is of great importance as well. The senior member of a state's House or even Senate delegation can mean receiving greater deference on policy matters from other members and greater influence over how federal dollars are allocated within a state. Ultimately, Mr. Lau argues that in terms of individual influence, one might be better off as a senior member of the minority party than a junior member from the majority party.

Second, Mr. Lau says it is important to know that most legislators are people who work very hard to meet often unrealistic public expectations about what they can do. Although many may see their representatives as being out of touch with their constituents, most members of Congress work hard for 3 or 4 days a week in Washington before flying home for 3 or 4 days of work in the home state or district before starting the next week and doing it all over again. Despite that, Mr. Lau says that most constituents think their representatives are not home enough. "There's a misunderstanding of how hard a job it is to be a legislator," Lau says. "It is easy for a challenger to argue that a member of Congress isn't home enough, but these are people who are expected to deliver and the only way to deliver is to be in Washington, D.C. a lot of the time pushing for constituent interests." It is a tough and demanding tightrope that members have to walk, with challengers always ready to pounce on the slightest perceived imbalance in the amount of time a member spends at events and meetings at home. After a decade of working for several members of Congress on both the government and campaign sides, Mr. Lau has come to admire as a special group the individuals who choose to serve in the national legislature.

However, this compromise was precisely what James Madison and the other founders of the Constitution had in mind when they attempted to set up a democratic government that would respect the rights of the minority and not be dominated by a simple majority. By compelling the Senate to enact the tax laws that affect student loans using a procedure that limits their duration to 10 years, the Democrats were forcing the Republicans, who controlled both the Congress and the presidency, to compromise. And the compromise may be a solution that neither party likes very well but that both parties can live with.

Is this compromise always the best solution? If not, how can Congress arrive at just and effective measures? Congress, as we have seen, has set up research, policy analysis, and audit agencies, created procedures, and hired staff in an attempt to enact the best measures in a world that is changing rapidly. While approval of the job Congress does may be very low (and it's even lower among young people), members of Congress care intensely about what you think of the job they are doing. And the greater the input from the people, the better Congress can represent and protect the diverse interests of its people. That reality means we have power over what the Constitution outlines as the most powerful branch of government . . . but only if we choose to exercise it.

YOUR LIST REVISITED

At the beginning of the chapter you were asked to think about what you might include on your own list of the Top 10 Most Important Things to Know About Congress. Now that you have read the chapter, take a moment to revisit your list. What, if anything, would you change about your list? Do you agree or disagree with the chapter list constructed by the author? What might you add or delete? Why?

KEY TERMS

Bicameral legislature 55
Bills 56
Caucus 63
Cloture 57
Collective action problems 59
Conference committees 61
Congressional Budget Office (CBO) 60
Constituents 60
Delegate 66
Discharge petition 67
Elastic clause 55
Filibuster 57
Gerrymandered 69
Impeach 56
Incumbent 57
Iron triangles 63
Joint committees 61
Logrolling 68
Majority Leader 64
Markup 67
Minority Leader 64
Necessary and proper clause 55
Party conferences 63
Pork-barrel spending 59
Rules Committee 64
Select committees 61
Seniority 62
Speaker of the House 63
Standing committees 61
Trustee 66
Unanimous consent agreements 56
Veto (presidential veto) 68
Ways and Means Committee 61

CHAPTER REVIEW QUESTIONS

10. According to James Madison in *Federalist No.51*, why is Congress likely to be the most powerful branch?
9. What are the key differences between the House of Representatives and the Senate described in the Constitution?
8. In what ways is Congress beset by collective action problems?
7. What role do staff agencies play in running Congress?
6. What is the purpose of the committee system in Congress?
5. What is the role of the Speaker of the House, and why is the Speaker so powerful?
4. Differentiate between the trustee and delegate modes of representation.
3. Explain the key stages of the legislative process.
2. Why are so many congressional incumbents reelected?
1. Why are approval ratings for Congress so low?

SUGGESTED READINGS

- Arnold, R. Douglas. *The Logic of Congressional Action.* New Haven, CT: Yale University Press, 1990.
- Cox, Gary W., and Mathew D. McCubbins. *Legislative Leviathan: Party Government in the House*, 2nd ed. New York: Cambridge University Press, 2007.
- Dodd, Lawrence C., and Bruce I. Oppenheimer, eds. *Congress Reconsidered*, 9th ed. Washington, DC: CQ Press, 2008.
- Hamilton, Lee H. *How Congress Works and Why You Should Care.* Bloomington, IN: Indiana University Press, 2004.
- Jacobson, Gary C. *The Politics of Congressional Elections*, 7th ed. New York: Longman, 2008.
- Madison, James, Alexander Hamilton, and John Jay. *The Federalist Papers,1787–1788* (#55, #57, #62, and #63). Available online at: http://thomas.loc.gov/home/histdox/fedpapers.html.
- Mayhew, David R. *Congress: The Electoral Connection*, 2nd ed. New Haven, CT: Yale University Press, 2004.
- Murray, Alan S., and Jeffrey H. Birnbaum. *Showdown at Gucci Gulch.* New York: Vintage, 1988.
- Shepsle, Kenneth A. "The Changing Textbook Congress" in John E. Chubb and Paul E. Peterson, eds., *Can the Government Govern?* Washington, DC: The Brookings Institution, 1989.
- Sinclair, Barbara. *Unorthodox Lawmaking: New Legislative Processes in the U.S. Congress,* 3rd ed. Washington, DC: CQ Press, 2007.

SUGGESTED FILMS

- *Mr. Smith Goes to Washington* (1939)
- *All the King's Men* (1949)
- *Advise and Consent* (1962)
- *The Candidate* (1972)
- *The Seduction of Joe Tynan* (1979)
- *The Distinguished Gentleman* (1992)
- *The People and the Power Game: The Elected* (1996)
- *The Contender* (2000)
- *Legally Blonde 2: Red White and Blonde* (2003)
- *Charlie Wilson's War* (2007)

SUGGESTED WEBSITES

- **Congress.org:** http://www.congress.org/
- **National Journal Online:** http://www.nationaljournal.com/
- **Roll Call:** http://www.rollcall.com/
- **The Center for Responsive Politics:** http://www.opensecrets.org/politicians/index.php
- **The Cook Political Report:** http://cookpolitical.com/
- **The Dirksen Center:** http://www.dirksencenter.org/
- **The Hill:** http://www.hillnews.com/
- **Thomas:** http://thomas.loc.gov/
- **U.S. House of Representatives:** http://www.house.gov/
- **U.S. Senate:** http://www.senate.gov/

ENDNOTES

[1]Joint Committee on Taxation, *Present Law and Analysis Relating to Tax Benefits for Higher Education* (JCX-35-08), April 29, 2008.

[2]As originally ratified, the Constitution provided that senators would be chosen by state legislatures, but the Seventeenth Amendment, ratified in 1913, provided for direct election of senators.

[3]Presidents are chosen by the Electoral College (or by the House of Representatives if no candidate receives a majority in the Electoral College), and members of the Supreme Court are nominated by the president and confirmed by the Senate.

[4]Until the ratification of the Seventeenth Amendment in 1913, Senators were chosen by state legislatures. The Seventeenth Amendment provided for direct election of U.S. Senators.

[5]A few of the smallest states (Alaska, Delaware, Montana, North Dakota, South Dakota, Vermont, and Wyoming) have only one House member, and so House members from these states represent all citizens in their state rather than those in a smaller legislative district.

[6]David Nather, "Senate Races Against the Nuclear Clock on Judges," CQ Weekly Online (May 30, 2005), 1440–1443, available at: http://library.cqpress.com/cqweekly/weeklyreport109-000001700754 (accessed July 10, 2009).

[7]Joseph J. Schatz and David Clarke, "Congress Clears Stimulus Package," CQ Weekly (February 16, 2009), 352–356.

[8]Congressional Budget Office, "Health Care: Estimates for March 2010 Health Care Legislation" (accessed May 20, 2011). http://www.cbo.gov/publications/collections/health.cfm

[9]Alex Wayne, "Fall Agenda: Social Security Overhaul." CQ Weekly Online (September 5, 2005), 2319–2319, available at: http://library.cqpress.com.libproxy.csun.edu:2048/cqweekly/weeklyreport109-000001843141 (accessed July 10, 2009).

[10]Matthew Daly, "Senate GOP Votes to Allow Murkowski to Keep Her Committee Post," HuffPost Politics (September 22, 2010), available at: http://www.huffingtonpost.com/2010/09/22/murkowski-committee-post_n_735355.html (accessed October 11, 2010).

[11]Patrick O'Connor, "Republican Freshmen Get Plum Posts," *Washington Wire* (December 10, 2010), available at: http://blogs.wsj.com/washwire/2010/12/10/republican-freshmen-get-plum-posts/ (accessed May 20, 2011).

[12]For more on this history and line of argument, see Kenneth Shepsle, "The Changing Textbook Congress," in John Chubb and Paul Peterson, eds., *Can the Government Govern*? (Washington, DC: Brookings Institution, 1989), 238–266.

[13]David S. Cloud, "THE LAST STRETCH: Big Risk for Margolies-Mezvinsky," CQ Weekly Online (August 7, 1993), 2125–2125, available at: http://library.cqpress.com.libproxy.csun.edu:2048/cqweekly/WR103402222 (accessed July 12, 2009).

[14]Ibid.

[15]For more on this idea, see R. Douglas Arnold, *The Logic of Congressional Action* (New Haven, CT: Yale University Press, 1990), 100–104.

[16]For more on this line of argument from James Madison, see *Federalist Papers #57*.

[17]E. J. Dionne, Jr., *Why Americans Hate Politics* (New York: Touchstone, 1991), 11.

Chapter 4

THE PRESIDENCY

Top Ten List

10 Article II of the Constitution lays out the minimal qualifications for the office of president, the nature of the office, and the means of selection.

9 Presidents are the only truly national officials, with correspondingly high and unique expectations placed on their shoulders.

8 The powers of the presidency were crafted in distrust, but they have evolved to meet the need for modern executive action.

7 Presidents fill multiple foreign policy roles as commander in chief, chief diplomat, and head of state.

6 Presidents serve as chief executive of the executive branch.

5 Presidents are expected to function as chief legislator, policymaker, and head of their political parties.

4 Presidential power is primarily the power to persuade and bargain.

3 Presidential power is limited by a variety of factors.

2 Presidents must govern successfully and campaign continuously to win reelection.

1 Presidents have substantial control over their Cabinets.

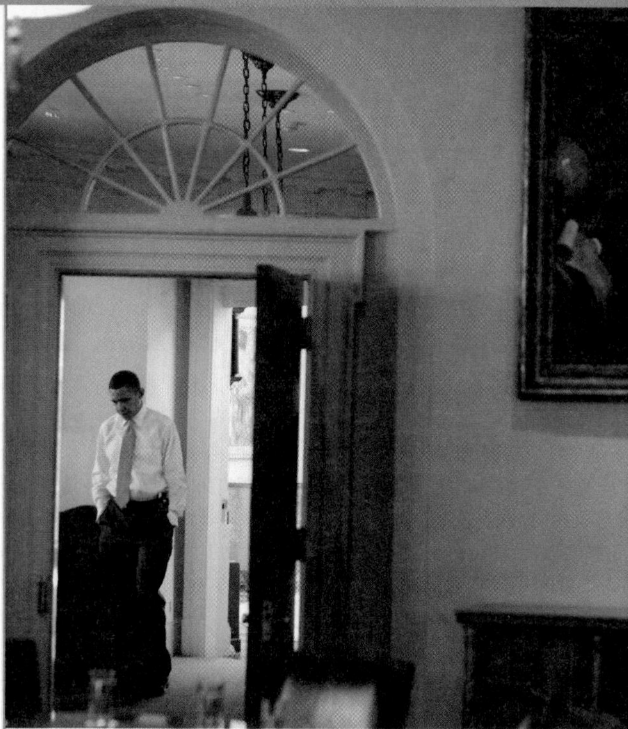

Presidents must constantly make life-altering decisions for millions of people at home and abroad, often with no good choices or clear outcomes. And no matter what a president does, he must ultimately decide alone and in the absence of certainty. In this way, the presidency is a powerful yet lonely place to be. Shown here, President Barack Obama walks through the outer oval office in between healthcare meetings in 2010.

YOUR LIST

Before you read this chapter, take a few moments to think about what you might include on a list of the Top 10 Most Important Things to Know About the American Presidency. At the end of the chapter you will be asked to compare and contrast your list with the one supplied in this chapter.

INTRODUCTION

Imagine you had to face an apparently sudden set of conflicts in your family, circle of friends, or larger community, ones that threatened the well-being of people involved and whose potential solutions were also tragically in conflict. Then imagine you were being held primarily responsible for solving all those conflicts, with little assistance and much resistance from the people involved. The expectations are high, but your real powers to affect the situation may be low, and pleasing all involved is probably impossible. You may feel alone and isolated in your responsibility.

President Obama and the forty-three men who have preceded him as president are all too familiar with such scenarios, ones that involved not just localized tensions, but often situations that shaped the whole world. In early 2011, President Obama was confronted with a sudden humanitarian crisis in Libya, where he had to decide whether or not to use American forces to prevent a massacre of civilians by the Libyan government, with all the costs and risks involved in such a decision. He chose to intervene and, in so doing, faced a good amount of public skepticism and congressional criticism. Even members of Obama's own party were not supportive of the president's decision.[1] One Democratic representative, Dennis Kucinich (OH), went so far as to ask whether Obama's actions in regard to Libya amounted to an impeachable offense:

> President Obama moved forward without Congress approving. He didn't have Congressional authorization, he has gone against the Constitution, and that's got to be said. . . . Such an action—that involves putting America's service men and women into harm's way . . . is a grave decision that cannot be made by the president alone. . . . [and] would appear on its face to be an impeachable offense.[2]

President Obama has confronted equally tense issues on the domestic front. For instance, disagreements between the president and members of Congress over the budget repeatedly threatened to shut down the federal government in 2011 and leave thousands without pay and certain government services. Equally contentious were the battles over healthcare reform that consumed much of Obama's first year and a half in the White House and put him at odds with many representatives and senators.

Presidents must constantly make life-altering decisions for millions of people at home and abroad, often with no good choices or clear outcomes. And no matter what a president does, even with the substantial power of the presidency behind him, he must ultimately decide alone and in the absence of certainty. In this way, the presidency is a powerful yet lonely place to be.

As children, we are often told that the president of the United States is one of the most powerful individuals in the entire world. While it is true that presidents have a range of powers to fundamentally reshape the world in which we live, the power they exercise is often fragile and limited by the structures of our political system. In addition, presidents confront great public expectations that often lead to public frustration when they fail to keep a promise or when their choices lead to both good and bad outcomes. In this chapter, we examine the reality of the American presidency and the question at the heart of this office. How does a president meet the expectations of the American (and world) public in an office that seems powerful on its face but that is constrained by a variety of factors—both constitutional and otherwise?

Article II of the Constitution lays out the minimal qualifications for the office of president, the nature of the office, and the means of selection.

The qualifications for the presidential office set down by the authors of the Constitution in Article II were few in number, simply requiring an individual to be at least 35 years of age, to be a natural-born U.S. citizen, and to have at least 14 years of continuous residency in the United States. These requirements were designed to ensure a basic level of life experience and a meaningful attachment to the United States. The more complex constitutional debates were over the nature of the office (singular or plural) and the means of selection.

The founders specified that the president be chosen for a 4-year term not through direct popular vote or by the legislature, but via the indirect system of the **Electoral College**. Through this unique mechanism, each of the fifty states is given the ability to appoint a group of presidential electors, who make that state's choice for who will become president. The number of electors is based on the state's number of U.S. House members and senators. To win the presidency, a candidate must receive at least 270 of the 538 electoral votes.

Electoral College Each of the 50 states is given the ability to appoint a group of presidential electors, who make that state's choice for who will become president.

Importantly, these electors are not "free voters." In virtually every case, their choice is guided by which candidate won the majority of direct popular votes in their state. However, that direct vote is modified in two ways. First, electoral votes are "winner take all"—meaning that in all but two states, Maine and Nebraska, the majority vote winner gets all the electoral votes of a state, while the "loser" gets none.[3] Second, the electoral votes overrepresent the voice of smaller states, due to equal representation of all states in the U.S. Senate. This system was designed to place a control on the direct voice of the public, while at the same time working to prevent a monarchical executive (which could have potentially transpired through congressional or direct public selection of the executive).[4]

If this Electoral College system is largely a modified "rubber stamp" for the direct public voice, why do some people see it as a problem, a practice in need of reform or abolition? Because occasionally—for instance in 1876, 1888, and most recently in 2000—the winner of the national popular vote has lost the Electoral College vote, leading to controversy and complaints about the "undemocratic" result.[5] Shortly after the 2000 election when Al Gore won the popular vote but George W. Bush won the Electoral College vote and thus the presidency, Gallup found that the majority of Americans supported eliminating the Electoral College:

> There is little question that the American public would prefer to dismantle the Electoral College system, and go to a direct popular vote for the presidency. In Gallup polls that stretch back over 50 years, a majority of Americans have continually expressed support for the notion of an official amendment of the U.S. Constitution that would allow for direct election of the president.[6]

9 Presidents are the only truly national officials, with correspondingly high and unique expectations placed on their shoulders.

A crucial feature of the presidential selection system is that presidents are chosen independently of Congress, giving presidents an autonomous claim to public support and legitimacy. Why is this important for power? First, presidents are not dependent on Congress for gaining or keeping their office. Unlike prime ministers in parliamentary systems, presidents are not chosen by, nor can they be easily removed by, legislative action. According to Article II, the only way Congress can remove a president from office is through **impeachment** and conviction for "high crimes and misdemeanors." In order to remove a president, the House of Representatives must first impeach the president, a process that is somewhat analogous to indictment by a grand jury. Just as the power of impeachment is the sole power of the House, the power to convict and remove a president from office is the sole power of the Senate (Article II, section 4).

Impeachment Article II, section 4, gives this power to the House of Representatives. The power to impeach is analogous to the power of indictment exercised by a grand jury. In order to be removed from office, the president must be convicted by the Senate.

Two presidents in American history have been impeached by the House (President Andrew Johnson and President Bill Clinton), but no president has ever been convicted and removed from office by the Senate. In 1998, for example, President Clinton was impeached by the House on charges of perjury, obstruction of justice, and the abuse of power stemming from scandals involving a female intern.[7] The Senate, however, voted against conviction, and President Clinton, like President Johnson before him, remained in office.[8]

The second impact of choosing presidents separately from Congress is that it gives them independent, and unique, public legitimacy. Only the president can claim to be chosen by a national process, by all the people. Only the president can claim a national mandate, with all the power—and responsibility—that goes along with such unique authority. Presidents, particularly since Theodore Roosevelt, have used the "bully pulpit" (the platform their position affords them to speak out) and their election to claim a public mandate for action on particular issues.[9] President Obama used his election as a claim for policy change, and he passed a major healthcare reform bill. But that law has been fiercely contested, and its passage cost him much political capital. It also helped to shift control of the House of Representatives to the Republicans in the 2010 midterm elections.[10]

One of the least controllable aspects of a president's work is the larger political environment in which they rise to power. Presidents must operate within the economic conditions, social mores, and political culture of the present, not the ideal conditions they seek to achieve. If the economy is weak, for instance, presidents will have less ability to convince Congress to create and fund new programs. While the rhetoric of campaigning may encourage supporters to believe that all things (and changes) are possible, the realities of time and place inevitably bring many of those rhetorical visions down to earth.

Particularly as their term in office nears its end, presidents become concerned about their legacy, the permanent changes they will leave behind. Most presidents search for a way to do something new, to change the policy landscape in a positive way. It becomes a personal imperative with institutional implications, and it leads every president to inevitably seek to be a change agent, creating the frequent tension between expectations and actual conditions.

Who judges a president's legacy? Everyone from presidential historians and political scientists to the public at large does. Periodically, in the news you may see presidential rankings of the best and worst presidents. One of the first such rankings was conducted by historian Arthur Schlesinger of Harvard in 1948. Since then, historians, political scientists, pollsters, journalists, and others have followed his lead. In most of these rankings, George Washington, Abraham Lincoln, and Franklin Roosevelt rank at or near the top of the list, while Warren Harding, James Buchanan, Franklin Pierce, and Ulysses S. Grant tend to rank at or near the bottom. Table 4.1 compares the ten best and worst presidents from Schlesinger's 1948 survey with the ten best and worst from a more recent survey by the United States Presidency Centre in 2011.[11]

Not all presidents have welcomed these types of rankings. Historian David Donald, for instance, notes that in 1962 John F. Kennedy expressed enormous dissatisfaction with the way historians judged his predecessors:

> No one has a right to grade a President—even poor James Buchanan—who has not sat in his chair, examined the mail and information that came across his desk, and learned why he made his decisions.[12]

Table 4.1 **Rankings of the Best and Worst Presidents**

	Schlesinger	United States Presidency Centre (USPC)
	Ranking (1948, 29 Presidents) **10 Best Presidents**	**Ranking (2011, 40 Presidents)** **10 Best Presidents**
1.	Lincoln	1. F. Roosevelt
2.	Washington	2. Lincoln
3.	F. Roosevelt	3. Washington
4.	Wilson	4. Jefferson
5.	Jefferson	5. T. Roosevelt
6.	Jackson	6. Wilson
7.	T. Roosevelt	7. Truman
8.	Cleveland	8. Reagan
9.	J. Adams	9. Jackson
10.	Polk	10. Eisenhower
	10 Worst Presidents	**10 Worst Presidents**
20.	Hoover	31. G.W. Bush
21.	Harrison	32. Arthur
22.	Tyler	33. Taylor
23.	Coolidge	34. Harrison
24.	Fillmore	35. Fillmore
25.	Taylor	36. Johnson
26.	Buchanan	37. Tyler
27.	Pierce	38. Harding
28.	Grant	39. Pierce
29.	Harding	40. Buchanan

Source: Robert K. Murray, "Presidential Greatness," *Journal of American History* [1983], 540–541. United States Presidency Centre, Survey of U.S. Presidents, Results, available at: http://americas.sas.ac.uk/research/survey/overall.htm (accessed May 29, 2011). See also, Godfrey Sperling, "Rating our Presidents," *Christian Science Monitor*, January 14, 2005, available at: http://www.csmonitor.com/2005/0614/p09s01-cogs.html (accessed April 14, 2011).

But it is not only scholars and historians who have been asked to rank the best and worst presidents. Pollsters and journalists consistently ask the general public for their opinions as well. Table 4.2 shows the results of one such Gallup survey.[13]

A president's legacy is usually judged in retrospect, after he has left office. But presidents and their administrations often act in anticipation of such judgments. They want to take actions that do not simply maintain the status quo, but in fact

CHAPTER

Table 4.2 Top 10 Presidents According to a 2011 (

This Gallup survey was conducted February 2–5, 2011. Gallup askea adults in the United States, "Who do you regard as the greatest Unitea president?"

1. Ronald Reagan (19%)
2. Abraham Lincoln (14%)
3. Bill Clinton (13%)
4. John F. Kennedy (11%)
5. George Washington (10%)
6. Franklin Roosevelt (8%)
7. Barack Obama (5%)
8. No opinion (5%)
9. Theodore Roosevelt (3%)
10. Harry Truman (3%)

Source: http://www.gallup.com/poll/146183/Americans-Say-Reagan-Greatest-President.aspx (accessed May 25, 2011).

lead to a new policy or a changed environment. The particular type of change is a function of presidential interest and expertise, but presidents will usually search for a signature issue. Some will choose narrow initiatives; others will spread their efforts across a wide range of concerns.

The powers of the presidency were crafted in distrust, but they have evolved to meet the need for modern executive action.

Despite the image of immense power that now surrounds the presidency, the institution was (at least publicly and formally) framed for what appeared to be a much weaker role, in an atmosphere of suspicion and distrust and the imperative of preventing a monarchical government. When the founders of the Constitution met in Philadelphia in 1787, many of the delegates wanted to create a stronger executive than had existed under the Articles of Confederation, as discussed in Chapter 1. For the delegates, the chief challenge was the concern that the public would not support granting too much explicit authority to the president. The president's primary role was to "faithfully execute the laws." Yet the public image of executive power was King George III or British royal governors, who Americans had rebelled against. How could they create necessary executive authority without raising public fears of a new king? The solution was to create a single, indirectly elected president with broad roles and vaguely defined powers, sometimes shared with (and limited by) the Congress and the Supreme Court, not immediately threatening but open to expansion as future conditions might warrant.[14]

Table 4.3 **The Constitutional or Formal Powers of U.S. Presidents**

Article II is devoted to the executive branch. It grants power and authority to the head of the executive branch, the chief executive or president of the United States, in two broad areas—domestic and foreign affairs. The president's explicit constitutional powers are limited to the following, sometimes vague and often shared, powers:

- Oversee the execution and implementation of the law
- Ensure that the laws of the land are faithfully executed, consistent with the Constitution
- Oversee the various departments and agencies of the executive branch
- Appoint leaders of the executive branch department (with the advice and consent of the Senate), and work with these individuals to implement programs and policies passed by Congress
- Influence and participate in the legislative process, and set legislative priorities through inaugural addresses and State of the Union Addresses
- Veto legislation Congress passes
- Appoint Supreme Court justices and other federal judges (with the advice and consent of the Senate)
- Serve as the commander in chief of the armed forces
- Receive all foreign ministers and ambassadors
- Serve as the chief diplomat, the primary representative of the United States in the international arena; engage in informal discussions and negotiations with other world leaders; negotiate treaties; and establish "executive agreements" with the leaders of other nations

Separating and sharing powers between the legislative and executive branches was a radical and untested political choice for its time, but it ensured that American presidential power would not duplicate that of King George III; every executive action would require some cooperation or assent from the other branches of government. Sovereignty would be shared and thereby limited, in theory. The second solution was also innovative for the time: Assign a series of broad but vague roles to the executive, roles that could be used to expand power over time but which also appeared limited to the eyes of 1787. As Table 4.3 shows, the language of the Constitution grants few explicit presidential powers. Indeed, the nature and scope of the roles it does create has been debated from the Convention until today.

Presidents fill multiple foreign policy roles as commander in chief, chief diplomat, and head of state.

Commander in chief The president is the ultimate civilian commander of all the U.S. armed forces, and thus he is able to authorize use and deployment of military forces in combat or peacemaking roles.

One of the most important responsibilities for presidents has been foreign policy, an area in which presidents execute multiple roles. As **commander in chief** (the ultimate civilian commander of all the U.S. armed forces, and thus able to authorize use and deployment of military forces into combat or peacemaking roles), the president ensures civilian control of the government. George Washington's service as a general, and his respect for civilian authority, helped to assuage any concerns with allocating this role to presidents. In addition, however, the founders delegated to Congress the sole power to declare war.[15] With the power to declare war in one hand and the power to command and deploy troops in another, a permanent recipe for potential conflict is inevitable.

For example, in 1970 President Nixon authorized a secret bombing of Cambodia during the Vietnam War, which angered Congress and the public when it was discovered. Many in Congress saw it as an abuse of presidential war powers by President Nixon, and in response Congress passed the **War Powers Act of 1973**. This act limited the president's ability to deploy military forces, by demanding notification of Congress and legislative approval of funding for military deployments after 60 days. Congress has occasionally (but sparingly) used this withholding of funds as a means of controlling presidential war powers, as when it refused President Ford's efforts to continue military assistance to South Vietnam in 1975. However, oftentimes Congress has been unable to limit presidential actions—for instance, when President Clinton acted against Sudan and Afghanistan in 1998 after terrorist attacks in Kenya and Tanzania, or when President George W. Bush authorized a number of secret antiterrorist initiatives after 9/11 that went beyond current law.

War Powers Act of 1973 Law passed by Congress in the wake of the Vietnam War designed to curb the power of the president to unilaterally commit American troops and resources to international conflict.

The president is also expected to negotiate treaties and agreements with foreign nations, effectively making the president our **chief diplomat**, the chief representative and spokesperson for the United States in foreign affairs. The president's voice is usually the predominant force in foreign policy, as he can speak with one voice over the multiplicity of congressional viewpoints. Once again, however, this power is shared; all formal treaties must be approved by the U.S. Senate in order to be binding on the government.

Chief diplomat The president is the chief representative and spokesperson for the United States in foreign affairs.

President Jimmy Carter discovered with the Panama Canal treaty in 1977 that this process can be highly contentious, and Senate approval is not automatic. After the United States had maintained control of the Panama Canal since its completion in 1914, President Carter negotiated a treaty to return control of the canal to Panama by 1999. This was strongly opposed by a substantial number of senators as a weakening of American power and influence, and Carter only narrowly received approval for the treaty (and probably hurt his 1980 reelection chances in the process).[16]

The intent of all these power-sharing structures with Congress was to limit presidential autonomy and require the judgment of the more calm and deliberate chamber of the Congress, the U.S. Senate. In this way, executive authority would be substantial but not unlimited, a steady balance (it was hoped) between institutions.

6 Presidents serve as chief executive of the executive branch.

Another primary constitutional role, flowing out of the charge to "faithfully execute" the laws, is **chief executive**. Congress may pass the laws, but it falls to the president to direct their implementation through executive agencies. Much presidential

Chief executive The president controls and directs the executive branch and its various agencies.

Executive orders Administrative directives drawn from the president's formal discretionary powers, which have the force of law and can direct the actions of executive branch officials.

ability to shape public policy comes through this broad executive activity. For instance, President Obama's decision not to defend the 1996 Defense of Marriage Act (regarding same-sex marriage restrictions) in court has made it more vulnerable to being overturned.[17]

The chief executive also has the power to issue **executive orders**, administrative directives drawn from the president's formal discretionary powers, which have the force of law and can direct the actions of executive branch officials. These are typically based on underlying powers granted by congressional statute, involving a degree of presidential discretion in interpreting the application of the laws involved. Figure 4.1 shows the number of executive orders issued each year by presidents, beginning in the 1920s with Herbert Hoover. Modern presidents have used these orders with some frequency to shape issues that are too publicly controversial to allow direct congressional action. Presidents Reagan, Clinton, George W. Bush, and Obama have all issued executive orders redefining the government's ability to publicly fund abortions (in some cases, reversing past presidents' executive orders). In 2009, for instance, President Obama rescinded the Mexico City Policy—a ban on funding for health organizations that perform or counsel about abortion. The policy, also known as the "global gag rule," was originally put into place by President Reagan in 1984, reversed by President Clinton in 1993, and reinstated by President George W. Bush in 2001.[18]

Figure 4.1 **Number of Executive Orders per Year**

This figure shows the number of executive orders issued by presidents each year, beginning with President Herbert Hoover. What do you think may have caused the sharp decline in the number of executive orders after Franklin Roosevelt's presidency?

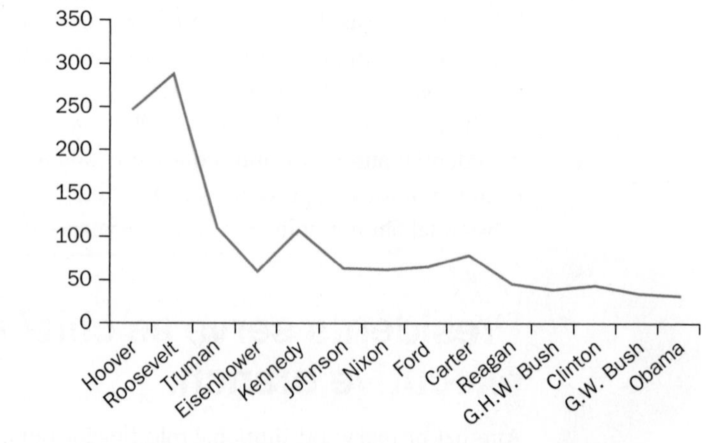

Source: Author's calculations of data from the National Archives, The Federal Register, Executive Orders. Available online at http://www.archives.gov/federal-register/executive-orders/.

Cabinet agencies The various administrative departments of the federal government.

Another key executive role, which highlights the sharing of powers, is the presidential responsibility for appointing ambassadors, federal court judges, and the heads of **Cabinet agencies**, the various administrative departments of the federal government. But it is not a singular decision—the president must gain the approval of the U.S. Senate for all high-level positions, and the Senate has limited presidents by rejecting some appointees. For example, the Senate rejected President Ronald Reagan's nomination of Robert Bork to the U.S. Supreme Court in 1987, forcing the president to submit a new nominee. In this way, a president must collaborate with Congress in choosing the leadership of the government.[19]

The power to grant pardons for legal convictions or charges is a role of some significance at particular times. A number of presidents have used this power to pardon soldiers in wartime, particularly President Abraham Lincoln during the Civil War. More recently, presidents have granted high-profile pardons to political figures, such as President Gerald Ford's pardoning of former President Richard Nixon in 1974 (after the Watergate scandal), President George H. W. Bush's pardon in 1992 of six Reagan administration officials involved in the Iran-Contra Affair, and President Clinton's controversial pardon of financier Marc Rich in 2001.[20] Despite pressure from many in his party, including Vice President Dick Cheney, President George W. Bush chose not to pardon former Cheney aide Lewis "Scooter" Libby, opting instead to commute his sentence.[21]

Presidents are expected to function as chief legislator, policymaker, and head of their political parties.

Veto The power of a president to prevent a bill passed by both houses of Congress from becoming law. Presidential vetoes can only be overridden by a two-thirds vote of both chambers, which is rare.

The arena of lawmaking is one in which the president's clear authority is actually the most limited, contrary to public perception of presidential power, making this one of their loneliest roles (high expectations and limited power). The only direct power granted to presidents in the lawmaking process is the presidential **veto** on legislation, the ability to reject an item of legislation, which nullifies the legislation unless overridden by a two-thirds vote of both the House and Senate. In the key area of passing laws, a president can put forward ideas and can reactively veto bills he or she disagrees with, but the rest is up to Congress. For example, while President Obama actively advocated for healthcare reform, the committees of Congress ultimately controlled the specific content of healthcare legislation, including the level and type of healthcare insurance coverage people could obtain (and who would pay for it).[22]

In addition to the legislative veto, the Constitution also requires the president to report to Congress each year on the "state of the Union." Particularly since President Woodrow Wilson in 1914, this has become a public speech before Congress that presidents now use to highlight their legislative ideas. It has become an important vehicle for introducing new initiatives and a way for the president to lobby the

Chief legislator The president's role in proposing a set of legislative initiatives to Congress on the major issues of the day.

public and thereby Congress to take new actions. It has also led to the presidential assumption of a role as **chief legislator**. From Theodore Roosevelt's presidency (1901–1909) to Barack Obama's, we have increasingly come to expect that presidents will take the lead in proposing a wide-ranging legislative agenda to Congress to solve the nation's contemporary challenges. Franklin Roosevelt definitively institutionalized this model of the modern president as legislative creator and leader, and a president without a policy agenda is seen to be a weak president.

In line with our expectations of policy leadership, we also expect presidents to be the active "head" of their political party, leading and guiding efforts to define and achieve its platform. Some presidents, such as Ronald Reagan in the 1980s and Franklin Roosevelt in the 1930s, embraced that role with relish and controversy, while other presidents, like Jimmy Carter, sought to be more independent and had a more contentious relationship with their political party.[23] This role as head of the party may be both an important and uneasy part of a president's responsibilities.

When it comes to achieving legislative change, presidents have become actors as well as reactors, thanks to specific policy responsibilities often assigned by Congress (as in the Budget Act of 1921, which requires presidents to submit an annual federal budget proposal to Congress). Presidents cannot directly control Congress, but they are now expected to be regular public initiators of legislative proposals and advocates for their passage during the steps of the legislative process.

Presidents begin with the now fully established norm of initiating some type of legislative program agenda, which is developed by their staff and/or executive branch agencies and is offered to Congress, either through speeches or in detailed statutory proposals. There is no set structure for how this occurs or what form the proposals take. Franklin Roosevelt sent Congress a fully developed set of proposals on banking and securities reform in 1933. President Clinton made a very involved (and ultimately unsuccessful) semipublic effort to draft a healthcare reform proposal from the White House. President Obama left it to Congress to craft the details of his healthcare law. Thus, in general, there is no one established process or model for initiating policy change.

One specific area of explicit policy responsibility for presidents is the national budget. Since 1921, Congress has specifically required that presidents draft an annual budget proposal. While in no way binding on Congress' actions, this budget document (which has now grown to a detailed multivolume set of books) can provide a starting point for debate and a vehicle for the president to highlight and advocate for his new initiatives. This creates both a developmental and advocacy role for initiative taking in the critical area of public finance. For presidents who either seek to expand government activity (as President Obama did in 2009–2010) or reduce its cost and scope (as President Reagan attempted to do in the 1980s), crafting the proposed national budget gives them a clear role in the policy process of working for such change.

Once a presidential agenda is on the table, presidents continue to function as actors in the process through ongoing communication with Congress, particularly with committees (and their chairs) that are directly responsible for particular policy areas. Modern presidents have official White House liaisons with Congress. Presidential staffers are informally entrusted with lobbying members of Congress on particular bills. Presidents also invite members of Congress, on occasion, to the White House for direct talks. Again, there is no "required" model for presidential involvement in influencing congressional activity; it tends to be a matter of individual choice and style. Some presidents, like Lyndon Johnson, lobbied Congress personally and persistently; Ronald Reagan relied often on his staff; and Jimmy Carter's efforts with Congress suffered because neither he nor his staff built effective relations with the House and Senate, particularly during his first year in office in 1977.

Once Congress has passed a bill, it comes to the president for approval or a veto. The veto, though a reactive power, also has substantial influence. It can force Congress to reconstruct a proposal or to drop an issue altogether. Many presidential vetoes are sustained, forcing either compromise or defeat onto the supporters of a bill. In this way, presidents can take on at least some negotiating power and indirect legislative authority. As a result, presidents are both actors and reactors in the process of making laws.

Presidential power is primarily the power to persuade and bargain.

Because the explicit official powers of a president are limited and ill-defined at times, particularly with regard to lawmaking, presidents must rely heavily on unofficial influence, or persuasion. This point was made most forcefully by scholar Richard Neustadt in his now classic book *Presidential Power*. After an exhaustive examination of the modern presidency, Neustadt concludes that the president's primary power is not the power to command, but the power to persuade and bargain: "The essence of a President's persuasive task is to convince such men that what the White House wants of them is what they ought to do for their sake and on their authority."[24]

As Neustadt notes, if a president has to resort to commanding, he looks weak, in large part because his explicit constitutional powers are limited. Instead, the most effective presidents are those who work hard to convince Congress, the public, and other political forces that a particular action is necessary or justified. Presidents must persuade and bargain because they rarely have the power to command. They can only propose ideas and hope that Congress is receptive. They must also work to persuade the public to get behind their ideas and put its own persuasive pressure on Congress to act, leading to the need for a "permanent campaign" mode of operating the presidency. This is why Franklin Roosevelt would have "fireside chats" on the radio to explain his ideas to the public. Congress will support an idea if it feels the public demands it, and presidents have learned that they must educate the public in some cases if they expect the public to move Congress. Effective presidents have often used their role as head of their political party to focus and support their persuasive efforts in policymaking.[25]

Just how can the president persuade someone in Congress to act in his favor? As Neustadt notes, he can effectively persuade or bargain using the tools and influence he has at his disposal. The Constitution, for example, gives the president the power to wield influence over the implementation of laws. Local projects or government facilities can either lose or gain funding through the discretionary action of executive agencies when laws or programs are implemented. The idea is ultimately horse-trading—something is given or taken away in order to persuade a member of Congress to cast a particular vote. While often criticized by the public as a corruption of the public interest, such exchanges are a common currency in the policy process, and unlikely to be discarded even by presidents who rail against the evils of political compromise. Much of the content of the 2009 Economic Stimulus bill was a result of such "persuasion by funding."[26]

On the public side, presidents can and do often persuade by "going public," through the media, for purposes of mobilization and power. In the age of multimedia communications, presidential ability to do this has become widespread through such tools as television, radio, social media sites, and the White House's own Web site, whitehouse.gov. It is a mark of the Web's twenty-first century importance that media analysts have now begun to regularly grade the quality of the White House Web site on a variety of criteria.[27] All of this is occurring because any president who wants to maintain his influence must follow the public into whatever communications media it is using as its dominant sources of both information and social exchange. To not do so is to risk being left behind—and thereby left unheard and without influence.

3 Presidential power is limited by a variety of factors.

While presidents have the power to persuade and bargain, their power is limited in a variety of ways that make the president less powerful in some respects than their counterparts in other nations. One of the crucial power differences between a presidential system and a parliamentary system, for example, is the lack of control over one's political party, either in the legislature or among the public. Once again, this lack of presidential control is by design and intent, growing out of the suspicion of executive power.

In a parliamentary system, prime ministers can dictate the votes of their party members in most situations. Why? Because if a party member chooses to vote against the prime minister's position, he or she can be "denied the whip," thrown out of the party, and probably not reelected to parliament. Thus, most party members follow the prime minister's direction on parliamentary votes. An American president has no such authority. Presidents cannot control or remove the party label from a member of Congress, even of their own party. They are elected separately and cannot directly command votes or affect tenure in the legislature. When presidents actively work against the reelection efforts of members of their own party, as Franklin Roosevelt did in 1938 with a number of Democratic U.S. senators, the results often backfire. FDR's "purge" campaign, like smaller efforts by Ronald Reagan in the 1980s, was not only unsuccessful, it resulted in political opposition to his policies that limited his success in the years that followed. This lack of authority forces presidents to rely on unofficial control and persuasion to shape congressional action by members of their own party.

Presidents also lack the ability to firmly command the broader organization of the political party to which they belong. American political parties are not unitary, hierarchical organizations. Instead, like much of the American political system, power is broadly divided and diffused in a fifty-state federal structure. Each state's branch of the national party guards its independence, including its ability to nominate party candidates of its choice for office. From Congress to party organization, presidents must negotiate with their fellow party members; they do not and cannot unilaterally command them.

Patronage The use of governmental or state resources to encourage people to vote in a certain way or to reward electoral support.

Civil service Governmental employees, except those in the military.

Merit system A system in which an individual must show competence to be hired and under which they can only be fired for cause (not political party affiliation).

In the past, presidents could influence party members with the power of patronage. **Patronage** is the ability to give or withhold a government position or benefit in exchange for the recipient's political loyalty in voting or other political actions. Up until the 1880s, presidents could award a wide variety of government jobs based on political party membership, in what became known as the "spoils system" (to the victor belong the spoils of war or conflict). President William Henry Harrison was hounded on his deathbed in 1841 by such job-seekers, and it was the assassination of President James Garfield by a disappointed office-seeker in 1881 that finally led to the creation of the **civil service** to limit presidential patronage power. From the 1880s until today, this civil service has expanded to include most federal employees under its **merit system**, in which an individual must show competence to be hired and can only be fired for cause (not political party affiliation).

2 Presidents must govern successfully and campaign continuously to win reelection.

In order to gain and maintain their power and authority, presidents must practice two conflicting but symbiotic roles: campaigner and governor. These two imperatives demand different focuses, skills, and concerns. Our early presidents faced less pressure for constant campaigning, but presidents today must be permanently concerned with how the public will perceive their actions. Thus, the line between campaigning and governing is much less defined than it was in the 1790s. The use of television advertising, Websites, candidate debates, and the campaign finances needed to support these activities all contribute to an unceasing "campaign" orientation to governance. Many analysts have come to call this phenomenon of campaign techniques being used not just during the election process, but throughout a president's term to achieve power and policy change as the "**permanent campaign.**"[28]

Permanent campaign This phrase refers to the notion that in order to govern successfully, modern presidents must campaign continually while in office.

Why are campaigning and governing different? When presidents run for office, they must make appeals that will gain attention and votes on Election Day. They must think about public opinion constantly and how ideas and proposals will be perceived by the public and communicated by the media. They must have the communicators and the receivers in mind at all times. This can mean that ideas are simplified or promises are made in a very broad manner. Television ads amplify this bias, as they force ideas to be framed in visual and auditory form that can be communicated and understood in a 30-second time frame. This builds the assumption that problems have clear solutions, that issues are black and white rather than complex, and that presidents have the power to solve the issues if they are elected. All of these assumptions are flawed when applied to the realities of governance.

The emphasis on campaigning has also grown because of the president's evolving role as a chief legislator. Because the president is expected to propose a programmatic agenda, and because its success depends on persuasion, building and shaping public opinion has become a necessary presidential activity. It is only by having the public mobilized on an issue that the president can gain political leverage on members of Congress to convince them to support a program or bill. Public appeals through the media, with a coordinated message, become a key tool of power. As a result, modern presidents have not only a press secretary but also a communications director to ensure that their executive branch is taking a unified position on an issue or controversy and is selling that position in a clear and vigorous manner. Such structures and objectives resemble the staff of an ad agency and its product campaigns, not a deliberative process of governance.

Governing is a very different activity from campaigning in terms of its particular demands. There is often a high degree of complexity in formulating the specifics of legislation or regulation. Much of what is actually produced is a product of highly specific negotiation with members of Congress, their staffs, and civil servants who will administer the laws or regulations. Final government actions are frequently the product of compromise, producing less than the original campaign promises. President Obama's efforts at healthcare reform illustrate the difference between presidential speeches and aspirations on the one hand and the specificity and complexity of negotiating a bill in Congress that will have a majority of votes and public support on the other. The latter process often produces a compromised result, which is disappointing to the more committed supporters and opponents in a debate.

In essence, legislative/executive shared governance is often complex, messy, unpredictable, and incomplete. This discordance with the clarity of a campaign message and promise is at the root of much public frustration with the presidency and our political process more generally. Yet the dynamics of our institutional structure of separated powers makes this uneasy marriage of campaigning and governance almost inevitable. Presidents create expectations to further their election but then enter an institution that often dashes those expectations against the realities of congressional compromise and resistance. Balancing these campaign expectations and governing realities is one of the key tasks of presidents today.

Presidents have substantial control over their Cabinets.

One area where presidents do have substantial power is in guiding and commanding their Cabinet secretaries. Cabinet members are appointed by the president, although this power is shared with the Senate under the "advise and consent" clause of Article II of the Constitution. They can be removed at will, with no appeal to the Senate.

The American presidential Cabinet has evolved over time in concert with the executive branch. In our early presidencies under Washington and Adams, we had four Cabinet departments: War, State, Treasury, and an Attorney General who would eventually head a Justice Department. As Table 4.4 shows, today we have Cabinet agencies and secretaries for everything from Agriculture to Homeland Security. Typically, these departments have formed out of public demands for continuing national government attention to a particular issue. But as the Cabinet has grown, the relative individual influence of its members with the president has decreased; only the four original Cabinet secretaries mentioned have access to the president on a regular basis, making them an "inner Cabinet" in the eyes of many analysts.[29]

What does this mean in terms of power? It means that executive decision making is ultimately carried out by an individual (the president) in many cases, rather than a collective group (the Cabinet). While presidents can theoretically use their Cabinet as a deliberative decision-making body, they rarely do so. Cabinet meetings are usually only "show-and-tell" sessions, reports and statements instead of active debate and decision. Cabinet secretaries often find they have minimal contact with the president, despite their position. As many secretaries have found out, their services can be dispensed with quickly if their views or statements no longer serve the president's purposes.[30]

"Going native" A process by which Cabinet appointees' sympathies and identification over time flow more to the agency they manage than to the president who appointed them.

The major difficulty and resistance that a Cabinet secretary can create for a president occurs when their loyalty rests more with their department's interests than the larger agenda of the president; this is often described as **"going native,"** a process by which appointees' sympathies and identification over time flow more to the agency they manage than to the president who appointed them. The presidency has responded to the potential dual loyalties of Cabinet secretaries (and the agencies themselves) by advocating successfully for the creation of their own dedicated

Table 4.4 Cabinet Departments and Cabinet Rank Agencies and Offices

Department/Agency/Office	Year Established	Website
Department of State	1789	www.state.gov
Department of the Treasury	1789	www.treasury.gov
Department of Defense	1789 (originally Department of War)	www.defenselink.mil
Department of Justice	1789 (Attorney General's Office; full Department of Justice in 1870)	www.usdoj.gov
Department of the Interior	1849	www.doi.gov
Department of Agriculture	1889	www.usda.gov
Department of Commerce	1903	www.commerce.gov
Department of Labor	1913	www.dol.gov
Department of Health and Human Services	1953	www.hhs.gov
Department of Housing and Urban Development (HUD)	1965	www.hud.gov
Department of Transportation	1966	www.dot.gov
Department of Energy	1977	www.energy.gov
Department of Education	1979	www.ed.gov
Department of Veterans Affairs	1988	www.va.gov
Department of Homeland Security	2002	www.dhs.gov
Council of Economic Advisors (Cabinet rank)	1946	www.whitehouse.gov/administration/eop/cea
Environmental Protection Agency (EPA) (Cabinet rank)	1970	www.epa.gov
Office of Management and Budget (OMB) (Cabinet rank)	1974	www.whitehouse.gov/omb
United States Trade Representative (Cabinet rank)	1963	www.ustr.gov
US Ambassador to the United Nations (Cabinet rank)	1945	www.usunnewyork.usmission.gov
White House Chief of Staff (Cabinet rank; leads the Executive Office of the President)	1953 (creation of official position)	www.whitehouse.gov/administration/staff/bill-daley
The Vice President (Cabinet rank)	1787	www.whitehouse.gov/administration/vice_president_biden

Source: www.whitehouse.gov.

Table 4.5 The Executive Office of the President (EOP)

This office was created in 1939 specifically to give presidents a staff of officials who would directly support the president's work on an increasing range of responsibilities. The EOP is made up of the following offices:

- Council of Economic Advisers
- Council on Environmental Quality
- Domestic Policy Council
- National Economic Council
- National Security Council
- Office of Administration
- Office of Management and Budget
- Office of National Drug Control Policy
- Office of Science and Technology Policy
- Office of the United States Trade Representative
- President's Intelligence Advisory Board and Intelligence Oversight Board
- White House Military Office
- White House Office

The White House Office includes the following:

- Advance
- Appointments and Scheduling
- Office of Cabinet Affairs
- Chief of Staff's Office
- Office of Communications
- Council on Women and Girls
- Office of Energy and Climate Change Policy
- Office of the First Lady
- Office of Health Reform
- Homeland Security Council
- Office of Legislative Affairs
- Office of Management and Administration
- Office of National AIDS Policy
- Oval Office Operations
- Office of Political Affairs
- Office of Presidential Personnel
- Office of Public Engagement and Intergovernmental Affairs
- Office of the Press Secretary
- Office of Social Innovation
- Office of the Staff Secretary
- Office of Urban Affairs Policy
- Office of the White House Counsel
- White House Fellows

Source: www.whitehouse.gov.

staff: the Executive Office of the President (EOP), which was established in 1939. As Table 4.5 shows, the EOP now comprises hundreds of staff who report solely to and serve only the president. In this way, the presidency has evolved to give the president one area of government where authority is complete and undivided. Given the many other limits on presidential power, the EOP has become an important source of power and influence.

CONCLUSION

While it should be clear from this chapter that presidents face many limitations and challenges in working to exercise their authority and that they confront a kind of tragic loneliness in their role, our history also shows the powerful individual influences of the men who have held the office. Their initiatives and leadership have led us into, and

THEIR LIST

An Insider's View

MICHAEL DUKAKIS

Former Massachusetts Governor, Democratic Presidential Nominee, 1988

When I spoke with Gov. Dukakis, I asked him what he thinks are the most important things to know about being a chief executive and what follows is his list.

10. The administrative leadership team you select is crucial to your success. You want a mix of professional and geographic backgrounds, as well as a group that mirrors the larger society. You should make the Cabinet a focal point of organization, using it as your principal policy team, with close access and little separation from the Chief Executive. There should be few special assistants and no "special offices" to confuse the locus of authority over policy areas. You also need good administrative liaisons and staffers out in the "field" with the agencies.

9. Your leadership team should also have strong public sector experience in dealing with the process of politics, including management, media and political skills. Transportation Secretary Ray Lahood is a good example of this kind of choice by President Obama.

8. Framing a clear vision, and keeping public focus on that vision, is also very important. The health care issue reveals how challenging this can be to convey to the public clearly, with the misunderstandings over Medicare's status as a public program being an example. A president must frame a world vision as well, given their unique foreign policy leadership role.

7. You need to be a good listener, and stay connected with your own organization as well as the country at large. You need to be vigilant in avoiding the threat of being "walled off" by staff or security, so that you keep a sense of the concerns of average citizens—or even your own executive structure. Former Transportation Secretary Frederico Pena would hold a regular "lunch lottery" in his agency, where the winners would have a 90 minute lunch meeting to directly share any concerns or ideas with him. Secretary Pena found this extremely valuable in informing his work.

6. In dealing with Congress or a state legislature, you need to involve members from the beginning in crafting policy initiatives. You need them to metaphorically "buy stock" in the idea from the beginning, so that they are willing to work on its behalf in the legislative process.

5. You, and those who work for you, must personally and professionally embody an ethic of integrity.

4. You should pursue a non-confrontational foreign policy, based on listening and not lecturing. We now live in a multi-polar world, where successful foreign relations will involve building consensus and being respectful.

3. A sense of humor, including about oneself, can be very important.

2. You need to be firm but consistent in the policies you pursue.

1. In your media interactions, you need to always convey a sense of confidence and leadership. For example, in this time of recession, it's very important for President Obama to highlight real concrete recovery actions (road building, reconstruction, etc.) in his public appearances.

out of, wars, expanded civil rights, protected our natural environment, and provided support for those in need. Presidents can reshape both the nation and the world, for both good and ill, by their choices. But these choices are made in an environment of permanent political struggle. And it is because of this ongoing tension over power that the identity and personality of each president takes on a special relevance.

Every president must wrestle with the contradictions between the desire to exercise leadership and achieve policy change and the many institutional constraints that our Constitution and political processes place on presidential authority. Some presidents (such as Calvin Coolidge in the 1920s) have adjusted to the constraints. But most presidents since Franklin Roosevelt have chafed under the institutional limitations on presidential power and have sought to resist and overcome them in the name of policy change and leadership.

Individual presidents' ability to succeed in the struggle for power is also shaped by the executive branch they lead, as well as the public who elected them to office. Depending on contemporary conditions and/or the particular issue being contested, executive branch workers may work either to further presidential initiatives or resist them in some fashion. Similarly, the public at large may either seek and support a powerful president or resist the "imperial" expansion of presidential power—sometimes on different issues being advocated by the same president. This unpredictability contributes to the permanent uncertainty of presidential power.

What this has meant for presidents is that they must be "dual-minded"—they must continually be thinking in both campaign and governance modes in order to achieve and maintain power among the public and use it to achieve concrete policy objectives in the Congress and their own executive branch. The institutional constraints on direct presidential power also mean that they must rely on persuasion for much of their power, as it is based on negotiation and not on powers of direct command or lawmaking.

The fundamental reality of the presidency is of an institution created in suspicion, limited by separation from the legislative process, reliant on influence and persuasion for expanding its power, and constrained by the operations of the executive branch, the forces of history, and the imperatives of leaving a legacy. Yet, it is also the reality that people can and do matter and that one person's character, persistence, and skill can make a difference in the office. And it is the tension between these forces, the individual presidents and the institutions and processes they must navigate, that have helped to define both the office and our country. It is a sometimes lonely but always a powerful responsibility.

YOUR LIST REVISITED

At the beginning of the chapter, you were asked to think about what you might include on your own list of the Top 10 Most Important Things to Know About the American Presidency. Now that you have read the chapter, take a moment to revisit your list. What, if anything, would you change about your list? Do you agree or disagree with the chapter list constructed by the author? What might you add or delete? Why?

KEY TERMS

Cabinet agencies 85
Chief diplomat 83
Chief executive 84
Chief legislator 86
Civil service 89
Commander in chief 82
Electoral College 77
Executive orders 84
"Going native" 91
Impeachment 78
Merit system 89
Patronage 89
Permanent campaign 90
Veto 85
War Powers Act of 1973 83

CHAPTER REVIEW QUESTIONS

10 How is distrust of power responsible for the structure of the presidency outlined in Article II of the Constitution?

9 How has the process of selecting the president shaped the power of the office?

8 How have the powers of the presidency evolved to meet the needs of modern executive action?

7 Explain the multiple foreign policy roles of the president.

6 How does the executive branch both enhance and limit presidential power?

5 What role do presidents play in the lawmaking process, and how do they interact with Congress?

4 In what ways does presidential power depend on persuasion?

3 What power and influence do presidents have over their political parties?

2 What is the relationship between campaigning for the presidency and governing as the president?

1 Describe the relationship between presidents and their Cabinets.

SUGGESTED READINGS

- Cronin, Thomas E. (ed.). *Inventing the American Presidency.* Lawrence, KS: University Press of Kansas, 1989.
- Edwards, George W. III, and Stephen Wayne. *Presidential Leadership*, 8th ed. Belmont, CA: Wadsworth Publishing, 2009.
- Hopkins, David A. *Presidential Elections: Strategies and Structures of American Politics*, 12th ed. Lanham, MD: Rowman and Littlefield Press, 2007.
- Jones, Charles O. *The Presidency in a Separated System*, 2nd ed. Washington, DC: Brookings Institution Press, 2005.
- Light, Paul C. *The President's Agenda*, 3rd ed. Baltimore, MD: Johns Hopkins University Press, 1998.
- Milkis, Sidney M., and Michael Nelson. *The American Presidency: Origins and Development, 1776–2007.* Washington, DC: CQ Press, 2007.
- Nelson, Michael. *The Evolving Presidency: Landmark Documents, 1787–2008*, 3rd ed. Washington, DC: CQ Press, 2007.
- Neustadt, Richard E. *Presidential Power and the Modern Presidents*, rev. ed. New York: The Free Press, 1991.
- Pfiffner, James P. *The Modern Presidency*, 6th ed. Belmont, CA: Thomson Wadsworth, 2010.
- Tulis, Jeffrey. *The Rhetorical Presidency.* Princeton, NJ: Princeton University Press, 1988.

SUGGESTED FILMS

- *Primary* (1960)
- *Crisis* (1963)
- *All The President's Men* (1976)
- *The Final Days* (1989)
- *The War Room* (1993)
- *Truman* (1995)
- *The West Wing* (1999–2006)
- *13 Days* (2000)
- *Journeys with George* (2003)
- *Staffers '04* (2004)

SUGGESTED WEBSITES

- **American Experience**: http:// www.pbs.org/wgbh/amex/presidents
- **American Presidency Project at the University of California**: http:// www.presidency.ucsb.edu
- **American President, an On-line Reference Resource**: http://millercenter.org/president
- **C-SPAN**: http:// www.c-span.org
- **Center for the Study of the President and Congress**: http:// www.thepresidency.org
- **Executive Branch and federal government**: http:// www.usa.gov
- **History Channel, Timeline of Presidents**: http:// www.history.com/topics/the-us-presidents
- **National Archives: Presidential Libraries:** http:// www.archives.gov/presidential-libraries/
- **The Obama Presidency, minute-by-minute coverage**: http:// www.politico.com/politico44
- **White House web site**: http:// www.whitehouse.gov

ENDNOTES

[1]John Bresnahan and Jonathan Allen, "Liberal Democrats in an Uproar over Libya Action," *Politico*, March 19, 2011, available at: http://www.politico.com/news/stories/0311/51595.html (accessed May 22, 2011).

[2]Benjy Sarlin, "Dennis Kucinich: Obama's Libya Attack an Impeachable Offense," *TPM: Talking Points Memo*, March 21, 2011, available at: http://tpmdc.talkingpointsmemo.com/2011/03/dennis-kucinich-calls-says-libya-attack-an-impeachable-offense-for-obama.php (accessed May 22, 2011).

[3]Maine and Nebraska do not use the winner-take-all system used by the other states; instead, they use a system of proportional allocation of votes. For a brief overview, see "U.S. National Archives and Records Administration," available at: http://www.archives.gov/federal-register/electoral-college/faq.html#mystate (accessed May 22, 2011).

[4]Frances Symes, "Why Do We Have an Electoral College?" *Congress.org*, available at: http://www.congress.org/news/2010/11/01/why_do_we_have_an_electoral_college (accessed May 22, 2011).

[5]John Diaz, "Electoral College Should be Scrapped," *San Francisco Chronicle: SF Gate,* May 22, 2011, available at: http://www.sfgate.com/cgi-bin/article.cgi?f=/c/a/2011/05/22/INEF1JHP1B.DTL&tsp=1 (accessed May 22, 2011).

[6]"Americans Support Proposal to Eliminate Electoral College System," *Gallup*, January 5, 2001, available at: http://www.gallup.com/poll/2140/Americans-Support-Proposal-Eliminate-Electoral-College-System.aspx (accessed May 22, 2011). See also "Americans Support Proposal to Eliminate Electoral College System," *Gallup*, November 2, 2004, available at: http://www.gallup.com/poll/13918/Public-Flunks-Electoral-College-System.aspx (accessed May 22, 2011).

[7]U.S. Joint Committee on Printing (September 2006). "Impeachment Proceedings," *Congressional Directory*, available at: http://frwebgate.access.gpo.gov/cgi-bin/getdoc.cgi?dbname=109_congressional_directory_interim_sep06&docid=109thin_txt-77 (accessed May 22, 2011).

[8]For more information on impeachment, conviction, and removal, see "Impeachment," United States Senate," available at: http://www.senate.gov/artandhistory/history/common/briefing/Senate_Impeachment_Role.htm#4 (accessed May 22, 2011).

[9]"American President: Theodore Roosevelt, Domestic Affairs," *The Miller Center of Public Affairs*, 2011, available at: http://

millercenter.org/academic/americanpresident/roosevelt/essays/biography/4 (accessed May 22, 2011).

[10]Kevin Sack, for instance, noted that "virtually every House Democrat from a swing district who took a gamble by voting for the health law made a bad political bet. Among 22 who provided crucial yes votes from particularly risky districts, 19 ended up losing on Tuesday. That included all five members who voted against a more expensive House version last November and then changed their votes to support the final legislation in March." "Health Care Vote Only Part of Democrats Vulnerability," *New York Times*, November 4, 2010, available at: http://www.nytimes.com/2010/11/04/us/politics/04health.html (accessed May 22, 2011).

[11]In 1948, Arthur Schlesinger polled 55 scholars to determine how they would rate the presidents. Robert K. Murray, "Presidential Greatness,"*Journal of American History* [1983], 540–541. United States Presidency Centre, Survey of US Presidents, Results, available at: http://americas.sas.ac.uk/research/survey/overall.htm (accessed May 29, 2011). See also Godfrey Sperling, "Rating our Presidents," *Christian Science Monitor*, January 14, 2005, available at: http://www.csmonitor.com/2005/0614/p09s01-cogs.html (accessed April 14, 2011).

[12]David H. Donald, *Lincoln* (New York: Simon and Schuster, 1995), p. 13.

[13]This Gallup survey was conducted February 2–5, 2011. Gallup asked 1,015 adults in the United States, "Who do you regard as the greatest United States president?" Source: http://www.gallup.com/poll/146183/Americans-Say-Reagan-Greatest-President.aspx (accessed May 25, 2011).

[14]For a good account of the issues and tensions surrounding the presidency at the Constitutional Convention, see Thomas E. Cronin, ed., *Inventing the American Presidency* (University Press of Kansas, 1989).

[15]U.S. Constitution, Article I, section 8, and Article II, section 2.

[16]"American President: Biography of Jimmy Carter," *The Miller Center of Public Affairs*, 2011, available at: http://millercenter.org/president/carter/essays/biography/print (accessed May 22, 2011).

[17]As former George H. W. Bush Solicitor General Ted Olson stated, this decision is "going to be persuasive in federal courts . . . even the government, who had a responsibility to defend the statutes if it could find a basis for doing so, felt that a 'heightened scrutiny' does apply." Jake Tapper, "Obama Administration Drops Legal Defense of 'Marriage Act,'" *ABC News*, February 23, 2011, available at: http://abcnews.go.com/Politics/obama-administration-drops-legal-defense-marriage-act/story?id=12981242 (accessed May 22, 2011).

[18]Rob Stein and Michael Shear, "Funding Restored to Groups that Support Abortion," *Washington Post*, January 24, 2009, available at: http://www.washingtonpost.com/wpdyn/content/article/2009/01/23/AR2009012302814.html?hpid=topnews (accessed May 22, 2011).

[19]It is worthy of note that a president's power to remove current appointees is not shared; he or she may remove appointees at will without congressional approval. But even here, Congress must approve a replacement.

[20]A full list of presidential pardons by administration can be found at the Department of Justice Web site: http://www.justice.gov/pardon/actions_administration.htm (accessed May 20, 2011).

[21]In his memoir former President George W. Bush noted that Cheney became angry in 2007 when he refused to pardon Libby. See *Decision Points* (New York: Crown/Random House, 2010).

[22]Lori Grant, "The Congressional Committees System and Health Care Reform," *Healthcare Musings*, March 18, 2009, available at: http://www.healthcaremusings.com/2009/03/18/the-congressional-committee-system-and-healthcare-reform/ (accessed May 18, 2011).

[23]Julian E. Zelizer, "Treat Your Democrats Well," *Newsweek*, September 17, 2010, available at: http://www.newsweek.com/2010/09/17/obama-needs-to-be-a-better-party-leader.html (accessed May 1, 2011).

[24]Richard Neustadt, *Presidential Power: The Politics of Leadership* (New York: John Wiley and Sons, 1960), p. 30.

[25]Richard Neustadt, *Presidential Power and the Modern Presidents: The Politics of Leadership from Roosevelt to Reagan* (New York: Free Press, 1991).

[26]Kathy Gill, "Economic Stimulus Package Has a Little Something for (Almost) Everyone," *About.com Guide*, January 26, 2009, available at: http://uspolitics.about.com/b/2009/01/26/economic-stimulus-package-has-a-little-something-for-almost-everyone.htm (accessed May 22, 2011); Greg Hitt, "Senate Begins Horse-Trading Over Stimulus Bill," *The Wall Street Journal*, January 30, 2009, available at: http://online.wsj.com/article/SB123323991367328771.html (accessed May 21, 2009).

[27]"Wired White House Looks to Harness New Media," *PBS NewsHour*, March 29, 2010, available at: http://www.pbs.org/newshour/bb/politics/jan-june10/whitehouse_03-29.html (accessed May 15, 2011); Claire Cain Miller, "How Obama's Internet Campaign Changed Politics," *New York Times*, November 7, 2008, available at: http://bits.blogs.nytimes.com/2008/11/07/how-obamas-internet-campaign-changed-politics/ (accessed May 2, 2011).

[28]This phrase was used most notably by Sidney Blumenthal in his book *The Permanent Campaign: Inside the World of Elite Political Operatives* (Boston: Beacon Press, 1980). See also Joe Klein, "The Perils of the Permanent Campaign," *Time*, October 30, 2005, available at: http://www.time.com/time/columnist/klein/article/0,9565,1124237,00.html (accessed May 19, 2011).

[29]The inner-outer Cabinet dichotomy is attributed to political scientist Thomas Cronin, *The State of the Presidency* (Boston: Little, Brown, 1985).

[30]See David Greenberg "The Sorry Lot of a Bush Cabinet Secretary," *Slate*, November 22, 2004, available at: http://www.slate.com/id/2110032/ (accessed May 23, 2011).

Chapter 5

THE BUREAUCRACY

Top Ten List

10 Bureaucracy is all around us, and it plays a major role in our daily lives.

9 Bureaucratic organizations come in many shapes and sizes and serve different functions.

8 Most bureaucrats are employed at the state and local levels.

7 The federal bureaucracy started small and grew along with the new nation.

6 The development of the contemporary American bureaucracy is the result of reaction to external events.

5 Recurring efforts to reform the bureaucracy have had limited success.

4 The bureaucracy is overseen by many institutions using many different oversight mechanisms.

3 Regulatory politics is more important and also more democratic than most people think.

2 There are a wide variety of reasons why bureaucratic organizational behavior does not match policymakers' intentions.

1 Most American citizens are ambivalent about bureaucracy.

The explosion of the *Deepwater Horizon* oil rig in April 2010 led to one of the worst environmental disasters in U.S. history. As a result of the disaster, government officials reorganized the bureaucratic agency known as the Minerals Management Service, which had handled both the leasing rights and the regulation of off-shore oil drilling. While the Deepwater Horizon incident provides a dramatic example of a bureaucratic failure, most bureaucracies actually perform quite well and are a critically important part of government that affects our everyday lives. Shown here, President Barack Obama speaks during a visit to an oil spill recovery staging area in Theodore, Alabama, 56 days after the oil spill began.

YOUR LIST

Before you read this chapter, take a few moments to think about what you might include on a list of the Top 10 Most Important Things to Know About the Bureaucracy. At the end of the chapter you will be asked to compare and contrast your list with the one supplied in this chapter.

INTRODUCTION

When the *Deepwater Horizon* oil rig exploded on April 20, 2010, the incident and the subsequent oil spill became one of the worst environmental disasters in U.S. history. The explosion killed eleven workers and injured many others. And, before the well-head was capped nearly 3 months later, an estimated 5 million barrels of crude oil had spilled into the Gulf of Mexico. At the same time that environmentalists, commercial fishermen, and others assessed the damage, much attention was also paid to how government could have allowed this catastrophe to happen and what government ought to do about preventing a similar tragedy in the future.

At the time of the explosion and spill, the agency responsible for both granting offshore oil drilling leases and for regulating those engaged in offshore drilling was the Minerals Management Service. Many argued that the agency personnel responsible for providing offshore drilling rights had become too cozy with those in the industry who were to be regulated. Therefore, one of the first things governmental officials determined after the explosion was that the functions of leasing oil-drilling rights and the regulation and enforcement of oil drilling had to be split.

The Minerals Management Service was renamed the Bureau of Ocean Energy Management, Regulation and Enforcement (BOEMRE), and several independent divisions within BOEMRE were established: one to focus on the leasing of drilling and exploration rights, one to focus on revenue collection, and one to focus on safety and enforcement. In explaining these changes, the new director of BOEMRE, Michael Bromwich, said, "This reorganization is much more than just moving boxes around." He continued, "It is about a comprehensive review and a fundamental change in the way that these agencies operate."[1] BOEMRE's Web site explains that "the reorganization and internal reforms that BOEMRE is implementing are designed to remove the complex and sometimes conflicting missions of the former Minerals Management Service by clarifying and separating these missions across three agencies and providing each of the new agencies with clear areas of focus and new resources necessary to fulfill those missions."[2]

The reorganization of the Minerals Management Service may not have made headlines around the world, but it underscores the importance of bureaucratic organization and form in affecting real policy outcomes. The reorganization was undertaken because the agency had not effectively regulated and enforced environmental and workplace safety standards in its current configuration. By separating the leasing of drilling rights from their regulation, administration officials believed both tasks would be carried out in a way more consistent with the public interest.

The *Deepwater Horizon* incident is a dramatic example, but bureaucracy impacts our lives every day. Indeed, most average citizens' experience with government is with a bureaucracy of one form or another. The Post Office, a public school administration, the Social Security Administration, and the military are all examples of public-sector bureaucracies carrying out public policies. And, the example of the

Minerals Management Service notwithstanding, most bureaucracies actually perform quite well and are a critically important part of government today.

Bureaucracy is all around us, and it plays a major role in our daily lives.

Bureaucracy A complex system of organization that employs standardized rules, procedures, communication, and organizational controls for achieving public good.

Political scientists spend a lot of time talking about Congress, the president, elections, and political parties, but the reality is that almost all of the interactions average citizens have with government are interactions with bureaucracies. The term **bureaucracy** refers to a complex system of organization that employs standardized rules, procedures, communication, and organizational controls for achieving public good.

We not only interact with bureaucracies, we also experience the effect of bureaucracies indirectly when we buy meat at the grocery store (inspected by the U.S. Department of Agriculture), when we apply for student loans (the process is regulated by the Department of Education), and when we drive on public roads (built and maintained by various agencies of government). In order to understand the variety of ways in which we are impacted by bureaucracies, it is important to get a sense of the scope of bureaucracy and to differentiate between different bureaucracies in different sectors and at different levels of government.

Bureaucracies are not unique to the public sector. Most people belong to various organizations like community groups, youth leagues, and churches that are bureaucracies. Large private corporations like Google, General Motors, and Cisco are also bureaucracies that impact your daily life. They exhibit many of the same characteristics and dysfunctions as public-sector bureaucracies. As a result of these perceived and real dysfunctions, more and more of the functions of government are being "outsourced" to nonprofit organizations and private-sector firms. For instance, private security firms and defense and intelligence contractors have been involved in helping to carry out the United States military missions in Iraq and Afghanistan. Here at home, nonprofit organizations use government grant dollars to deliver social services in local communities, and various levels of government have privatized services previously delivered by government agencies, including trash collection and even incarceration of prisoners. And, of course, the national, state, and local governments all employ agencies of various sorts to carry out their mission.

Because organizations at different levels may be influenced by different sets of political actors (officeholders, the media, interest groups, etc.), it is not uncommon to have bureaucratic organizations at the national and more local levels either replicating one another's work or even working at cross-purposes. For instance, in recent years, the state of California sought to impose new, tougher emissions standards on automobile manufacturers that would apply to all cars sold in California. In 2007, the U.S. Environmental Protection Agency (EPA) denied California's request to impose tougher standards on carbon dioxide emissions, arguing that allowing each state to impose its own standards would create an "unenforceable patchwork of environmental law."[3] In June 2009, however, the EPA, under the direction of the Obama administration, reversed course and granted California (and thirteen other states) the right to force manufacturers to meet the more stringent emissions standard.[4]

Bureaucratic organizations come in many shapes and sizes and serve different functions.

Line agencies Organizations that directly deliver a service to citizens, such as the U.S. Postal Service or each state's Department of Motor Vehicles.

Staff agencies Agencies that indirectly serve the public by providing support and advice to line agencies.

In the 1930s, sociologist Max Weber outlined the six major characteristics of a bureaucracy (see Table 5.1).[5] However, although bureaucracy is omnipresent, not all governmental bureaucracies are the same. There is great variation in the size, shape, and function of bureaucratic organizations in government. Some bureaucratic organizations exist to provide services to the public, while other organizations exist to provide services to other bureaucracies. Thus, a first distinction we can make in the functions of bureaucracies is a distinction between "line" agencies and "staff" agencies. **Line agencies** are the organizations that directly deliver a service to citizens, such as the U.S. Postal Service or your state's Department of Motor Vehicles. **Staff agencies** are agencies that indirectly serve the public by providing support and advice to line agencies.

Table 5.1 Weber's Six Key Characteristics of a Bureaucracy

Hierarchy	A formal hierarchy must exist; each level controls the level below and is controlled by the level above; this is the basis of central planning and decision making.
Rules	Rules govern management; the top power figures in the bureaucracy make the rules and decisions that must be followed at all levels.
Function	Organization is key to proper function. Work should be done by specialists, and members organized by skill so as to keep similar individuals together.
Focus (in or up)	If the mission is an "in focus," the goal is to serve the needs of members (market share and high profits). If the mission is an "up focus," the goal is to profit stockholders and similarly powerful people.
Impersonal	Refers to employment standards and relationship with customers; requires equal treatment of all employees and customers.
Qualification	Like impersonal, refers to employment standards; employment within the bureaucracy relies on qualifications rather than connections; dismissal requires just cause.

Source: Max Weber, Wirtschaft und Gesellschaft, part III, chap. 6, pp. 650–678. 1922 (English translation published in Somerville New Jersey Bedminster Press, 1968).

An example of a staff agency is the Office of Personnel Management (OPM). OPM's Web site states the purpose of the agency at the top of the page: "Recruiting, Retaining and Honoring a World-Class Workforce to Serve the American People."[6] The stated purpose of OPM is not some direct product or service for the American people; rather, its purpose is to ensure that the workforce that does directly serve the American people is the best and most productive that can be found. Staff agencies like OPM can be found at all levels of government, and staff personnel (like a human resources director or a budgeting director) can be found within line agencies.

Even among line agencies, governmental organizations are distinguished based on the kinds of policies they are responsible for and the kinds of publics they serve. A **clientele agency** is an agency that serves a particular industry, group, or constituency. The Department of Labor and the Department of Education are examples of clientele agencies. These agencies are a way that powerful groups in society seek to make their previous policy gains more permanent.

Clientele agency An agency that serves a particular industry, group, or constituency.

Sometimes, a clientele agency will include within it (or work with) a regulatory agency. **Regulatory agencies** are established to issue regulations or rules that have the force of law. The Occupational Safety and Health Administration (OSHA) is an example of a regulatory agency that is located within the Department of Labor. OSHA's mission is to "ensure safe and healthful working conditions for working men and women by setting and enforcing standards and by providing training, outreach, education and assistance."[7] OSHA promulgates rules and regulations related to workplace safety, and it also enforces compliance, sometimes by fining corporations for failure to meet safety standards.

Regulatory agencies Agencies established to issue regulations or rules that have the force of law.

Another way to distinguish between governmental organizations is to distinguish between various organizational forms. The names of various governmental organizations provide some clues as to their differing functions. There are governmental departments, agencies, bureaus, commissions, and corporations. **Departments** are the largest units of bureaucratic organization and, at the federal level, the heads of departments are referred to as "Secretary" and are part of the president's **Cabinet**. These officials and many of their subordinates are nominated by the president and confirmed by the Senate. Departments are made up of many agencies and bureaus, smaller organizations that specialize in particular functions and tasks for which a department is responsible. Figure 5.1 shows the organizational chart for the U.S. Department of Veterans Affairs (VA). As you can see, the VA includes several subbureaus and agencies, such as the Veterans Health Administration.

Departments The largest units of bureaucratic organization.

Cabinet The informal designation of the group who are the heads of the major departments in the federal government

In some cases, agencies or bureaus may exist independent of a full department. A couple of the more well-known examples of **independent agencies** are the Environmental Protection Agency (EPA) and the Central Intelligence Agency (CIA). These independent agencies are usually supervised by a single director who is appointed by the president and confirmed by the Senate, just as department secretaries are.

Independent agencies Agencies or bureaus that exist independently of a full department and are usually supervised by a single director who is appointed by the president and confirmed by the Senate.

Figure 5.1 Department of Veterans Affairs Organizational Chart

Like all departments, the U.S. Department of Veterans Affairs (VA) is made up of many agencies and bureaus—smaller organizations that specialize in particular functions and tasks. The VA includes several sub-bureaus and agencies, such as the Veterans Benefits Administration, Health Administration, and National Cemetery Administration.

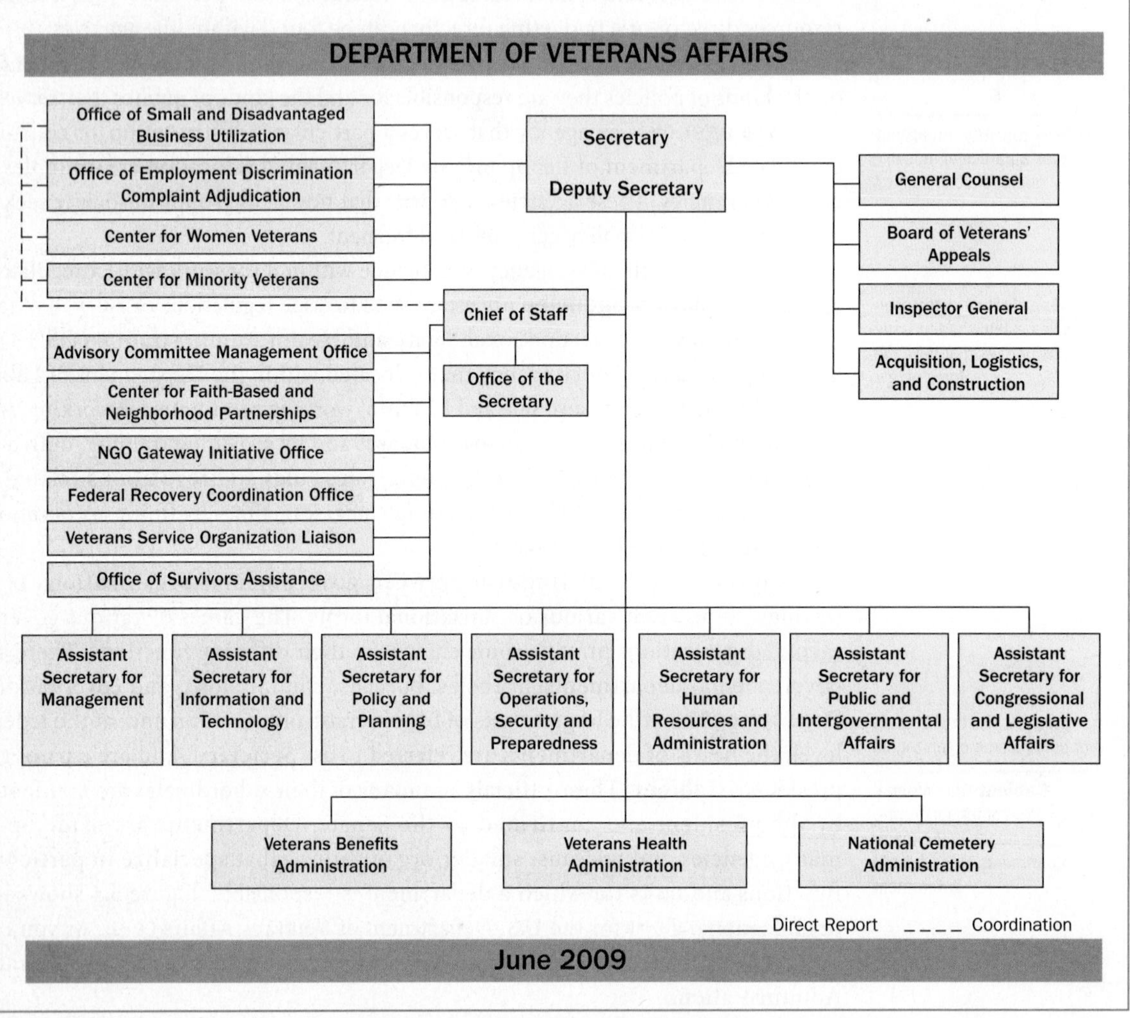

Source: U.S. Department of Veterans Affairs http://www.va.gov/landing_organizations.htm (accessed November 7, 2010).

Independent commissions and boards Organizations that are structured so as to be sealed off, to some extent, from political influence by legislators and executives.

Independent commissions and boards are another form of organization. These organizations are structured so as to be sealed off from political influence by legislators and executives, at least to some extent. Some examples of these organizations are the Federal Election Commission (FEC), the Securities and Exchange Commission (SEC), and the Federal Reserve Board (FRB). During the 2008 presidential campaign, amidst the turmoil in international financial markets, Senator John McCain, the Republican presidential nominee, called on President Bush to fire the chairman of the SEC, Christopher Cox. There was only one problem. The president does not have the power to fire the chair of the SEC, although he could have asked him to resign from the commission.[8] The intention behind keeping commissioners independent of the political process is to avoid just such a scenario where commissioners are making important decisions regarding policies or even investigations under pressure from an elected official seeking to do what is popular in the short term.

Government corporation An organization that provides "market-oriented public service"and that generates roughly enough revenue to cover its expenses.

Finally, there are **government corporations**. The Congressional Research Service defines a government corporation as an organization that provides a "market-oriented public service" and that generates roughly enough revenue to cover its expenses.[9] The most well-known examples of government corporations include the U.S. Postal Service (USPS) and AMTRAK. Government corporations are frequently derided by critics as being inefficient and as rating poor in terms of customer service when compared with private-sector corporations. But these critiques are at least partly unfair, as government corporations are frequently established in the first place to provide a public service that is deemed important even if it may not be economically efficient. The USPS, for instance, is required by law to deliver a first-class piece of mail from one end of the country to the other for the same low price (44 cents in 2011).

Most bureaucrats are employed at the state and local levels.

In order to get a sense of the size and scope of bureaucracy in American political life, we can look at how many people are employed by government by sector. As Figure 5.2 shows, the vast majority of people employed by government are employed at the state and local levels. In 2007, nearly 14.2 million of the 22.1 million civilian government employees worked for local government organizations. Education is, by far, the largest employer at the state and local levels. More than 7.8 million of the local government workers were employed in elementary and secondary education, and nearly 2.4 million of the 5.2 million state workers were employed in higher education.[10] Local government is also the fastest-growing sector in government employment. Figure 5.3 shows employment over the past three decades at the federal, state, and local levels. Uniformed military employment has declined, federal civilian employment has been

Figure 5.2 Employment by Level of Government (in thousands), 2007

The vast majority of people employed by government are employed at the state and local levels. In 2007, for instance, nearly 14.2 million of the 22.1 million civilian government employees worked for local government organizations.

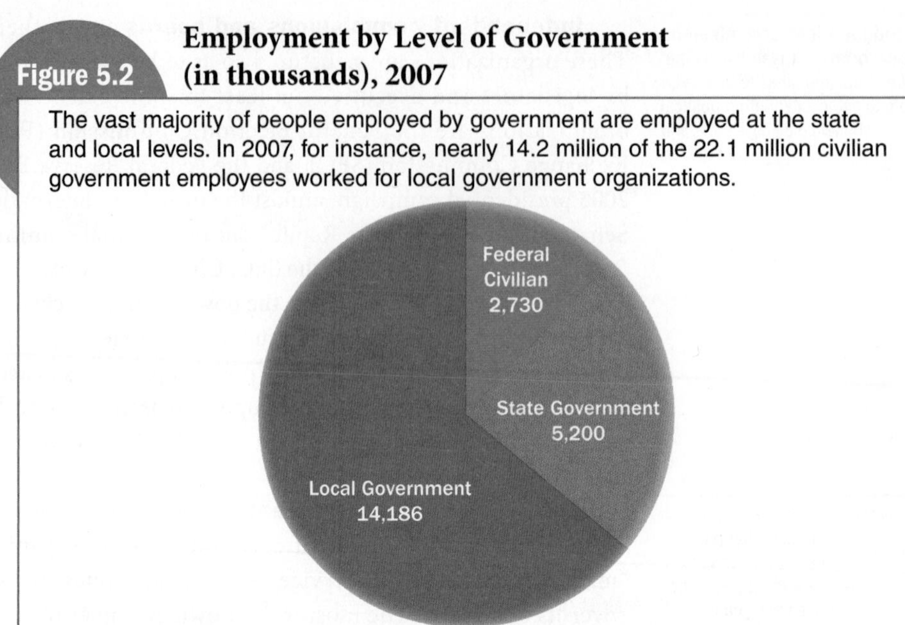

Source: U.S. Bureau of the Census, Governments Division, Federal, State, and Local Governments, Public Employment and Payroll Data, Table 450.

Figure 5.3 Employment by Level of Government (in thousands), 1982–2007

Over the last three decades, uniformed military employment has declined, and federal civilian employment has been essentially flat. In contrast, employment by state and local governments has grown.

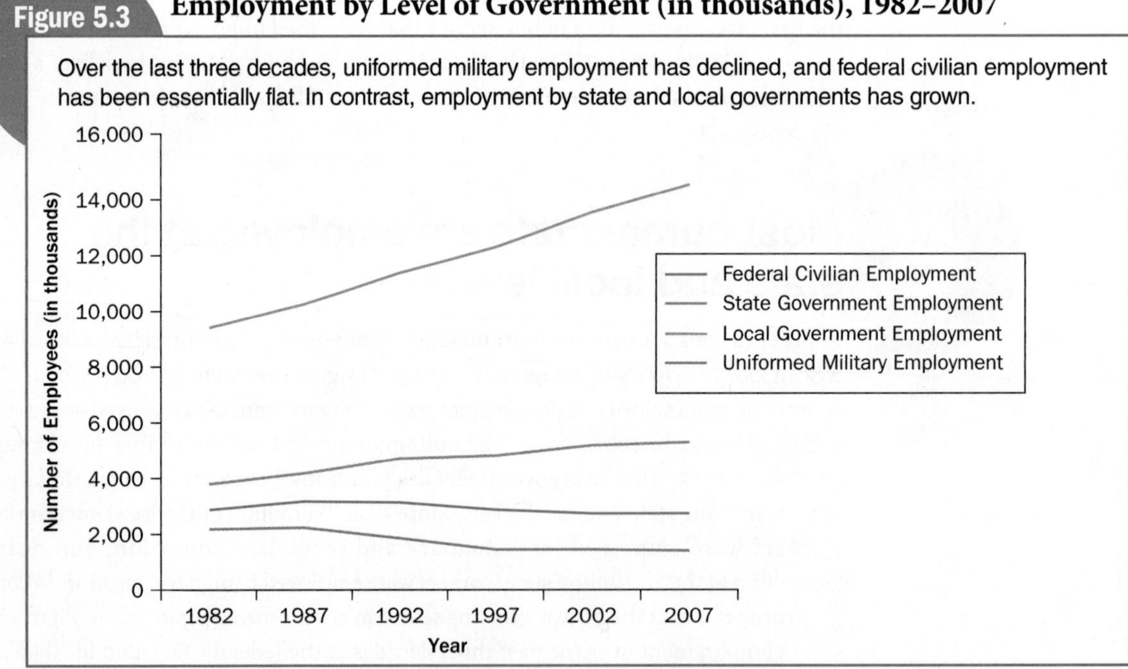

Source: U.S. Bureau of the Census, Governments Division, Federal, State, and Local Governments, Public Employment and Payroll Data, Table 449. U.S. Office of Personnel Management, Historical Federal Workforce Tables

Figure 5.4 **Federal Civilian Employment Compared with U.S. Population, 2006**

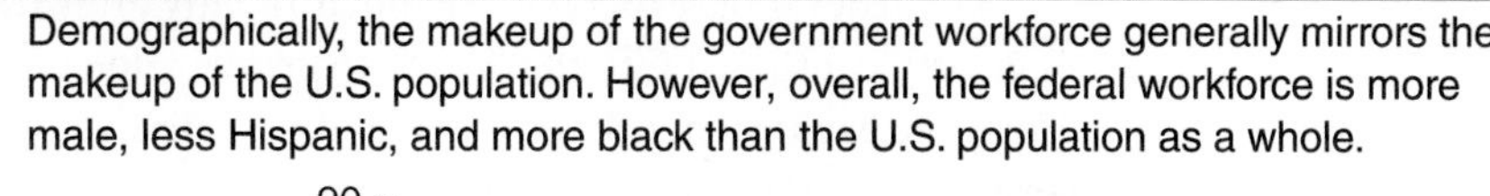

Demographically, the makeup of the government workforce generally mirrors the makeup of the U.S. population. However, overall, the federal workforce is more male, less Hispanic, and more black than the U.S. population as a whole.

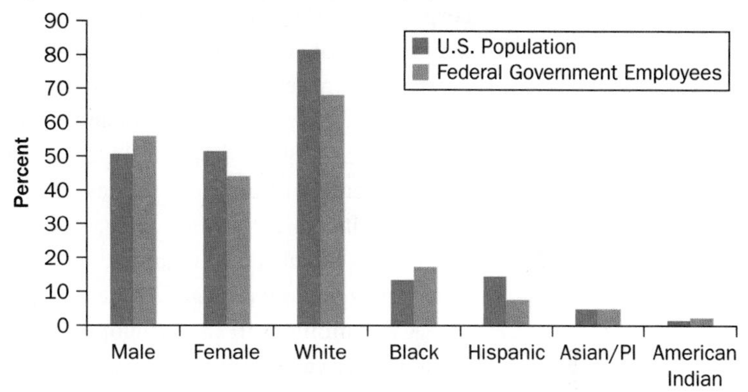

Source: Author's calculations of data found at U.S. Office of Personnel Management, Central Personnel Data File. Annual Estimates of the Resident Population by Sex, Race, and Hispanic Origin for the United States: April 1, 2000 to July 1, 2009 (NC-EST2009-03).

essentially flat for 25 years, and employment by state and local governments has grown.

Demographically, the makeup of the government workforce mirrors the makeup of the U.S. population, but not perfectly. The Office of Personnel Management in the Executive Office of the President collects data on federal civilian (nonpostal) employees. Figure 5.4 compares some of the demographic characteristics of the federal workforce with the American population. Overall, the federal workforce is more male, less Hispanic, and more black than the U.S. population as a whole.

7 The federal bureaucracy started small and grew along with the new nation.

The founders of the Constitution, particularly Madison and Hamilton, were aware of the fact that good administrators were an important part of a good government. William Richardson even argues that the founders considered the emergence of a group of virtuous civil servants necessary for our democracy.[11]

The first Congress created only three federal departments: the Departments of State, Treasury, and War, each headed by a Secretary. In 1790, during President Washington's first term, the federal government employed about 2,000 people, the greatest number serving in the postal service. Even during the country's westward expansion in subsequent decades, the federal bureaucracy remained small. At that time, the main role of the federal bureaucracy was the collection of revenue at ports and recording land deeds and citizenship records. [12]

The federal bureaucracy expanded rapidly after the Civil War, and the pace of growth continued into the twentieth century due mainly to population growth, economic expansion, urbanization, and industrialization. The emergence of large corporations, transportation and energy problems, and the rise of mass production led to issues of corporate dominance and influence over the economy, requiring a greater governmental role in economic regulation. Congress became more assertive in regulating interstate commerce and working conditions.

Patronage The practice of handing out government jobs on the basis of political loyalty rather than objective measures of expertise or experience.

Until the 1880s, federal employees received their positions by way of **patronage** appointments and political parties. The employees were directly responsible to elected politicians, and when changes occurred as a result of elections—for instance, if a new president was inaugurated or power changed hands from one party to another—a large number of government employees would find themselves out of work.

A key moment in the development of a professionalized bureaucracy in the United States came about as a result of the assassination of President James Garfield on July 2, 1881 by a disgruntled lawyer whose expectation of a government job never materialized. Consequently, the **Pendleton Act of 1883** was passed, and the modern civil service was created. Under this new system, hiring, promotions, and pay were based on demonstrated measures of employee performance and merit rather the old practice of patronage. The mandate of this newly created **civil service** system was to hire based on merit, institute efficiencies in the daily operation of bureaucracies, and treat employees fairly.

Pendleton Act Enacted in 1883, it declared officially that government jobs should be handed out on the basis of merit.

Civil service A system of governmental employment based on merit in which employees cannot be fired without legitimate cause related to job performance.

In 1923, as a result of further reforms and the increasing clout of unions in the United States, the Classification Act was passed, which permitted legislators and agency administrators to define the tasks and responsibilities of each agency. Personnel specialists then determined the qualifications required to perform the different components associated with these tasks and create an appropriate wage and pay scale.[13]

6 The development of the contemporary American bureaucracy is the result of reaction to external events.

By 1925, the number of federal agencies had grown to 170, and the number of employees had increased to over 6,000.[14] After the stock market crash of 1929 and the onset of the Great Depression, the country experienced years of record high unemployment and economic stagnation, which led to the election of President Franklin D. Roosevelt and the rise of the New Deal.

Under New Deal legislation, the federal bureaucracy experienced its greatest growth, asserting the federal government's role in managing the economy and implementing efforts to alleviate unemployment and poverty. In 1935, for example, Congress created Social Security to provide income and sustenance to senior citizens and widows of deceased workers. The federal government, during this same period, created the Works Progress Administration and Civilian Conservation Corps and instituted price control policies. By the end of Roosevelt's presidency in 1945, many Americans accepted and expected the federal government's involvement in the management of the economy and that meant an increasingly large and visible role for the federal government in ways that impacted the daily lives of Americans.

The government's role continued to expand in the 1950s with the creation of the Department of Health, Welfare, and Education, and in the 1960s with the creation of the Department of Housing and Urban Development. Among other things, Michael Harrington's book *The Other America* brought to light the racial and income disparity in America, leading President Lyndon B. Johnson to successfully promote the Great Society, which entailed a broad range of social programs focused on the alleviation of the consequences of poverty and inequality in the United States. The Social Security Act of 1965 created the Medicare and Medicaid system, the healthcare system for the elderly, the disabled, and the poor.[15]

The subsequent energy crisis in 1973 and persistent economic stagnation during the 1970s forced policymakers to rethink the expansion of federal social and economic programs. In the late 1970s and early 1980s, most notably during the administration of President Reagan, political discourse shifted toward a more limited role for government. With respect to bureaucracy, President Reagan specifically focused on what he called a "War on Waste," arguing that the federal bureaucracy was too inefficient. In the 1990s, influenced by Osborne and Gaebler's book *Reinventing Government* (1993),[16] President Clinton declared that "the era of big government is over" and focused on diminishing "red tape" and unnecessary procedural rules and regulations in an attempt to reempower public bureaucracies to serve the public.

Recurring efforts to reform the bureaucracy have had limited success.

With the growth of American bureaucracy, bureaucratic reform has become a recurring theme in American public administration. The first and most significant reform restructuring the executive branch was recommended by the President's Committee on Administrative Management and was enacted in 1939. This committee was also known as the **Brownlow Committee**, named after the chair, Louis Brownlow.

Brownlow Committee Formally known as The President's Committee on Administrative Management, this committee recommended sweeping organizational changes for the executive branch in 1937.

As government grew rapidly during the New Deal era, amidst the crisis of the Great Depression, there was limited time for planning. Many believed that the policies of the New Deal era had created an executive branch that was unmanageable. The Brownlow Committee's report called for a reorganization of the executive branch from a managerial perspective. Brownlow argued that the president must have professional staff members in order to be able to carry out his tasks, to deal with complex policy and administrative issues, and to have direct control over bureaucratic matters. Overall, the committee recommended a major reorganization of the federal bureaucracy and the creation of the **Executive Office of the President**, a conglomeration of offices meant to directly assist the president in managing the executive branch. Congress ultimately passed the Reorganization Act of 1939, which was based on the Brownlow Committee's recommendations.[17]

Executive Office of the President A conglomeration of offices meant to directly assist the president in managing the executive branch.

Hoover Commission In the late 1940s, this commission was established to reduce the number of government agencies created during World War II. However, it actually recommended an increase in the capacity of the Executive Office of the President.

During World War II, government agencies continued to multiply. In the late 1940s, the first **Hoover Commission** was established to take action to reduce the number of government agencies created during World War II. The commission took its name from former President Herbert Hoover, who was appointed by President Harry Truman to chair the commission. The commission's finding was that governmental administrative machinery worked at cross-purposes, creating redundancies and inefficiencies. As a result, in contrast to its initial charter, the commission actually recommended an increase in the capacity of the Executive Office of the President by strengthening the Bureau of Budget. The commission also recommended more discretionary power for the president over the presidential organization and staff and the creation of the position of White House Chief of Staff. One of the key outcomes of the commission was the Reorganization Act of 1949 and the establishment of the Department of Health, Education, and Welfare in 1953.

Hoover Commission II In 1955, this commission recommended eliminating nonessential government services and activities and made the case that the federal government should not be in competition with private enterprise.

The second Hoover Commission (**Hoover Commission II**) in 1955 recommended eliminating nonessential government services and activities. And it went on to state that the federal government should not be in competition with private enterprise. In actuality, the recommendations of the second Hoover Commission accomplished very little compared with the first commission.

President's Private Sector Survey on Cost Control (PPSSCC) Also known as the Grace Commission, it concluded in its 1984 report that the U.S. government was wasting billions of dollars every year on bureaucratic inefficiencies.

In 1982, the **President's Private Sector Survey on Cost Control (PPSSCC)**, chaired by J. Peter Grace and composed of prominent business figures, produced forty-seven reports aimed at identifying areas in need of reform and reduction in government size and scope of operations. However, the Grace Commission, as it was known, failed to include the participation and perspectives of employees. As a result, the General Accounting Office and the Congressional Budget Office refused to accept the findings in the commission's reports, and, without political traction, President Reagan was unable to use them to effectively make any meaningful changes.

Reinventing government A sweeping set of reforms employed during the Clinton administration aimed at streamlining governmental processes, making the federal bureaucracy more efficient, and focusing bureaucratic efforts on clients and outcomes rather than processes.

The most recent government reform initiative, known as **reinventing government**, began in 1993, when President Bill Clinton launched the National Performance Review. It aimed to make government more efficient and change the culture and practices of the national bureaucracy by empowering employees and managers to actually initiate solutions to problems. The reinvention movement sought to shift the bureaucratic culture from being one based on rules and processes to one based on outcomes and results. The George W. Bush administration shifted away from "reinvention" towards "contracting out" and pushing many agencies to become more reliant on third-party providers of goods and services through special contracting processes.

The bureaucracy is overseen by many institutions using many different oversight mechanisms.

With all the different departments, agencies, bureaus, commissions, and public-sector corporations out there, you might wonder who oversees the many bureaucracies of the federal government to make sure the bureaucracy is implementing policy in a manner that is consistent with the wishes of elected officials and the public. The answer is that the bureaucracy serves many masters and, as a result, many institutions and the American public all oversee the bureaucracy.

Most people know that the president has some responsibility for overseeing the bureaucracy, and with good reason. Article II of the Constitution begins by asserting that "the executive Power shall be vested in a President of the United States of America." The president also has the power to make appointments to the highest offices within the bureaucracy subject to the "advice and consent" of the Senate. Even though it is not explicitly stated in the Constitution, presidents have interpreted the various powers above to mean they have the power to issue executive orders, which are legally binding commands to those in the bureaucracy to carry out the law in a particular way. Executive orders cannot violate the Constitution or a law enacted by Congress, but so long as they remain within those bounds, presidents have relatively wide latitude to unilaterally require bureaucrats to follow the president's preferences.

Contrary to conventional wisdom, however, presidents do not have the sole authority to oversee the bureaucracy. Congress also has substantial formal authority to oversee the executive branch. Most federal bureaucracies exist in the first place because they are authorized by an act of Congress. Congress has also created the Government Accounting Office (GAO), an auditing arm of Congress, whose job it is to regularly investigate and audit what government agencies are doing and how well they are doing it. Perhaps more importantly, Congress must act every year to fund these bureaucracies: to pay for the buildings that house them, to pay for the services they render, and to pay the employees who work in them. This means that Congress can use this control over funding to influence bureaucratic outcomes.

Police-patrol versus fire-alarm oversight A distinction between two forms of congressional oversight of the bureaucracy. In police-patrol oversight, Congress patrols for violations of congressional preferences in settings like hearings. In fire-alarm oversight, legislators respond to complaints from groups and individuals about agency actions.

Political scientists Mathew McCubbins and Thomas Schwartz argue that members of Congress engage in two different kinds of oversight: **police-patrol oversight** and **fire-alarm oversight**. McCubbins and Schwartz explain that police and firefighters look for problems (crime and fires, respectively) in different ways. The police patrol around looking for problems, while firefighters wait at the firehouse for someone to ring an alarm. Drawing on this metaphor, they argue that members of Congress engage in both of these tactics in searching for bureaucratic violations of congressional policy preferences. They "patrol" by holding hearings, calling in bureaucrats to testify, and by requiring bureaucracies to provide them with regular reports on their progress. But they also set up elaborate "fire-alarm" mechanisms by requiring bureaucrats to be transparent and open and deliberate in their decision-making processes and, in some cases, by requiring consultation with important groups before making a decision or taking action. These groups then have the option of "sounding an alarm." McCubbins and Schwartz argue that this kind of "fire-alarm" oversight is more efficient for members of Congress, as they can just deal with bureaucratic issues likely to be of electoral concern.[18]

Oversight of the bureaucracy is thus conducted by institutions and persons both inside and outside of government. Courts can, and sometimes do, exercise the power of judicial review over agency actions. Interest groups keep a close eye on agency actions and register their "alarm" both directly to agencies and indirectly to powerful allies in Congress and in the White House. The media serve a watchdog role over the bureaucracy, engaging in investigative reports of bureaucratic action. The bureaucracy is also overseen by average citizens, who are given frequent opportunities to express their own sentiments, and most bureaucracies seek comments and invite complaints from their clients and consumers. Finally, bureaucracies oversee themselves. Most bureaucracies of significant size have large evaluation programs, audit operations, and Inspectors General offices whose job it is to investigate wrongdoing, abuse of power, and misuse of public funds.

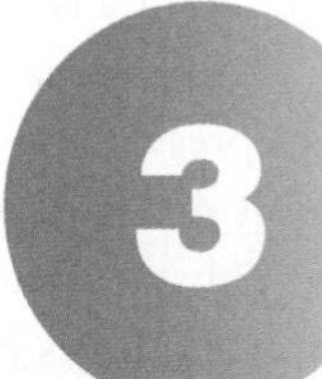

Regulatory politics is more important and also more democratic than most people think.

Rulemaking The process by which agencies create regulations that have the force of law.

Most of the work done by the federal government to protect consumers, public health, and the environment, and to ensure workplace safety is done by regulatory agencies. Congress creates regulatory agencies and empowers them with **rulemaking** authority to create "rules" and regulations that have the force of law, very often with broad guidelines: for example, to make the water cleaner, to ensure that the meat purchased at the grocery store is safe to consume, or to make sure airplanes flying across the country are safe.

Since rules have the force of law, they are the subject of intense political disputes. Part of the reason for the intensity of these disputes is that industries may incur significant new costs and lives are often at stake. Cornelius Kerwin and Scott Furlong compiled data on the number of final rules issued each year and the number of pages they take up in the Federal Register by year; the data are plotted in Figure 5.5. As you can see, the number of final rules issued each year has declined slightly over time, but the total number of pages added to the Federal Register has increased. Not surprisingly, there is also substantial variation in the types of agencies engaging in more or less rulemaking under a given presidential administration.[19]

3 Regulatory politics is more important and also more democratic than most people think.

Figure 5.5 **Number of Final Rules and Pages Added to the Federal Register, by Year**

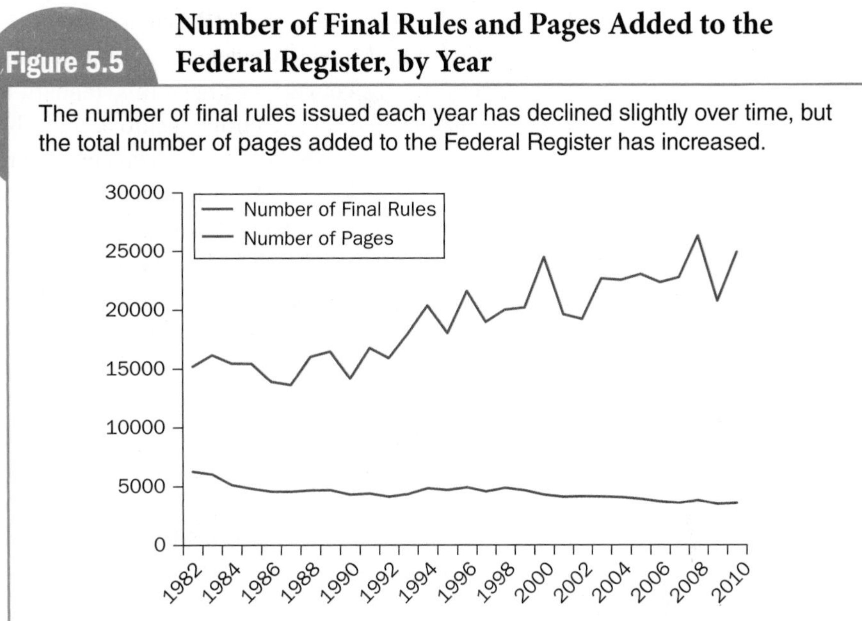

Source: Federal Register. Data available at: http://www.federalregister.gov/uploads/2011/07/History-Charts-7-27-2011-All.pdf

Another reason for intense political disputes over rules is that the bureaucrats who are responsible for making these important rules are not democratically elected. For the most part, they are civil servants. Many argue that the growing power of regulatory agencies has been problematic in part because bureaucrats are not elected and are not subject to popular review by the people, so there is no clear way for citizens to hold them accountable for the impactful decisions they make.[20]

Largely in response to this kind of critique, Congress enacted the Administrative Procedures Act (APA) of 1946 and has since included agency-specific procedures in much rulemaking authorizing legislation. The APA effectively acts as a backup statute for agencies that do not have their own procedural requirements for openness. According to Martin Shapiro, there are two key ways in which the APA scheme injects a healthy degree of democratic accountability into rulemaking. First, the APA requires "notice and comment." This means an agency that is thinking about engaging in rulemaking must provide ample notice of the area in which it is considering making a rule, and it must disclose the text of the proposed rule. Additionally, the agency must provide ample opportunities for affected individuals, groups, and the general public to submit comments and objections to the agency.

A second way in which the APA scheme provides for accountability is that it makes possible judicial review of agency actions deemed to be "arbitrary and capricious." Over time, the courts interpreted this standard to mean that agencies had to prove they had taken public comments into account by responding to all of them. And all this back-and-forth thus created a rulemaking record that courts could then review to see if the agency's action was, in fact, "arbitrary and capricious."[21]

The Negotiated Rulemaking Act, which was first passed in 1990, represents a more recent democratizing innovation in rulemaking. Negotiated rulemaking basically adds a series of steps in which the various stakeholders in a rulemaking proceeding attempt to develop some consensus over the shape of a new rule prior to a traditional rulemaking procedure. The idea behind negotiated rulemaking is that the process might be less conflicted, might take less time, and might be less costly in terms of litigation if the interested parties can have an opportunity to negotiate and agree to a deal ahead of a traditional rulemaking process. While it is not yet clear that negotiated rulemaking has made the process any more expeditious,[22] it is clear that negotiated rulemaking processes provide yet another opportunity for public participation in regulatory politics.

2 There are a wide variety of reasons why bureaucratic organizational behavior does not match policymakers' intentions.

Ideally, policymakers like legislators would settle on a policy decision, and those charged with carrying out the policy would carry it out exactly as policymakers intended. But there are several reasons why we see a gap between policy intentions and implementation. Motivating employees in the public sector can be challenging, the goals of a policy are not always as clear as they might be, and policies are not always carried out by personnel employed directly by the government.

As discussed earlier, there have been many attempts to reform public bureaucracies in American political history. Effective management of public bureaucracies depends upon many factors, including structure, culture, type of services provided, and management's ability to motivate employees. However, the motivation of public employees is not as easy as it sounds. Because the public sector does not have profit or revenues as its singular goal, assessing the merit or productivity of particular employees can be very difficult, if not impossible. In addition, the civil service protection that is given to public-sector employees seeks to restrict the ability of public managers to be arbitrary and capricious in their decisions over hiring, firing, promotion, etc. As a result, these managers have less flexibility than private-sector managers and little ability to use incentive mechanisms, including financial rewards.

Hierarchy of needs theory Developed by psychologist Abraham Maslow, this theory suggests that people are motivated by their desire to satisfy specific needs; physiological needs (e.g., food and water) are the most primary, followed by safety needs, social belonging needs, esteem needs, and, at the top, self-actualization needs.

One of the most popular motivational theories, proposed by psychologist Abraham Maslow, is the **hierarchy of needs theory**. Maslow suggested that people are motivated by their desire to satisfy specific needs. The hierarchy of these needs is presented such that physiological needs (e.g., food and water) are the most primary, followed by safety needs, social belonging needs, esteem needs, and, at the top, self-actualization needs. Maslow stipulated that although physiological needs dominate, once those are met, other motives drive people's actions.[23] The relevance of Maslow's theory for employees in the public sector is that managers have to find ways to empower employees strangled by bureaucratic red tape and develop procedures to allow them to achieve self-actualization. One mechanism that has energized and encouraged public-sector civil servants has been the creation of the merit pay system. [24]

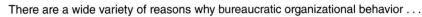

Merit pay system A system in which compensation is based, at least in part, on performance and in which performance bonuses are handed out to those performing better on the basis of some set of measurable indicators.

The Civil Service Reform Act of 1978 introduced, for the first time, a **merit pay system** of monetary incentives for public employees to strive for higher productivity and performance improvement. Under this system, the selection, promotion, and retention of government employees is based on their qualifications, work performance, and level of knowledge and expertise, as well as performance management. Effective performance management includes activities to ensure that all organization goals are met consistently; this method of employee evaluation allows managers to incentivize high performers.

Another reason implementation of a policy does not always match policymakers' intentions is that politicians do not always take implementation issues into consideration in designing policy. In fact, many politicians consider bureaucracies and the inability of these entities to successfully carry out policies as a detriment to their own reelection and, consequently, denounce bureaucrats and public servants. Bureaucrats work in a highly politicized environment, which often hinders a bureaucracy's effectiveness.

Policy implementation is problematic and cumbersome for several reasons. First, federal bureaucracies are often given multiple and contradictory goals. We see this very often in policy areas where a particular industry is being regulated. On the one hand, the agency wants to police the industry to make sure it is safe for workers, consumers, etc. But, on the other hand, the agency may also want to ensure the economic viability of the industry, and this may be at odds with the first set of goals. Second, the responsibility for implementing various policies is often spread out across many bureaucratic agencies, which makes it difficult to determine what agencies should be held accountable for whatever results occur. Third, many federal policies are implemented at the state and municipal levels, making them more difficult to monitor. Fourth, fragmentation and faulty coordination of decision making, whether in Congress or the state legislature, further diffuses accountability. Finally, as discussed earlier, many federal and local programs rely on contractors to deliver goods and services because contracting out can be much less expensive and can free governments from taking on long-term liabilities like pensions and healthcare for retired workers. However, the interests of the contractors are not necessarily the same as those of the bureaucrats or policymakers.[25]

1 Most American citizens are ambivalent about bureaucracy.

At least in the abstract, most Americans believe that government is too big, we are taxed too much, and that government does not respond efficiently, quickly, or effectively to the public's problems. Particularly in recent years, we have seen declining confidence in America's public institutions. For instance, over the last decade, the USA Today/Gallup Poll has asked respondents "which of the following will be the biggest threat to the country in the future: big business, big labor, or big government?" Every time the question has been asked, more Americans see "big government" as the greatest threat, with 55 percent expressing this view in March 2009 amid a financial meltdown caused, at least in part, by the risky investment practices of big banks and insurance companies.[26]

At the same time, however, citizens hold fairly positive views of their interactions with particular federal agencies. In his widely cited polemic on public administration, Charles Goodsell[27] reviews many different public opinion polls on citizens' views of government and bureaucracy. Goodsell finds that, in poll after poll, citizens express a significant degree of satisfaction in their experiences with local, state, and federal government agencies ranging from local fire departments and public schools to public transportation and the U.S. Postal Service. Indeed, one of the studies cited by Goodsell asked respondents to compare their satisfaction with their interactions with private-sector corporations in addition to their satisfaction with their interactions with public-sector agencies and found little in the way of differences in customer satisfaction. Believe it or not, this study even found fairly solid customer satisfaction among citizens dealing with the IRS![28]

As noted above, citizens tend to believe they are taxed too much and get too little for their money, so we would expect them to want to see cuts in the major areas of federal spending and activity. But the largest categories of federal spending, by far, are national defense, Social Security, Medicare, and Medicaid, and voters generally do not want any of these categories of spending to be cut. At the state level, most money is spent on healthcare, education, and the criminal justice system. Again here, most voters believe they are overtaxed but do not approve of cuts in any of these areas.

In short, voters suffer from a sort of schizophrenia with regard to government and bureaucracy. We tend to be satisfied with the particular interactions we have with government bureaucracies at the national, state, and local levels, but we do not have a high regard for government and bureaucracy in the abstract. The roots of this ambivalence are probably as old as the nation itself. The American Revolution was a fight against a distant, centralized government that was perceived to be taxing people too much and delivering little in the way of services in return. It may rightly be said that Americans have not yet squared that negative perception of government with the high levels of satisfaction they have in their day-to-day dealings with public-sector bureaucracies.

THEIR LIST

An Insider's View

BRYCE YOKOMIZO

Public Servant, Los Angeles County Department of Public Social Services

Bryce Yokomizo recently retired from nearly 35 years of public service in Los Angeles County. Most of Mr. Yokomizo's career was in the Los Angeles County Department of Public Social Services (LADPSS) and, more recently, he served as the deputy chief executive officer for the County of Los Angeles. Over his years of service to LADPSS, he was an entry-level welfare worker, disaster services worker, staff assistant, fraud investigator, employment program manager, the community relations director, the director of welfare fraud investigations, the governmental relations director, the budget director, the San Fernando Valley and West Los Angeles district welfare director, the chief of Medicaid services, and the director of LADPSS. We asked Mr. Yokomizo how he got involved in working in the public sector and what he thought were the most important things to know about bureaucracy.

Mr. Yokomizo said that when he began his career in 1974, many had discouraged him from work in civil service, and he had a negative view of the public sector as well. Born in the baby-boomer generation, Mr. Yokomizo was a sociology major in college, a choice that dismayed his parents, who encouraged him to be an engineer or scientist or employed in some other lucrative profession.

It was a time, like today, where many had disdain for those working in the public sector and perceived bureaucrats as being lazy and inefficient. At first, he did not intend to stay in the public sector, but he was drawn by the prospect of what he thought was a solid paycheck—$659 per month! Over time, however, Mr. Yokomizo came to have tremendous respect for those working in the public sector. "For the most part, I found myself surrounded by so many really smart and dedicated people—people who taught me so much," he said.

Asked what he thought students should know about the bureaucracy, Mr. Yokomizo made two key points. First, for students interested in a career in the public sector, Mr. Yokomizo said they should not fear change, but see change as new opportunities to grow. He said the way he had moved up in the bureaucracy over the years was to always be willing to take on new assignments, which gave him new perspectives that helped him better understand the organization and especially the people and communities the organization serves. Mr. Yokomizo explained that the diversity of positions and exposure to various different bureaucratic procedures and people really allowed him to gain the knowledge and experience to become the director of a large social service agency.

The other point Mr. Yokomizo thought students should know is that the bureaucracy is filled with hard-working people who really care about what they are doing. While it is true that the public sector has its share of waste and inefficiency, it is no more true in the public sector than it is in the private sector. He went on to say, "Regardless of the disdain and cynicism the public has for bureaucracy, we have established standards of behavior based on ethical fairness. Our benchmark is to always treat people, the community we serve, and our employees for that matter, well and fairly. Fairness and transparency are valuable aspects of what bureaucratic agencies have to offer. We, in bureaucratic agencies, are in a very unique and powerful position, because if we do our jobs right, we can positively enrich the lives of those we serve."

Since his official retirement, Mr. Yokomizo has remained as busy as ever. He teaches classes in public administration and continues to work as a consultant for Los Angeles County on various projects. He works with public-sector bureaucracies and serves the public interest by teaching, sharing, and preparing the next generation of public administrators. He is proud to have worked in the public sector throughout his career and urges students interested in making a difference in their communities to look past the cynicism he once shared about the public sector. Like Mr. Yokomizo, you may find a career that is a pleasant surprise.

CONCLUSION

The average citizen has a fairly negative impression of governmental bureaucracies, and the term itself has a negative meaning in popular usage. But we have also seen that bureaucratic forms of organization are used in the interest of fairness, equity, and efficiency, and the reality is that we tend to regard the specific experiences we have with public-sector bureaucracies more positively than our abstract negative view of bureaucracy would suggest.

In its simplest definition, a bureaucracy is a complex form of organization that employs a division of labor and specialization. In practice in the United States, bureaucracy has taken many forms over time. In the nineteenth century, the United States employed a more politicized and, from a negative perspective, more corrupt, form of bureaucracy. Throughout the twentieth century, public-sector bureaucracies in the United States became more professionalized and unionized with the rise of a civil service system that covered more federal, state, and local employees over time. As we moved into the twenty-first century, the bureaucracy tried to "reinvent" itself by becoming more client-driven and by generally adopting more private-sector management practices where applicable.

Whatever shape it takes, it is clear that bureaucracy matters. How organizations are structured, how their personnel are chosen and trained, and what procedures they adopt to allow for public influence have a tremendous impact on how we all experience government. Debates regarding the size and shape of bureaucracy also continue to be a major theme in American politics.

Since the 1980s, whether Republican or Democrat, almost every president (and every major presidential candidate) has promised to reform the American bureaucracy. In the 2008 election, for instance, then candidate Barack Obama released a government reform agenda that stated, "in many areas of the federal government there is too much Washington bureaucracy—too many layers of managers, and too much paperwork that does not contribute to directly improving the lives of the American people."[29] Similarly, his Republican opponent John McCain promised a "top to bottom review of every federal bureaucracy [that] yields great reductions in government."[30] Despite the fact that reforms have met with varying degrees of success, future candidates are likely to continue to discuss ways to reform the bureaucracy.

YOUR LIST REVISITED

At the beginning of the chapter, you were asked to think about what you might include on your own list of the Top 10 Most Important Things to Know About the Bureaucracy. Now that you have read the chapter, take a moment to revisit your list. What, if anything, would you change about your list? Do you agree or disagree with the chapter list constructed by the author? What might you add or delete? Why?

KEY TERMS

Brownlow Committee 109
Bureaucracy 101
Cabinet 103
Civil service 108
Clientele agency 103
Departments 103
Executive Office of the President 110
Government corporation 105
Hierarchy of needs theory 114
Hoover Commission 110
Hoover Commission II 110
Independent agencies 103
Independent commissions and boards 105
Line agencies 102
Merit pay system 115
Patronage 108
Pendleton Act 108
Police-patrol versus fire-alarm oversight 111
President's Private Sector Survey on Cost Control (PPSSCC) 110
Regulatory agencies 103
Reinventing government 110
Rulemaking 112
Staff agencies 102

CHAPTER REVIEW QUESTIONS

10 What are the key characteristics of bureaucracy?

9 How has bureaucratic change reflected external events in society over time?

8 Identify the various types of agencies, and explain why there are so many different bureaucratic forms.

7 What are some of the ways in which the bureaucracy is overseen by other branches of government?

6 What are the key historical differences between administration in the nineteenth and twentieth centuries in the United States?

5 Was "reinventing government" really a reinvention or was it something old in a new package? Why or why not?

4 Is bureaucratic employment growing fastest at the national, state, or local level? Why?

3 How did the Pendleton Act and the Civil Service Reform Act of 1978 change personnel management in the public sector?

2 What are the ways in which public participation is made a part of rulemaking?

1 According to Maslow, what is the hierarchy of needs, and what does it mean for bureaucracies?

SUGGESTED READINGS

- Denhardt, Robert. *In the Shadow of Organization.* Lawrence: Regents Press of Kansas, 1981.
- Derthick, Martha. *Agency Under Stress.* Washington, DC: Brookings Institution, 1990.
- Goodsell, Charles. *The Case for Bureaucracy.* Washington, DC, CQ Press, 2004.
- Janis, Irving. *Groupthink.* Boston: Houghton Mifflin, 1983.
- Light, Paul. *The Tides of Reform: Making Government Work, 1945–1995.* New Haven, CT: Yale University Press, 1997.
- Osborne, David, and Ted Gaebler. *Reinventing Government: How the Entrepreneurial Spirit Is Transforming the Public Sector.* New York: Plume, 1993.
- Radin, Beryl. *Accountable Juggler.* Washington, DC: CQ Press, 2002.

- Weber, Max. The Theory of Social and Economic Organization. London: W. Hodge, 1947.
- Wilson, James Q. Bureaucracy: What Government Agencies Do and Why They Do It. New York: Basic Books, 1991.
- Wilson, Woodrow. "The Study of Administration," November 1, 1886, essay available online at: http://teachingamericanhistory.org/library/index.asp?document=465.

SUGGESTED FILMS

- *Hands Over the City* (1963)
- *Paperland: The Bureaucrat Observed* (1979)
- *The River* (1984)
- *Brazil* (1985)
- *Office Space* (1999)
- *Thirteen Days* (2000)
- *Path to War* (2002)
- *The Hitchhiker's Guide to the Galaxy* (2005)
- *The Office (television show)* (2005–)
- *Parks and Recreation (television show)* (2009–)

SUGGESTED WEBSITES

- **Citizens Against Government Waste:** http://www.cagw.org/
- **Government Accountability Office:** http://www.gao.gov/
- **Government Printing Office:** http://www.gpoaccess.gov/
- **National Association of Schools of Public Affairs and Administration:** http://www.naspaa.org/
- **National Conference of State Legislatures:** http://www.ncsl.org/
- **National Governor's Association:** http://www.nga.org/
- **National Whistleblowers Center:** http://www.whistleblowers.org/
- **Office of Personnel Management:** http://www.opm.gov/
- **Recovery.gov—Tracking the Money:** http://www.recovery.gov/
- **Regulations.gov:** http://www.regulations.gov/

ENDNOTES

[1]Michael Bromwich quoted in CNN Wire Staff, "U.S. Splits Up Offshore Regulators After Oil Disaster." CNN.com (January 19, 2011), available at: http://www.cnn.com (accessed April 23, 2011).

[2]See http://boemre.gov (accessed April 23, 2011).

[3]John M. Broder and Peter Baker, "Obama's Order is Likely to Tighten Auto Standards." *New York Times* (January 25, 2009): A1, available at: http://www.nytimes.com/2009/01/26/us/politics/26calif.html (accessed November 7, 2010).

[4]Deborah Zabarenko, "UPDATE 2-US EPA Approves California Auto Emissions Standard." *Reuters* (June 20, 2009), available at: http://www.reuters.com/article/idUSN3044688920090630 (accessed November 7, 2010).

[5]Max Weber, *Wirtschaft und Gesellschaft*, part III, chap. 6, pp. 650–78. (NJ: Bedminster Press Somerville, 1968).

[6]See http://www.opm.gov/index.asp (accessed November 7, 2010).

[7]See http://osha.gov/about.html (accessed November 7, 2010).

[8]Jeff Mason, "McCain says he would fire Republican SEC chief Cox," *Reuters* (September 18, 2008), available at: http://www.reuters.com/article/idUSN1841507620080918 (accessed November 7, 2010).

[9]Kevin R. Kosar, "Federal Government Corporations: An Overview," *Congressional Research Service* (Updated January 31, 2008), available at: http://assets.opencrs.com/rpts/RL30365_20080131.pdf (accessed November 7, 2010).

[10]U.S. Bureau of the Census, *Statistical Abstract of the United States*, 2010, Table 450.
[11]William D. Richardson, *Democracy, Bureaucracy, and Character*. (Lawrence, KS: University Press of Kansas, 1997).
[12]Ibid.
[13]Stephen Goldsmith, "How Rules Demean Public Workers," *Governing* (November 2010): 56.
[14]Paul C. Light, *The True Size of Government* (Washington, DC: Brookings Institution, 1999).
[15]Michael Harrington, *The Other America*. (New York: MacMillan, 1962).
[16]D. Osborne and T. Gaebler, *Reinventing Government*. (New York: Penguin Books, 1993).
[17]J. Shafritz and E.W. Russell, *Introducing Public Administration* (New York: Longman, 2010).
[18]Mathew D. McCubbins and Thomas Schwartz, "Congressional Oversight Overlooked: Police Patrols Versus Fire Alarms," in Mathew D. McCubbins and Terry Sullivan, eds., *Congress: Structure and Policy* (New York: Cambridge University Press, 1987), pp. 426–440.
[19]Cornelius M. Kerwin and Scott R. Furlong, *Rulemaking: How Government Agencies Write Law and Make Policy*, 4th ed. (Washington, DC: CQ Press, 2011), Chapter 1.
[20]The most well-know expression of this argument is one made by Theodore Lowi in *The End of Liberalism*. (New York: W. W. Norton, 1979).
[21]This summary is drawn from Martin Shapiro, *Who Guards the Guardians?* (Athens, GA: University of Georgia Press, 1988).
[22]See for instance, Cary Coglianese, "Assessing Consensus: The Promise and Performance of Negotiated Rulemaking," in *Duke Law Journal*, 46 (6, April 1997): 1255–1349; Ellen Siegler, "Regulating Negotiations and Other Rulemaking Processes: Strengths and Weaknesses from an Industry Viewpoint," in *Duke Law Journal*, 46 (6, April 1997): 1429–1443; and Cary Coglianese and Laurie K. Allen, "Does Consensus Make Common Sense? An Analysis of EPA's Common Sense Initiative," *Environment* (January–February, 2004): 10–24.
[23]You can learn more about Abraham Maslow's hierarchy of needs by accessing his original work, such as *Toward a Psychology of Being* (Van Nostrand Reinhold, 1968), *Motivation and Personality* (first edition, 1954, and Harper & Row, second edition, 1970), and *The Further Reaches of Human Nature* (Penguin, 1971). Also see one of the many brief introductions, such as Janet A. Simons, Donald B. Irwin, and Beverly A. Drinnien, "Maslow's Hierarchy of Needs," in *Psychology—The Search for Understanding* (New York: West Publishing Company, 1987). Also available online at: http://honolulu.hawaii.edu/intranet/committees/FacDevCom/guidebk/teachtip/maslow.htm
[24]J. Shafritz, S. Ott, and S. Y. Jang, *Classics of Organization Theory* (Florence, KY: Wadsworth Publishing, 2010).
[25]John Dululio, Jr., *Principled Agents: Cultiural Bases of Behavior in a Federal Government Bureaucracy*. The Berkeley Symposium, available at: http://jpart.oxfordjournals.org/content/4/3/277.full.pdf (accessed November 25, 2010).
[26]Data collected from The Polling Report (online) at http://pollingreport.com/institut.htm (accessed December 12, 2010).
[27]See Chapter 2 of Charles T. Goodsell, *The Case for Bureaucracy: A Public Administration Polemic*, 4th ed. (Washington, DC: CQ Press, 2004).
[28]Mary-Jo Hall, "The American Customer Satisfaction Index," *The Public Manager*, 31 (1, Spring 2002): 23–26, available online at: http://findarticles.com/p/articles/mi_m0HTO/is_1_31/ai_n25050742//?tag=content;col1.
[29]Tom Shoop, "Obama Pledges to fire managers, cut redundant programs," *Government Executive.com*, September 22, 2008, available at: http://www.govexec.com/dailyfed/0908/092208ts1.htm (accessed June 2, 2011).
[30]John McCain, "McCain Outlines Vision for First Term," *Real Clear Politics*, May 15, 2008, available at: http://www.realclearpolitics.com/articles/2008/05/mccain_outlines_vision_for_fir.html (accessed June 2, 2011).

Chapter 6

THE JUDICIARY

Top Ten List

10 The U.S. judiciary shares traits with courts of other countries.

9 Federal and state courts differ in the number and type of cases they hear.

8 There are three tiers in the federal court system: District, Appellate, and Supreme.

7 The Supreme Court is unique.

6 The law that courts apply comes from all three branches of government.

5 Judicial power in the United States has grown over time.

4 Although not elected, justices are accountable to the citizenry.

3 Justices have a good deal of discretion when it comes to deciding controversial issues and questions.

2 The power of judges is limited by the inherent constraints of the judicial system.

1 Citizen support for the U.S. Supreme Court is high.

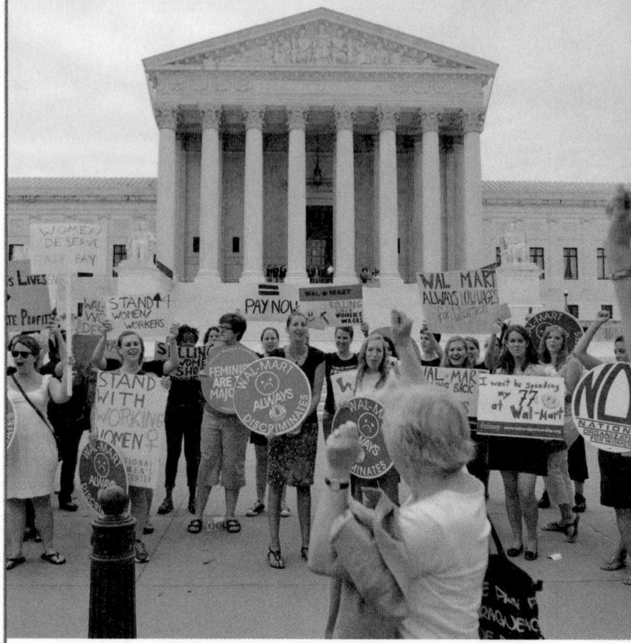

Shown here, demonstrators gather outside the U.S. Supreme Court in 2011 to protest the Court's Wal-Mart sex discrimination class action lawsuit decision. Courts lie at the center of the drama where individuals, organizations, and companies resolve conflicts. These conflicts involve questions vital to our private and public lives: questions of property rights, family ties, compensation for wrongs, criminal guilt, and the breadth of legitimate governmental activity. What is the proper balance between maintaining an independent judiciary with the freedom to follow the rule of law and a judiciary that is held accountable as a policymaker in a democratic nation?

YOUR LIST

Before you read this chapter, take a few moments to think about what you might include on a list of the Top 10 Most Important Things to Know About the Judiciary. At the end of the chapter you will be asked to compare and contrast your list with the one supplied in this chapter.

INTRODUCTION

American television is filled with legal shows: *Judge Judy* and her fellow TV judges fill the daytime hours, while courtroom dramas occupy the evening. In 2009, *Law and Order* completed its twentieth, and final, season, making it the longest running crime drama on American television. Readers are also intrigued by the law—every year American authors publish new legal thrillers, and the best of these stories often become big screen hits. Dramatized accounts of law are not alone in capturing the public's attention. A review of daily newspapers, of the 24-hour news channels, or of the news page of your favorite Web browser will show that this interest carries over to the impact law has in our daily lives. This should come as no surprise. These representations, fictional and real, are stories of conflicts awaiting resolution, the essence of a good story. How could we not be interested?[1]

Courts are at the center of the drama where conflicts are resolved. These conflicts involve questions vital to our private and public lives, questions of property rights, familial ties, compensation for wrongs, criminal guilt, and the breadth of legitimate governmental activity. According to Harold Laswell's classic definition of politics—"who gets what, when, and how"—many of these conflicts concern political questions, drawing courts into the policymaking process.

In a recent work, Richard A. Posner, Circuit Judge of the U.S. Court of Appeals for the Seventh Circuit, described a judge's job with this in mind: "A pragmatic judge assesses the consequences of judicial decisions for their bearing on sound public policy as he conceives it. But it need not be policy chosen by him on political grounds as normally understood."[2] So while judges do make policy, the politics of the judiciary are different from those of Congress or the president.[3] We would never expect a judge to respond to public opinion in deciding a case before her; rather, we expect the courts to resolve conflicts using a set of preexisting norms collectively known as "the law."

The challenges posed by a legal institution resolving political questions forms the framework for this chapter. It presents us with two key questions: How do the politics of the judiciary differ from those of Congress and the presidency? And what is the proper balance between maintaining an independent judiciary that is free to follow the rule of law and a judiciary that is held accountable as a policymaker in a democratic nation? We cannot address these important questions, however, until we have a basic understanding of the American judicial system.

10 The U.S. judiciary shares traits with courts of other countries.

Dispute resolution processes are found in all cultures and have existed for millennia. Whether it be children using "rock, paper, scissors," the activity of a university's conduct board, or a criminal trial, communities have developed methods for resolving the disputes that inevitably arise among their members, hoping to resolve the conflicts without violence.

Courts Formal organs of government that resolve disputes using rules of law.

While all societies have processes for resolving disputes, not all have formalized these in **courts**, formal organs of government that resolve disputes using rules of law.[4] In order for this to happen, it is necessary for courts to be recognized as distinct entities, independent from other governmental actors, so that citizens can be assured that judicial decisions are based on law and not on the political whims of the governing authorities.[5] The decisions of these bodies are binding on all parties and are enforced by the government.

Institutions that meet this definition are found in countries throughout the world. The following cases involve claims by individuals against companies in three different countries: Scotland, Japan, and the United States.[6]

- A man's luggage was lost by an airline. Rather than accept the minimal amount he was offered as compensation, he sued the airline for damages he suffered as a result of its negligence. The court awarded him a sum substantially larger than he had originally been offered by the airline.
- A man who cancelled his contract for language lessons sued the school for charging him a higher-than-agreed-upon rate upon his cancellation. The court found the school's cancellation policy to be illegal and required the school to pay the **plaintiff**, the man in this case who signed up for the lessons and filed the lawsuit.
- A man whose wife suffered life-altering injuries when her car rolled over sued the maker of the automobile for knowingly producing a defective product. The trial court awarded him both compensatory and punitive damages. **Compensatory** (or actual) **damage** is money awarded in a civil suit to compensate an injured party for direct losses or injuries sustained; **punitive damage** is money awarded to punish or deter the wrongdoer from behaving in the same way again.[7]

Plaintiff The person who initiates or files a lawsuit.

Compensatory (or actual) damages Money awarded in a civil suit to compensate an injured party for direct losses or injuries sustained.

Punitive damages Money awarded to punish or deter the wrongdoer from behaving in the same way again.

In all three of these cases, the trial courts resolved the conflicts described according to each nation's laws, awarding damages to the plaintiffs. Even though the plaintiff prevailed in all three cases, the process by which the courts in these three nations—Scotland, Japan, and the United States, respectively—reached this conclusion differs a good deal.[8] It is important to keep in mind that despite some similarities, legal systems around the world each have their own unique and rich histories, and the U.S. system is no different in this regard.

The legal system in the United States developed from the common law tradition brought to America by British colonists almost 400 years ago. In a **common law system**, conflicts that come before a court are decided based largely on previous judicial decisions, a practice known as **stare decisis**, Latin for "let the decision stand."[9] These past decisions are known as **precedents**. Common law differs from the civil law systems used by many other countries in the world. Whereas common law systems trace their roots back to England, civil law regimes tend to be rooted in Roman law and the Napoleonic code.[10] In a **civil law regime**, the conflicts that come before the courts are decided

Common law system Conflicts that come before a court are decided based largely on previous judicial decisions.

Stare decisis Latin for "let the decision stand"; the process of deciding cases based largely on previous judicial decisions.

Precedents Past judicial decisions of courts used to resolve current conflicts.

Civil law regime Conflicts that come before the courts are decided according to an extensive code or set of laws; less attention is paid to past court decisions.

according to an extensive code or set of laws. Each case is analyzed with reference to the appropriate section of the code, and less attention is paid to past decisions of courts.[11]

Today, the distinction between common law and civil law systems has become somewhat blurred. In the United States, most law has been codified in statutes enacted by Congress, state legislatures, and local governing authorities. The process by which judges make their decisions in interpreting these statutes, however, still relies largely on precedent. As a result, the decisions of courts carry more weight, generally giving the U.S. judiciary more political power than it would have in a civil law system.[12]

9 Federal and state courts differ in the number and type of cases they hear.

The United States has two levels of courts, state and federal, which are authorized to hear different cases. While state courts operate similarly to federal courts, they handle more cases. Any conflict coming before a court in the United States must fall within that court's **jurisdiction**, or authority to hear the case. In some cases, state and federal courts can share jurisdiction, referred to as concurrent jurisdiction, but in many instances a case will fall under the jurisdiction of one system or another. Jurisdiction generally varies by geography (for instance, a conflict from the state of Wyoming will not be heard in a court in Illinois), by subject matter (for instance, in Article III the U.S. Constitution specifies that the federal courts can hear cases that deal with the Constitution, federal law, and treaties, not cases dealing with state laws or state constitutions), and by the parties involved (similarly, Article III specifies that cases involving certain parties like ambassadors can be heard in federal court).

Jurisdiction The authority of a court to hear and decide a case.

Table 6.1 provides a summary of federal jurisdiction. Most federal suits involve a **federal question** related to federal law, the U.S. Constitution, or treaties. Examples include the challenge brought by environmentalists in 2006 under the Endangered Species Act to protect the spotted owl from harm caused by logging, federal criminal charges brought against drug traffickers, and the 2000 antitrust suit brought against Microsoft by the U.S. government. **Diversity of jurisdiction** cases make up a substantial portion of federal suits. These are cases that would otherwise go to a state trial court but go into federal court because they involve litigants of different states and/or countries. Most of these cases are personal injury suits between individuals or corporations of two different states.[13]

Federal question A lawsuit related to federal law, the U.S. Constitution, or treaties.

Diversity of jurisdiction These cases make up a substantial portion of federal suits. They are cases that involve litigants of different states and/or countries.

State courts hear cases involving their respective state constitutions and laws and, unless there is a conflict with the U.S. Constitution, are the final voice on their state's law. While there is overlap in the type of laws enacted by states and the federal government, states alone are primarily responsible for family law, matters involving juveniles, real estate, and probate (the process of administering an estate and the last

Table 6.1 **Jurisdiction of Federal Courts as Defined in Article III of the Constitution**

Subject Matter Jurisdiction—Cases involving:

- the U.S. Constitution, federal laws, and treaties (**federal questions**)
- ambassadors, public ministers, and consuls
- admiralty and maritime law

Party Jurisdiction—Cases involving:

- the United States
- two or more states
- a state and citizens of another state*
- citizens of different states (**diversity of jurisdiction**)
- citizens of the same state claiming lands under grants of different states
- a state, or the citizens thereof, and foreign states, citizens, or subjects

**Per the Eleventh Amendment, federal courts do not have jurisdiction in cases in which a state is sued by citizens of another state, domestic or foreign.*

Table 6.2 **2008 Caseload Comparison of Filings in Federal and State Courts**

	Civil Cases (Trial Courts)	**Criminal Cases (Trial Courts)**	**Intermediate Courts of Appeal**	**Courts of Last Resort**
50 States and Puerto Rico	19,373,089* (Includes civil, domestic relations, and juvenile)	21,292,567*	169,967*	63,350*
Federal Courts	245,427**	55,860**	66,618**	87***

Sources: * Court Statistics Project, *State Court Caseload Statistics: An Analysis of 2008 State Court Caseloads* (National Center for State Courts 2010), Tables 1, 10—Reported Filings.

**Administrative Office of the United States Courts, *Federal Judicial Caseload Statistics: March 31, 2009* (Washington, DC, 2009).

***2009 Chief Justice's Year-End Report on the Federal Judiciary (Data on number of cases argued in 2008/2009 term).

will and testament of a deceased person). Both federal and state courts hear criminal cases as well as those involving personal injury and contracts.

The decisions of the federal courts have a vital influence on our daily lives, but the large majority of conflicts that come before courts in the United States each year are heard in state courts (see Table 6.2). In FY 2008, for example, the state courts processed almost 80 times more civil cases and over 300 times more criminal complaints than the federal courts.[14]

8 There are three tiers in the federal court system: District, Appellate, and Supreme.

The federal judiciary is a three-tier system. As Figure 6.1 shows, the U.S. **district courts** are the **trial courts** at the base of the system with two levels of **appellate courts** above: the courts of appeal make up the middle tier, and the U.S. Supreme Court sits at the top.[15]

District courts Courts at the base or the lowest tier of the three-tiered U.S. federal court system. These courts hear cases that involve original jurisdiction.

Trial courts Most often the courts of original jurisdiction.

Appellate courts Courts in the middle tier of the federal court system. These courts have jurisdiction to hear any case appealed from the lower federal (or district) courts.

Original jurisdiction Granted to a court to hear a case for the first time.

The district courts hear cases that involve **original jurisdiction**, which simply means they are the first courts to hear and decide a dispute (i.e., the case "originates" in this court). The jurisdiction of the federal courts is described in some detail in Article III, section 2, of the Constitution. The district courts have the ability to hear and decide two specific types of cases: federal questions and diversity of jurisdiction cases that involve litigants of different states and/or countries.

There are ninety-four district courts in the United States.[16] Each state has at least one such court, with three of the most populous states (California, New York, and Texas) having four. Cases are assigned to courts according to geographic jurisdiction. For instance, a federal trial involving an incident that occurred in Miami Beach, Florida, will be heard in the Southern District of Florida.

Figure 6.1 Organizational Chart of the Federal Judiciary

The federal court system has three tiers; trial courts are at the bottom, and the highest appellate court, the United States Supreme Court, is at the top.

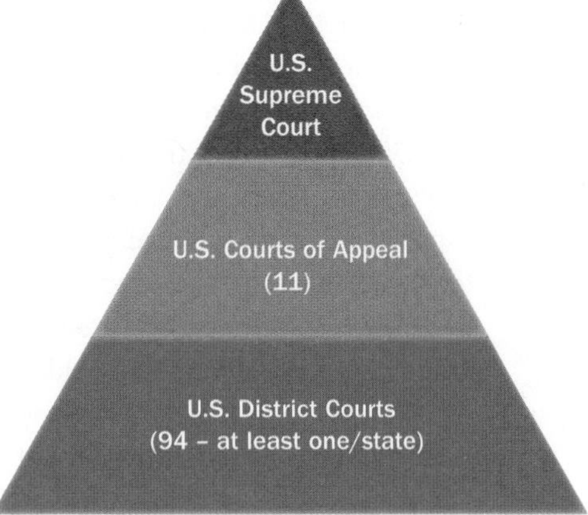

Criminal law Reflects the collective will of the citizenry; when an individual violates a criminal law, lawyers representing society at large bring the suit.

Civil law Involves conflicts of a noncriminal nature; in federal court, these are likely to include cases involving contracts, personal injury, and bankruptcy.

U.S. Courts of Appeal Courts at the middle tier of the three-tiered U.S. federal court system. These courts hear cases on appeal from the lower courts.

Appellate jurisdiction Refers to the authority of a court to hear a case on appeal from a lower court.

Circuits Refers to the thirteen courts of appeal located within one of eleven numbered geographic boundaries. Most of these appellate courts hear cases on appeal from district courts.

U.S. Court of Appeals for the Federal Circuit One of the thirteen courts of appeal in the United States. Unlike the other twelve, this appellate court has nationwide jurisdiction based on subject.

Adversarial process In this system, each side in a conflict argues its position before a neutral third party who makes the final decision.

Cases that come to trial in district courts concern either criminal or civil law. **Criminal law** represents the collective will of the citizenry. When an individual violates a criminal law, he or she is harming not only the victim (and very possibly himself) but also society at large. Therefore, criminal cases are brought to court by lawyers from the U.S. Attorneys' Offices on behalf of the citizenry. One of the best-known federal criminal cases was the trial of Timothy McVeigh, the Oklahoma City bomber. Mr. McVeigh was tried and convicted in the U.S. District Court for the District of Colorado on eleven charges of murder and conspiracy in the 1995 bombing of the Alfred P. Murrah Federal Building in Oklahoma City, Oklahoma.[17] Over 150 people, including 19 children, were killed by his actions. McVeigh was sentenced to death, and on June 11, 2001, he became the first convict to be executed by the federal government in 38 years.

Civil law involves conflicts of a noncriminal nature. In federal court these are likely to include cases involving contracts, personal injury, and bankruptcy.[18] Individual plaintiffs bring these cases to court. In 1990, for example, Ray Repp, the plaintiff, brought a copyright suit against Andrew Lloyd Webber, the defendant, claiming Webber had used a portion of Repp's music in a theme from *Phantom of the Opera*. When this case came before a jury, Webber presented part of the evidence in person, playing portions of the song on a piano. The jury found Webber's defense more convincing than Repp's claim and determined that no copyright infringement had occurred.[19]

For most cases, district court action marks the end of the conflict.[20] However, for the cases in which there is a legitimate question of law, the losing party can choose to appeal. Fifteen percent of the cases decided in the district courts in FY 2008 were appealed to a **U.S. Court of Appeals**. The U.S. Court of Appeals is the middle tier of the federal court's three-tier system (see Figure 6.1). Unlike the district courts, these courts hear cases on **appellate jurisdiction** (simply, the authority of a court to hear a case on appeal from a lower court).

There are currently thirteen courts of appeal located within one of eleven numbered **circuits**, or the D.C. Circuit (see Figure 6.2).[21] The thirteenth court of appeals is the **U.S. Court of Appeals for the Federal Circuit**, which has nationwide jurisdiction based on subject. All other courts of appeal hear cases from district courts within their geographic circuit or territory.

Unlike district or trial courts, in appellate courts in the United States there is no jury; no witnesses are called or evidence presented. The facts of the case as established at the trial are not subject to appeal.[22] Rather, justices on the appellate level determine if the law was appropriately interpreted and applied in the trial court. To help in determining this, an **adversarial process** is employed, with attorneys presenting arguments for their respective sides in the form of written briefs. In many cases, these are followed by oral argument in which the attorney for each party is given a set period of time to present an argument and to respond to questions from the justices.

An example may help to clarify the distinction between trial and appellate processes. In a case tried in the Federal District Court for the Northern District of

8 There are three tiers in the federal court system: District, Appellate, and Supreme.

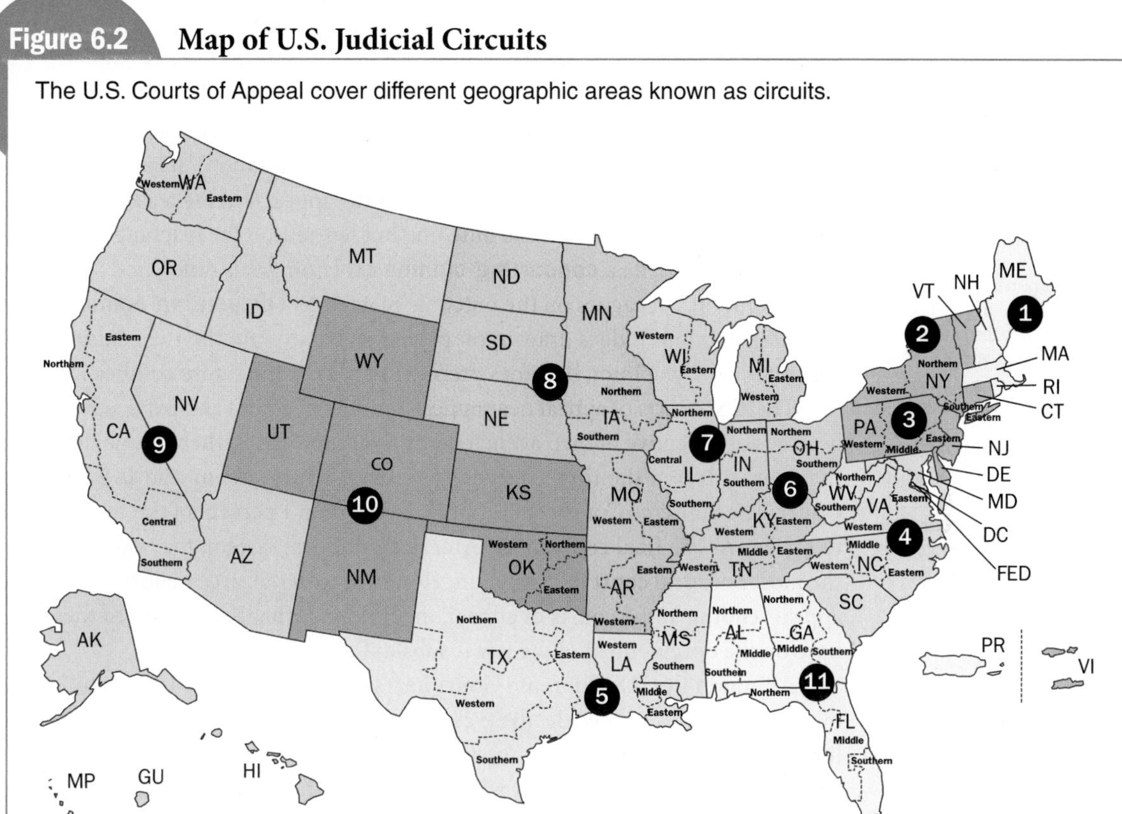

Figure 6.2 Map of U.S. Judicial Circuits

The U.S. Courts of Appeal cover different geographic areas known as circuits.

Source: http://www.uscourts.gov/courtlinks/

Georgia and appealed to the Eleventh Circuit, Ernest Gibbs was charged with committing robbery.[23] His conviction was based in part on confessions that he had given to the FBI. Before trial, Mr. Gibbs filed a motion to exclude the confessions. His attorney argued that they could not have been given voluntarily because of Mr. Gibbs's limited literacy skills; this motion was denied, the trial took place, and Mr. Gibbs was found guilty. He appealed, and the question of law that the Eleventh Circuit considered was whether Mr. Gibbs's confession had been taken in violation of his Fourth and Fifth Amendment rights. This is a question of law since it requires an interpretation of the Constitution. Determination of the process by which the confession was given is a factual question; whether or not this process violated Mr. Gibbs's constitutional rights was a question of law. The Eleventh Circuit panel found that the circumstances surrounding the confession did not violate Mr. Gibbs's constitutional rights and that his confession was properly admitted as evidence.

One other major difference between trial and appellate courts is that justices on appellate courts hear cases in panels, whereas judges on trial courts sit alone. Judges for courts of appeal sit in panels of three. All nine justices of the U.S. Supreme Court sit together to hear appeals.

Majority opinion Judicial findings that reflect the view of the majority of the justices on the outcome of the appeal.

Concurring opinion An opinion written by a justice that agrees with the outcome but whose reasoning differs.

Dissenting opinion An opinion written by a judge who differs with his or her colleagues on the outcome.

U.S. Supreme Court This court is the most powerful court in the nation. It hears appeals in less than 1 percent of the cases it is asked to review.

Justices decide the question being appealed and issue their findings in the opinion of the Court (oftentimes referred to as a **majority opinion**). It reflects the view of the majority of the justices on the outcome of the appeal and the reasons for this outcome. If a justice agrees with the outcome but her reason for reaching this outcome differs, she may write a **concurring opinion** explaining this difference. A judge who differs with his colleagues on the outcome may write a **dissenting opinion**. In writing these opinions judges draw upon precedents to explain their conclusions.[24] The current majority opinion becomes precedent for deciding future conflicts.

The U.S. courts of appeal hear appeals from trial courts and from administrative hearings of executive branch agencies. For a very few cases, there is one more step—the apex or top of the three-tiered U.S. federal court system, the **U.S. Supreme Court**. The Supreme Court hears appeals in less than 1 percent of the cases it is asked to review. As the final court in the American political system, the Supreme Court is the most powerful court in the nation. However, with the large majority of all federal appeals ending at the courts of appeal, the influence that the justices of these courts have on the development of the law is substantial.

Although the U.S. Supreme Court hears only 80 to 120, or less than 1 percent, of the cases it is asked decide, these cases tend to be the most well-known of the millions of cases decided in the country each year. For this reason, the remainder of the chapter focuses a good deal on what happens in the Supreme Court of the United States, which has become the final arbiter of what the Constitution means.

The Supreme Court is unique.

Like other appeals courts, the U.S. Supreme Court hears cases on appeal and answers questions of law. Despite this similarity, there are two things in particular that set the Supreme Court apart from the other courts in the federal judicial system.

First, unlike decisions of the federal district courts, which affect only their state, or the decisions of the courts of appeal that affect only their circuit, decisions of the U.S. Supreme Court are the law of the land. For example, nearly two decades ago two people who applied to the University of Michigan filed a suit against its admissions policy that ranked applicants using a 150-point scale, giving an automatic 20 points to any member of an underrepresented minority. Five justices of the Supreme Court decided that this admissions policy violated the Fourteenth Amendment guarantee that "[n]o state shall . . . deny to any person within its jurisdiction the equal protection of the laws."[25] Since that time, all public universities in the nation have been forced comply.

The second factor that sets the Supreme Court apart, and one that magnifies the Court's power, is the discretion it has in choosing which cases to hear. The district courts and courts of appeal must hear all legitimate conflicts that are brought before them. The Supreme Court must hear all cases that come before it under its original jurisdiction, but these cases are very few in number.[26] All other cases come to the Court under its appellate jurisdiction. Over time, Congress has all but eliminated mandatory appellate jurisdiction, so that today almost all of the Supreme Court's caseload is discretionary. This enables the justices to hear only those cases they consider to be most important.

Writ of certiorari Latin term meaning "to be informed"; is issued by the U.S. Supreme Court to a lower court when agreeing to review the case coming from that lower court.

Each year thousands of parties ask the Court to hear their appeal by filing a petition for a **writ of certiorari**. These petitions ask the Supreme Court to issue an order to the lower court to send the record of the case to the Supreme Court for further review. Over 8,200 such petitions were filed in the 2008/2009 term, the large majority (over 80 percent) being petitions filed by indigents, usually prison inmates, who file their petition for free via a simplified process.[27]

Cert pool Each participating Supreme Court justice assigns one or more clerks to review each petition and to make recommendations to the justices about which cases to hear.

Rule of Four If four or more Supreme Court justices want to hear a case, it is put on the court's docket.

Once the petitions are received by the Clerk of the Supreme Court, they are sent to each justice's office for review. Since 1972 most of the justices have participated in the **cert pool** in which each participating justice assigns one or more clerks to work with law clerks from the other offices to review each petition and to make recommendations to the justices about which cases to hear.[28] If four or more justices want to hear a case, it is put on the Court's docket under a time-honored norm called the **Rule of Four**. The Court then issues the writ of certiorari.

Of the thousands of petitions that have been filed in recent years, the Court has heard arguments and issued full opinions in fewer than 100, or less than 1 percent of all petitions filed.[29] This raises a question that has intrigued political scientists: What factors do the justices use in deciding which cases to hear? The official rules of the Supreme Court say that the Court will hear those cases in which there is a conflict between decisions of lower courts on a question of federal law or a case that raises "an important question of federal law that has not been, but should be, settled by this Court." But this does not give us the whole story.

To better answer this question, scholars have studied which justices vote to hear which cases. Four variables make it more likely that a justice will vote to hear a case: if there is a conflict between lower courts, if the United States is a petitioner, if the case runs counter to the ideology of the granting justice, and if there are numerous petitions from other interested parties encouraging the Court to hear the case.[30]

Briefs Documents filed with the Supreme Court that outline the facts of the case, the law to be applied, and the legal argument that each side is making.

Amicus curiae (friend of the court) brief Brief filed with an appellate court by a person or organization that is not a party to the case but that wishes to bring information on the conflict to the court's attention.

Once a case has been accepted, the parties are notified and are given a deadline for filing of **briefs**. These documents outline the facts of the case, the law to be applied, and the legal argument that each side is making. The case is then scheduled for oral argument. Other individuals or groups who are interested in the outcome of a case may ask for permission to file additional briefs known as **amicus curiae (friend of the court) briefs** that raise additional legal arguments for the Court to consider. The most contentious of Supreme Court cases attract numerous amicus briefs. In the 1992 case of *Planned Parenthood v. Casey*, almost fifty briefs were filed representing hundreds of parties. This is not surprising in light of the fact that at the time many felt this case could result in the overturning of the 1973 case *Roe v. Wade*, which dealt with abortion.[31]

Once briefs have been filed, the case is ready for oral argument.[32] Except in extraordinary circumstances, each party is allowed 30 minutes to make its oral argument before the Court, which since the post–Civil War period has consisted of nine justices—the **Chief Justice** (currently John Roberts), who is appointed by the president and confirmed by the Senate, is the presiding justice on the court.[33] The eight **Associate Justices** (currently, and in order of appointment: Antonin Scalia, Anthony Kennedy, Clarence Thomas, Ruth Bader Ginsburg, Stephen Breyer, Samuel Alito, Sonia Sotomayor, and Elena Kagan) are also appointed by the president and confirmed by the Senate; they have the same responsibilities as the Chief Justice as it pertains to cases, but fewer or different administrative responsibilities.

Chief Justice The presiding justice on the Supreme Court appointed by the president and confirmed by the Senate.

Associate Justices These eight justices are appointed by the president and confirmed by the Senate. They have the same responsibilities as the Chief Justice as it pertains to cases, but different administrative responsibilities.

During the oral argument, the nine justices sit on the bench in order of seniority, with the Chief Justice in the center and the others alternating in from left to right. While the attorneys for either side will be given a chance to begin their argument, the majority of the 30 minutes is filled with justices peppering the attorneys with questions on the case. When the U.S. government is a party to the case, it is represented by the **Solicitor General's** staff. She or he is a senior staff person in the Department of Justice and plays a key role in determining which cases to appeal and how to shape appellate arguments for the U.S. government.[34]

Solicitor General Senior staff person in the Department of Justice; when the U.S. government is a party to a case, he or she plays a key role in determining which cases to appeal and how to shape appellate arguments.

After a case has been argued, the justices meet alone in conference. The cases are discussed, a vote is taken, and a justice is assigned to write the opinion for the Court. In those cases in which the justices are unanimous in their decision, or in which the Chief Justice is in the majority, he assigns himself or an Associate Justice in the majority to write the opinion. If the Chief is in the minority, the most senior member who voted with the majority assigns the opinion.

The justice who writes the opinion for the court has an important duty. The opinion must be written so as to reflect the views of the court in a way that keeps the majority intact. Further, the way in which the opinion is written is important for the future, since each majority opinion sets a precedent for future cases. As with all appeals courts, justices may also choose to write concurring or dissenting opinions.

6 The law that courts apply comes from all three branches of government.

Although we generally think of Congress as the "lawmaking" branch of government, all three branches actually make law: *statutory law* comes from Congress, *administrative law* from the executive branch, and common and *constitutional law* from the courts. The result of law coming from various sources is that in any one substantive area of law (education, disability rights, national security) "the law" is a mixture of statutes, regulations, and court decisions. Further, because of the common law tradition of the American legal system, court decisions are also important in determining the meaning of statutory and regulatory law.

In a Supreme Court decision involving the meaning of the Age Discrimination in Employment Act of 1967, Justice Kennedy's majority opinion made extensive reference to the statute and to Equal Employment Opportunity Commission (EEOC) regulations. He also cited twenty past decisions of the U.S. Supreme Court.[35] This heavy use of precedent reinforces the power of the courts.

Although Congress and executive branch agencies try to write laws as clearly as possible, there will always be a need for interpretation. Do EPA clean air regulations apply to the actions of a particular industry? Will the No Child Left Behind Act allow a state to apply its own assessment criteria? Do the IRS regulations regarding charitable contributions apply to a certain organization? Answers to these questions require judges to interpret laws. If Congress or the executive branch agency feels that a judge has misinterpreted their statute or regulation, they can correct this error by enacting a new, clearer law or regulation.[36] In these instances, any action by the judiciary that runs contrary to the will of the other branches can be corrected, checking the judicial power of statutory or regulatory interpretation.

Judges of the federal courts also interpret one other source of law in resolving disputes: the U.S. Constitution. Even more than statutes or regulations, the Constitution is written in broad terms. What does it mean to say that "due process" shall not be violated? And what qualifies as "interstate commerce"? The federal justices interpret these general clauses and apply them to the challenges that come before them. Unlike the interpretation of statutes and regulations, however, the decisions of justices regarding the meaning of the Constitution can only be overturned by a constitutional amendment, a difficult and cumbersome process. This difference makes constitutional law the area of law in which the courts are most powerful.

Judicial power in the United States has grown over time.

The power granted to the courts as defined by the Constitution has changed little since 1789.[37] However, the power of the federal judiciary in practice has grown exponentially since that time, particularly in cases involving equitable remedy and judicial review.

The power of federal trial courts is most often exercised through juries. However, in conflicts in which an aggrieved person is asking the court to grant an **equitable remedy**, the judges act alone. In these cases, a plaintiff is not asking for monetary damages, but rather is asking the court to take a specific action, such as issuing an injunction or a restraining order, to correct a problem. These remedies are

Equitable remedy A plaintiff asks the court to take a specific action, such as issuing an injunction or a restraining order, to correct a problem.

awarded by trial judges and can have long-ranging political effects. Federal judges have mandated environmental cleanups, dictated conditions in prisons, and required agencies to follow certain hiring practices.

Perhaps the best-known use of equity powers by federal district court judges resulted from the U.S. Supreme Court decision of *Brown v. Board of Education* (1954). The year after the Court issued this decision declaring segregation in public schools to be unconstitutional, the Court issued a second opinion (*Brown II*) that dealt with implementation in which Chief Justice Warren sent these cases back to the district courts, requiring them to oversee local desegregation plans.[38] Federal courts in 1789 also had the authority to fashion equitable remedies, but the increased scope of governmental activity and the application of constitutional liberties to states through the Fourteenth Amendment (not enacted until 1868) has greatly increased the power of federal district courts in imposing resolutions in many local conflicts.[39]

Judicial review The authority of a court to invalidate actions of other governmental actors, if these actions are in violation of the nation's constitution.

The power of federal courts to exercise judicial review has also expanded over time. **Judicial review** is the authority of a court to invalidate actions of other governmental actors, if these actions are in violation of the nation's constitution. While all courts have this power, a decision by a lower court that a federal action is unconstitutional will likely be appealed to the U.S. Supreme Court, the final judicial authority in these questions. Interestingly, while courts exercise this power fairly regularly today, it is not among the powers of the judiciary mentioned in the Constitution. The founders considered granting this power to the courts and then decided against it. According to Madison's notes on the Constitutional Convention, only nine of the fifty-five delegates supported judicial review.[40] As a result, the judiciary did not have this power until Chief Justice John Marshall claimed it in 1803, in arguably the most famous and influential case in American history, *Marbury v. Madison.*

In 1800, after the Federalist Party had lost both the presidency and Congress to the Jeffersonians, it tried to increase its influence in the judicial branch by creating additional judgeships and appointing Federalists to the open slots. When the Jeffersonians refused to deliver commissions to some Federalist appointees, William Marbury sued. Marshall, a Federalist appointee himself, denied the petition and declared a section of the Judiciary Act of 1789 to be unconstitutional. While he is remembered for claiming this power for the Court, this was the one and only time that Marshall exercised judicial review over a federal action in over 34 years on the bench. It wasn't until after the Civil War that the Supreme Court began to use this power more freely, and this was predominantly to strike down state actions. As of 2007, the Supreme Court has declared 174 federal statutes and 973 state acts to be unconstitutional.[41] As Figure 6.3 shows, most of these decisions were issued during the latter half of the twentieth century.[42]

The power of the court to strike down the acts of Congress and the executive branch is seldom discussed by the public, but it is arguably one of the most controversial powers assumed since the founding. By asserting this power, the U.S. Supreme Court has made itself the chief interpreter and arbiter of the Constitution. This raises

Figure 6.3 **Number of Federal and State Statutes Declared Unconstitutional by the U.S. Supreme Court**

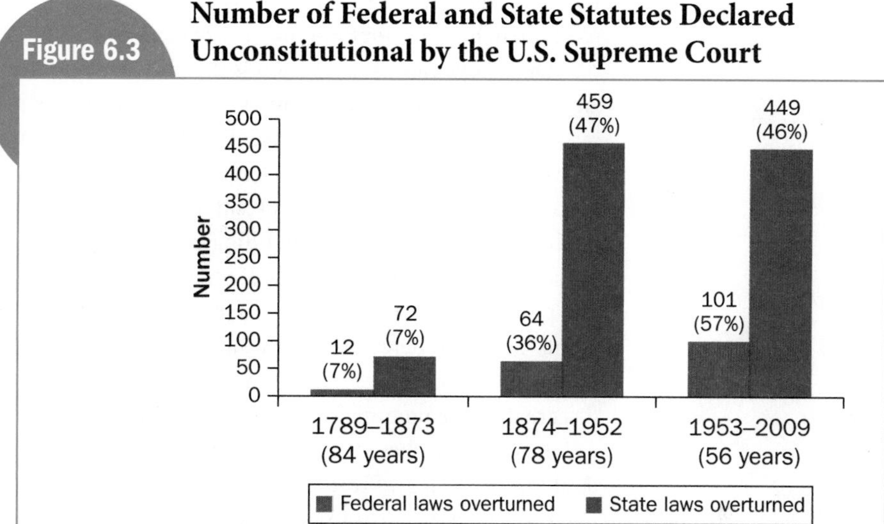

Source: Based on data found in David O'Brien, *Storm Center: The Supreme Court in American Politics* (New York: WW Norton, 2011), p. 31.

several questions, including: Should the judiciary have this power over two coequal branches of government? Was this the intention of the founders of our Constitution? Is it democratic for nine unelected people who cannot be voted out of office to have the power to say what the Constitution means?

4 Although not elected, justices are accountable to the citizenry.

It should be clear by now that the actions of the federal courts make them political institutions. They exercise decisions about "who gets what, when, and how" just as the legislative and executive branches do. However, there is one essential difference between the justices and the officials in the other two branches of government. Federal judges are not elected. Further, these judges have lifetime appointments. The judiciary is the only one of the three branches of the federal government whose members hold policymaking powers without any direct accountability to the voters.[43]

There are, however, various ways in which the federal courts are indirectly checked by the other two branches of government. Congress has constitutional authority over the judiciary in several ways. First, it controls the purse strings; this includes the budget for the judicial branch. In addition, Article III of the U.S. Constitution grants Congress control over both the structure of the courts (only the Supreme Court is required by constitutional language) and over the jurisdiction of the courts. Congress determines which cases they can hear.[44] Finally, Congress can remove judges through the process of impeachment. These checks have not been used often, but this does not mean they have no effect.

One check that is used often is the judicial appointment process established by Article II, section 2, of the Constitution requiring the president to "nominate, and by and with the advice and consent of the senate, [to] appoint . . . judges of the Supreme Court" and of the district courts and courts of appeal. In choosing whom to nominate to the federal bench, presidents consider a variety of factors. These include qualities one would consider in filling any position: experience, skill, merit, and ethical standards. Other qualities come into play as well. Factors such as political party and political reward for past service may be considered. Further, contemporary presidents have considered ethnic, racial, and gender balances in their nominations. And finally, presidents consider a nominee's view of a judge's role and, to the degree it is discernable, the nominee's ideological position.

Exactly how these factors are combined depends largely on the individual president (see Table 6.3). President Jimmy Carter, for example, was the first president to make a deliberate effort to place women and minorities on the bench.[45] As Table 6.3 shows, other presidents have followed his lead. President Ronald Reagan, a Republican, was known for choosing judges who not only shared his partisan affiliation (a common trait for all presidential nominees) but also judges who shared his ideological perspective.[46]

Once a nominee is chosen, his or her name is submitted to the Senate. The influence of this body is greatest in district court appointments. Since the jurisdiction of district courts covers one and only one state, senators from that state have a particular interest in who fills the positions. So, when the name of a district court nominee arrives at the Senate Judiciary Committee, senators from the nominee's state are notified. If one of the senators disapproves of the nominee, no hearing is held on the nominee, a practice called **senatorial courtesy**. This encourages presidents to consult with senators before making district court nominations to avoid delay after the nomination is sent to the Senate.[47]

Senatorial courtesy A practice that sometimes occurs in the U.S. Senate when a federal district court nominee is appointed by the president. Once the name is submitted to the Senate Judiciary Committee, senators from the nominee's state are notified. If one of the senators disapproves of the nominee, no hearing is held.

Upon receiving the nomination, the Senate Judiciary Committee investigates the nominee and holds a public hearing to assess the nominee's qualifications. The senators look at the same criteria as the president. They are concerned with experience, intelligence, and judicial temperament and also with a judge's ideology and judicial philosophy. And while senators take their oversight responsibilities seriously, the large majority of presidential nominees to lower federal court are recommended by the Judiciary Committee and approved by the full Senate. Once appointed, federal justices serve for life.

The 103 justices who have served on the Supreme Court since 1789 have averaged over 16 years of service in that position. This is a longer term than any president except Franklin Delano Roosevelt and more years of service than most members of Congress. Considering the important political role these men and women play, it should be no surprise that their nominations have often been contested. One-fourth of all presidential nominations to the Supreme Court have failed.[48]

 Although not elected, justices are accountable to the citizenry.

Table 6.3 **U.S. District Court Appointees by Administration**

	W. Bush (%)	Clinton (%)	Bush (%)	Reagan (%)	Carter (%)
Occupation					
Politics/ Government	13.4	11.5	10.8	13.4	5.0
Judiciary	48.3	48.2	41.9	36.9	44.6
Large Law Firm (25+)	18.8	16.1	25.6	17.9	13.8
Medium Law Firm (5–24)	10.0	13.4	14.9	19.0	19.3
Small Law Firm (1–4)	6.1	8.2	4.8	10.0	13.0
Professor of Law	1.1	1.6	1.4	.7	.5
Experience					
Judicial	52.1	52.1	46.6	46.2	54.0
Prosecutorial	47.1	41.3	39.2	44.1	38.1
Neither	24.9	28.9	31.8	28.6	31.2
Gender					
Male	79.3	71.5	80.4	91.7	85.6
Female	20.7	28.5	19.6	8.3	14.4
Ethnicity/Race					
White	81.6	75.1	89.2	92.4	78.2
African American	6.9	17.4	6.8	2.1	13.9
Hispanic	10.0	5.9	4.0	4.8	6.9
Political Identification					
Democrat	8.0	87.5	6.1	4.8	91.1
Republican	83.1	6.2	88.5	91.7	4.5

Source: Reprinted from Judicature, the journal of the American Judicature Society. Goldman, Sheldon, Sara Schlavoni, Elliot Slotnick, © 2009.

Clearly, the judicial selection process operates as a check on who is appointed. Even when combined with other congressional checks, we must ask, is this enough? This question becomes even more important when we consider that many of the important questions that come before these men and women require the justices to apply laws that are not as clear as we might think to situations that are fraught with political implications.

3 Justices have a good deal of discretion when it comes to deciding controversial issues and questions.

When a conflict comes before a court we expect decisions to be made in accordance with the law, which is assumed to be an objective standard that gives a right answer. The answer should be the same regardless of one's political ideology. Whether a judge is a liberal or a conservative should not matter. Most of the time the work of trial and appellate courts meets this expectation. Of the thousands of cases processed by the federal courts each year, few raise political controversies. There are times, however, when the question of how a law applies to a set of circumstances is not so clear.

In a 2006 employment discrimination suit, for example, a federal trial court judge in the District of Columbia was asked to determine if a transgendered employee could raise a claim of sex discrimination based on gender identity, a question that the framers of the statute may never have considered (*Schroer v. Library of Congress*). The judge determined that Ms. Schroer could raise such a claim; the case went forward and she won her suit against her employer.

The vague language of the Constitution can raise even more questions. For instance, in 1989 the Supreme Court was asked to determine if a Texas law prohibiting the burning of the American flag infringed on First Amendment free speech rights. Five justices of the Court said the flag-burning statute was unconstitutional, while four justices disagreed, finding that the American flag was a unique symbol that must be protected (*Texas v. Johnson*). Which answer is "right"?

Divided opinions open up the possibility that the law alone is not all that is involved in judicial decision making. For the past 75 years, political scientists have tried to determine what other nonlegal factors may affect these decisions. When the law is not clear, what do judges use to help them reach decisions? Scholars have varied in their explanations, but many have found ideology to be a contributing factor. This raises questions about whether there is sufficient accountability, given that in a democracy people should have the ultimate role in making political decisions.[49]

2 The power of judges is limited by the inherent constraints of the judicial system.

Judicial power is restricted by limits specifically delineated in the Constitution, like jurisdiction, but also by constraints that are intrinsic to the context within which the federal courts operate. First, courts are reactive institutions; they must wait for someone to bring a conflict to them in the form of a case or controversy.

Once a case reaches a court, there are other limitations on the justices. Primary among these is the judiciary's lack of enforcement power. If a judge issues a decision that the affected public finds unacceptable, there is a chance that the decision may not be followed. Knowing this, federal courts must consider the impact on their legitimacy of issuing orders that are ignored on a regular basis. By and large, the only "power" that the federal courts have is the power of persuasion. They must be able to convince not only the other branches but also the general public of the reasonableness of their decisions if they are to maintain their authority.[50]

Consider, for example, the slow implementation of the Supreme Court decisions prohibiting school prayer.[51] Dolbeare and Hammond (1971) found that 10 years after the initial decisions, public schools across the county included Bible reading and prayer in their daily routines.[52] Following up on this study, McGuire (2008) found that there continues to be resistance to complying with Supreme Court decisions regarding organized religion in public schools, most particularly in southern school districts.[53] In a study of University of North Carolina undergraduates, McGuire found almost 25 percent of students from southern schools reported that organized prayer was still conducted in their schools.

Judicial activism Role adopted by a judge who is willing to use his or her authority to influence public policy, especially to protect rights established in the U.S. Constitution.

Judicial restraint Role adopted by a judge who sees his or her job as limited to making only those decisions that are essential to a resolution of the conflict before the court.

There is one final set of constraints that operate on justices, which is the concept of the role of judges. Judges generally adopt one of two role orientations, **judicial activism** or **judicial restraint**. These roles fall at opposite ends of a continuum. A judge who adopts a more restrained view sees his job as limited to making decisions that are essential to a resolution of the conflict before him. The more a decision involves questions of policymaking, the less likely he is to reach that decision. A classic example of restraint can be found in Justice Felix Frankfurter's dissenting opinion in *West Virginia Board of Education v. Barnette* (1943), a case in which the majority struck down a West Virginia statute that allowed schools to expel any student who would not recite the Pledge of Allegiance. In dissent, Justice Frankfurter found that no matter how much he personally disliked the legislation, the state legislature was acting within its power and the law should not be struck down.

Judges who are willing to be more activist in their decisions see the role of the judge differently. While they recognize the importance of democratic decision making, they are also concerned with the rights protected in the U.S. Constitution. When they find that these rights are being infringed by the legislature or the executive, as did the majority in *Barnette*, they are willing to use judicial power to provide this protection.[54]

Citizen support for the U.S. Supreme Court is high.

The limited democratic accountability of the Supreme Court justices might lead one to assume that the Court is distrusted by the American public, but this is not so. The Court certainly rates higher than Congress. As Figure 6.4 shows, slightly more than half of U.S. residents approve of the job that the justices of the Supreme Court are doing compared to under 20 percent who approve of the way Congress is handling its job.

While approval of the Court over the years has tended to rank higher than the other two branches of government, the statistics may even underestimate the level of support for the nation's high court.[55] Poll questions such as these tend to

Figure 6.4 **Approval Ratings for the U.S. Supreme Court and Congress**

The U.S. Supreme Court has substantially more approval from the American public than does the U.S. Congress.

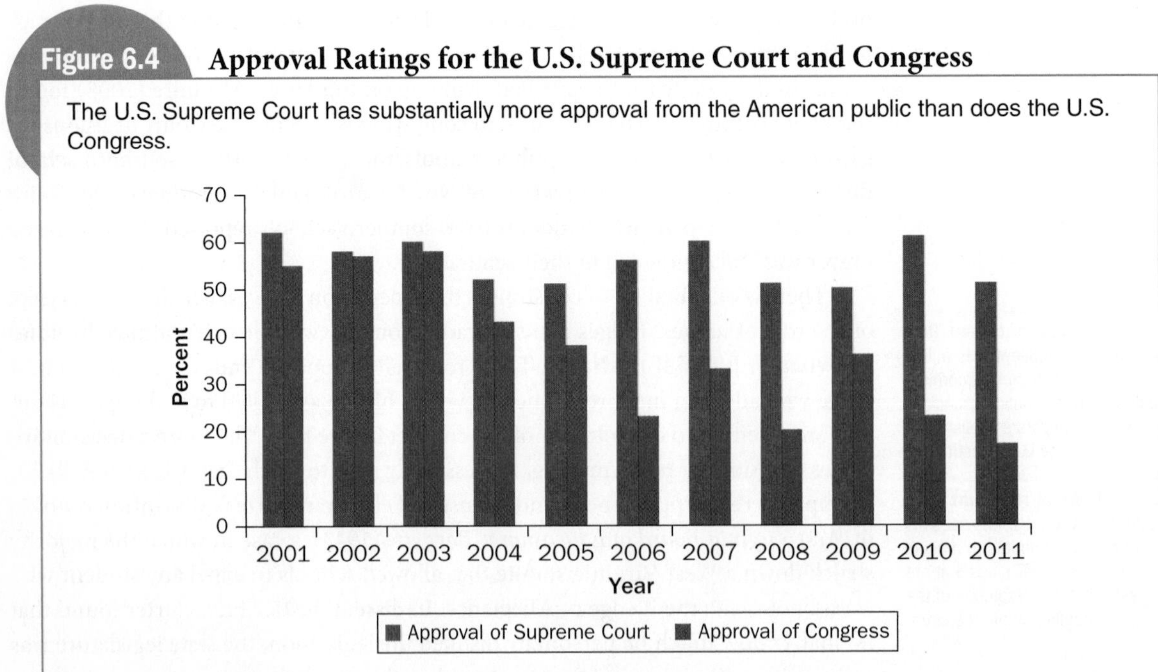

Source: Lydia Saad, "Supreme Court Starts the Term with 51% Approval Rating," Gallup, October 6, 2010. Available on-line at: http://www.gallup.com/poll/143414/Supreme-Court-Starts-Term-Approval.aspx
Frank Newport, "Congressional Approval at 17%," *Gallup*, April 21, 2011. Available online at: http://www.gallup.com/poll/147227/Congressional-Job-Approval.aspx

measure public support for what the Court is currently doing. What happens when researchers look at more deep-seated feelings of loyalty to the institution?

The Supreme Court provided an excellent opportunity to test this question in 2000 when it issued its opinion in *Bush v. Gore*. In this decision, the Court determined that the recount of presidential ballots being conducted in Florida could not continue, effectively ending the election. George W. Bush became the forty-third president of the United States. There was a great deal of controversy over this decision, and public opinion reflected this. "Among Republicans, approval of the Court between August 2000 and January 2001 jumped from 60 percent to 80 percent, according to a Gallup poll, but among Democrats it fell from 70 percent to 42 percent."[56]

An institution that must depend on goodwill to carry out its decisions would be in serious trouble if this were a true measure of public support. Recent scholarship, however, shows that loyalty to the Court changed little as a result of this decision. Survey respondents' answers to several questions that assess deep-seated commitment to the Court as an institution showed that between 1995 and 2001 loyalty to the Supreme Court actually increased by a small but statistically significant percentage.[57] It appears that even when citizens do not agree with the Court's decisions, general support for the institution does not waver. On the whole, Americans are comfortable with the role that the U.S. Supreme Court plays in the government.

CONCLUSION

This chapter began with a central question: What is the proper balance between maintaining an independent judiciary that is free to follow the rule of law and a judiciary that is held accountable as a policymaker in a democratic nation? Now, we may have enough information to begin to answer this question. We have seen that the rule of law is an essential attribute of a democracy. Citizens must know that laws exist to guide public behavior and that these laws will be applied equally to all. Ultimately, it is the job of the courts to ensure that this occurs.

The institutional structure of the federal courts and the lifetime appointments of federal judges help to ensure that judges are independent and not swayed by popular political opinion when resolving the conflicts that come before them. Applying the law to these conflicts is not always an easy job, however, for the law is not always clear. Some of the conflicts that come before the nation's courts reflect aspects of the law that are ambiguous and require more discretion on the part of judges.

There has been public reaction in recent years to what some perceive as an over-reaching judiciary in such cases. By and large these attacks are prompted by disagreement with the substance of certain court decisions, leading some to ask whether unelected, lifetime appointees should be making these decisions in a democracy. On the other hand, a different sort of challenge to a democracy arises when such attacks are aimed at the institution of the judiciary, an institution that is essential to maintaining the rule of law.

THEIR LIST

An Insider's View

NANCY GERTNER

Federal Judge, U.S. District Court of Massachusetts

Judge Nancy Gertner was appointed to the U.S. District Court, District of Massachusetts, by President Bill Clinton in 1994. She received her B.A. from Barnard, her M.A. in Political Science from Yale, and her J.D. from Yale Law School. As an attorney in private practice for over 20 years, Judge Gertner was well known for her work in criminal defense and civil rights. In 2008, she was honored by the ABA's Section of Individual Rights and Responsibilities as a recipient of the Thurgood Marshall award. Recently I had the opportunity to visit with Judge Gertner in her chambers at the Moakley Federal Courthouse in Boston. Judge Gertner spoke about the federal judiciary, reflecting in particular on the three most important things she, as someone who has devoted her life to the law, thinks people should know about the American court system.

Judge Gertner spoke first about the place of the federal courts in relation to the states. She noted that while the federal courts are courts of limited jurisdiction, "it's a limited jurisdiction that has been growing as the national power grows. . . . Although there's a federal system and a state system there are myriad examples of the federal court dealing with state issues." For example, cases involving state actions can come to the federal courts through habeas corpus petitions or discrimination statutes or as challenges under the U.S. Constitution. Further, federal judges interpret state law when presented with diversity of jurisdiction cases. The line between federal and state authority is not always so clear.

The absence of a clear delineation between federal and state authority is further complicated by the three-tiered structure of the federal courts. This implies a hierarchy, with the cases moving from the trial courts up to the Supreme Court; the law as defined by the Supreme Court is then applied by the lower courts. While this is generally the way the process works, Judge Gertner noted ways in which this simplified view can be misleading. In speaking of some Supreme Court opinions, for example, she noted that they "have proven to be very difficult to unpack. What you find is a lot of Supreme Court decisions on these issues and local courts virtually not knowing what the next step will be." Further, the model implies that federal law is nationalized and consistent throughout the United States. However, Judge Gertner remarked, "individual courts of appeals are actually quite independent," and "a gun case in Montana looks different than a gun case in Massachusetts." When one considers the few cases that the U.S. Supreme Court takes every year, the system may not be as nationalized as we always think.

As a lifetime appointee to the federal bench, Judge Gertner also spoke about the basic assumption that federal judges are not accountable. While they may not be directly accountable through elections as judges in some states are, she said, "with 24/7 media coverage I think we're all accountable in a way I don't think we've been before. And while . . . you're not going to do things or not do things because of what the impact will be on the press coverage . . . there is no question that it has an impact. . . . And that's not a bad thing." Once again, a clear line in theory is somewhat blurred in actual practice.

Judge Gertner's experience not only provides insight into the operation of the federal courts but it also gives her a wealth of cases from which to draw in providing examples. As proof that the decisions of federal courts are both vital and interesting, Judge Gertner's docket contains approximately fifty cases in which record companies are suing students for Internet piracy under the 1998 Digital Millennium Copyright Act (DMCA). A hearing was recently scheduled on the constitutionality of the act's implementation, and several students moved to allow narrowcasting of this hearing to viewers across the Internet. Judge Gertner granted their motion and the record companies appealed. Both questions, whether narrowcasting should be allowed and whether the implementation of the DMCA is constitutional, are of vital interest for future generations.

Studies on the courts have determined that familiarity does not breed contempt. Those who are familiar with courts are more likely to be supportive of these institutions.[58] Informed citizens will not always approve of the job that courts do, but they will be able to distinguish between criticism of policy and criticism of the institution. The ability to do so is a sign of a mature citizenry and is essential to guaranteeing the independence of the courts that is so essential to maintaining the rule of law.

In 2005, retired Associate Justice Sandra Day O'Connor spoke of the dangers of politically charged attacks on the judiciary. "That is why, [Alexander] Hamilton says, judicial independence is especially important in the American system, but as the Founders knew, statutes and constitutions don't protect judicial independence—people do[.]"[59]

YOUR LIST REVISITED

At the beginning of the chapter you were asked to think about what you might include on your own list of the Top 10 Most Important Things to Know About the Judiciary. Now that you have read the chapter, take a moment to revisit your list. What, if anything, would you change about your list? Do you agree or disagree with the chapter list constructed by the author? What might you add or delete? Why?

KEY TERMS

Adversarial process 128
Amicus curiae (friend of the court) brief 131
Appellate courts 127
Appellate jurisdiction 128
Associate Justices 132
Briefs 131
Cert pool 131
Chief Justice 132
Circuits 128
Civil law 128
Civil law regime 124
Common law system 124
Compensatory (or actual) damages 124
Concurring opinion 130
Courts 124
Criminal law 128
Dissenting opinion 130
District courts 127
Diversity of jurisdiction 125
Equitable remedy 133
Federal question 125
Judicial activism 139
Judicial restraint 139
Judicial review 134
Jurisdiction 125
Majority opinion 130
Original jurisdiction 127
Plaintiff 124
Precedents 124
Punitive damages 124
Rule of Four 131
Senatorial courtesy 136
Solicitor General 132
Stare decisis 124
Trial courts 127
U.S. Courts of Appeal 128
U.S. Court of Appeals for the Federal Circuit 128
U.S. Supreme Court 130
Writ of certiorari 131

CHAPTER REVIEW QUESTIONS

10 How does a common law system differ from a civil law system?

9 How does federal court jurisdiction differ from state court jurisdiction?

8 How is the federal court system organized?

7 In what ways is the U.S. Supreme Court unique?

6 Describe two ways in which the power of the federal courts has grown since 1789.

5 In what ways do the courts apply law that comes from all three branches of government?

4 What checks are provided in the U.S. Constitution against abuses of judicial power?

3 Describe the appointment process for federal judges.

2 What are the inherent limits to judicial power?

1 Are Americans generally supportive of the U.S. Supreme Court? Why or why not?

SUGGESTED READINGS

- Baum, Lawrence. *American Courts: Process and Policy*, 6th ed. New York: Houghton Mifflin, 2007.
- Bork, Robert. *The Tempting of America*. New York: Free Press, 1997.
- Cardozo, Benjamin. *The Nature of the Judicial Process*. New Haven, CT: Yale University Press, [1921] 1960.
- Carter, Lief, and Thomas Burke. *Reason in Law*, 8th ed. New York: Pearson Longman, 2009.
- Lewis, Anthony. *Gideon's Trumpet*. New York: Vintage, [1964] 1989.
- O'Brien, David. *Storm Center*, 9th ed. New York: Norton, 2011.
- Rosenberg, Gerald. *The Hollow Hope: Can Courts Bring About Social Change?* 2nd ed. Chicago: University of Chicago Press, 2008.
- Segal, Jeffrey, and Harold Spaeth. *The Supreme Court and the Attitudinal Model*. New York: Cambridge University Press, 1993.
- Slotnick, Elliot, ed. *Judicial Politics: Readings from Judicature*. Washington, DC: CQ Press, 2005.
- Williams, Juan. *Thurgood Marshall: American Revolutionary*. New York: Three Rivers Press, 2000.

SUGGESTED FILMS

- *Twelve Angry Men* (1957)
- *Witness for the Prosecution* (1958)
- *Anatomy of a Murder* (1959)
- *Judgment at Nuremberg* (1961)
- *To Kill a Mockingbird* (1963)
- *A Man for All Seasons* (1966)
- *The Verdict* (1982)
- *A Few Good Men* (1992)
- *Philadelphia* (1993)
- *Erin Brokovich* (2000)

SUGGESTED WEBSITES

- **American Bar Association:** http://www.abanet.org/
- **Federal Courts:** http://www.uscourts.gov/
- **Findlaw for Legal Professionals:** http://lp.findlaw.com/
- **Law School Admissions Council:** http://lsac.org/
- **Legal Information Institute at Cornell Law School:** http://www.law.cornell.edu/
- ***New York Times* on the Supreme Court of the United States:** http://topics.nytimes.com/topics/reference/timestopics/organizations/s/supreme_court/index.html
- **Oyez—U.S. Supreme Court Media at Northwestern University:** http://www.oyez.org/
- **Supreme Court of the United States Blog:** http://www.scotusblog.com
- **Supreme Court of the United States:** http://www.supremecourtus.gov/
- ***Washington Post* Courts Site:** http://www.washingtonpost.com/wp-dyn/nation/courts/

ENDNOTES

[1]Many scholars have looked at the interplay between popular culture and the law. See the works of Michael Asimow of the UCLA Law School. For a discussion of the challenge that popular culture creates for the law, see, Kimberlianne Podlas, "Should We Blame Judge Judy? The Messages TV Courtrooms Send Viewers, *Judicature* 86: 38–43 (2000).
[2]Richard Posner, *How Judges Think* (Boston: Harvard University Press, 2008), p. 13.
[3]"Courts" and "judiciary" are used interchangeably in this text.
[4]Further, it should be noted that even in countries with highly developed judicial systems, alternative modes of dispute resolution also exist.
[5]For a discussion of the relationship between judicial independence and the rule of law, see Stephen B. and Barry Friedman, eds., *Judicial Independence at the Crossroads: An Interdisciplinary Approach* (Thousand Oaks, CA: Sage Publications, 2002). Individual country studies can be found in Pilar Domingo, "Judicial Independence: The Politics of the Supreme Court in Mexico," *Journal of Latin American Studies* 32: 705–735 (2000); Albert P. Melone, "The Struggle for Judicial Independence and the Transition Toward Democracy in Bulgaria," *Communist and Post-Communist Studies* 29: 231–243 (1996); and E.M. Salzberger and Paul Fenn, "Judicial Independence: Some Evidence from the English Court of Appeal," *The Journal of Law and Economics* 42: 831–847 (1999).
[6]Tim Koopmans, *Courts and Political Institutions: A Comparative View* (Cambridge: UK Cambridge University Press, 2003).
[7]Findlaw Legal Dictionary available online at: http://dictionary.findlaw.com/definition/damage.html.
[8]In a work that looks at courts in the United States and Europe, Koopmans (2003, 1) points out another similarity between the courts of different nations: "I hope to show that it is far from easy to determine the borderline between the scope of judicial and political activities." The challenges posed by courts making policy in a democracy are not unique to the United States.
[9]See Westlaw's law.com for a definition of common law. www.dictionary.law.com.
[10]See Westlaw's law.com for a definition of civil law. www .dictionary. law.com.
[11]William Tetley, "Mixed Jurisdictions: Common Law vs. Civil Law (Codified and Uncodified)," Unif. *Law Review and La. Law Review* (published in three parts, 1999–2003). Also available online at: www.mcgill.ca/files/maritimelaw/mixedjur.pdf (accessed June 3, 2011).
[12]For a discussion of the ways in which civil and common law systems are more similar than this general distinction might indicate, see Mary Garvey Algero, "The Courses of Law and the Value of Precedent: A Comparative and Empirical Study of a Civil Law State in a Common Law Nation,"*Louisiana Law Review* 65: 775–822 (2005).
[13]Damages in diversity cases must exceed $75,000 to be filed in federal court (U.S. Code Title 28, Part IV, Ch. 85 §1332(a)).
[14]State data also include cases from Puerto Rico. Federal data also include cases from Puerto Rico as well as Guam, the Northern Mariana Islands, and the Virgin Islands.
[15]This "three tier" structure is also used in thirty-nine states, with trial courts being divided between courts of general jurisdiction, having authority to hear a wide variety of cases, and courts of limited jurisdiction. Eleven states have only trial courts and a supreme court.
[16]This section describes Article III courts, those established pursuant to Article III of the Constitution. There are also Article I courts, those that Congress may establish under power granted

in Article I, section 8, of the Constitution. Article I courts have limited jurisdiction and the judges may be chosen differently than Article III judges; further, they serve for a limited period of time. Article I courts include bankruptcy courts, Territorial Courts, the U.S. Court of Appeals for the Armed Forces, the U.S. Court of Appeals for Veterans Claims, the U.S. Court of Federal Claims, and the U.S. Tax Court.

[17]Federal Judge Richard Matsch ordered the trial be moved from Oklahoma to a federal district court in Colorado to avoid bias in jury selection.

[18]Civil law, a description of a general kind of law, should not be confused with a civil law regime, a legal system, discussed above.

[19]Jesse McKinley, "Jury Vindicates Andrew Lloyd Webber," *New York Times*, December 16, 1998, available online at: http://www.nytimes.com/1998/12/16/nyregion/jury-vindicates-andrew-lloyd-webber.html.

[20]Most cases in district court are disposed of without trials. In FY 2008, trials took place in 2 percent of civil cases and for less than 1 percent of criminal defendants.

[21]There is also a Federal Circuit. This is a unique court that hears appeals from courts throughout the country on specialized topics, including patents and government personnel claims.

[22]Courts of Appeal cannot set aside findings of fact from the lower court unless they are "clearly erroneous" (Federal Rules of Civil Procedure 53(a)(6)).

[23]*United States v. Ernest Romond Gibbs, Jr.*, 2007 U.S. App. LEXIS 15320,*; 237 Fed. Appx. 550.

[24]*United States v. Virginia*, a 1996 Supreme Court case challenging the single-sex admissions policy of Virginia Military Institute, provides an example of all three types of opinions. This case and others cited in this chapter can be found at Findlaw, Cornell.edu or Oyez. Complete URLs for these sites are at the end of this chapter.

[25]*Gratzer v. Bollinger* 529 U.S. 244 (2003).

[26]The Court decided approximately 170 cases under its original jurisdiction in the first 200 years of its existence [Anne-Marie Carstens, "Lurking in the Shadows of Judicial Process: Special Masters in the Supreme Court's Original Jurisdiction of Cases," *Minnesota Law Review* 86: 625–725, p. 639. (2002)]. These cases take little of the Court's time since special masters are appointed to hear and decide the preliminaries on these conflicts. See Carstens for a discussion of this process.

[27]For further discussion, see for instance Melanie Wachtell and David Thompson, *An Empirical Analysis of Supreme Court Certiorari Petition Procedures* 16 Geo. Mason U. L. Rev. 237, 241 (2009).

[28]Each justice has four clerks (with the Chief Justice having a fifth) who work in their chambers assisting the justices in their duties of researching and writing. Most clerks serve for one year; these positions are highly sought after by the most promising law school graduates from the nation's most elite institutions. Over the last 30 years, almost 40 percent of the clerks were graduates of Harvard or Yale law schools [David O'Brien, *Storm Center* 8th ed. (New York: Norton, 2008), p. 136]. See Artemus Ward and David Weiden, *Sorcerers' Apprentices: 100 Years of Law Clerks at the United States Supreme Court* (New York: New York University Press, 2006) for an in-depth review of the role of law clerks in the Supreme Court.

[29]These numbers have dropped substantially in the last 20 years [Erwin Chemerinsky, "The Shrinking Docket," *Trial* 32: 71–72 (1996)].

[30]Gregory Caldeira and JohnWright, "Organized Interests and Agenda Setting in the U.S. Supreme Court," *American Political Science Review* 82: 1109–1127 (1988).

[31]*Roe* was not overturned in this case, although the Supreme Court allowed more restrictive abortion regulations to be implemented.

[32]You can listen to oral arguments online at Oyez.com. Oral arguments are not televised, however. The justices allow no cameras in the courtroom.

[33]The number of justices on the U.S. Supreme Court is determined by Congress. The number has changed throughout U.S history, but has been set at nine since the post–Civil War period.

[34]See Lincoln Kaplan, *The Tenth Justice: The Solicitor General and the Rule of Law* (New York: Knopf, 1987) and Richard Pacelle, *Between Law and Politics: The Solicitor General and the Structuring of Race, Gender, and Reproductive Rights* (College Station, TX: Texas A&M Press, 2003) for an in-depth discussion of the Office of the Solicitor General.

[35]*Federal Express Corporation v. Holowecki* (2008).

[36]Congressional passage in January 2009 of an amendment to Title VII of the Civil Rights Act of 1964 in response to the Supreme Court's decision in *Ledbetter v. Goodyear Tire and Rubber* (2007) provides a recent example. Scholarly analysis of such judicial-legislative dialogue can be found in Miller and Barnes (2004), especially articles by Lawrence Baum and Lori Huasegger ("The Supreme Court and Congress: Reconsidering the Relationship") and by Thomas Burke ("The Judicial Implementation of Statutes: Three Stories about Courts and the Americans with Disabilities Act") in Mark Miller and Jeb Barnes, *Makingpolicy, Making Law: An Interbranch Perspective* (Washington, DC: Georgetown University Press, 2004).

[37]See Article III of the U.S. Constitution.

[38]The effectiveness of the *Brown* decision and implementation by the United States district courts has been debated. See Rosenberg (1991).

[39]See C. K.Rowland, "The Federal District Courts," in John B. Gates and Charles A. Johnson, *The American Courts: A Critical Assessment* (Washington, DC: CQ Press, 1991) for a thorough discussion of the work of federal district courts.

[40]Max Farrand, ed., *The Records of the Federal Convention of 1787* (New Haven, CT: Yale University Press, 1911). Madison's *Notes* are also available online at: http://avalon.law.yale.edu/subject_menus/debcont.asp.

[41]O'Brien, 2008, 31

[42]Figure 6.3 also shows that the Supreme Court has always been more willing to strike down state statutes than federal statutes.

[43]This could also be said about the federal bureaucracy within the executive branch, although the bureaucracy is ultimately accountable to the president.

[44]There is one exception to this statement: The original jurisdiction of the Supreme Court is established in the Constitution.
[45]Sheldon Goldman, *Picking Federal Judges: Lower Court Selection from Roosevelt through Reagan* (New Haven, CT: Yale University Press, 1997), p. 282.
[46]O'Brien, 2008, 71. There have been numerous works written on the judicial selection process. For the district courts, see Goldman 1997; for the courts of appeal, see Donal R. Songer, Reginald S. Sheehan, and Susan B. Haire, *Continuity and Change on the United States Courts of Appeals* (Ann Arbor, MI: University of Michigan Press, 2000); for the Supreme Court, see Christine Nemacheck, *Strategic Selection: Presidential Nomination of Supreme Court Justices from Herbert Hoover through George W. Bush* (Charlottesville, VA: University of Virginia Press, 2007).
[47]It should be noted that this process has varied over time, sometimes being bipartisan and other times allowing only the majority-party senators to participate in the blue-slip process.
[48]Over the last 20 years, there has also been increasing conflict over nominees to lower courts. See Sheldon Goldman, "Assessing the Senate Judicial Confirmation Process: The Index of Obstruction and Delay," *Judicature* 86: 251–257 (2003); O'Brien 2008, 42.
[49]See Jeffrey Segal and Harold Spaeth, *The Supreme Court and the Attitudinal Model* (New York: Cambridge University Press,1993) for the attitudinal theory, Lee Epstein and Jack Knight, *The Choices Justices Make* (Washington, DC: CQ Press,1988) on strategic decision making, and Cornell Clayton and Howard Gillman, *Supreme Court Decision-making* (Chicago: University of Chicago Press,1993) for a deeper look at historical institutionalism.
[50]For a comprehensive study of compliance, see Charles Johnson and Bradley Canon, *Judicial Policies: Implementation and Impact* (Washington, DC: CQ Press,1984).
[51]*Engel v. Vitale* in 1962 prohibited formal Bible reading in public schools, while *Abington v. Schempp* (1963) found organized prayer in public schools to be unconstitutional.
[52]Kenneth Dolbeare and Phillip Hammond, *The School Prayer Decision: From Court Policy to Local Practice* (Chicago: University of Chicago Press, 1971).
[53]Kevin McGuire, "Public Schools, Religious Establishment, and the United States Supreme Court: An Examination of Policy Compliance,"*American Politics Research* 37: 50–74 (2009).
[54]For a discussion of the complexity of the concept of judicial activism, see Lief Carter and Thomas Burke's description of Canon's six dimensions of activism in *Reason in Law*, Updated 7th ed. (New York: Longman, 2007), p. 117.
[55]Unfortunately, almost no research has been done on support for the federal courts at either the district or circuit levels. Research on state courts may give us some insight into public support for federal trial courts (Sara C. Benesh, "Understanding Public Confidence in American Courts," *Journal of Politics*, 68 (3, 2006): 697–707.
[56]Jeffrey Rosen citing Howard Gillman in "A Majority of One," *New York Times Magazine*, June 3, 2001, available online at: http://www.nytimes.com/2001/06/03/magazine/a-majority-of-one.html.
[57]James Gibson, Gregory A. Caldeira, and Lester Kenyatta Spence, "The Supreme Court and the U.S. Presidential Election of 2000: Wounds, Self Inflicted or Otherwise?" *British Journal of Political Science*, 33 (4, 2003): 535–556.
[58]Benesh, 2006; Gibson et al., 2003
[59]Transcript accessed at floridabar.org.

Chapter 7

CIVIL LIBERTIES AND CIVIL RIGHTS

Top Ten List

10 The nature of the separation of church and state provided by the establishment clause of the First Amendment has been debated since the founding.

9 The government places limits on the free exercise of religion.

8 Liberties are not absolute; freedom of expression may be limited in several instances, including times of crisis.

7 Expression that is libelous, slanderous, or obscene may be limited.

6 The right to privacy is inferred from the text of the Constitution.

5 The Constitution includes protections for criminal suspects, defendants, and convicts.

4 The equal protection clause of the Constitution forbids racial and ethnic discrimination.

3 Civil rights laws prohibit racial and ethnic discrimination in commerce.

2 Gender discrimination sometimes violates the Constitution and civil rights laws.

1 Some carefully designed affirmative action programs are constitutional.

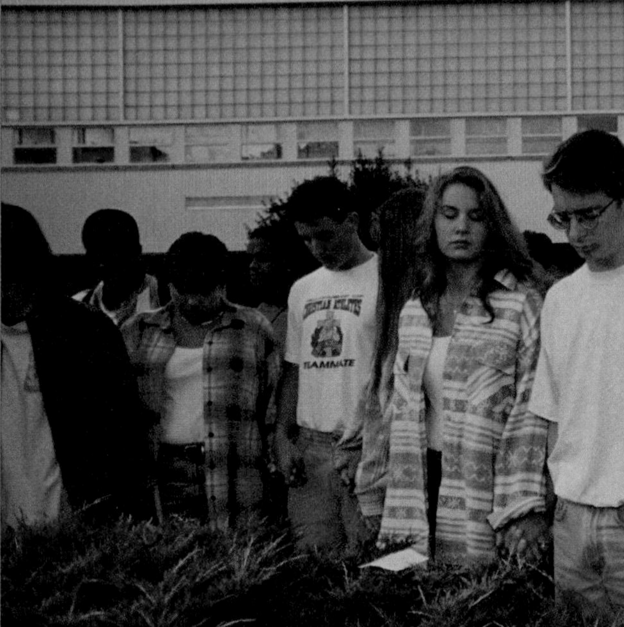

Shown here, students at a high school in Annandale, Virginia share a moment of prayer outside of the school. Education officials often face a dilemma when it comes to religion. If they ban religious practice, they may be accused of curtailing civil liberties. If they allow religious practice, they may be accused of supporting a particular religion. The difficulty of the school bureaucrats mirrors the difficulty that judges have had in dealing with this issue and others related to civil liberties and civil rights.

YOUR LIST

Before you read this chapter, take a few moments to think about what you might include on a list of the Top 10 Most Important Things to Know About Civil Liberties and Civil Rights. At the end of the chapter you will be asked to compare and contrast your list with the one supplied in this chapter.

INTRODUCTION

You apply to law school, but you're rejected. A friend of yours who has lower grades and test scores, but who is a member of a minority, is accepted. Is that fair? Is that legal? If you apply to medical school, can the admissions office take your race or gender into account? Do you have the right to pray in school? Can you stop a racist from going on TV to try to persuade young people to become bigots? If you are unsure about the answers to these questions, you are not alone. Citizens of the United States are guaranteed many civil liberties and civil rights. But the biggest problem with enforcing these rights and liberties is that many people don't know what they are.

One study found that only one in four Americans can name more than one of the five freedoms guaranteed by the First Amendment, while more than half could name at least two members of the fictional Simpson family. [1] The study also found that more people could name the three "American Idol" judges than First Amendment rights![2]

In this chapter, we will explore some of the basic freedoms Americans enjoy, or what are often called civil liberties and civil rights. **Civil liberties** are constitutional and legal guarantees of people's freedoms. They are freedoms that people enjoy and that government cannot suppress. The most well-known are those contained in the Bill of Rights, which enumerates some of the most important liberties we enjoy (see Table 7.1). **Civil rights**, by contrast, are constitutional guarantees of equality and rights of citizenship. They guarantee equal protection under the law, so that people cannot be discriminated against based on demographic characteristics such as race, gender, or age. These rights stem primarily from the Fourteenth Amendment and from laws passed by Congress.[3]

Civil liberties Constitutional and legal guarantees of people's freedom.

Civil rights Constitutional and legal guarantees of equality and rights of citizenship.

Understanding the distinction between liberties and rights and becoming familiar with some of the basic liberties and rights Americans enjoy is only the first step. As you study the **First Amendment rights** of freedom of religion, speech, press, and peaceful assembly, it will quickly become clear to you that not only is there widespread disagreement about what each clause means, but our interpretation has also changed over time. This is true not just of the First Amendment, but of all the rights and liberties we enjoy. Throughout the chapter we will come back to this issue and ask you to think about how you would interpret these rights and liberties and how they might be reframed in the future.

First Amendment rights Freedom of religion, speech, press, and peaceful assembly.

The nature of the separation of church and state provided by the establishment clause of the First Amendment has been debated since the founding.

In a letter to a Baptist congregation in Connecticut in 1802, President Thomas Jefferson declared that there is "a wall of separation between church and state." It is one of his most cited lines (many people think, incorrectly, that it is a quotation

Table 7.1 **Key Liberties and Rights Protected in the Constitution and Bill of Rights**

Article/ Amendment	Text of Article/Amendment	Explanation
Article I, section 9	The privilege of the Writ of Habeas Corpus shall not be suspended, unless when in Cases of Rebellion or Invasion the public Safety may require it. No Bill of Attainder or ex post facto Law shall be passed.	Provides for writ of habeas corpus—written orders issued that determine if a person is being unlawfully detained Prohibits bills of attainder—legislative act declaring a person/ group guilty of crime and punishing them without a trial Prohibits ex post facto law—criminal law applied to acts committed prior to passage of a law
Article III, section 2	The Trial of all Crimes, except in Cases of Impeachment, shall be by Jury; and such Trial shall be held in the State where the said Crimes shall have been committed.	Guarantees trial by jury in state where crime is committed
Article III, section 3	Treason against the United States, shall consist only in levying War against them, or in adhering to their Enemies, giving them Aid and Comfort. The Congress shall have power to declare the Punishment of Treason, but no Attainder of Treason shall work Corruption of Blood, or Forfeiture except during the Life of the Person attainted.	Defines treason and discusses punishment
First Amendment	Congress shall make no law respecting an establishment of religion, or prohibiting the free exercise thereof; or abridging the freedom of speech, or of the press; or the right of the people peaceably to assemble, and to petition the Government for a redress of grievances.	Guarantees freedoms of speech, press, and assembly
Second Amendment	A well regulated Militia, being necessary to the security of a free State, the right of the people to keep and bear Arms, shall not be infringed.	Provides for the right to bear arms
Third Amendment	No Soldier shall, in time of peace be quartered in any house, without the consent of the Owner, nor in time of war, but in a manner to be prescribed by law.	Prevents forced housing of soldiers without the owner's consent

(continued)

Table 7.1 **(Continued)**

Article/ Amendment	Text of Article/Amendment	Explanation
Fourth Amendment	The right of the people to be secure in their persons, houses, papers, and effects, against unreasonable searches and seizures, shall not be violated, and no Warrants shall issue, but upon probable cause, supported by Oath or affirmation, and particularly describing the place to be searched, and the persons or things to be seized.	Prohibits unreasonable search and seizure
Fifth Amendment	No person shall be held to answer for a capital, or otherwise infamous crime, unless on a presentment or indictment of a Grand Jury, except in cases arising in the land or naval forces, or in the Militia, when in actual service in time of War or public danger; nor shall any person be subject for the same offence to be twice put in jeopardy of life or limb; nor shall be compelled in any criminal case to be a witness against himself, nor be deprived of life, liberty, or property, without due process of law; nor shall private property be taken for public use, without just compensation.	Forbids trial except after grand jury indictment, double jeopardy, punishment without due process, compelling an individual to be a witness against him- or herself, and the government from taking private property for public use without just compensation
Sixth Amendment	In all criminal prosecutions, the accused shall enjoy the right to a speedy and public trial, by an impartial jury of the State and district wherein the crime shall have been committed, which district shall have been previously ascertained by law, and to be informed of the nature and cause of the accusation; to be confronted with the witnesses against him; to have compulsory process for obtaining witnesses in his favor, and to have the Assistance of Counsel for his defense.	Provides for a right to a speedy, public trial for criminal offenses; trial by jury
Seventh Amendment	In Suits at common law, where the value in controversy shall exceed twenty dollars, the right of trial by jury shall be preserved, and no fact tried by a jury, shall be otherwise re-examined in any Court of the United States, than according to the rules of the common law.	Ensures a trial by jury in civil cases
Eighth Amendment	Excessive bail shall not be required, nor excessive fines imposed, nor cruel and unusual punishments inflicted.	Prohibits excessive bail

from the Constitution). A couple of days after writing it, he rode down Pennsylvania Avenue to the House of Representatives, where he attended a Congressional prayer service, something he occasionally did during his presidency. Jefferson's mixed message about the proper relationship between the government and religion foreshadowed the ambivalence and lack of clarity that has characterized American constitutional law regarding the **establishment clause**, the First Amendment provision that provides for the separation of church and state.

Establishment clause First Amendment provision that requires separation of church and state.

The first clause of the First Amendment prohibits Congress from passing any law that would "establish" a religion. So it is clear that the Constitution bans any sort of official church of the United States. But it isn't clear just how far this ban goes. Does it mean that the government cannot give any aid to religion at all? Many people argue that the First Amendment has put into place a high, impermeable barrier between church and state, while others argue that the government may fund all sorts of religious institutions and activities, so long as it does not favor particular religious groups. The Supreme Court has repeatedly tried, and failed, to write clear guidelines for government officials to decide how much, if any, taxpayer money can be spent in support of religion.

We do know that some amount of support of religion will be allowed by the courts. For instance, chaplains are employed and supplied by the U.S. military, in prisons, and even in Congress. Government employees receive a paid holiday on Thanksgiving, a day on which the president ritually proclaims the nation's thanks to God. Most important, at least from a financial point of view, religious institutions such as churches and temples usually are not required to pay any property tax. Many of them would not be able to stay open if they had to pay the same tax as other property owners.[5]

However, courts have forbidden the government from providing other kinds of support to religion. This issue has been especially contentious in the field of education. Perhaps the most controversial question in this area has been that of the place of prayer in the classroom. Up until the 1960s, the public schools in New York (like most states) required teachers to begin the day with a prayer. The Board of Education adopted a prayer which it termed "nondenominational," that is, acceptable to all religions. ("Almighty God, we acknowledge our dependence upon Thee, and we beg Thy blessings upon us, our parents, our teachers and our country. Amen.") Any children who did not want to participate would be allowed to remain silent. But some students and parents objected. Why should the state be paying teachers to lead any prayers? Wasn't this a violation of the Constitution's ban on establishment of religion?

The Supreme Court agreed that it was. In the case of *Engle v. Vitale*,[6] in 1962, Justice Hugo Black ruled that "when the power, prestige and financial support of government is placed behind a particular religious belief, the indirect coercive pressure upon religious minorities to conform to the prevailing officially approved religion is plain." Prayers led by teachers were an instance of established religion and therefore unconstitutional.

Over the next decades the Court ruled that practices such as posting the Ten Commandments, setting aside time for silent prayer, and prayers at graduations and football games in public schools were also violations of the establishment clause. Aid to private schools that were sponsored by religions was also ruled unconstitutional, although some noneducational aid, such as transportation and medical care, was allowed.[7]

As school districts lost one lawsuit after another because of religious activities taking place in their schools, principals and superintendents figured that the best way to avoid legal trouble was to simply ban these activities. But sometimes it is not clear if a practice is an official support of religion or a free exercise of it. In truth, a practice can be both an instance of free exercise and of establishment.

In 1996, The Good News Club applied to the Milford, New York, school district for permission to hold after-school Bible study classes for children in the school building. Other, nonreligious groups (such as the Boy and Girl Scouts) commonly got permission for these types of activities. However, the superintendent turned down the Good News Club, since he was afraid that the use of a government building would involve taxpayer funds, and the location of the class might imply endorsement of the Bible club by the school. The club then sued, and the Supreme Court agreed with the Bible club. If a school opens its classrooms up for after-school activities to various groups, it cannot refuse to do so for religious groups. The Court ruled that to ban them would be an unconstitutional infringement on their freedom to meet and discuss their views.[8]

This case is a good example of the dilemma that education officials sometimes face regarding establishment of religion. No matter what they do they will get sued! Allow the club to meet, and they will be accused of supporting religion. Ban it, and they will be accused of curtailing civil liberties. The difficulty of the school bureaucrats reflects the difficulty that judges have had in dealing with the establishment clause. After dozens of Supreme Court decisions, we still do not have clear guidelines as to how much support the government may give to religion. Rather than a "wall" of separation between church and state, we have a blurry moving line.

The government places limits on the free exercise of religion.

In addition to prohibiting an "establishment of religion," the First Amendment also contains what is known as the **free exercise clause**, which provides protection for practicing the religion of one's choice. Today, few Americans believe that the government can punish people for expressing their religious views. However, there are disputes when it comes to religious practices. Religions sometimes mandate activities (sacrifice of animals, for example) that many people find objectionable. If a majority want to ban such a practice, or force believers to perform acts they see as sinful (such

Free exercise clause First Amendment protection of the right to practice the religion of one's choice.

as serving in the military or paying taxes), does the free exercise clause protect the freedom of the believers to act or not act as their religion commands? In most cases, the answer is *no*, but there are important exceptions.

In the case of *Wisconsin v. Yoder* (1972), a religious group argued that their children should be exempt from the compulsory school law.[9] The Amish believe that they should live apart from American society, with its materialist, self-centered temptations. They avoid the use of electricity, internal combustion engines, and modern farm machinery. As you might expect, children with these sorts of beliefs can face a tough time in school. Their dress, their manner of speaking, their lack of familiarity with music, movies, television, and sports make them the targets of ridicule and peer pressure.

Wisconsin, like all states, has a compulsory school law. The Amish agreed that their kids should attend public school in order to learn how to read, write, and do fundamental math but that anything taught beyond eighth grade was not just superfluous, but potentially harmful. They argued that to force them to send their children to high school would be devastating to their religion and their children and that they should be exempt from the Wisconsin law. In 1972, Chief Justice Burger wrote an opinion of the Court that supported the Amish. Wisconsin's requirement of "compulsory formal education after the eighth grade would gravely endanger if not destroy the free exercise of the Amish families' religious beliefs." The Amish community did not receive any government aid and did not have a high crime rate or other social problems that might make it a detriment to the other citizens of the state. Therefore, the Court ruled that if enforcement of the law would seriously hurt the religion, while granting the exception caused no harm to the rest of the people of the state, the exception was mandated by the Constitution.[10]

By 1990, it seemed that the Supreme Court had settled on a "no harm, no foul" rule. If enforcing a law would seriously hinder or prohibit a religious practice, and granting an exception to the law caused no harm to the public, then the law would not be enforced in that context. But in that year the Court announced that moving forward it would take a strict approach to making exceptions.

The case that set the new precedent involved the use of an illegal hallucinogenic drug, peyote, by Native Americans in a religious ceremony. A drug abuse counselor was fired from his job when his employer found out that he smoked peyote. Out of a job, he then applied to the state of Oregon for unemployment benefits, but he was turned down because he had lost his job through his own fault (use of an illegal drug).[11] But he argued that he had not done anything wrong. He was not a recreational drug user or a pusher. He ingested peyote as a part of a religious ceremony. No one alleged that his practice was anything but sincere and limited to his church's ritual.

In *Employment Division, Department of Human Resources of Oregon v. Smith* (1990), the Court ruled in favor of Oregon because the state's law against hallucinogenic drug use was a reasonable one and it was not passed with any intent to harm a religion. This case raises several questions. If we make an exception here, where does it end? Can people refuse to pay taxes, refuse to obey environmental laws, child labor laws, and laws against sex discrimination because of religion?[12]

Liberties are not absolute; freedom of expression may be limited in several instances, including times of crisis.

Most Americans are proud of their ability to express themselves as they want, without worrying that the government will punish them. But almost everyone agrees that there have to be some limits to this freedom. Government regulates expression every day by, for example, requiring silence in courts and forbidding perjury (lying). One of the great arguments of American society has been, where should we draw the lines? What kinds of expression, in what circumstances, should be censored? It has always been widely accepted that the right to **freedom of expression**, a First Amendment protection of all forms of communication, is valuable, but there continue to be sharp disagreements about the limits to that right.

Freedom of expression First Amendment protection of all forms of communication.

The Supreme Court was forced to confront this problem in the early twentieth century. At that time many Americans were afraid that anarchists (those who are opposed to government and seek to abolish or diminish state authority) and Communists were preparing to assassinate officials and commit sabotage. These fears grew after the United States entered World War I. With feelings of nationalism and fear running high, Congress passed several laws that restricted the rights of opponents of the war to voice their objections. A number of protestors were arrested and convicted of breaking these laws, and a few of them appealed their convictions to the Supreme Court.

Supreme Court Justices Oliver Wendell Holmes and Louis Brandeis developed a standard for judging such cases in the early twentieth century. They rejected the idea that freedom of expression is absolute. Speech that instigates criminal behavior may be punished. In addition, they argued, sometimes speech itself might be a criminal act (in Holmes's famous example, falsely shouting "Fire!" in a crowded theater so as to cause a panic is certainly a crime). In each case judges should consider the circumstances in which the expression occurs (falsely shouting "Fire!" on a deserted beach would obviously not be a crime). The critical "question in every case is whether the words used are used in such circumstances and are of such nature as to create a clear and present danger that they will bring about the substantive evils that Congress has a right to prevent. It is a question of proximity and degree." Known as the **clear and present danger test**,[13] this is the standard now used by American courts that allows restrictions on speech, if the speech will lead directly to criminal acts.

Clear and present danger test A standard used by the Supreme Court that allows restrictions on speech, if the speech will lead directly to criminal acts.

There have been times, especially when the nation has felt threatened, when judges have abandoned the clear and present danger test and used another standard,

Bad tendency test A standard used by the Supreme Court that allows restrictions on speech that would probably lead to the performance of criminal acts.

often called the **bad tendency test**. This test allows restrictions on speech that would probably lead to the performance of criminal acts. In response to the threat posed by communism in the late 1940s and 1950s, Congress and the states passed laws that, in effect, made advocacy of Marxist ideas illegal. People who were convicted under these laws argued that they were unconstitutional.[14] Using a version of the bad tendency test, in *Dennis v. United States* (1951) Chief Justice Vinson argued that if a group is planning to violently overthrow the government, then the authorities have the responsibility to prevent that from happening.[15]

This interpretation of the First Amendment was widely approved at first, but within a few years many Americans began to wonder if the adoption of the bad tendency test was really a good move. The problem with the bad tendency test was that it allowed for too many convictions of harmless, often quite patriotic, citizens. By the late 1950s the Supreme Court had reversed itself,[16] and it once again began to apply the clear and present danger standard, as it has ever since.

Preferred freedoms doctrine First Amendment rights are fundamental to a free society and receive heightened protection from the courts.

When presented with First Amendment cases today, the Court generally invokes the **preferred freedoms doctrine**. This doctrine holds that because First Amendment liberties are vital to a democratic, free society, whenever an individual claims that his or her First Amendment rights have been infringed, the burden will fall on the government to prove that its policy is necessary and narrowly designed so as to restrict freedom as little as possible.

Since we now know that the American Communist movement would never amount to much, it is perhaps too easy for us to side with those who, a generation or two ago, advocated for the clear and present danger standard. But consider what the use of that standard means today. When the Ku Klux Klan calls for the expulsion from the United States of African Americans, when skinheads call for the incarceration (and worse) of homosexuals, when antiabortion protestors call for the death of doctors and nurses, their speeches, Web sites, videos, and newsletters are usually protected under the current interpretation of the First Amendment. Should such **hate speech**, which urges violence or oppressive behavior toward a group, be tolerated in the marketplace of ideas? At what point, if ever, can we say that an idea has had its chance and has failed? On the other hand, if we should punish hate speech, how should we decide what constitutes hate speech? How much of a bad tendency is enough to warrant censorship? Who should decide?

Hate speech Expression that urges violence or oppressive behavior toward a group.

Expression that is libelous, slanderous, or obscene may be limited.

Freedom of expression is not only limited in times of crisis. American courts have ruled that **slander** (a false and harmful spoken statement), **libel** (a false and damaging publication), false advertising, breaches of confidentiality, copyright violations, and radio and television broadcasts are subject to government regulation, regardless

Slander A false and harmful spoken statement.

Libel False and damaging publication.

Prior restraint Censorship of expression before it reaches the public.

of any proof of clear and present danger or bad tendency. The First Amendment has also been interpreted to mean that the government may not use **prior restraint** to stop the distribution of a publication or production in advance. If there is to be punishment for the expression, it must come after the public has had a chance to read or hear the material.

The difficult question confronted by the Supreme Court in most of these cases is when and how to draw the line between speech that is protected and speech that is not protected. The well-known case of *New York Times v. Sullivan* (1964) helps illustrate this dilemma. This case concerned an ad in the *New York Times* that alleged the arrest of Martin Luther King, Jr. in Alabama was part of a campaign to destroy King's work for equal rights. The Montgomery city commissioner, L. B. Sullivan, claimed that the allegation defamed him personally and filed a libel action against the *Times*. In this instance, the Court had to weigh whether the advertisement was protected speech or unconstitutional. In a 9–0 opinion in favor of the *Times*, the justices found that "the First Amendment protects the publication of all statements, even false ones, about the conduct of public officials except when statements are made with **actual malice** [with knowledge that they are false or in reckless disregard of their truth or falsity]."[17]

Actual malice In order for a public official to prove libel, he or she must prove a statement was made with knowledge that it was false or with reckless disregard of the statement's truth or falsity.

Obscene expression Sexually explicit speech or publication that has as its prime or only purpose sexual arousal.

Another type of material that has raised many difficult First Amendment concerns is pornography. Debates have raged for a half century about whether it should be regulated, and if so, how? In legal terms, pornography is **obscene expression**, that is, speech or publication that has as its prime or only purpose the stimulation of sexual arousal. While American judges have almost always found that pornography is not protected by the First Amendment, they have had a lot of problems in defining just what pornography is.

In 1957, in *Roth v. United States*,[18] the Supreme Court ruled that material would be considered obscene only if:

1. The "dominant theme" of material as a whole was obsessively concerned with sex.
2. The work would strike the average person as "prurient," that is, as being excessively concerned with sex.
3. There was no redeeming social value to the material.

This standard meant that fewer restrictions could be placed on sexually explicit works, but the courts still had to figure out what was "prurient," what the "average" person would find offensive, and what was redeeming in value. Those questions proved to be very difficult to answer. This led Justice Potter Stewart to say that the courts should give up trying to come up with a specific standard to decide what was obscene. Even if he could not define pornography, he famously declared, "I know it when I see it."[19]

After 16 years of struggling with difficult cases, the Supreme Court decided in *Miller v. California* (1973) to shift much of the problem back to the states.[20] Instead of continuing to try to come up with national standards of obscenity, the

Court decided to allow for different standards in different localities. Thus, what could be shown to an audience in New York City might be censored in places like West Virginia or Utah. This did not mean that local governments could restrict access to any material at all; they still had to follow the guidelines that had been announced in the *Roth* case. However, these were clarified a bit with the addition of the **LAPS test**. Sexually explicit material would not be considered obscene if the content contained serious **L**iterary, **A**rtistic, **P**olitical, or **S**cientific value. If, after following these guidelines, local judges and juries found material to be obscene, then it could be banned, and its distributors and producers could be punished.

LAPS test Sexually explicit material is not considered obscene if it contains literary, artistic, political, or scientific value.

Most of the First Amendment cases we have discussed involved actions by the states (such as California), not the federal government. Yet, the first words of the First Amendment are "*Congress* shall make no law. . .." State governments are not mentioned, and for a long time it was thought that the Bill of Rights did not apply to state governments. However, in the twentieth century the Supreme Court, in a series of cases, ruled that most of the Bill of Rights and other rights contained in the U.S. Constitution protect Americans from actions by all levels of government. The Fourteenth Amendment, which had been ratified after the Civil War, applied these rights to the states through a process known as **incorporation**. At first only a few rights were thought to be important enough to be incorporated (such as freedom of speech), so the process became known as "**selective incorporation**." Gradually, almost all the Constitution's rights were applied to the states through the Fourteenth Amendment.

Incorporation The states are bound to respect rights guaranteed by the U.S. Constitution.

Selective incorporation The process by which parts of the Bill of Rights were applied to the states through the Fourteenth Amendment.

6 The right to privacy is inferred from the text of the Constitution.

The Ninth Amendment of the Bill of Rights states that "the enumeration in the Constitution of certain rights shall not be construed to deny or disparage others retained by the people." That is, we have other rights besides those that are specified in the text of the document. In the twentieth century, many judges and political theorists argued that the **right to privacy**, the right to conduct one's life without government interference, is one of these "other rights."

Right to privacy The right to conduct one's life without government interference. It is one of the implied rights protected by the Ninth Amendment.

Privacy is essential in a liberal society. Americans want the liberty to live their lives as they please, and they do not want agents of the government snooping into their affairs. Liberalism, the political theory underlying the Constitution, values freedom of the individual and thus limits the authority of the government over the private sphere. However, while that authority is limited, it is not absent. Private choices can have public consequences (as with child pornography, for example). Thus, even if we accept that the right to privacy is strongly implied by the Constitution (and not everybody accepts that premise), the problem remains: Where do we draw the line?

In 1965 Connecticut still had on its books a law that forbade the use of contraceptives by anyone, including people who were married. In the case of *Griswold v. Connecticut*,[21] the Supreme Court ruled that, at least as far as married couples were concerned, enforcement of this law was a violation of the right to privacy. Justice William Douglas wrote that although the privacy of family life is not specifically included in the Bill of Rights, we can see that the founders wanted to protect the home from unreasonable intrusions. The right to privacy is clearly implied by several of the amendments.[22] Since *Griswold*, the Court has extended the right of privacy to areas beyond contraception. One of the most controversial and well-known areas is abortion.

In Texas in 1969, it was a crime to have or perform an abortion in almost all cases. Norma McCorvey, a pregnant 21-year-old single woman who wanted an abortion, obtained the help of lawyers who were working for women's rights, and she sued to challenge the law as an infringement of her right to privacy. In 1973, in the case of *Roe v. Wade*,[23] the Court ruled in her favor (though by that time McCorvey had long since given birth). Justice Harry Blackmun wrote the opinion of the Court, in which he explained that issues of reproduction are intensely private and that the state should not interfere with fundamentally private matters unless it had very compelling reasons for doing so. Texas had argued that it did have such a reason: protection of human life. Blackmun acknowledged that the state had the responsibility to protect lives and that the right to privacy surely did not include the right to take a person's life. According to Blackmun's research, "person" was traditionally used in the law to refer to people who had been born, but there was a gray area in the last weeks of a normal pregnancy, in which the fetus is viable (can live outside the womb). So Blackmun decided that abortions should be up to the woman up to the point of viability. After that, the state would have the power to prohibit abortions unless the mother's life was in danger.

Roe v. Wade set off a major political battle that has continued to this day. Since 1973, all Republican candidates for president have vowed to appoint justices to the Supreme Court who will overturn the decision, and Democratic candidates have promised to appoint justices who will defend it. Although the Court has become more conservative, it has continued to support the major findings of *Roe* in large part because the case rests on the right to privacy.[24]

Another controversial issue related to the issue of privacy is that of homosexual relations. Through most of American history the states made sexual relations between members of the same gender illegal. But in 2003, in *Lawrence v. Texas*, the Supreme Court ruled that the government did not have a good reason to regulate individuals' private sexual behavior. As long as they were not harming anyone, and minors were not involved, adults' private, consensual sexual conduct could not be considered a crime.[25]

The Constitution includes protections for criminal suspects, defendants, and convicts.

The great dilemma of criminal law is: How do we give law enforcement authorities enough power so that they can protect people from being hurt by criminals, while at the same time limiting that power so it isn't abused? The power of the government to search, imprison, and even execute innocent people was a major concern of the founders. Almost half of the Bill of Rights—the Fourth, Fifth, Sixth, and Eighth Amendments—is devoted to protecting the rights of criminal suspects, defendants, and convicts (see Table 7.1).

Probable cause Reason to think that it is likely that someone is guilty or in possession of evidence.

Warrant A document issued by a court authorizing a search or arrest.

The courts have interpreted the Fourth Amendment's search and seizure clause to mean that the police must have **probable cause**, or reason to think that someone is guilty or in possession of evidence, in order to look through someone's belongings or to arrest somebody. Often it is necessary to search and arrest a suspect on the spot, in which case the officers must retroactively explain why they had probable cause. If time permits, however, the police must get a **warrant**, a document issued by a court authorizing a search or arrest, before proceeding. To do this, they must apply to a judge, who is supposed to review the reasons that the officers give for the action they want to take and then decide if there is enough evidence to proceed.

But what if a cop wants to arrest a suspect *before* a crime is committed? That question has given the courts some difficulty. In 1963, a member of the Cleveland police department noticed three men on the sidewalk outside a store. The officer thought that their behavior was suspicious, so he watched them for a while until he became convinced that they were "casing" the store and were about to rob it. He then approached them, identified himself as a cop, and proceeded to frisk them. When he did, he found that two of the men were carrying guns, so he arrested them. Terry, one of the men, was then convicted on a charge of carrying a concealed weapon. On appeal, he argued that the search had been unconstitutional. He had been merely looking in the store window with his friends. The police officer did not see their weapons, nor did he overhear them planning a robbery, so how can the search have been reasonable? What was the probable cause?

In *Terry v. Ohio*, the Supreme Court ruled that, given the circumstances, the police officer's search of Terry had been reasonable. If an officer is justified in believing that an individual is armed and dangerous, "he is entitled for the protection of himself and others in the area to conduct a carefully limited search of the outer clothing" of the suspects to search for weapons.[26] But who is suspicious? There have been countless instances in which African American and Latino men have been stopped and searched when they have been innocently shopping or just waiting for a bus. Many studies have shown that police often engage in "ethnic profiling" (sometimes unconsciously), so behavior that would not be thought at all suspicious if performed by a white man or woman is considered suspect when seen in African American and Hispanic men.

These rules regarding searches and arrests are very important because if the police do not follow them, the evidence that they gather will be permanently excluded from all court proceedings. According to the **exclusionary rule**, announced in the case of *Mapp v. Ohio* in 1961, any evidence obtained in violation of the Fourth Amendment must be thrown out, no matter how important it is. The exclusionary rule prevents many unreasonable searches and arrests, and it ensures that proper procedures will be more often followed in interrogations. But it does have a social cost. Evidence that could be used to detain and punish criminals gets thrown out of court, and some guilty people go free, oftentimes committing more crimes.

Exclusionary rule Evidence obtained by law enforcement authorities illegally cannot be used in a criminal case.

According to the Sixth Amendment, anyone prosecuted for a crime is entitled to a lawyer. But in many cases, poor people cannot afford to hire attorneys. Up until 1963, they were usually left to try to defend themselves in court. But in the case of *Gideon v. Wainwright*,[27] the Supreme Court ruled that the government must provide legal defense to people who cannot afford to pay for lawyers themselves. Unfortunately, the "public defenders" are often overworked and have limited resources.

Finally, as anyone who has watched television knows, when suspects are arrested they must be told of their right to an attorney and of their Fifth Amendment right to not answer questions.[28] These rights stem largely from the well-known 1966 case *Miranda v. Arizona*. While almost 50 years later most Americans support this right, what many do not realize is that several aspects of the Miranda ruling continue to be debated today. Consider, for instance, the 2010 case of *Berghius, Warden v. Thompkins*. Chester Thompkins, a murder suspect, was questioned by police for nearly 3 hours. He was not only advised of his Miranda rights but given a copy of them to read. Thompkins refused to waive his Miranda rights either orally or in writing. Toward the end of his interrogation the police asked Thompkins "if he prayed to God?" When Thompkins answered "yes," the officer then asked, "do you pray to God to ask for forgiveness for shooting that boy down?" Once again Thompkins answered, "yes." Thompkins later claimed that his refusal to waive his rights orally or in writing was an indication that he had invoked his right to silence. He, therefore, maintained that his voluntary responses to the questions regarding prayer amounted to coercion and were a violation of his right against self-incrimination.

In a controversial 5–4 decision that pitted liberal justices against conservatives, the Court sided with the police. Writing for the majority, Justice Anthony Kennedy stated:

> a suspect who has received and understood the Miranda warnings, and has not invoked his Miranda rights, waives the right to remain silent by making an uncoerced statement to the police. Thompkins did not invoke his right to remain silent and stop the questioning. Understanding his rights in full, he waived his right to remain silent by making a voluntary statement to the police.[29]

The equal protection clause of the Constitution forbids racial and ethnic discrimination.

The word *discrimination* often has a negative meaning. When most people hear it, they think of racist and sexist behavior. But governments must practice discrimination all the time. To discriminate is to treat different categories of things or people differently. Thus, when the government denies certain rights to convicts or children or the insane, or refuses to hire people who lack relevant skills, it is discriminating, but it is doing so in ways that almost everyone would consider rational. What the Constitution forbids is **invidious discrimination**, discrimination that is irrational and harmful. The **Fourteenth Amendment** to the Constitution, which passed after Emancipation and the Civil War, was written to ensure that the freed slaves and their descendants had the full rights of citizenship. Soon after the amendment was ratified, the Supreme Court made it clear that the "equal protection of the laws" applied not just to African Americans, but to members of all ethnic groups (although not to women).

Invidious discrimination Harmful, irrational discrimination.

Fourteenth Amendment Guarantees citizenship to all born or naturalized in the United States; mandates equal protection of the laws.

But within a couple of decades the membership of the Supreme Court changed. And by the 1890s, the Supreme Court had almost entirely stopped meaningful enforcement of the Fourteenth Amendment in racial discrimination cases, most notoriously in ***Plessy v. Ferguson*** (1896).[30] In *Plessy*, the Court ruled in favor of a Louisiana law that required segregation of passengers on trains. So long as both races had some access to public services, the Court said that segregation would be considered "**separate but equal**" and thus constitutional. Thus the state and federal governments were free to pass "**Jim Crow**" **laws**, which mandated separation of the races, not just in government facilities, but also in private businesses. The right to vote, supposedly protected by the Fifteenth Amendment, was nullified through poll taxes, literacy tests, and violent acts designed to keep African Americans from voting. By the end of the nineteenth century, much of the United States had adopted an apartheid system, which is a social and political policy of strict separation of the races.

Plessy v. Ferguson An infamous 1896 ruling in which the Supreme Court upheld racial segregation in private businesses, especially railroad cars.

Separate but equal A rule that segregation would be constitutional so long as both races had some access to public services.

Jim Crow laws Racial segregation required by law.

One of the most important changes to ever occur in American law came in the middle of the twentieth century, when the Supreme Court announced a standard of review known as **strict scrutiny**, which said that if a policy seemed to treat members of historically oppressed minority groups (such as African Americans) differently from the majority, then that policy was automatically suspect and was assumed to violate the **equal protection clause** of the Constitution, which requires that the states not discriminate against groups of people. The burden would be on the government to show that it had a "compelling" objective and that the challenged policy was the only way to reach that goal. The Court's decision to use *strict scrutiny*

Strict scrutiny A presumption that laws infringing on fundamental rights or treating historically oppressed groups differently are unconstitutional, unless there are compelling reasons for upholding them.

Equal protection clause Fourteenth Amendment provision that requires the states not to discriminate against groups of people.

meant that many kinds of racially discriminatory public policies were open to legal challenge. The first and most important of these were educational practices.

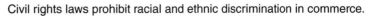

Throughout the South, and in some other parts of the country, in the 1950s public schools were racially segregated by law and regulation. This system was challenged by the NAACP in ***Brown v. Board of Education of Topeka, Kansas***.[31] The question put to the Court by Thurgood Marshall, the lawyer for the Brown family, was whether Topeka could justify racial segregation. He argued that the system was harmful to the children. By separating students based on race, the schools were teaching racism. Black children were getting the message from their government that there was something wrong with them, so much so that they needed to be kept away from the white students. Because of the terrible lessons it taught (as well as the more obvious material harm it caused), Marshall argued that racial segregation was inherently unjust and a violation of the Fourteenth Amendment.[32]

Brown v. Board of Education of Topeka, Kansas Landmark Supreme Court decision in 1954 declaring that segregation in public education is unconstitutional. This decision overturned *Plessy v. Ferguson* (1896).

Without dissent, the Supreme Court agreed. The 1954 decision in *Brown v. Board of Education* meant that explicitly racial segregationist laws and regulations would now be struck down by the federal courts. Over the next few years the legal framework of the American apartheid system was dismantled. Hospitals, public transportation, and all other government services and property had to be integrated. Some states even had laws that forbade marriage between people of different races, and these laws were struck down.[33]

3 Civil rights laws prohibit racial and ethnic discrimination in commerce.

The end of legally enforced segregation did not mean, however, that segregation and other racist practices came to a halt. For a long time after the *Brown* decision, American society was almost as segregated as it was before 1954. Simply because ***de jure* discrimination** (discrimination that is mandated by law) no longer existed did not mean that individuals and businesses discontinued their racist policies. ***De facto* discrimination** persisted in fact, regardless of law or regulation.

***De jure* discrimination** Discrimination that is mandated by law.

***De facto* discrimination** Discrimination that exists in fact, regardless of the law.

Privately owned shops, hotels, restaurants, and other businesses could, and frequently did, refuse service to African Americans, Latinos, Native Americans, Jews, and other groups they wanted to exclude. In other cases, service was limited; so, for example, minority group members would be given only take-out orders at restaurants, or the back seats of buses, or they would be banned from using the restrooms. Perhaps even more important, private employers discriminated, so that racial and ethnic minorities were paid lower wages, denied promotions, or not hired at all. Blatant discrimination was legal in the housing industry as well.

Civil Rights Act of 1964 The first effective civil rights legislation. With passage of this law, discrimination in stores, hotels, and restaurants became illegal, as did racist practices in hiring and promotion.

Private *de facto* discrimination was not made illegal until the mid-1960s, when a coalition of liberal Democrats and Republicans was strong enough to pass the **Civil Rights Act of 1964**, the first effective civil rights legislation.[34] With passage of this law, discrimination in stores, hotels, and restaurants became illegal, as did racist practices in hiring and promotion. *De facto* discrimination did not, of course, disappear, but it was greatly reduced.

2 Gender discrimination sometimes violates the Constitution and civil rights laws.

The Fourteenth Amendment was written to protect the rights of African Americans as they freed themselves from the vestiges of slavery. But the text of the amendment does not specify equal protection for African Americans, or ex-slaves. It says that the government shall not deny equal protection to any "person." Very soon after the amendment was adopted, judges were faced with the question of what the words "person" and "equal protection of the laws" meant. Advocates of women's rights argued that the Fourteenth Amendment should be read literally. No one denied that women were persons, but women had few legal or political rights.

It took women's rights advocates a hundred years to convince the Supreme Court to expand its reading of the Fourteenth Amendment and protect the rights of women. In 1973, in the case of *Frontiero v. Richardson*, the Supreme Court finally extended the amendment to women by ruling that the government had violated Sharron Frontiero's rights by providing different benefits for the husbands and the wives of armed forces personnel.[35] Although the justices agreed that the government must pay men and women equally, they did not agree on a standard by which to judge future cases of **sex discrimination**, the process of treating males and females differently. The more conservative members of the (all-male) Court thought that applying the strict scrutiny standard would be going too far, because they believed it was reasonable to have some policies that treated males and females differently.

Sex discrimination The practice of treating females and males differently.

Justice William Brennan skillfully maneuvered to create a majority who would support a middle position between those advocated by the liberals and conservatives. This middle approach came to be called **intermediate scrutiny**. Laws and regulations that treated males and females differently would be allowable only if they were needed to achieve an important governmental objective. These laws would be more carefully scrutinized than most policies examined by the courts, but not as strictly as racial classifications. It soon became apparent that very few sexually discriminatory policies could survive intermediate scrutiny.

Intermediate scrutiny Standard used by the Supreme Court that allows gender/sex discrimination only if it is needed to achieve an important government objective.

Title VII of the Civil Rights Act has been effective in forcing employers to pay women and men equally for equal work. Before 1964, it was common for males and females to work at the same job but with the men receiving significantly higher pay. It was not unusual for women with greater skills and responsibilities to be paid much less than men who had less developed skills and fewer responsibilities. More often, women were not hired or promoted at all by many businesses. With enforcement of the Civil Rights Act, these policies became illegal.[36]

1 Some carefully designed affirmative action programs are constitutional.

In spite of the major gains made since the U.S. government began to take some action against *de jure* violations of civil rights in the 1950s, African Americans, Latinos, and women continue to suffer the effects of discrimination. Women receive only about four-fifths of the pay of men, and African Americans and Hispanics have significantly lower incomes than whites, are less likely to graduate from college, and less likely to own a home. American minority group members have shorter life expectancies and higher infant mortality rates than white Americans.[37]

Affirmative action Positive steps taken to make up for past discrimination against minorities and/or women.

To help remedy this, the federal government, along with several states, began to implement **affirmative action** programs, which were designed to make up for past discrimination against minorities and women and increase their numbers in employment and education. Most aspects of affirmative action were not initially controversial; they consisted of efforts to increase applications and reduce harassment. But over time, these programs became highly divisive.

Civil rights advocates had long argued that each person should be judged on his or her merits, and that one's race, ethnicity, or gender was irrelevant. They had often quoted from Justice Harlan's famous dissent in *Plessy v. Ferguson* that "our Constitution is color-blind and neither knows nor tolerates class among citizens."[38] Now, however, civil rights advocates began to argue that the government *should* take race, ethnicity, and gender into account in situations where past discriminatory practices continued to work to the disadvantage of these groups. One solution to this was to mandate quotas, numerical requirements for hiring in jobs or admitting students to schools. If, for example, 20 percent of the adults in a state were African American, then about 20 percent of the people hired to be, for instance, state police officers should also be African American. Preferential treatment would come into play if, in order to fill the quota, lower scores or lesser qualifications would be accepted from minority group applicants.

In 1973, Allan Bakke, a white man, applied to the Davis Medical School that was part of the state of California's public education system. He was rejected, but over a dozen minority students were accepted with scores that were lower than his.[39] Bakke argued that his civil right to be treated equally by the school had been violated, and he sued to be admitted. He claimed that he had been rejected simply because of racial discrimination. If he had been black or Hispanic, he would have been accepted, but because he was white, he was not. He felt that he was being made to pay for the wrongs done by the state to minority group members, even though he himself was guilty of nothing.

In *University of California v. Bakke,* a divided Supreme Court ruled that the affirmative action program used by the medical school in this case was *suspect* because it employed racial and ethnic classification. Thus, the Court would use *strict scrutiny* in examining the policy. The affirmative action program used a rigid quota that guaranteed admission of a set number of minority applicants, no matter how poor their scores were (and some of them were shockingly bad). So Bakke won, and the program was struck down as a violation of the equal protection clause. But Justice Lewis Powell went on to say that this did not mean that all preferential treatment programs were also unconstitutional. Those that took race and ethnicity into account, without setting strict quotas, could well be approved by the Court.

Since the 1970s, the Supreme Court has become more conservative and skeptical of affirmative action, but it has continued to uphold the central ruling in *Bakke*. In the case of *Grutter v. Bollinger* (2003), the Court upheld the affirmative action program used by the law school at the University of Michigan. There, race or ethnicity was taken into account in evaluating each application, and minority status could be considered a "plus" factor, along with other factors, such as coming from a poor family or overcoming a physical handicap. Justice Sandra O'Connor (a moderately conservative Republican on the Court at the time) wrote that affirmative action programs such as that used by the Michigan law school could pass the strict scrutiny test so long as they were designed to remedy past discrimination. She concluded the majority opinion of the Court by noting that 25 years had passed since the *Bakke* decision and that another 25 years would probably be necessary for affirmative action to completely destroy the vestiges of racial discrimination. After that, she suggested, the program should come to an end.

CONCLUSION

Freedom and equality are important political values to almost all Americans. However, we often disagree about just what those terms mean and which should be given priority when they conflict with one another. We want to have freedom of speech, but we don't want people to be allowed to say harmful things. We want to be safe from criminals, but we don't want to be harassed by the police. We want everyone to be treated equally, but we cannot agree on what constitutes equal opportunity. These are but a few examples of the many debates regarding rights and liberties that have persisted in the United States since the founding.

Yet, it is important to recognize that these debates reflect our changing interpretation of our rights and liberties. Today's debates about regulation of hate speech and affirmative action may fade away, just as earlier debates about censorship of communists and Jim Crow laws did, but they are sure to be replaced by fresh arguments about how we should balance liberty and security and how we should define equality. While interracial marriage is not widely debated today, for instance, same-sex marriage is. While six states and one district (Connecticut, Iowa, Massachusetts, New Hampshire, Vermont, New York, and the District of Columbia) recognize same-sex marriage, the federal government does not. The Supreme Court has yet to speak on this issue, but many lower courts have. As a result, most observers feel it is only a matter of time before a same-sex marriage case finds its way into the court of last resort.

 Some carefully designed affirmative action programs are constitutional.

THEIR LIST

An Insider's View

MATTHEW J. BYRNE, ESQ.

Judge and Attorney, New York

Matthew J. Byrne, Esq. is one of the youngest judges elected to the bench in New York. He has served over 16 years as Suffern Village Justice. Judge Byrne is also a practicing attorney and a partner in Balsamo, Byrne, Cipriani, and Ellsworth and a former assistant county attorney. Based on his varied service in the legal profession, particularly in the areas of civil and criminal matters, I asked Judge Byrne what, from his perspective, are the most important things he thinks people should know about civil liberties and civil rights in the United States.

> One of the things I believe that is most important to understand about civil liberties and civil rights is the manner in which the protections found in the Constitution affect us all, even in ways we may never appreciate. This is especially true in the area of criminal justice, most specifically, the 4th, 5th, and 6th Amendments to the Constitution. These guarantee all of us protection from an overreaching government. This is true whether we're speaking of a parking ticket or a charge of murder. Obviously, we place the murder trial in a higher level of importance, but the constitutional application is the same.
>
> A pet peeve of mine is when we hear at times that somebody "got off on a technicality." The Constitution is not a technicality. Sometimes it protects bad people, but we have to be willing to allow that to happen in exchange for the protection of all of the innocent people out there who may be on the receiving end of governmental/police impropriety, whether intentional or negligent.
>
> Another aspect of constitutional law that may be lost on many people is something that is in and of itself foundational. Simply said, the purpose of the Constitution, the reason why our founders adopted this document, was to LIMIT government. There was a great level of suspicion on the part of our founders in developing an all too powerful government. So much of the Constitution consists of provisions that place practical, systemic, and structural limitations on our government that have stood the test of time and resulted in landmark and controversial Supreme Court decisions.
>
> Another more practical approach to understanding the development of constitutional jurisprudence over the generations is to have an appreciation for and understanding of our nation's history. If you can understand what was happening historically, you can understand perhaps what might have been motivating the Supreme Court in making some of its landmark decisions related to civil liberties and civil rights. While we would like to think the Court is above it all, the justices certainly can be swayed by the real demands of the times and the societal challenges that are taking place. We hope that the Court's decisions are nonetheless grounded in a sound interpretation of the Constitution. This may at times be up for debate, but the practical realities that have a role in the Court's decision making processes, are not.

While same-sex marriage is a civil liberties issue most people have heard about, there are liberties and rights issues that will undoubtedly be major concerns in the next few years that few of us today can even imagine. As legal scholar Jeffrey Rosen writes, "in the next 10 or 15 years, as technology and science continue to advance . . . the Supreme Court will, in all likelihood, be asked to decide a fascinating array of divisive issues (including brain fingerprinting and genetic screening) that are now only dimly on the horizon."[40] These debates will reflect the changing political culture of our society. However, for these debates to truly reflect the values of the people themselves, the people themselves must know their rights and liberties and enter into the debate through active political participation.

YOUR LIST REVISITED

At the beginning of the chapter you were asked to think about what you might include on your own list of the Top 10 Most Important Things to Know About Civil Liberties and Civil Rights. Now that you have read the chapter, take a moment to revisit your list. What, if anything, would you change about your list? Do you agree or disagree with the chapter list constructed by the author? What might you add or delete? Why?

KEY TERMS

Actual malice 157
Affirmative action 165
Bad tendency test 156
Brown v. Board of Education of Topeka, Kansas 163
Civil liberties 149
Civil rights 149
Civil Rights Act of 1964 163
Clear and present danger test 155
***De facto* discrimination** 163
***De jure* discrimination** 163
Establishment clause 152
Equal protection clause 162
Exclusionary rule 161
First Amendment rights 149
Fourteenth Amendment 162
Free exercise clause 153
Freedom of expression 155
Hate speech 156
Incorporation 158
Intermediate scrutiny 164
Invidious discrimination 162
Jim Crow laws 162
LAPS test 158
Libel 157
Obscene expression 157
Plessy v. Ferguson 162
Preferred freedoms doctrine 156
Prior restraint 157
Probable cause 160
Right to privacy 158
Selective incorporation 158
Separate but equal 162
Sex discrimination 164
Slander 156
Strict scrutiny 162
Warrant 160

CHAPTER REVIEW QUESTIONS

10 What is the establishment clause, and why has it been debated since the nation's founding?

9 According to the Court's ruling in *Wisconsin v. Yoder*, can states require students to attend school after eighth grade if it violates their religion? Why or why not?

8 Explain the differences between the clear and present danger test and the bad tendency test. Which test is used by the Supreme Court today?

7 Give two examples of a type of speech that can be prohibited under the Constitution. Why can these types of speech be prohibited?

6 Where in the Constitution is the right to privacy found? Explain your answer.

5 In what ways does the Bill of Rights protect those accused of a crime?

4. What clause in the Fourteenth Amendment has been useful in helping to combat racial, ethnic, and sex discrimination? How has the clause been useful?

3. What is the difference between *de jure* and *de facto* discrimination? Which is more difficult to outlaw? Why?

2. When is gender discrimination permissible? Which level of scrutiny do cases involving gender discrimination receive from the courts?

1. What was the significance of the Supreme Court's decision in *University of California v. Bakke* (1978)? Why do you think the Supreme Court was divided in its decision?

SUGGESTED READINGS

- Carson, Clayborne, David Garrow, Gerald Gill, Vincent Harding, and Darlene Clark Hine. *The Eyes on the Prize Civil Rights Reader.* New York: Penguin Books, 1991.
- Chamallas, Martha. *Introduction to Feminist Legal Theory.* Gaithersburg, MD: Aspen Law and Business, 1999.
- Donnelly, Jack. *Universal Human Rights in Theory and Practice.* Ithaca, NY: Cornell University Books, 2003.
- Gerstmann, Evan. *Same-Sex Marriage and the Constitution.* Cambridge: Cambridge University Press, 2003.
- Katz, Leo. *Bad Acts and Guilty Minds.* Chicago: University of Chicago Press, 1987.
- Kluger, Richard. *Simple Justice: The History of Brown v. Board of Education and Black Americas Struggle for Equality.* New York: Knopf, 2004.
- Lewis, Anthony. *Freedom for the Thought We Hate.* New York: Basic Books, 2007.
- Perry, Barbara. *The Michigan Affirmative Action Cases.* Topeka, KS: University of Kansas Press, 2007.
- Rhode, Deborah. *Speaking of Sex: The Denial of Gender Inequality.* Boston: Harvard University Press, 1999.
- Toobin, Jeffrey. *The Nine: Inside the Supreme Court.* New York: Anchor Books, 2008.

SUGGESTED FILMS

- *To Kill a Mockingbird* (1962)
- *Gideon's Trumpet* (1980)
- *A Soldier's Story* (1984)
- *Mississippi Burning* (1988)
- *The Long Walk Home* (1990)
- *Guilty By Suspicion* (1991)
- *Dead Man Walking* (1995)
- *The People vs. Larry Flynt* (1996)
- *Not for Ourselves Alone: Elizabeth Cady Stanton & Susan B. Anthony* (1999)
- *The Cider House Rules* (1999)

SUGGESTED WEBSITES

- **Avalon Project: Documents in Law, History, and Diplomacy:** http://avalon.law.yale.edu/subject_menus/diana.asp.
- **Balkinization (progressive-leaning legal blog):** http://balkin.blogspot.com/.

- **FindLaw: US Supreme Court Center:** http://supreme.lp.findlaw.com/.
- **First Amendment Center:** http://www.firstamendmentcenter.org/.
- **Legal Information Institute (Cornell Law School):** http://www.law.cornell.edu/.
- **Oyez: US Supreme Court Media:** http://www.oyez.org/.
- **Scotusblog: Supreme Court of the United States Blog:** http://www.scotusblog.com/.
- **Slate: Jurisprudence:** http://www.slate.com/articles/news_and_politics/jurisprudence.html.
- **University Law Review Project (full-text articles):** http://www.lawreview.org/.
- **Volokh Conspiracy (libertarian-leaning legal blog):** http://volokh.com/.

ENDNOTES

[1]"Homer Simpson, Yes; First Amendment? "Doh!" *Editor and Publisher,* March 1, 2006, available online at: http://www.editorandpublisher.com/Departments/Top%20Stories/homer-simpson-yes-first-amendment-doh-41790-.aspx.

[2]For a complete review of the results of the McCormick Freedom Museum study, see http://www.freedommuseum.us/Press.aspx.

[3]Article I of the Constitution grants Congress the power to do this.

[4]Daniel L. Dreisbach, *Thomas Jefferson and the Wall of Separation Between Church and State* (New York: New York University Press, 2002), pp 21–22.

[5]*Walz v. Tax Commission of the City of New York,* 397 US 664 (1970).

[6]*Engle v. Vitale,* 370 US 421 (1962).

[7]*Lemon v. Kurtzman,* 403 US 602 (1971).

[8]*Good News Club v. Milford Central School,* 533 US 98 (2001).

[9]*Wisconsin v. Yoder,* 406 US 205 (1972).

[10]Ibid.

[11]*Employment Division, Department of Human Resources of Oregon v. Smith,* 494 US 872 (1990).

[12]Ibid.

[13]*Schenk v. U.S.,* 249 US 47 (1919).

[14]*Dennis v. United States,* 341 US 494 (1951).

[15]Ibid. Vinson adopted this approach from Judge L. Hand, who said the following: "'In each case . . . [we] must ask whether the gravity of the 'evil,' discounted by its improbability, justifies such invasion of free speech as is necessary to avoid the danger.' . . . the Supreme Court, in a plurality opinion written by Chief Justice Vinson . . . adopted Judge Hand's formulation of the legal rule." See David R. Dow and R. Scott Shieldes, "Rethinking the Clear and Present Danger Test," available at: http://www.law.indiana.edu/ilj/volumes/v73/no4/04.html (accessed May 21, 2011).

[16]*Yates v. United States,* 354 US 298 (1957).

[17]See, for instance, http://www.oyez.org/cases/1960-1969/1963/1963_39.

[18]*Roth v. United States,* 354 US 476 (1957).

[19]*Jacobellis v. Ohio,* 378 US 184 (1964).

[20]*Miller v. California,* 413 US 15 (1973).

[21]*Griswold v. Connecticut,* 381 US 479 (1965).

[22]Ibid.

[23]*Roe v. Wade,* 410 US 113 (1973).

[24]*Planned Parenthood of Pennsylvania v. Casey* 505 US 833 (1992). In this case the Court allowed some restrictions on abortion, but reaffirmed women's right to reproductive freedom.

[25]*Lawrence v. Texas,* 539 US 533 (2003).

[26]*Terry v. Ohio,* 392 US 1 (1968).

[27]*Gideon v. Wainwright,* 372 US 335 (1963).

[28]*Miranda v. Arizona* 384 US 436 (1966).

[29]Frank James, "Supreme Court Miranda Ruling Favors Police," National Public Radio, June 1, 2010, available at: http://www.npr.org/blogs/thetwo-way/2010/06/supreme_court_miranda_ruling_f.html (accessed May 21, 2011).

[30]*Plessy v. Ferguson,* 163 US 537.

[31]*Brown v. Board of Education of Topeka,* 347 US 483 (1954).

[32]Richard Kluger, *Simple Justice* (New York: Vintage Books, 1975).

[33]*Loving v. Virginia,* 388 US 1 (1967).

[34]Daniel Rodriquez and Barry Weingast, "The Positive Political Theory of Legislative History: New Perspectives on the 1964 Civil Rights Act and Its Interpretation," *University of Pennsylvania Law Review,* 151 (3, April, 2003): 1452–1497.

[35]*Frontiero v. Richardson,* 411 US 677 (1973).

[36]It is important to note that despite gains, in some sectors and locations women and men still do not receive equal pay for equal work. See, for instance, http://www.pay-equity.org/info-time.html.

[37]T. A. LaVeist, "Racial segregation and longevity among African Americans: an individual-level analysis," *Health Services Research* 38 (6, Pt 2, December 2003): 1719–1733, doi:10.1111/j.1475-6773.2003.00199.; R. S. Levine, J. E. Foster, R. E. Fullilove, et al., "Black-white inequalities in mortality and life expectancy, 1933-1999: Implications for healthy people 2010," (2001)

[38]*Plessy v. Ferguson,* 163 US 537 (1896).

[39]*Regents of the University of California v. Bakke,* 438 US 265 (1978).

[40]Jeffrey Rosen, "Roberts v. The Future," *New York Times Magazine,* August 28, 2005.

Chapter 8

CAMPAIGNS AND ELECTIONS

Top Ten List

10 Most modern democracies are representative.

9 Democratic elections must be open to all citizens, offer meaningful choice and informed deliberation, and be fair, free, and frequent.

8 The United States holds more frequent elections with more choices than other modern democracies.

7 To win an election, a candidate must make efficient use of time and money.

6 Candidates with an appealing message and skilled staff are critical to a successful campaign.

5 Candidates secure their parties' nomination in primary elections and caucuses before running for office.

4 Both party nominees and independent candidates can compete in the general election.

3 The Electoral College determines the outcome for the presidential race in the general election.

2 Most of the elections that occur in the United States take place at the state and local levels, but the majority are not competitive.

1 The cost of winning is a major concern people have about the health of U.S. elections.

Shown here, Minnesota Representative Michelle Bachmann and former Massachusetts Governor Mitt Romney participate in a debate prior to the start of the 2012 Republican presidential primaries. Debates are a key opportunity during an election cycle for voters to get to know candidates and learn about their positions on key issues that affect the United States. Despite the magnitude of the issues confronting the nation, however, voter turnout in elections remains very low when compared with turnout in other countries. This has led scholars and observers to become increasingly concerned about the structure and health of the country's electoral institutions.

YOUR LIST

Before you read this chapter, take a few moments to think about what you might include on a list of the Top 10 Most Important Things to Know About Campaigns and Elections. At the end of the chapter you will be asked to compare and contrast your list with the one supplied in this chapter.

INTRODUCTION

"Midterm Turnout Could Shatter Records." This was the headline in the NBC News blog "First Read" on the eve of the historic 2010 midterm election.[1] The "First Read" blog was reporting on turnout projections made by Michael McDonald, a professor at George Mason University, who used early voting data and other statistics to predict that a "record breaking 90-million people" would vote in the midterm election the following day.[2] **Voter turnout**, defined as the percentage of eligible voters who cast a ballot in a given election, had previously reached a record high for a midterm election in 2006 when 86 million Americans went to the polls.[3]

Voter turnout The percentage of eligible voters who cast a ballot in a given election.

As it turned out, McDonald was not far off the mark. In the months following the election, he and other analysts examined the voter turnout statics from various states and concluded that in fact 89.1 million people had voted.[4] While this level of participation is accurately described as "historic," it is important to note that it translates into just 40.9 percent of the voting-eligible population in the United States. Put another way, in this historic midterm election, with so many important issues at stake, almost 60 percent of eligible voters in the United States did not even bother to go to the polls.

So how does this compare with voter turnout in other established democracies? According to most scholars and observers, the answer is, "not well." Voter turnout in the United States tends to be quite low when compared to Europe, Oceania, and Asia. In Western Europe, for instance, since 1945 an average of 77 percent of eligible voters have cast ballots, compared with 50 percent in the United States.[5]

The comparatively low level of voter turnout in the United States is just one of many issues that are of concern to scholars and observers. Stephen Wayne, a respected author and lecturer on the American political system, for instance, points to "fraudulent, error-prone and discriminatory voting practices; high costs and unequal resources for those running for office; [and] short, compartmentalized, and negative media coverage."[6] Wayne asks, "is this any way to run a democratic election?"[7] In this chapter, we will examine the structure, health, and future well-being of one of the most important institutions in any democracy, the American electoral and voting process.

10 Most modern democracies are representative.

The ancient Greeks practiced a form of direct democracy in which the people ruled directly and made public policy decisions themselves without the "benefit" (or what the Athenians might have seen as the drawback) of elected officials or representatives. We still see examples of direct democracy practiced at the state and local levels in some parts of the United States.

New England town meetings A common practice in many small New England towns, whereby residents gather together to decide issues of policy.

Two of the most well-known examples of direct democracy are the **New England town meetings**, where residents gather together to decide issues of policy,

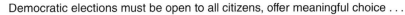

Initiatives In nearly every election cycle, voters in almost half the states are asked to indicate their support or opposition to a particular measure at the voting booth.

and **initiatives**. In nearly every election cycle voters in almost half the states are asked to participate in state ballot initiatives where they indicate their support or opposition to a particular measure at the voting booth. During the 2010 election, for instance, millions of voters across the country were asked to cast votes on issues ranging from healthcare to taxation to whether marijuana should be legalized. In total, 155 measures were on the ballots in thirty-six states.[8]

Despite the number of ballot measures, today direct democracy is far from the norm. This is due in part to the fact that direct democracy would not only be impractical but nearly impossible in a country as large, complex, and diverse as the United States and other modern democracies. As a result, democracies today are representative democracies, in which the voters select people to represent them in office and to make and implement public policy decisions on their behalf. The processes by which people choose others to represent them in office are **elections**. The people selected, those who win election, are empowered to act in the name of their **constituents**, or the people in their district whom they represent. They are empowered to make decisions and to set and implement policy. And if their constituents are satisfied with their job performance, they may be reelected in the next election.

Elections The process by which voters select people to represent them in office.

Constituents The people whom elected officials represent.

Democratic elections must be open to all citizens, offer meaningful choice and informed deliberation, and be fair, free, and frequent.

Elections may be an essential institution in a democracy, but that doesn't mean that all elections are democratic. In 2007, Central Asia's most populous nation, Uzbekistan, held presidential elections that were widely criticized for being undemocratic. Islam Karimov, the nation's only president since the country's independence from Soviet rule, won 88.1 percent of the vote. According to the election monitoring watchdog of the Organization for Security and Cooperation in Europe (OSCE), the election was "held in a strictly controlled political environment, leaving no room for real opposition." As a result, the OSCE concluded that the election "generally failed to meet . . . commitments for democratic elections."[9]

Likewise, in 2010, the Belarus government reported that President Aleksandr Lukashenko won reelection to a fourth term of office with 79.7 percent of the vote. The United States refused to recognize the election results after the OSCE reported that the elections were "marred by the detention of most presidential candidates and hundreds of activists."[10]

Both of these cases raise an important question: What are the basic standards an election in Uzbekistan, Belarus, or the United States, for that matter, must meet in order to be considered democratic? Political theorists Robert Dahl, Stephen Wayne,

William Hudson, and others have studied this issue in depth and identified four criteria critical to democratic elections.

Universal suffrage The right of all adult citizens to vote.

First, in order to be considered democratic, all citizens must be given the opportunity to participate in and influence the outcomes of elections. In short, **universal suffrage**, or the right of all adult citizens to vote, is an essential component of democratic elections.

Second, voters must be given a meaningful choice. One of the major criticisms in Uzbekistan in 2007 was that the opposition candidates who ran against President Karimov were not serious contenders and were placed on the ballot solely to give the election an appearance of fairness. When the vote was tallied, each of his three opponents received approximately 3 percent of the vote to his 88 percent.

Third, voters must also be given the chance to deliberate and have an open discussion about what policies their government should pursue. In order to deliberate, citizens need access to basic information and knowledge. Finally, a fourth essential element of democratic elections is that they must be fair, free, and frequent. According to Dahl, this means that "elected officials are chosen in frequent and fairly conducted elections in which coercion is comparatively uncommon."[11] For example, national elections in the United States are held every two years.

The question for Americans is not just whether other countries like Uzbekistan or Belarus live up to these standards, but whether we do ourselves. Throughout the remainder of the chapter, we will discuss several issues related to the American electoral process. As we do, consider how we are living up to these important standards. Where are we succeeding? Where are we faltering? And, how we can do better?

8 The United States holds more frequent elections with more choices than other modern democracies.

Turnout statistics support the contention that Americans not only pay more attention to the presidential election than any other elections, they actually vote in much larger numbers as well. Consider that in the 2008 presidential election, more than 132 million Americans voted. This is 45 million more than turned out to vote in the highly contentious 2010 midterm elections.[12] There are many reasons why more people tend to tune in and turn out in presidential election years, including the amount of comparative media interest, money spent, the fact that the president has a higher-profile job than those running in midterm elections, and so on.

American citizens are asked to go to the polls more frequently and vote for more candidates than many of their counterparts in other democratic nations. As Table 8.1 shows, in 2009 residents of Los Angeles County were asked to go to the polls eight times between March and July. During the previous year, they were expected to turn

Table 8.1

Number of County Elections in Los Angeles County by Year (2007–2009)

Year	Number of Elections	Elections (Dates)
2009*	8	32nd Congressional Special General (7/14)
		Special School District Elections (6/30)
		Palos Verdes Peninsula Special Election (6/23)
		Southern Pasadena USD Special Election (6/19)
		Special Statewide & Consolidated Elections (5/19)
		San Marino USD Special Parcel Tax Election (5/5)
		Arcadia USD Board of Education election (4/21)
		26th State Senate Special Primary Election (3/24)
2008	4	Maywood City Recall & Special Election (12/9)
		Presidential General Election (11/4)
		Primary Election (6/3)
		Presidential Primary Election (2/5)
2007	8	55th State Assembly Special Primary (12/11)
		Consolidated Elections (11/6)
		Lynwood City Special Recall Election (9/25)
		37th Congressional Special General (8/21)
		37th Congressional Special Primary (6/26)
		Wiseburn School District Special Election (6/12)
		Special Elections (6/5)
		39th State Assembly Special Primary (5/15)

**Data Updated as of August 2009.*

Source: County of Los Angeles, Registrar-Recorder/County Clerk, http://rrcc.co.la.ca.us/elect/pdownrslt.html-ssi (accessed August 2009).

out four times.[13] And Los Angeles County is not an anomaly. In some parts of the country citizens are asked to go to the polls even more regularly. It is no wonder that, as Ivor Crewe writes, "the average American is entitled to do far more electing—probably by a factor of three or four—than the citizen of any other democracy."[14]

Not only do Americans go to the polls more frequently than citizens in most countries, but oftentimes citizens are asked to cast their votes for candidates for many offices. The result is a "long ballot." In Thurston County, Washington, in 2008, citizens were asked to cast votes for candidates in thirty-one races (everyone from the president to the county public utilities commissioner), three ballot initiatives, and three propositions.[15] It is not surprising that some citizens cast ballots only for the offices at the "top of the ticket" and leave the other offices at the so-called "bottom of the ticket" blank. The number of elections in Los Angeles County and the sheer number of votes citizens in Thurston were asked to cast in 2008 raise an important question: Are we asking too much of voters? If you lived in Los Angeles County or Thurston County, how many of these elections would you have participated in?

If the frequency and sheer number of elections make it difficult for voters to make well-informed and deliberate decisions, then why do we have this system? The answer stems from the federal structure of the U.S. government. The fact that the United States has national, state, and local governments means that not only are citizens asked to cast ballots for multiple federal officials, they are also asked to cast ballots for local and state officials as well. The United States also offers **staggered elections** both on a national and local level. Members of the U.S. Senate serve six-year terms, but only one-third of the U.S. Senate is up for election every two years. Staggered elections help ensure stability and maintain a more deliberative legislative body that is less subject to the whims of opinion. Yet, these principles come at a cost, and our challenge as Americans is how we can honor these founding principles without overwhelming voters.

Staggered elections Only one-third of the U.S. Senate is up for election every two years. Staggered elections help ensure stability and maintain a more deliberative legislative body that is less subject to the whims of opinion.

To win an election, a candidate must make efficient use of time and money.

We have already established that the sheer number of elections held in the United States annually can be daunting for voters asked to participate in all of them. They can also be exhausting for candidates, who, in order to win any election, even the most local, must campaign vigorously. A **campaign** is an attempt by a candidate to gain the support of backers and voters to help win election to political office. A basic definition like that, however, underplays the amount of effort candidates and the people who work for them go through in order to win political office. A successful campaign makes use of five major resources: time, money, message, the candidate, and people.[16] All of these resources are scarce and must be monitored closely and employed as efficiently and skillfully as possible to maximize their benefits.

Campaign An attempt by a candidate to gain the support of backers and voters to help win election to political office.

Time is key in a campaign and, much as in life, there is seldom enough of it. The calendar of the U.S. election cycle has expanded over time as candidates seek to improve their chances with electors. Today, for example, most presidential candidates start campaigning at least three to four years before the election. This is essential if they are going to visit key states, raise funds, earn name recognition, and do all the other things required to make a viable run for the presidency. And the fact is, early politicking occurs not only at the presidential level but in other national, state, and local races as well. Take Larry Kissell, for instance, who was elected Congressman from North Carolina's 8th District in 2008. Kissell began campaigning the day after he lost in 2006. What Kissell realized is something all winning candidates know: time is a critical resource and something that must be maximized to outcampaign, outwork, and outfundraise your opponent.[17]

A second important and controversial resource of campaigns is money. The simple truth is—from the presidential level down to local sheriffs—money is required to do everything from buying advertising time and paying those people working for the campaign to helping transport the candidate to and from campaign speeches and paying for polling data. The cost of the 2008 presidential election topped a record-breaking $1 billion, the most money spent on a presidential election in American history. The following year, the mayor of New York City, Michael Bloomberg, spent more than $100 million running for reelection. This brought total spending on his three successful bids for mayor in 2001, 2005, and 2009, to an astonishing $250 million or "the equivalent of what Warner Brothers Studio spent on the latest Harry Potter film."[18]

Although money plays a key role in helping candidates get their message out and campaigns have become much more expensive over time, the 2010 midterm election underscores the fact that even in politics money isn't everything. As we saw that year, many of the wealthiest self-funded candidates lost, including former Hewlett-Packard CEO Carly Fiorina, who ran for the U.S. Senate in California; former CEO of the World Wide Wrestling Federation Linda McMahon, who ran for the Senate in Connecticut; and Democrat Jeff Greene, who ran for the Senate in Florida. In fact, the Center for Responsive Politics reports that fewer than one in five of the fifty-eight candidates who spent more than half a million dollars on their own campaign in 2010 won.[19]

6 Candidates with an appealing message and skilled staff are critical to a successful campaign.

As important as time and money are, they usually do not suffice in the absence of a candidate with a message that resonates. In fact, a campaign that lacks adequate funding and time at the outset may be able to make up for the scarcity of these resources with an attractive candidate and a strong message. During the first nine months of 2007, for example, Hillary Clinton raised over $90 million. Despite this,

Clinton finished third in the Iowa caucuses.[20] Many people suggest that in addition to the superb way in which his campaign organized that state, Barack Obama also won because he was a candidate with an attractive message of hope and change that resonated with many more voters.

Incumbent A candidate for office who currently holds the seat.

In addition to an appealing message, another factor that heavily influences the outcome of an election is incumbency. An **incumbent** is a candidate who currently holds the seat. Generally speaking, incumbents have a significant advantage over their challengers. For one, they enjoy the perks of office; these include staff, budget, free postal mailings, and the ability to "bring home the bacon," or get tangible results for their districts. Second, they have the luxury of time their opponents may not. Once elected, they serve full-time and can devote 100 percent of their energy to the position, unlike their challengers who are more apt to be balancing a run for office with a full-time job. Third, they have visibility: They are more frequently interviewed in the local press, more likely to make appearances, and have more general name recognition than their challengers. Fourth, they have a campaign organization in place from their last successful race for the same office. Fifth, as Table 8.2 shows, they have

Table 8.2 Incumbent Advantage

The charts below show the enormous financial advantage enjoyed by incumbents. That's one of the reasons reelection rates are so high—incumbents generally don't have to work as hard to get their name and message out.

Senate

Type of Candidate	Total Raised	Number of Candidates	Average Raised
Incumbent	$332,518,265	30	$11,083,942
Challenger	$141,207,301	152	$928,995

House

Type of Candidate	Total Raised	Number of Candidates	Average Raised
Incumbent	$636,396,176	420	$1,515,229
Challenger	$296,927,277	1,115	$266,302

Source: Based on data released by the FEC on February 02, 2011. Figures include all candidates who have filed reports. Center for Responsive Politics, http://www.opensecrets.org/overview/incumbs.php.

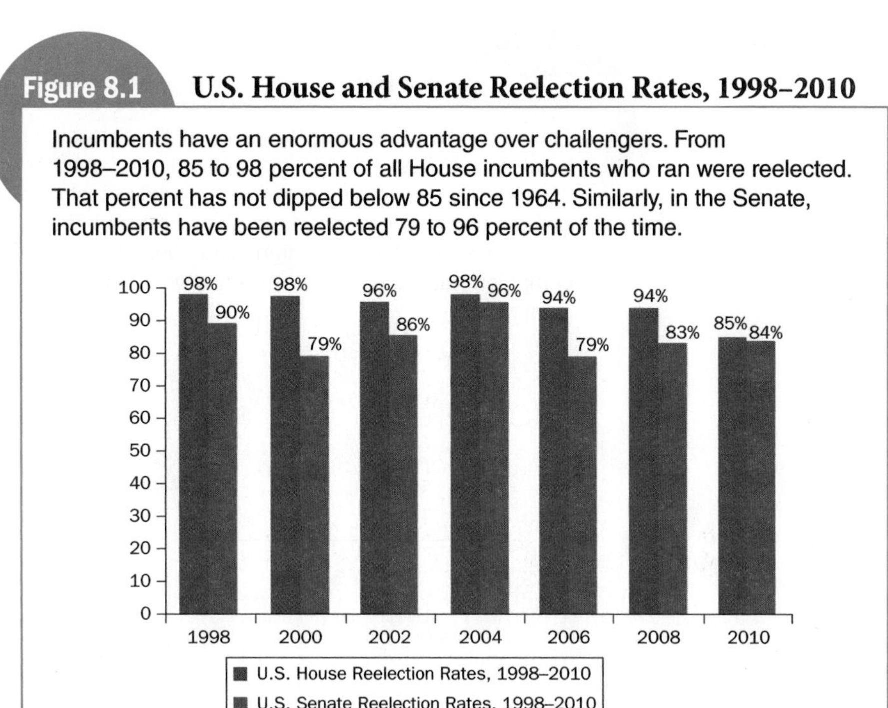

Figure 8.1 U.S. House and Senate Reelection Rates, 1998–2010

Incumbents have an enormous advantage over challengers. From 1998–2010, 85 to 98 percent of all House incumbents who ran were reelected. That percent has not dipped below 85 since 1964. Similarly, in the Senate, incumbents have been reelected 79 to 96 percent of the time.

Source: Center for Responsive Politics, http://www.opensecrets.org/bigpicture/reelect.php

the all-important ability to raise on average far more money as a sitting official than their challengers can. On average, challengers for House seats were outspent by incumbents by more than $1.2 million. Challengers for Senate seats were outspent by incumbents by more than $10 million.[21]

These incumbent advantages are meaningful because they translate into votes. As Figure 8.1 indicates, in the 12 years from 1998 to 2010, 85–98 percent of all incumbents who ran in the House were reelected. That percentage has not dipped below 85 since 1964. Similarly, in the Senate over the same twelve-year period, incumbents have been reelected between 79 to 96 percent of the time.[22] These numbers show that the odds are generally not in favor of challengers.

Figure 8.2 shows that in addition to the candidate, the key people in a campaign include the campaign manager, media consultant, fund-raiser, pollster, press aide, scheduler, researcher, speech writer, lawyers, field workers, volunteers, interns, and the like. While most campaigns have a manager, pollster, media consultant,

Figure 8.2 **Structure of a Modern Campaign**

The key people in a campaign include the campaign manager, media consultant, fundraiser, pollster, press aide, scheduler, researcher, speech writer, lawyers, field workers, volunteers, and interns. While most campaigns have a manager, pollster, media consultant, fundraiser, and staff director, the actual number of people working for a campaign differs depending on how many resources the campaign has available (especially money) and whether it is a national, state, or local race.

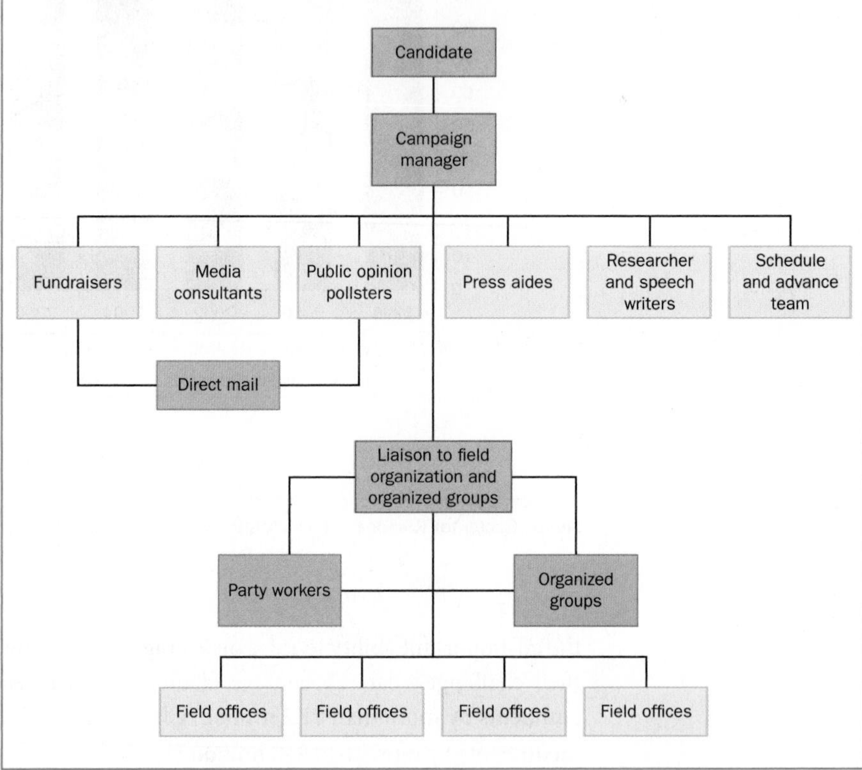

Source: Louis Sandy Maisel, Mark D. Brewer. *Parties and Elections in America: The Electoral Process.* Rowan and Littlefield Publishing (2008) p. 244

fund-raiser, and staff director, the actual number of people working for a campaign differs depending on how many resources the campaign has available (especially money) and whether it is a national, state, or local race. Local campaigns tend to have anywhere from a few dozen to hundreds of campaign workers, state candidates thousands, and national campaigns upwards of tens of thousands.[23]

Candidates secure their parties' nomination in primary elections and caucuses before running for office.

Primary elections Elections in which voters go to the polls to choose the nominee for a political party.

Open primaries Elections in which all registered voters can decide on the day of the election in which party's election they will participate.

Closed primaries Elections in which only party members can participate.

Caucuses Meetings in which members of a party gather to choose their party's nominee.

Political candidates representing major and minor parties must obtain their parties' nomination before they can compete in general elections. **Primary elections** are elections in which voters go to the polls to choose the nominee for a political party. There are two major types of primary elections. As Table 8.3 shows, some states, such as Ohio, hold **open primaries** in which all registered voters can decide on the day of the election in which party's election they will participate. **Closed primaries** are elections in which only party members can participate.[24]

Some states do not hold primaries. Instead, these states choose party nominees through a caucus process. **Caucuses** are meetings in which members of a party gather to choose their party's nominee. The first and most important caucus in the country every four years is held in Iowa. The caucus is important because it gives the candidates who win a psychological boost and increases the likelihood the media will dub the winner "front-runner"—a label that can help as the candidates move to the next battleground.

During the Iowa caucuses, registered Republicans and Democrats gather together to discuss the candidates and vote for their party's nominee. In both parties, the purpose of the vote is to select delegates to attend a county convention. These delegates in turn select delegates to go to the congressional district state convention, and those delegates choose the delegates that go to the national convention. The Iowa caucuses have often played a key role in determining who the nominee of a party will (or will not) be. In 2008, for instance, then Senator Barack Obama surprised many when he won the Iowa caucuses. The momentum Obama got coming out of Iowa helped propel him forward in his quest to become the nominee of the Democratic Party that year.

Just how Obama went from being the junior senator from Illinois to winning the Iowa caucus and ultimately securing the Democratic Party's nominee for president will be used to illustrate the three major steps in the presidential nomination process: the announcement, the quest for delegates, and the formal nomination at the party's **national nominating convention**.

National nominating convention An assembly of party delegates where the formal nomination of a candidate takes place.

Announcement: Senator Barack Obama formally announced his intention to seek his party's nomination for president on May 2, 2007. Standing on the steps of the Old State Capitol in his hometown of Chicago, Illinois, Obama evoked his hero Abraham Lincoln as he announced his intention to run for president less than two years after being sworn into the U.S. Senate. Obama was not the only Democrat seeking the Democratic nomination that year. Indeed, several Democrats threw their hats into the ring, including the much better funded Senator from New York, Hillary

Table 8.3 Types of Primaries in Each State

State	Closed	Open	Other	State	Closed	Open	Other
Alabama		X		Montana			X
Alaska	X			Nebraska	X		
Arizona	X			Nevada	X		
Arkansas		X		New Hampshire			X
California			X	New Jersey			X
Colorado	X			New Mexico	X		
Connecticut	X			New York	X		
Delaware	X			North Carolina	X		
District of Columbia	X			North Dakota		X	
Florida	X			Ohio			X
Georgia		X		Oklahoma	X		
Hawaii	X			Oregon	X		
Idaho		X	X	Pennsylvania	X		
Illinois			X	Rhode Island	X		X
Indiana		X		South Carolina		X	
Iowa	X		X	South Dakota	X		
Kansas	X		X	Tennessee		X	
Kentucky	X			Texas		X	
Louisiana	X		X	Utah	X		
Maine	X			Vermont		X	
Maryland	X			Virginia		X	
Massachusetts			X	Washington		X	
Michigan		X		West Virginia			X
Minnesota		X		Wisconsin		X	
Missouri		X		Wyoming	X		

Source: FairVote Voting and Democracy Research Center http://www.fairvote.org/?page=1801.

Clinton, former U.S. Senator from North Carolina John Edwards, Governor of New Mexico Bill Richardson, U.S. Senator Joe Biden, U.S. Senator Chris Dodd, and Representative Dennis Kucinich, among others.

Winning Delegates: In order to win the nomination, candidates have to win the majority of votes cast at their party's convention. The people at the convention who cast the votes are called **delegates**. The two most common ways in which candidates get delegates are through the party caucuses and primary elections. In 2008, the Iowa caucuses were held in January. After spending millions of dollars on campaign advertisements and an inordinate amount of time campaigning and organizing campaign workers on his behalf, Obama shocked everyone by winning 38 percent of the vote to Edwards' 30 percent and Clinton's 29 percent. Although Clinton received just 9 percent less support than Obama, the results impacted her candidacy because she failed to meet expectations.

Delegates The people at the convention who cast the votes.

Just five days later, the candidates for the 2008 nomination descended on New Hampshire for the first-in-the-nation primary. They then competed in a flurry of caucuses and primaries during the first several weeks of the year, culminating on February 5, 2008 in "**Super Duper Tuesday**," when an unprecedented twenty-three states held their primaries simultaneously.

Super Duper Tuesday The Tuesday in February during a presidential election year when an unprecedented twenty-three states hold their primaries simultaneously.

One potential problem with open primaries came to light during the 2008 primary season. Conservative talk show host Rush Limbaugh launched what was dubbed "Operation Chaos." Limbaugh went on the air and urged his Republican supporters to vote for Hillary Clinton in the Democratic primary. In the process of beefing up his ratings, he also managed to create disarray in the Democratic Party by extending the heated contest between Clinton and Obama. Subsequent to his call, Clinton won the Ohio, Indiana, and Texas primaries (but ultimately lost the nomination). It remains unclear whether her success in these primaries was related to Limbaugh's efforts or whether other factors came into play, but it raises the question of whether an open primary encourages or discourages a more democratic process.

Nominating Convention: The two major parties hold national nominating conventions every four years, usually in the late summer or early fall. In 2008, the Democrats had only two-and-a-half months to unify a party that had been badly splintered between two popular candidates. In the end, however, Obama was formally nominated at the Democratic National Convention in Denver, Colorado, on August 28.

The Republican Party held its convention in St. Paul, Minnesota, from September 1 to September 4. Unlike the Democrats, Republicans had from March until early September to unify the party behind their nominee, Senator John McCain. On the fourth day of the convention, McCain delivered a speech in which he formally accepted his party's nomination.

Beyond the nomination of their candidate for president, national conventions also allow party members from across the country to gather together to take care of other party business. Most importantly, for instance, the convention gives party members an opportunity to adopt the **party platform** (a formal written statement of where the party stands on key issues). It also gives members the chance to unify the

Party platform A formal written statement of where the party stands on key issues.

party faithful behind the ticket and introduce the party's presidential and vice presidential ticket to the rest of the world.

Both party nominees and independent candidates can compete in the general election.

General election The contest between candidates who have either succeeded in winning the nomination of their party or who are running independently.

Third party Minor party

Once each major party selects its nominee, the real battle gets underway. The **general election** is the contest between candidates who have either succeeded in winning the nomination of their party or who are running independently. Although voters who identify as independents made up approximately 30 percent of the electorate in 2008, independent candidates who have a real shot at winning the presidency are historically rare.[25] During the 2008 presidential election, in addition to the two major party candidates, there were at least eleven **third-party** (or minor-party) and six independent candidates with ballot status in at least one state. The Constitution Party nominated Chuck Baldwin, the Green Party nominated Cynthia McKinney, and the Libertarian Party nominated Bob Barr. These were just three of the third-party nominees in 2008. Few had name recognition, and as a group they received little press coverage and few votes.

Historically, most independent candidates for president form party organizations to support their run. One of the most well-known examples of this is H. Ross Perot, the Texas billionaire businessman who formed the Reform Party shortly after his unsuccessful bid for the presidency in 1992. The Reform Party successfully elected former wrestler Jesse Ventura as governor of Minnesota in 1998. Since that time, the party has weakened considerably and been beset by problems of infighting. This is typical of these types of parties that are formed generally to support one candidate or one primary cause.

While third-party or independent candidates in the United States have little chance of winning the presidency, they can often have an impact by drawing public attention to an issue or set of issues, increasing turnout by bringing people to the polls who might otherwise not vote, and underscoring discontent with the major parties and their candidates.

The Electoral College determines the outcome for the presidential race in the general election.

Electoral College A slate of electors within each state and the District of Columbia that cast the ultimate vote for president on behalf of voters.

The method by which a candidate for president wins the White House sounds deceptively simple: The person who wins the majority of **Electoral College** votes goes on to become president. Yet many Americans aren't quite clear as to how the process in fact works. When citizens go into the voting booth on Election Day, they are not voting for the president directly, but rather they are voting for a slate of electors within each state and the District of Columbia.[26] As Table 8.4 shows, electors ultimately cast the vote for president on our behalf.

For the most part, the Electoral College has functioned well. However, it is possible to have an election in which no candidate wins a majority of the Electoral

Table 8.4 The Electoral College (in brief)

1. Each state is allotted 1 elector for each U.S. Representative and Senator (for example, if California has 52 representatives in the House and 2 senators, it gets 54 Electoral College votes; the District of Columbia receives 3 electors—the same number as the least populous state). The total number of electoral votes is 538.
2. Most electors are nominated at state party conventions.
3. On Election Day, voters in each state cast their ballot for a slate of electors representing their choice of presidential ticket. The electors' names do not appear on the ballot, but when a voter cast a vote for John McCain in 2008, she cast a vote for a Republican slate of electors; likewise, another voter who cast a ballot for Barack Obama actually voted for a Democratic slate of electors.
4. The slate of electors for the presidential ticket that receives the most votes is appointed, and all the electoral votes for that state go to those candidates (i.e., if the popular vote goes to the Republicans, then the slate of Republican electors is appointed). Thus, it is in most states a "winner-take-all" system. The person/presidential slate with the most votes, gets all the Electoral College votes (except in Maine and Nebraska).*
5. A candidate needs to win a majority of Electoral College votes (270) to be elected president.
6. If no candidate wins a majority of these votes, the election is "thrown into the House," and the House will choose the president. In this instance, the names of the three candidates are given to the House, and each state gets 1 vote.
7. In December, in a largely ceremonial gesture, the electors cast their ballots for president and vice president. The electors are expected to follow the popular vote in their state. On rare occasions, a few electors have voted for another candidate. When this happens, the elector is sometimes referred to as a "faithless elector." By some accounts, this has occurred less than 160 times in American history.** One of the most recent occurrences was said to be in 2004 and was actually a result of a mistake when an elector pledged to Democratic candidate John Kerry supposedly accidentally cast a ballot for Kerry's vice presidential running mate Senator John Edwards. Approximately twenty-six states have legislation to punish faithless electors.
8. The Electoral College votes are counted at a Joint Session of Congress the following January, and the president is officially elected.
9. The president is then sworn into office in late January.

*You can read more about Maine and Nebraska's alternative systems at: http://archive.fairvote.org/e_college/me_ne.htm.

**You can read more about "Faithless electors" at: http://archive.fairvote.org/e_college/faithless.htm

Table 8.5

Presidential Elections in Which the Candidate with the Most Votes Lost the Electoral College and the Presidency

Year	Winner of Popular Vote	Winner of Electoral College Vote
1824	Andrew Jackson	J.Q. Adams
1876	Samuel Tilden	Rutherford B. Hayes
1888	Grover Cleveland	Benjamin Harrison
2000	Albert Gore	George W. Bush

College votes. In this case, the election goes to the House of Representatives, where the president is chosen. This occurred in both the election of 1800 (when the House chose Thomas Jefferson over Aaron Burr) and the election of 1824 (when the House chose John Quincy Adams over Andrew Jackson). There is also a second possibility (shown in Table 8.5) in which the winner of the popular vote does not win in the Electoral College. This happened most recently in 2000, when Al Gore won the most popular votes but George W. Bush won in the Electoral College.

Many people assumed that the 2000 election might be the end of the Electoral College or result in reform. But, so far, no proposal has gained traction. Among the most popular reform proposals are the following:

- A popular election in which the winner of the popular vote wins the presidency, and the Electoral College is eliminated entirely. The Electoral College, however, is a requirement specified in Article II of the Constitution, so eliminating it would take a constitutional amendment, which is not an easy thing to do.
- A proportional plan. Most states award electors based on the "**winner-take-all system**" in which the candidate who wins a particular state receives all of the state's Electoral College votes. If states instead awarded electoral votes on a proportional basis, mathematically the winner of the popular vote would always be reflected in the vote outcome of the Electoral College.

Winner-take-all system The candidate who wins a particular state receives all of the state's Electoral College votes.

Most of the elections that occur in the United States take place at the state and local levels, but the majority are not competitive.

During the 2008 election, the race for president consumed the vast majority of the media attention—but it was not the only election going on at that time. On Election Day 2008, citizens of thirty-five states elected a U.S. senator, and all 435 seats in the House of Representatives were up for grabs. Many of these elections received minimal media coverage, suffered from low turnout rates, and were among the least competitive in the nation.[27] If the situation is less than desirable for U.S. Senate and House races, it is near deplorable at the state and local levels, where there are tens of thousands of seats to be filled.

Midterm elections Elections that occur midway through a president's term (nonpresidential election years).

Off-year elections Elections held in the United States that occur in odd-number years. These elections are generally for the selection of local and municipal offices rather than major state or federal offices.

Low levels of turnout for subnational races become most clear when you consider the relative turnout rates for **midterm** or **off-year elections**. Levels of turnout decrease across the board, but it is instructive to consider differences among one subset of the population, such as young people ages 18 to 29. In advance of the 2009 off-year election, for instance, columnist and author E. J. Dionne speculated that young people would probably not turn out in as large numbers for the 2009 and 2010 elections as they had during the 2008 presidential election.[28] His prediction is supported by a good deal of data which show that whereas turnout among 18- to 29-year-olds was roughly 51 percent in 2004 and 53 percent in 2008, it tends to be about half of that (20 to 25 percent) for midterm elections such as 2006 and 2010 and even less than that for off-year elections like 2007 and 2009.[29]

These races are also characterized by a general lack of competitiveness. This can be seen most clearly by the enormous rate of incumbency reelection. Even in the dramatic midterm election of 2010 when Republicans took the House of Representatives, approximately 85 percent of incumbents were reelected.[30] Although most political experts attribute the lack of competitiveness in local races to redistricting, a recent survey by The Pew Research Center found that the majority of the public "lack a sense as to whether the elections in their own House districts are competitive . . . [and are] only dimly aware of the debate over how boundaries are drawn for legislative districts."[31]

The incumbency reelection rates and the comparative lack of media coverage and participation at the state and local levels mean that there is something of a general lack of competitiveness that pervades many (but not all) of these contests. This is complicated by the fact that the rules regarding who can run, how candidates' names appear on the ballot, who can register and ultimately vote, when and how elections (below the national level) occur, and the role of the parties differ from state to state.

As scholars David Magleby and Paul Light note, state and local governments play a vital role in all of our lives:

> Many of the critical domestic and economic issues facing the United States are decided by state and local officials. . . . how schools are run, where roads and bridges are built, how land is used, what social services are provided to who . . . they regulate our driving, our occupations, our families . . . they decide what constitutes criminal behavior and how it should be charged, tried, and punished."[32]

Given this, it is troubling that elections for these offices tend to be less than competitive. It is also important to think about whether, given their characteristics, these key state and local elections meet the requirements for democratic elections discussed earlier: equal opportunity, meaningful choice, chance for deliberation, and fair, free, and frequent elections.

The cost of winning is a major concern people have about the health of U.S. elections.

In 2009, New York City Mayor Michael Bloomberg spent close to $100 million on his reelection campaign. Across the Hudson, New Jersey Governor Jon Corzine spent about a quarter of that, approximately $24 million. Nevertheless, in doing so Corzine still spent nearly three times as much as his Republican challenger, Chris Christie. And, unlike Bloomberg, Corzine lost the race.[33] As staggering as these amounts are, they pale in comparison to the almost $1 billion candidates for president spent on the 2008 election.

These figures help explain why the high cost of running for and winning office in the United States remains a primary concern of election observers and experts. They also help explain why there has been so much focus on the issue of **campaign finance reform**, or efforts in the United States to curb or regulate the role of money in political campaigns. These efforts date back to the early twentieth century and the **Tillman Act** of 1907 (the first piece of legislation in the United States prohibiting monetary contributions to national campaigns by corporations) and have continued through to the early twenty-first century with the **Bipartisan Campaign Reform Act** of 2002 (often referred to as either the BCRA or McCain-Feingold law), which regulates the financing of political campaigns. In fact, it was the McCain-Feingold law that was at issue in the key 2010 Supreme Court case ***Citizens United v. Federal Election Commission (FEC)***.

Campaign finance reform Efforts to limit or otherwise regulate the amount of money spent on election campaigns.

Tillman Act Enacted in 1907, this was the first piece of legislation in the United States to prohibit monetary contributions to national campaigns by corporations.

Bipartisan Campaign Reform Act (BCRA) Passed in 2002, this piece of legislation regulates the financing of political campaigns.

Citizens United v. Federal Election Commission (FEC) A 2010 Supreme Court case in which in a 5–4 ruling the Court ruled that key portions of the BCRA were unconstitutional.

The Citizens United case stemmed from a film entitled *Hillary: The Movie* produced during the 2008 presidential election by Citizens United, a conservative not-for-profit organization. The film questioned whether then presidential candidate Hillary Clinton would make a good president. The FEC argued that section 203 of the BCRA forbids corporations or labor unions from funding such types of communication. In a highly anticipated decision, the Supreme Court ruled 5–4 in favor of Citizens United, finding that key portions of the BCRA were unconstitutional. As Justice Anthony Kennedy wrote in his majority decision, "if the First Amendment has any force, it prohibits Congress from fining or jailing citizens, or associations of citizens, for simply engaging in political speech."[34]

The decision was so controversial that in an unprecedented move, President Obama condemned the Court's ruling during his 2010 State of the Union speech, noting:

> Last week, the Supreme Court reversed a century of law to open the floodgates for special interests—including foreign corporations—to spend without limit in our elections. Well I don't think American elections should be bankrolled by America's most powerful interests, or worse, by foreign entities.[35]

 The cost of winning is a major concern people have about the health of U.S. elections.

Citizens United remains one of the most discussed and controversial Supreme Court decisions of the last several years in part because it deals with an issue at the heart of American democracy—free and fair elections. Critics of the Court's ruling have called it "the most serious threat to American democracy in a generation,"[36] while supporters have countered that the Court stood up for the First Amendment and that the decision will make elections more fair and competitive.[37]

Regardless of where you stand on this particular case, the prevailing sense remains that money is corrupting our political process. Primary among the concerns expressed is the notion that people and groups with money have undue influence on the electoral process. Is it, for instance, a coincidence that both Bloomberg and Corzine are millionaires? A related concern is the fact that candidates and public officials are now almost required to spend an inordinate amount of time fund-raising if they hope to have a chance at gaining or maintaining public office. When you consider that the people who usually win office are those who spend the most, a candidate's focus on fund-raising is at once understandable and a source of concern. As Stephen Wayne notes, "the general perception today is that government is for sale to the highest bidder."[38]

While the potential corrupting influence of money in elections may be a source of uneasiness, it is not the only aspect of the U.S. electoral process of concern. As we have seen in this chapter and elsewhere in this text, low levels of voter knowledge and participation, voting methods and procedures, the role of the news media, negative advertising, interest groups, political action committees, and the incumbency advantage are just a few of the many areas of the U.S. electoral process that commentators and scholars suggest may be in need of reform.

CONCLUSION

The introduction referenced a question posed by scholar Stephen Wayne: "Is this any way to run a democratic election?" Put another way, how good a job are we doing electing representatives? By now you should have learned enough about the basics of the American electoral process to begin to form your own judgments regarding the health and well-being of the system and to consider which aspects might be in need of reform.

One way to answer these questions is to consider how well we are doing living up to the criteria required for fair and democratic elections: equal opportunity, meaningful choice, open deliberation, and fair, free, and frequent elections. When it comes to equality, for instance, does everyone have an equal opportunity to participate in the electoral process? A recent report by the Brennan Center suggests "a great many young people, particularly students, who want to vote are unable to do so because of legal or administrative barriers that make it extremely difficult or impossible to vote in their college communities."[39] And what about fairness? Is it fair,

THEIR LIST

An Insider's View

THOMAS DOHERTY

Partner, Mercury Public Affairs

Thomas Doherty is a partner in Mercury Public Affairs. Prior to joining Mercury, he served as executive director of "Victory '98" for the New York State Republican Committee, where he established campaign infrastructure, worked on fund-raising, scheduling, strategy, and press, as well as managed campaign staff for five statewide candidates. He also served as Governor George Pataki's (R-NY) deputy secretary of appointments and oversaw his Office of State and Local Government Affairs. In addition to his work in the governor's office, he has served as both an elected and appointed official in his local community.

Given all the time he has devoted to both managing campaigns and running for office, we asked Mr. Doherty what he thinks are the most important things to know about campaigns and elections. He suggested there are three things, in no particular order, that students should know about the reality of running for office in the United States.

First, the reality is that financing is critical to running a legitimate election. Or to put it another way, whether we like it or not, money matters a good deal. "Finances are," said Doherty, "the most important thing you have going for you. If you can self-fund your campaign, for example, this gives you a tremendous leg up. . . . Money carries you forward."

Second, in addition to money, candidates need a purpose or reason to run. This is closely related to the concept of credibility. "If a candidate is seeking to run," Doherty said, "they need to be able to tell people why they are running, what their purpose is, why their campaign and candidacy makes sense, why voters should choose them." In some cases, Doherty noted, the money comes first and the purpose follows; in others, the order is reversed.

Once candidates have these two things, both a reason to run and the funding necessary to do it, it is critical they put together a viable campaign organization. They need campaign managers, workers, pollsters, lawyers, schedulers, advisors, volunteers, and others who understand the campaign environment, know what it takes to run and win in that district, and are well equipped to assist the candidate in doing that. This includes working on everything from outreach, polling, and opposition research, to scheduling appearances, managing the press operations, fund-raising, and the myriad other things involved in putting together a successful campaign operation.

for instance, that candidates who are personally wealthy are more likely to run and win office in the United States than candidates who do not have access to similar monetary resources?

Although our system is far from perfect, it does have its virtues. Since its founding, the American electoral system has allowed the minority party to compete for power. And, even after a hard-fought race, transitions from one administration to the next are peaceful. In addition, citizens are encouraged to participate, candidates and parties can express their views, and voters have access to information about the candidates.[40] It is no surprise that in its 2010 "Freedom in the World" report, the Freedom House gave the United States a perfect score on its index of political rights.[41] It is important in a democracy to both acknowledge these areas of strength and to continue to work towards improving those areas where the system fails to measure up to our shared ideals.

YOUR LIST REVISITED

At the beginning of the chapter you were asked to think about what you might include on your own list of the Top 10 Most Important Things to Know About Campaigns and Elections. Now that you have read the chapter, take a moment to revisit your list. What, if anything, would you change about your list? Do you agree or disagree with the chapter list constructed by the author? What might you add or delete? Why?

KEY TERMS

Bipartisan Campaign Reform Act (BCRA) 188
Campaign 176
Campaign finance reform 188
Caucuses 181
Citizens United v. Federal Election Commission (FEC) 188
Closed primaries 181
Constituents 173
Delegates 183
Elections 173
Electoral College 184
General election 184
Incumbent 178
Initiatives 173
Midterm elections 187
National nominating convention 181
New England town meetings 172
Off-year elections 187
Open primaries 181
Party platform 183
Primary elections 181
Staggered elections 176
Super Duper Tuesday 183
Third party 184
Tillman Act 188
Universal suffrage 174
Voter turnout 172
Winner-take-all system 186

CHAPTER REVIEW QUESTIONS

10 In what type of democratic system do elections play a key role?

9 Explain the four major criteria elections must meet to be considered democratic.

8 What are two unique characteristics of U.S. elections?

7 Why does a candidate need to make efficient use of time and money to win?

6 Why do incumbents have an advantage in the U.S. system?

5 What is the major difference between primary and general elections?

4 Can independent candidates play a meaningful role in the general election? Why or why not?

3 How does the Electoral College determine the outcome of presidential elections?

2 Why aren't most of the elections at the state and local levels competitive?

1 Why are scholars and political scientists concerned with the health of U.S. elections?

SUGGESTED READINGS

- Anonymous. *Primary Colors: A Novel of Politics.* New York: Random House, 1996.
- Cramer, Richard Ben. *What It Takes: The Way to the White House.* New York: Random House, 1992.
- Crouse, Timothy. *The Boys on the Bus.* New York: Random House, 1973.
- Frank, Thomas. *What's the Matter with Kansas?: How Conservatives Won the Heart of America.* New York: Henry Holt, 2005.
- Heilemann, John, and Mark Halperin. *Game Change: Obama and the Clintons, McCain and Palin, and the Race of a Lifetime.* New York: Harper, 2010.
- Larson, Edward J. *Magnificent Catastrophe: The Tumultuous Election of 1800, America's First Presidential Campaign.* New York: Free Press, 2007.
- McGinnis, Joe. *The Selling of the President,* 1968. New York: Trident Press, 1969.
- Thompson, Hunter. *Fear and Loathing on the Campaign Trail 72.* San Francisco: Straight Arrow Books, 1973.
- Wayne, Stephen J. *Is This Any Way to Run a Democratic Election?* Washington, DC: CQ Press, 2011.
- White, Theodore. *The Making of the President, 1960.* New York: Harper, 1961.

SUGGESTED FILMS

- *The Last Hurrah* (1958)
- *The Manchurian Candidate* (1962)
- *The Candidate* (1972)
- *Bob Roberts* (1992)
- *Dave* (1993)
- *The American President* (1995)
- *Wag the Dog* (1997)
- *Bulworth* (1998)
- *Election* (1999)
- *The Contender* (2000)

SUGGESTED WEBSITES

- **American Association of Political Consultants:** http://www.theaapc.org/.
- **Campaigns and Elections: Politics Magazine:** http://politicsmagazine.com/.
- **CIRCLE: Center for Information and Research on Civic Learning & Engagements:** http://www.civicyouth.org/.
- **Columbia University: Campaigns & Elections:** http://library.columbia.edu/indiv/usgd/guides/federal/campaign.html
- **Election Law Blog:** http://electionlawblog.org/.
- **Federal Election Commission:** http://www.fec.gov/.
- **National Conference State Legislatures (NCSL):** http://www.ncsl.org/LegislaturesElections/tabid/746/Default.aspx
- **Politics1:** http://politics1.com/.
- **The Living Room Candidate:** http://www.livingroomcandidate.org/.
- **United States Election Assistance Commission:** http://www.eac.gov/.

ENDNOTES

[1]Carrie Dann and Domenico Montanaro, "Midterm could shatter records," *First Read from NBC News*, November 1, 2010, available online at: http://firstread.msnbc.msn.com/_news/2010/11/01/5390479-midterm-turnout-could-shatter-records.

[2]Michael McDonald, "2010 Turnout Rate and Early Voting Rate Forecasts," *United States Election Project*, November 2010, available online at: http://elections.gmu.edu/2010_vote_forecasts.html.

[3]Bob Guldin, *Choosing the President 2008: A Citizen's Guide to the Electoral Process* (Guilford, CT: The Lyons Press, 2008), p. 8.

[4]Michael McDonald, "2010 General Election Turnout Rates," *United States Election Project*, January 28, 2011, available online at: http://elections.gmu.edu/Turnout_2010G.html.

[5]"Voter Turnout," Historymania, available online at: http://www.historymania.com/american_history/Voter_turnout.

[6]Stephen J. Wayne, *Is This Any Way to Run a Democratic Election?* 3rd ed. (Washington, DC: CQ Press, 2007).

[7]Ibid.

[8]A. G. Sulzberger, "Voters face decisions on a mix of issues," *New York Times*, October 5, 2010, available online at: http://www.nytimes.com/2010/10/06/us/politics/06ballot.html?scp=8&sq=2010%20election%20propositions&st=cse.

[9]"Uzbekistan's elections labeled 'undemocratic,'" *Christian Science Monitor*, December 26, 2007, available online at: http://www.csmonitor.com/2007/1226/p11s01-wosc.html.

[10]"U.S. Condemns Belarus Crackdowns, Rejects 'Illegitimate' Election Results," *Bloomberg*, December 20, 2010, available online at: http://www.bloomberg.com/news/2010-12-19/protesters-police-clash-in-minsk-after-belarus-s-lukashenko-wins-election.html.

[11]Dahl, "What Political Institutions," *Political Science Quarterly*, v. 120, n. 2 (2005): p. 188.

[12]Michael McDonald, "Voter Turnout," *United States Elections Project*, available online at: http://elections.gmu.edu/voter_turnout.htm.

[13]This information is available from the County of Los Angeles Registrar-Recorder/County Clerk. Please visit the Web site online at: http://rrcc.co.la.ca.us/elect/pdownrslt.html-ssi.

[14]Ivor Crewe quoted in Matthew Justin Streb, *Rethinking American Electoral Democracy* (New York: Routledge, 2008), p. 11.

[15]This information was determined from a General Election Sample Ballot for Thurston County, Washington; the actual ballot may have differed somewhat. The sample ballot is available online at: http://www.co.thurston.wa.us/auditor/Elections/2008Elections/General/Sample_ballot.pdf.

[16]This section is drawn in part from a presentation, "NRCC Campaign Management School," January 2001, prepared by Greg Strimple, Mahoney, Strimple, Goncharenko LLC, a strategic management and polling firm with offices in New York City and Washington, DC.

[17]"The Campaign Manager: The World of Politics in Florida and Tampa Bay," available online at: http://campaignmanager.blogspot.com/2009/03/money-money-money-like-it-or-not.html (accessed 10/20/09).

[18]Michael Barbaro and David W. Chen, "Bloomberg Sets Record for His Own Spending," *New York Times*, October 23, 2009.

[19]Dave Levinthal, "Biggest Election Night Losers: Self-Funded Candidates," available online at: http://www.opensecrets.org/news/2010/11/biggest-losers-on-election-night-se.html.

[20]http://www.factcheck.org/askfactcheck/does_the_person_with_the_most_money.html.

[21]"Incumbent Advantage," Open Secrets, Center for Responsive Politics, available online at: http://www.opensecrets.org/overview/incumbs.php.

[22]"Reelection Rates over the years," Open Secrets, Center for Responsive Politics, available online at: http://www.opensecrets.org/bigpicture/reelect.php; "Why are Most Sitting Members of Congress Almost Always Reelected?" Citizens for US Direct Initiatives (CUSDI), available online at: http://www.cusdi.org/reelection.htm (accessed August 2009).

[23]Benjamin Ginsberg, Theodore Lowi, and Margaret Weir, *We the People: An Introduction to American Politics*, 6th ed., brief (New York: W.W. Norton, 2007), p. 361.

[24]For a complete list of states with open and closed primaries, see http://www.fairvote.org/?page=1801.

[25]Kathleen Hall Jamieson, *Electing the President 2008: The Insiders' View* (Philadelphia: University of Pennsylvania Press, 2009), p. 170.

[26]The Electoral College consists of electors who are nominated by their state political parties in the months prior to the election. The Constitution allows each state to determine the process for choosing the electors. The number of electors is determined by the number of members of the House of Representatives and the number of members of the Senate (currently 438 + 100 = 538 electors in the Electoral College). Electors who make up the Electoral College differ from party delegates who attend the political parties' conventions to choose the party nominee for president.

[27]It is important to note that the low levels of media coverage, turnout, and competitiveness vary greatly and are more prominent the lower you go on the ticket. As a result and as might be expected, coverage of Senate, House and gubernatorial races far exceeds that of races for attorney general and city council, for instance.

[28]E. J. Dionne, "Time to Reawaken Young Voters," *Washington Post*, October 19, 2009, available at: http://www.washingtonpost.com/wp-dyn/content/article/2009/10/18/AR2009101801463.html.

[29]You can access data on youth voting, engagement, and turnout at CIRCLE, the Center for Information and Research on Civic Learning and Engagement at: http://www.civicyouth.org/.

[30]"Incumbents Who Have Lost: Grayson, Feingold, Lincoln," *Politico*, November 2, 2010, available at: http://www.politico.com/news/stories/1110/44576.html.

[31]"Lack of Competition in Elections Fails to Stir Public: Most Have Heard Little or Nothing of Redistricting Debate," The Pew Research Center, October 27, 2006, available online at: http://people-press.org/report/294/lack-of-competition-in-elections-fails-to-stir-public.

[32]David Magleby and Paul Light, *State and Local Politics: Government By the People*, 14th ed. (New York: Pearson, 2009), p. 3.
[33]Jonathan McLeod, "Jon Corzine Fails to Buy New Jersey Race," *The Politic*, November 4, 2009, available online at: http://www.thepolitic.com/archives/2009/11/04/jon-corzine-fails-to-buy-new-jersey-election/.
[34]*Citizens United v. Federal Election Commission* 558 U.S. 08-205 (2010).
[35]You can see this segment of President Obama's speech as well as Justice Samuel Alito's reaction at: http://www.bing.com/videos/watch/video/alito-mouths-not-true-as-obama-criticizes-sup-ct-for-opening/fe9c991e7b06be404c00fe9c991e7b06be404c00-818394759203?cpkey=e9392de8-0010-470f-919b-5c6bdf086bab%7Cobama%20alito%20state%20of%20union%202010%7C%7C&q=obama%20alito%20state%20of%20union%202010.
[36]Jonathan Alter, "High Court Hypocrisy: Dick Durbin's got a good idea," *Newsweek* (Newsweek, Inc.), February 1, 2010, available at: http://www.newsweek.com/id/232147 (accessed May 21, 2011).
[37]Greg Stohr, "Corporate Campaign Spending Backed by U.S. High Court," *Bloomberg*, January 21, 2010, available at: http://www.bloomberg.com/apps/news?pid=20601110&sid=aU.fsorJbt3E (accessed May 21, 2011) ; Ed Rollins, "Another shock to the Washington system, CNN, January 22, 2010, available at: http://www.cnn.com/2010/OPINION/01/21/rollins.campaign.rules.obsolete/index.html (accessed May 21, 2011).
[38]Stephen J. Wayne, *Is This Any Way to Run a Democratic Election?* 3rd ed. (Washington, DC: CQ Press, 2007), p. 101.
[39]"Policy Brief on Student Voting," Brennan Center for Justice, available online at: http://www.brennancenter.org/page/-/d/download_file_10178.pdf.
[40]Louis Sandy Maisel, *American Political Parties and Elections: A Very Short Introduction* (Oxford: Oxford University Press, 2007), pp. 1–2, 146–147.
[41]See the Freedom House's report online at: www.freedomhouse.orgs or http://freedomhouse.org/template.cfm?page=22&year=2010&country=7944.

Chapter 9

POLITICAL PARTIES AND INTEREST GROUPS

Top Ten List

10 Political parties are essential institutions in democratic republics.

9 Despite George Washington's warning, political parties arose very early in American history and have continued to play a prominent role in American politics.

8 A two-party system provides for stability and accountability within a democratic system.

7 When third parties are successful, their agendas are co-opted by the two major parties.

6 By competing in elections and organizing government, political parties create the majorities essential to democracies.

5 Political parties have a hierarchical organization that is open to all citizens.

4 Interest groups and social movements provide avenues for political participation and are important to democratic society.

3 Interest groups pursue both economic and noneconomic interests.

2 Interest groups engage in a variety of strategies to achieve their goals, including grassroots campaigns and lobbying.

1 Despite their flaws, political organizations are a key way in which people can influence their government.

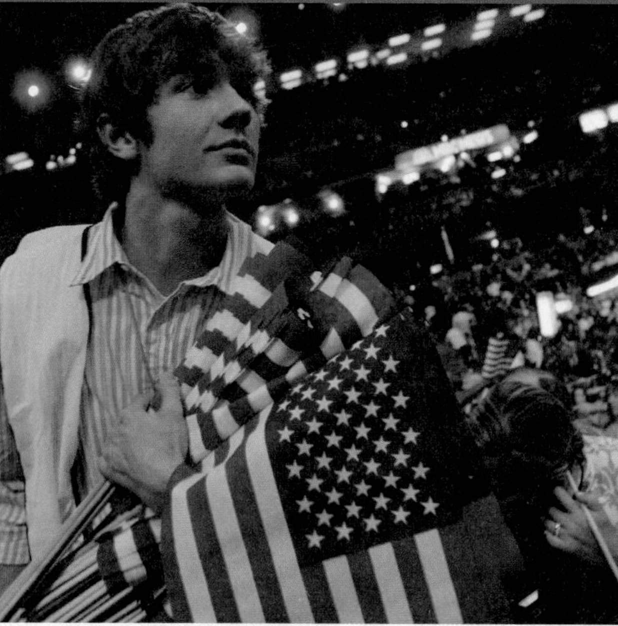

The goal of political parties is to win elections: They nominate candidates, campaign for their election, and thereby give voters a choice as to who will govern and, equally important, who will not govern. Campaigns have become the entry for many young people who want to have an influence on the nation's future. While working for a political party and a candidate they believe in, young people acquire the requisite knowledge and skills and meet people who can be helpful in starting and building a career in government and politics. Shown here, a volunteer hands out American flags to the crowd during the 2008 Democratic National Convention in Denver, CO.

YOUR LIST

Before you read this chapter, take a few moments to think about what you might include on a list of the Top 10 Most Important Things to Know About Political Parties and Interest Groups. At the end of the chapter you will be asked to compare and contrast your list with the one supplied in this chapter.

INTRODUCTION

Americans, for the most part, love and celebrate the virtues of freedom and democracy. They do not feel the same way about politics and political parties. Politics with its bargaining and trading seems like a compromise of principles, while parties, like interest groups and other political organizations, appear to be just another source of corruption. Yet politics and parties are essential to freedom and democracy. When in the later part of the twentieth century the nations of Eastern Europe, like Poland, threw off the tyrannical authoritarianism of Communist rule, they pointed proudly to their new party politics as proof of their freedom and democracy.

Young people, both college students and workers, played a prominent role in the political struggle for freedom in all of the nations of Eastern Europe. In America, it is election campaigns, not revolutionary movements, that have become the domain of the young in politics. Candidates must put together campaign organizations whose sole purpose is to win the nomination of a political party and ultimately the election. And while a candidate for national or statewide office may not be a 20-year-old, large numbers of his or her campaign staffers, as well as those working on behalf of the party directly, will be. Campaigns require long hours of work every day, and it is the young who have the stamina and the time to commit to so demanding a schedule.

Campaigns have thus become the entry for many young people who want to have an influence on the nation's future. It is often in campaigns, while working for a political party and a candidate they believe in, that young people acquire the requisite knowledge and skills and meet people who can be helpful in starting and building a career in government and politics, whether as a candidate for office, as a staff person for an elected official or interest group, or a political consultant.

10 Political Parties are essential institutions in democratic republics.

The late, great political scientist E. E. Schattschneider put the matter squarely: "Democracy is *unthinkable* in the absence of political parties."[1] Democracy had its origin as a form of popular government in ancient Greece, in the city-state of Athens, where all citizens could assemble in one place to make the decisions governing their lives.[2] Many theories of democracy continue to treat Athenian democracy as "true" democracy, but it is a form of government that can only exist in small towns in which all members of the community can meet in one place. Indeed, Schattschneider simply dismissed the Athenian model as a guide to democracy, calling it "pre-modern" with no relevance to the contemporary nation-state.

Schattschneider saw the world as it is and not as it was or as it might be ideally. Democracy in the modern world requires that citizens have the right to vote, that there be regular elections, that choices be freely made, and that elections be organized, so as to give the electorate an effective check on government. Political parties present voters with these choices. **Political parties** are organizations of ordinary citizens, popularly chosen, who come together around a common program of their design with the aim of electing individuals who will support that program in government. They are the most broadly based popular institutions in American life, as well as the most open and participatory. They are also the only organizations that put forward candidates for office and that can be held accountable by voters if their officeholders fail to perform as the people desire.

Political parties Organizations of ordinary citizens, popularly chosen, who come together around a common program of their design with the aim of electing individuals who will support that program in government.

Party platform A formal written statement of a political party's position on those key issues that it deems most important.

Every political party has a **party platform**, a formal written statement of the party's position on those key issues that it deems most important. Most party platforms argue for specific health, social, economic, environment, and foreign affairs policies. The party platform allows voters to predict what changes the party will make if its candidates win the election and to choose the party that most closely reflects their own values. Party platforms do not reflect the views of everyone, but they are designed to appeal to the widest proportion of voters in order to win the votes of a majority. The goal of the major parties is to win elections: They nominate candidates, campaign for their election, and thereby give voters a choice as to who will govern and, equally important, who will *not* govern.

Despite George Washington's warning, political parties arose very early in American history and have continued to play a prominent role in American politics.

The mass-based political party, which exists in all modern countries, is an American invention. The founders were not friendly toward any political organization, including parties, calling them **factions**. They saw all political organizations as narrowly self-interested enemies of the broader public good, and many like George Washington warned their fellow countrymen to beware the spirit of faction. But political parties arose very early under the Constitution during the presidency of Washington, and it was the very individuals warning against parties who resorted to them as the most useful way to advance their purposes.

Factions Narrowly self-interested political organizations, or a small group of people who share a common belief, interest, or opinion.

The nation's first political parties—the Federalist and Democratic-Republican parties—were primarily legislative parties dominated by members of Congress and state legislatures, which, at the time, controlled the process of nominating candidates for president. The modern political party—a popular institution with a broad base in the electorate in which citizens are directly involved in presidential nominations—came into existence in the 1820s.

The presidential campaign of Andrew Jackson in 1828 was the first to go directly to the people to seek their support for his candidacy. Jackson's backers organized a national party organization with party committees in all of the states, as well as one in Washington, and through it actively promoted his candidacy in the electorate at large. It produced a great outpouring of popular support and a decisive victory for Jackson in the first truly popular election of an American president. Jackson's party, which embraced the Jeffersonian ideal of limited government, was called the Democratic Party, and it became the model for all the national parties that followed.

During Jackson's presidency a second party, the Whigs, formed, and regular two-party competition for the White House became the norm in American politics. Martin Van Buren, a member of Congress from New York who served as Jackson's vice president and who succeeded him, argued that an organized two-party system removed the choice of president from the hands of an elite group in Congress and enabled citizens across the country to participate in the selection of the nation's chief executive. The Republican Party replaced the Whigs as the second major party in the political turmoil of the Civil War.

Since Jackson, American politics has been dominated by these two homegrown political parties—Democrats and Republicans (see Table 9.1). They have usually won all but a small fraction of the popular vote and almost all the Electoral College votes. Only two third-party candidates—George Wallace in 1968 and Ross Perot in 1992 and 1996—were able to win even 10 percent of the popular vote, and only Wallace won any electoral votes. If Table 9.1 included congressional and gubernatorial elections, the same two-party contest for office would be apparent. The system of two closely competitive major national parties has been the way in which American elections are fought and governments are organized at the national and state levels.

A two-party system provides for stability and accountability within a democratic system.

Multiparty system A political system in which getting a majority in government requires coalitions of two or more parties.

Two-party system A political system in which successful candidates for public office are nominees of one of two major parties.

Some scholars and political figures point out that the U.S. democratic system offers voters only two real choices and that a **multiparty system** would be more democratic. More parties would offer voters more choices. But more choices does not necessarily mean an electoral system that is more democratic or a democracy that is more *effective*. The virtue of a **two-party system** is precisely that it presents an either/or choice, which means that one candidate will normally win a clear majority of the vote and, in turn, a majority of the offices and the right to organize the government. In multiparty systems, getting a majority in government often requires coalitions of two or more parties in which the several parties must make compromises in their principles in order to work together. This can create confusion about who is responsible for what government does. In a two-party system, responsibility is generally clear. The party in power has to answer to the voters for what it has done, and voters can hold it accountable, as in 2006 when they voted Republicans out of office and in 2010 when they did the same to Democrats.

8 A two-party system provides for stability and accountability within a democratic system.

Table 9.1

Popular and Electoral College Votes by Party in Presidential Elections, 1960–2008

Presidential elections from 1960 through 2008 have been dominated by two political parties—Democrats and Republicans. In the 50 years covered in this table, only two third-party candidates—George Wallace in 1968 and Ross Perot in 1992 and 1996—were able to win even 10 percent of the popular vote, and only Wallace won any electoral votes.

Year	Popular Vote	Percent of Popular Vote			Electoral College Vote		
		Dem	Rep	Other	Dem	Rep	Other
1960	68,838,219	49.7	49.5	0.8	**303**	219	15[a]
1964	70,644,592	61.1	38.5	0.4	**496**	52	0
1968	73,211,875	42.7	42.7	13.6	191	**301**	46[b]
1972	77,718,554	37.5	60.7	1.8	17	**520**	1
1976	81,555,889	50.1	48.0	1.9	**297**	240	1
1980	86,515,221	41.0	50.7	8.3	49	**489**	0
1984	92,652,842	40.6	58.8	0.6	13	**525**	0
1988	91,594,809	45.6	53.4	1.0	111	**426**	1
1992	104,425,014	43.0	37.4	19.6[c]	**370**	168	0
1996	96,456,345	49.2	40.7	10.1[c]	**379**	156	0
2000	105,586,274	48.4[d]	47.9	3.7	266	**271**	0
2004	122,294,978	48.3	50.7	1.0	271	**286**	1
2008	132,889,600	52.9	45.6	1.5	**365**	173	0

[a]Electors from several southern states cast protest votes for U.S. Senator Harry Byrd (D-Virginia) though Byrd was not formally a candidate for president.
[b]George Wallace, as the candidate of the American Independent Party, carried several southern states.
[c]Ross Perot, as the candidate of the Independent Party, won a sizeable popular vote but carried no states and received no Electoral College votes.
[d]In 2000, Al Gore received a plurality of the popular vote, but George W. Bush won a majority in the Electoral College and thus became president.

Unified government A situation in which the same party controls all popularly elected branches of the national government.

Even with a two-party system, however, the question of responsibility is complicated in the United States by the separation of powers in the constitutional framework. When the three popularly elected branches at the national level—the president, House of Representatives, and Senate—are in the control of one party, it is called **unified government**. In this situation, it is easy for voters to know who is responsible for what is or is not done. But when the branches of government are controlled by different

Divided government A situation in which different parties control at least one branch of the national government: either the executive or one house of the legislature.

parties, a situation known as **divided government**, the party in control of one branch may blame the party in control of another branch (or the president) for whatever has gone wrong. This can create confusion for voters, who may not know whom to blame. It may also encourage voters to become more cynical and blame the government in general for not being able to get things done. At the national level, divided government has been the normal state of affairs in the United States since the late 1960s, which may explain in part why voter cynicism has grown over the years. But the problem here, if one exists, is in the constitutional design, not in the two-party system.

Those who want a multiparty system suggest that the current two parties and the state election laws those parties have enacted are the reasons we do not have more parties. It is, however, more complicated than that, because our two-party system is inherent in the design of our Constitution with its separation of powers and with representatives and senators chosen from **single-member districts** by **plurality elections**. This means that there can be only one winner in an election for president or a seat in Congress, and that the candidate who gets more votes than any other wins regardless of whether it is a majority of the votes cast.[3] Political scientists have shown persuasively that constitutional systems like ours with single-member districts and plurality elections will produce a two-party system, whereas a system of multimember districts and proportional representation will produce a multiparty system.[4]

Single-member districts A system, such as the one we have in the United States, where there can be only one winner in an election for president or a seat in Congress.

Plurality elections An electoral system, such as the one we have in the United States, where the person who gets the most votes wins; also known as the "first past the gate."

For all the apparent similarities in a given campaign, the differences between the two parties are long-standing, well known, articulated in their party platforms, and strongly embraced by their leadership.[5] They center on the role that the national government should play in the lives of American citizens and especially in the nation's economy. From the latter years of the nineteenth century until today, the Republicans have been the party of big business, have celebrated free markets and enterprise, and have sought minimal government regulation of the activities of the private sector. The Democrats, at least since Franklin Roosevelt's New Deal in the 1930s, have been the party of social concerns, calling for government to assure greater equality in the social condition and economic opportunities for all Americans. This difference means that the ideological center of political gravity in the Republican Party is to the right and in the Democratic Party it is to the left. These differences are more apparent after a party wins an election than they are in the contest for office, because the party will staff the government with its partisans from the right or left as well as supporters from the middle.

7 When third parties are successful, their agendas are co-opted by the two major parties.

Third parties in America typically have candidates who receive a small portion of the vote and are almost never of any importance in the outcome of elections. On occasion, however, a third party may emerge that taps into the values or grievances

Third parties Any party that is not one of the two major parties.

of large numbers of voters and can upset the results in a tight race by drawing votes away from one of the candidates of the major parties. When a third party succeeds in this way, the major parties commonly "listen" to what its voters seem to be saying and try to co-opt the issues of the third party in order to win over their voters for the major party.

In 2000, the Green Party nominated Ralph Nader as their presidential candidate. The Green Party focuses primarily on environmental issues, but Ralph Nader had acquired recognition and respect for his role as a consumer advocate. In the 1960s, automobiles lacked basic safety features. Nader pushed for inclusion of new safety measures—such as the seatbelt. His harsh criticism of the influence of wealthy corporations on the government attracted the support of the left wing of the Democratic Party. In the 2000 elections, Ralph Nader received 2.7 percent of the vote. The Democratic presidential candidate Al Gore won the popular vote but lost in the Electoral College by an extremely narrow margin. Republican candidate George W. Bush won. Many Democrats bitterly argued that Nader had stolen the election from Gore.

The third parties that draw enough votes to swing an election are commonly organized around a protest or cause. Their frustration is that, should they draw a sizeable vote in losing, one of the major parties will almost certainly capture the issues that proved so popular and eliminate any reason for the continued existence of the third party.[6] However, there are ideological third parties that present a broad platform and as a result remain in existence for longer periods of time. Today, the Libertarian Party is a successful example of one of these ideological parties. The party focuses primarily on local races, and as a result, hundreds of libertarians currently serve on school boards or fill positions within local governments such as mayor or sheriff. While they are unlikely to upset a presidential election, the libertarians participate significantly in local politics.

6 By competing in elections and organizing government, political parties create the majorities essential to democracies.

American political parties concern themselves with winning elections and building majorities in government. Parties organize and mobilize the electorate by forming consensus among their supporters and getting them to the polls on Election Day. They nominate candidates, fund campaigns, mobilize voters, organize government, and are accountable for how government performs. On the national level, they take positions on the most pressing issues, which they articulate in their party platforms.

Building consensus is not always an easy task for a couple of reasons. First, American parties are internally divided. Neither party is monolithically liberal or conservative. Both have broad and somewhat overlapping bases in the electorate that span a wide variety of social groups and interests. There are conservative Democrats and liberal Republicans as well as many of moderate views in both parties, and these groups within the party check pressures toward extremism. Furthermore, the Constitution assigns primary responsibility for the conduct of elections to state governments. In effect, this creates fifty state political systems each of which is different in some ways from the others. Each also has a degree of independence from the national political system. Democrats from rural Texas, therefore, may be more socially conservative than urban Democrats from California, and so they may completely disagree on an issue such as gay rights.

Secondly, the task of building consensus has become increasingly difficult for parties because they have weakened over time. There was a time in the nineteenth century when many urban and rural party organizations resembled a machine. They nominated candidates in caucuses that were closed to the rank-and-file. They printed ballots used in voting. They controlled thousands of public jobs used as patronage to reward a cadre of loyal party workers and exercised inordinate influence over public spending, such as the awarding of contracts for public construction. They also raised money in vast amounts from any source available.

Progressive movement A U.S. movement in the late nineteenth and early twentieth centuries that called for changes and reforms through governmental action.

Then, around the turn of the nineteenth century, reformers known as **Progressives** won passage of sweeping reforms of the party system that changed everything, from how candidates were nominated to how and from whom parties could raise money. These reforms replaced most patronage with a merit-based civil service system in public employment, and they changed the legal status of parties from being private associations to being quasi-public institutions more easily regulated by government. Although these reforms were much needed, they did signal a period of decline in the ability of political parties to control the nomination process.

Despite these challenges, political parties are able to form consensus and push through legislation at both the state and national level by reaching compromises. One notable example was the 2008 presidential election. Republican presidential nominee John McCain had a long history of crossing party lines to work with Democrats on specific issues. For example, he and Democratic Senator Russ Feingold initiated the Bipartisan Campaign Reform Act (2002), which regulated the financing of political campaigns in an attempt to reduce corruption and the influence of big money interests. McCain looked for supporters among independent voters and moderate Republicans. To appeal to hard-core conservatives and increase his support from within the Republican Party, he chose Alaska Governor Sarah Palin as his running mate in 2008. Similarly, after being elected, President Obama sought to appeal to moderate Democrats by nominating Hillary Clinton as Secretary of State.

 Political parties have a hierarchical organization that is open to all citizens.

5 Political parties have a hierarchical organization that is open to all citizens.

Modern political parties involve hundreds of thousands of workers and volunteers in the month-to-month work of politics and government during and between elections. On paper, the organizational structure of the political parties appears to be rigidly hierarchical, as shown in Figure 9.1, but in practice each level of party organization has a significant degree of independence from other levels, and much of the work falls to the lower levels.

The lowest levels of office, the precinct chairs, are often vacant and filled by volunteers—open to anybody willing to put in the time and energy needed to hand

Figure 9.1 Structure of Political Party Organizations

This figure shows the hierarchical structure of the two major political parties from voters at the bottom to the national committees at the top.

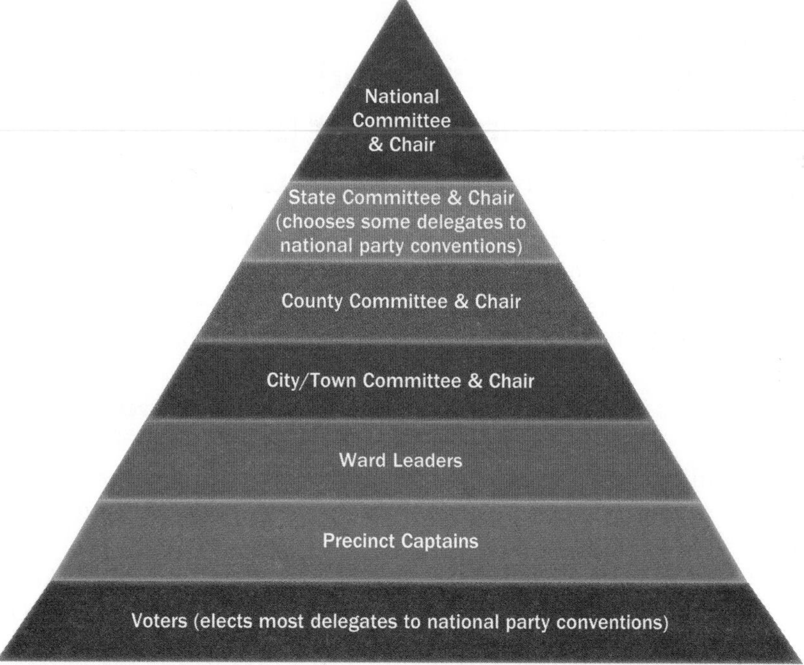

out leaflets or conduct voter registration drives. Precinct chairs can have a significant impact on local campaigns and on getting out the vote for state and national candidates as well. Precinct chairs can eventually work up to membership in county or state committees where they can wield significant influence on statewide and national campaigns. During elections, thousands more serve as **delegates** to state and **national party conventions** where candidates are nominated for president and vice president. In addition, millions of party members participate in party caucuses and primary elections to pick candidates to run for public office.

Delegates Individuals who are selected to represent the party at state or national party conventions.

National party conventions An assembly with delegates chosen from all of the states whose function is to nominate candidates for president and vice president and to oversee the governance of the party.

The only test for party membership is that voters declare themselves to be Democrats or Republicans.[7] The organization of parties, especially at the local level, is open and accessible to ordinary party members who wish to become involved. There is no better evidence of this than members of the religious right who in the mid-to-late 1970s joined local and state Republican Party committees and through them came to exert enormous influence on the national party. More recently, many Tea Party voters worked within the Republican Party rather than form a third party.[8] Participation in a political party, therefore, gives citizens a voice in the full range of decisions made by government and provides the most effective vehicle to achieve the ends set forth. Some voices may be more influential than others because some party activists have more experience and party service than others, but all can make themselves heard.

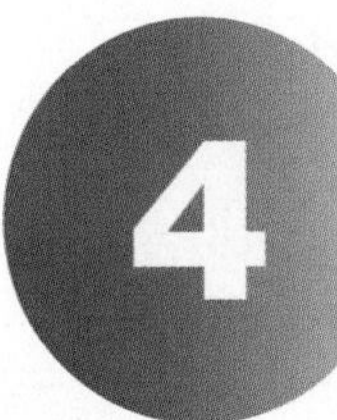

Interest groups and social movements provide avenues for political participation and are important to democratic society.

Political parties are not the only means, however, for political participation. Interest groups and social movements are not only numerous but prominent in a democratic society as open and diverse as ours. An **interest group** is an organization of individuals that promotes common social, economic, or political values. There are more than ten thousand interest groups in Washington, D.C. alone and thousands more in the various state capitals. Some are very large organizations that focus on a broad range of issues, such as the National Chambers of Commerce and the American Federation of Labor-Congress of Industrial Organizations (AFL-CIO), while others such as the National Rifle Association (NRA) may concentrate on a single issue.

Interest groups Organizations formed around narrow and specific economic or social interests to protect and advance the cause of their members.

Interest groups are an essential part of our system of representative democracy. They mirror in part the pluralistic and multicultural character of American society and bring that diversity to the political process in the nation and state alike. Interest groups are not abstract organizations detached from American life, but rather they represent Americans whose livelihood or way of life can be affected by changes in public policy. It is difficult to say for certain how many Americans are active in an interest or advocacy group at any one time, but given the many types of interest groups it is likely a substantial portion of the population.

Among the different types of interest groups are public interest groups (groups that promote and pursue a public issue that might otherwise not be on the agenda, e.g., Common Cause); economic groups (those with a primarily economic focus, such as the National Association of Manufacturers or the American Public Power Association); social or ideologically based groups (groups that are organized to promote a set of core ideological or political beliefs, e.g., The American Civil Liberties Union or the National Right to Life Committee); and labor unions (groups designed to provide workers with the power to bargain collectively with businesses and corporate bosses, e.g., the American Federation of Labor-Congress of Industrial Organizations or the Service Employees International Union).

You may know people in your family or friends who are active in a group such as these. If, for instance, you have a family member or friend who is a teacher, they are almost certainly a member of a teachers' union such as the American Federation of Teachers (AFT) or the National Education Association (NEA). Similarly, you may know someone who is a member of a public interest group, such as someone who cares about the environment and joins the Environmental Defense Fund or someone who is a member of the League of Women Voters, an organization which boasts chapters in every state across the nation.

What all these groups have in common is that they are civic organizations whose members are advocating for the values of its membership. By joining together and working collectively, these groups give members better access to state and national decision makers and help facilitate the functioning of democratic government.

In addition to political parties and interest groups, there are other types of collective groups that citizens can join to promote change and fight perceived injustice. Social movements are one important way in which this has occurred. The civil rights movement, for instance, arose from a widespread sense of injustice and mobilized large numbers of people to demand change. These types of movements have proven to be effective in dramatizing the importance of their cause and may achieve at least some of the changes sought by their leaders.

However, unlike parties and interest groups, social movements are not permanent institutions. Some, like the women's movement, achieve greater permanence by evolving into an interest group, like the National Organization for Women (NOW). NOW was founded in 1966 in response to the ruling of the newly established Equal Employment Opportunity Commission (EEOC) allowing organizations to specify a gender preference when advertising a job opening. In the 1970s, the organization grew, branching out into other issues related to women's rights. Today, NOW has assembled a membership of 500,000 individuals who advocate for equal pay and opportunities for women in the workplace, freedom from sexual harassment on the job, access to legal abortion, and the rights of lesbians.[9]

3 Interest groups pursue both economic and noneconomic interests.

Many interest groups strive to achieve goals related to the economy. Business groups can represent general business interests, such as chambers of commerce, or a subgroup, such as small companies or minority-owned firms. Professional associations focus on particular professions such as plumbers, carpenters, teachers, or doctors. You may well have heard of the American Medical Association (AMA). The organization often issues public recommendations and research results, as well as advertisements for or against certain health programs and government policies. Yet, the AMA also performs many services that you do not hear about: It provides education on ethical and legal issues, practical assistance for office management, and discounts on medical products for its membership. Its ads, activism in Washington, educational programs, public outreach, and slew of services advance the interests of medical professionals.

Trade associations represent the interests of a specific industry, such as the automobile manufacturers, home builders, farmers, or pharmaceutical companies. These organizations provide general services and tools to their members as well as political advocacy on the state and national levels. For example, the National Association of Home Builders (NAHB) provides legal assistance, data on home prices and building materials, social networking and educational opportunities in addition to many services, including advocating for the interests of homebuilders in Congress. In 2009, during the economic downturn caused by a credit crisis, the NAHB urged Washington to increase credit to home buyers and solve other problems consumers faced when trying to buy a home. Although these actions appeared to be aimed at helping home buyers, the NAHB supported these policies because it would help put "Americans back to work"—and in particular, advance the economic interests of their members and help ensure that they could afford to hire workers and build or remodel houses.[10]

Labor unions are another example of economic interest groups that work to further the interests of their members both at home and in Washington. Labor unions originally concentrated on organizing strikes to achieve better pay for their members. These strikes often erupted into bloodshed, with strikers attacking company managers, companies hiring agencies that killed strikers, or the government intervening with widespread arrests. But as the federal government began to protect workers' rights to organize in the twentieth century, labor unions branched out into political advocacy. The AFL-CIO emerged in the 1930s and is the largest and broadest trade union in the United States. Today, it has 3 million members who include steelworkers, pilots, truck drivers, teachers, farm workers, and firefighters. The AFL-CIO promotes health and safety in the workplace, healthcare for workers, and retirement security. While early labor unions often took a stand against immigration because immigrants could be hired to break strikes, the AFL-CIO now reaches out to organize and provide services to immigrant workers.

Noneconomic interest groups include a wide array of citizens groups organized around public interests, ideologies, or political and social issues. You've probably heard of or may even support single-issue or multiple-issue interest groups, such as the Sierra Club, Save the Children, or antitax organizations. Other groups serve broader or public interests shared by all citizens. Common Cause, for example, is a group that advocates for campaign finance reform, ethical behavior of office holders, and the accountability of government. Like the AMA, it tries to educate the public and spread awareness in order to bring pressure on political officials to enact laws that promote clean government. Other interest groups advance the values of religious, ethnic, or ideological groups. For instance, the National Association for the Advancement of Colored People (NAACP) played an active role in the civil rights movement.[11] And, the Moral Majority, a religious Christian group, helped secure Ronald Reagan's election to the presidency in 1980.

2 Interest groups engage in a variety of strategies to achieve their goals, including grassroots campaigns and lobbying.

The phone rings. A person from an association that fights cancer asks if they can rely on you to send out envelopes to your friends and neighbors asking for donations. Sound familiar? The call was likely part of a grassroots campaign, one of the major strategies interest groups use to exert pressure. If you go to the Web site of an interest group, you'll generally see a link entitled Take Action, Get Involved, or Advocacy where the site lists a series of actions members of the public can take to further their cause. These actions will often involve writing, e-mailing, or calling political officials. Sometimes they involve fund-raising, organizing meetings, or participating in educational events. Interest groups engage in grassroots organizing as a means of raising awareness and shaping public opinion.

In order to be effective, however, interest groups have to lobby all three branches of the government. The American Civil Liberties Union (ACLU) is an interest group that heavily relies on lobbying the courts. In fact, a good many of its members are lawyers who advocate for individual rights and liberties that they feel the Constitution provides but that are not likely to be protected by the courts. For example, in 1976 Frank Collin, the leader of a Chicago-based neo-Nazi group, sent a letter to the park district of the city of Skokie requesting a permit to march through one of the city's parks. A large percentage of Skokie residents had either survived the Holocaust themselves or were descendants of those survivors. After the city refused this and other requests by Collin, the case was taken up by the ACLU. In 1978, in *National Socialist Party of America v. Village of Skokie*, the Supreme Court ruled that Collin had the right to march, and the Village of Skokie had to issue his group a permit.[12]

Interest groups lobby Congress as well. It is in this context that they are most often deplored or portrayed as corrupt entities buying votes by offering gifts, vacations, and other incentives to members of Congress. In actuality, interest groups have the greatest impact on legislation by providing expert knowledge about the interests they represent (business, labor, agricultural, professional, and others) and of how changes in public policy affect those interests. The information interest groups provide to policymakers must of necessity be truthful, for if legislators and others cannot rely upon the accuracy of information provided by a group, the group will cease to have any influence. At the same time, the conclusions put forward by groups are understood to represent the interests of their members and not to be purely objective.

There are, of course, interest groups on all sides of any major policy issue, which means that the policy recommendations of one group are likely to be balanced by those of another, leaving decision makers better informed as to policy choices and their consequences for different groups in the population. Therefore, in testifying at congressional hearings, conducting research on specific areas such as automobile safety, and having lunch with members of Congress and their staffs to discuss a pressing issue, interest groups are increasing the likelihood that Congress will make a sound policy decision.

Finally, interest groups also lobby the bureaucracy because often laws do not cover important details. For example, the Equal Employment Opportunity Commission (EEOC) was established as part of the federal bureaucracy by the Civil Rights Act of 1964. It was charged with ending race and gender-based discrimination in the workplace. Yet, in 1966 the EEOC allowed organizations to specify a gender preference when advertising a job opening. As a result, the National Organization of Women (NOW) formed to exert pressure on this bureaucratic institution to implement what NOW perceived as the full meaning of the law.

Despite their flaws, political organizations are a key way in which people can influence their government.

Political parties and interest groups often get a bad rap. Critics argue, for instance, that interest groups distort the nation's politics by representing some interests but not all. Moreover, some argue there is a bias to the system of interest group representation in that it is more representative of upper-middle and upper-class interests than those of lower-income and poor Americans. Similarly, elected officials and party leaders are likely to be wealthier, better educated, and more often male and Caucasian than the average American. The criticisms are not restricted to issues of representation, however. Since Washington's Farewell Address, political parties in particular have been looked on with suspicion. By the Progressive era, parties in the United States were viewed as corrupt institutions in which cigar-smoking men in top hats made deals with the highest bidder. This image of parties as corrupt institutions has remained a key component of American political life.

No image is more popular among reformers and the news media than that of the independent voter who makes his or her decision without regard to party affiliation. Held to be the very model of the virtuous democratic citizen, the independent voter is depicted as actively engaged in and fully informed about issues, making up his or her mind free from the influence of political parties or interest groups, and acting solely on the basis of individual conscience. The image is charming. It is also at odds with the truth. Since the systematic study of voting behavior began in America more than 70 years ago, voters who call themselves independents have been found to be the least interested in politics, least informed about issues, and least likely to vote or take any part in politics.[13]

Political scientist E.E. Schattschneider wrote: "I suppose the most important thing I have done in my field is that I have talked longer and harder and more persistently and enthusiastically about political parties than anyone else alive."[14] To this extent Schattschneider is just one of many political scientists and scholars who have worked in favor of responsible party government and argued that "modern democracy is unthinkable save in terms of the party."[15] After reading more about political parties and interest groups, you should have a better sense of why so many who study American government have taken this position. Their argument is not that parties are perfect or they operate exactly as they should, rather that if they could be made more responsible and responsive, they are the best hope American citizens have of influencing the direction of the nation or of their state.[16]

While there are always voters who use elections to send a message to the major parties, there is also strong evidence to support the fact that if you do *not* vote for a candidate of one of the two major parties, you may be wasting your vote. Or worse yet, you may help the candidate you like least to win the election. In 2000, for instance, third-party candidate Ralph Nader captured millions of votes, most of which otherwise seem likely to have gone to the Democrat, Al Gore. Voters for Nader, despite their protestations to the contrary, helped to elect the Republican, George W. Bush.

Voters for third-party candidates commonly claim to be keeping faith with their principles and also of letting the major parties know that neither represents them. But elections are not about feeling good; they are about winning the majorities that will enable a party to govern. In a democracy, majorities rule; and, in American politics, only Democrats and Republicans have any chance to win a majority. This may be regrettable. Some would like to have more parties from among which to choose, but that is not the way the American system works. A two-party system, as we have said, is built into our constitutional arrangements. To get a multiparty system requires sacking our Constitution and adopting one that provides for a parliamentary system of government. Only one third party (the Republicans) ever became a major party, and this occurred at the time of the Civil War, which was so disruptive to the fabric of life in the nation that the political party system broke down completely. Since the Civil War, only one third party (the Progressives in 1912) has even finished second in a presidential race, and that was because the Republican party split in half and the Progressive half had Theodore Roosevelt as its nominee.

Federalism and ballot laws make matters even more difficult for minority parties by creating what amounts to a fifty-party system; each state's laws governing access to the ballot are somewhat different from the others. Third parties have to go to each state and meet its particular requirements to get their names on the ballot. This is time-consuming and expensive and almost guarantees a poor performance at the polls. And then there are the news media, which often treat election campaigns as horse races in which only two horses (the major parties) have a chance to win. With the major parties getting full coverage, it is extremely difficult for a third party to spread its message widely and inexpensively.

CONCLUSION

In the United States, political parties and interest groups are often derided as corrupt, inefficient, and biased. These types of criticisms go back to Washington's Farewell Address and continue today. At the same time, independence in terms of voting and party affiliation is often celebrated in the media and elsewhere. Whether you are talking about candidates from the left or the right, one of the most common themes you hear in modern campaigns is the promise to act in a bipartisan or nonpartisan way. For instance, in 1999, when he was running for president, George W. Bush said, "I reject the ugly politics of division, I'm a uniter, not a divider."[17] Similarly, after Democrats took control of the House in the 2006 election, Speaker Nancy Pelosi (D-CA) said, "We will work with Republicans in Congress and the administration in the spirit of partnership, not partisanship."[18] Both Barack Obama and John McCain made similar claims during the 2008 presidential election.[19] It is somewhat ironic that even the leaders of their respective parties have consistently promised to be less partisan. While these promises may sound attractive, and there is a history in the United States of deriding political organizations, these organizations play an important and often unheralded role in our system.

Modern democracy requires that citizens participate in periodic elections, that choices be freely made, and that elections be organized, so as to give the electorate the opportunity to hold their representatives accountable. Political parties are the primary organizations that present voters with these choices. These are organizations

THEIR LIST

An Insider's View

STANLEY ROSENBERG

State Legislator, Massachusetts

Stanley Rosenberg has been a Massachusetts state senator since 1991 and a state representative prior to that. Before entering the legislature, he was executive director of the Massachusetts Democratic Committee and, while in the legislature, has been a member of the state committee where he has chaired the campaign services committee.

He was asked what three things he thought you should know about political parties. Keep in mind that he is talking about political parties in Massachusetts where, in 2011, the Democrats had overwhelming majorities in both houses of the state legislature and (with one exception) held all of the major statewide and congressional offices. Party systems vary among the states, and the response of an insider from another state might be quite different from that of Senator Rosenberg, which follows:

"The first thing to know is that political parties stand alone as a venue where political activists can come together to influence both the selection of candidates and the making of public policy."

"Second, candidates for office will use the political party to help them get elected, but they also put together their own campaign organizations. Once elected, few ever face a serious challenge for reelection, and the party becomes less important to them. Also, in the legislature, the leaders are very powerful and control most of the things members want."

"Finally, parties in Massachusetts lack the tools and resources to hold officials accountable. At times, it can be useful to remind members what is in the party platform, but the legislative leadership has more political muscle than the party does."

"The political culture of the state is one that is more candidate-centered and leadership-centered than it is party-centered. I know other states are different, but I am not sure they are all that different."

made up of people who come together around a common program of their design with the aim of electing individuals who will support that program in government. To this extent, they are the most broadly based popular institutions in American life, as well as the most open and participatory. They are also the only organizations that put forward candidates for office and that can be held accountable by voters if their officeholders fail to perform as the people desire.

YOUR LIST REVISITED

At the beginning of the chapter you were asked to think about what you might include on your own list of the Top 10 Most Important Things to Know About Political Parties and Interest Groups. Now that you have read the chapter, take a moment to revisit your list. What, if anything, would you change about your list? Do you agree or disagree with the chapter list constructed by the author? What might you add or delete? Why?

KEY TERMS

Delegates 204
Divided government 200
Factions 197
Interest groups 204
Multiparty system 198
National party conventions 204
Party platform 197
Political parties 197
Plurality elections 200
Progressive movement 202
Single-member districts 200
Third parties 200
Two-party system 198
Unified government 199

CHAPTER REVIEW QUESTIONS

10 Why do political parties exist? Where did they come from?

9 Why does the United States have a two-party system?

8 Would it be possible to have a multiparty system in the United States? Why or why not?

7 What role do third parties play in American politics?

6 What challenges do political parties face in building consensus?

5 How are political parties organized and staffed?

4 What are the differences between political parties, interest groups, and political movements?

3 How many different types of interest groups are there? Why is it useful to distinguish between those interest groups that pursue economic interests and those that do not?

2 Explain some strategies interest groups use to achieve their goals.

1 Why are political parties so important to democracy and popular government? Would we be better off if there were no political parties? Why or why not?

SUGGESTED READINGS

- Beck, Michael Lewis, William G. Jacoby, Helmut Norpoth, and Herbert F. Weisberg. *The American Voter Revisited.* Ann Arbor: University of Michigan, 2008.
- Gerring, John. *Party Ideologies in America, 1828–1996.* Cambridge: Cambridge University Press, 1998.
- Gould, Lewis L. *Grand Old Party: A History of the Republicans.* New York: Random House, 2003.
- Green, John C., and Paul S. Herrnson, eds. *Responsible Partisanship? The Evolution of American Political Parties Since 1950.* Lawrence, KS: University Press of Kansas, 2002.
- Hetherington, Marc J., and William J. Keefe. *Parties, Politics, and Public Policy in America.* Washington, DC: Congressional Quarterly Press, 2007.
- Kelly, Christine A. *Tangled Up in Red, White, & Blue: New Social Movements in America.* New York: Rowan & Littlefield Publishers, 2001.
- LaRaja, Raymond. *Small Change: Political Parties & Campaign Finance Reform.* Ann Arbor, MI: University of Michigan Press, 2008.
- Milkis, Sidney M. *The President and the Parties: Transformation of the American Party System Since the New Deal.* New York: Oxford University Press, 1993.
- White, John Kenneth, and Jerome M. Mileur, eds. *Challenges to Party Government.* Carbondale, IL: Southern Illinois University Press, 1992.
- Witcover, Jules. *Party of the People: A History of the Democrats.* New York: Random House, 2003.

SUGGESTED FILMS

- *Mr. Smith Goes to Washington* (1939)
- *The Great McGinty* (1940)
- *State of the Union* (1948)
- *Born Yesterday* (1950)
- *The Last Hurrah* (1958)
- *Advise and Consent* (1962)
- *The Best Man* (1964)
- *Thank You for Smoking* (2005)
- *Boogie Man: The Lee Atwater Story* (2008)
- *Casino Jack* (2010)

SUGGESTED WEBSITES

- **Campaign Finance Institute:** http://www.cfinst.org/.
- **Democratic National Committee:** http://www.democrats.org/.
- **Electionline.org:** http://www.electionline.org/.
- **Green Papers:** http://www.thegreenpapers.com/.
- **Open Secrets, Center for Responsive Politics:** http://www.opensecrets.org/.
- **Political Resources on the Web:** http://www.politicalresources.net/.
- **Politics 1, Directory of U.S. Political Parties:** http://www.politics1.com/parties.htm.
- **Project Vote Smart, Interest Group Rating:** http://www.votesmart.org/official_five_categories.php?dist=issue_rating_category.php.
- **Project Vote Smart, Political Parties:** http://www.votesmart.org/resources.
- **Republican National Committee:** http://gop.com/.

ENDNOTES

[1]E. E. Schattschneider, *Party Government* (New York: Farrar and Rinehart, 1942), p. 1.

[2]The Greek philosopher Aristotle identified two forms of popular government, one a "republic" in which decisions were made in the general public interest and the other a "democracy" in which decisions were self-interested. Aristotle saw a republic as the virtuous form of popular government and democracy as a corruption of it. The authors of our Constitution shared Aristotle's understanding of democracy, which is why they spoke of establishing a republic, not a democracy. Today, the terms are used more or less interchangeably.

[3]A "plurality" means one candidate received more of the votes cast than any of the challengers. Most states' constitutions, like the federal constitution, also provide for single-member districts and plurality elections. A few states also require runoff elections between the two top vote-getters if neither receives a majority of the total vote.

[4]Proportional representation is a system for allocating votes so that the number of representatives a party receives is roughly proportional to the vote it received in the election. The Democratic Party uses a form of proportional representation in allocating delegates to its national party convention based on the share of the vote primary candidates receive in a given state.

[5]More and more Americans have come to appreciate that the two parties are different; the number of those who see important differences has increased dramatically since the mid-1990s.

[6]Although at this point the Tea Party is not an official party, choosing instead to operate within the confines of the Republican Party, some members of the movement have expressed concern about being co-opted or having their message compromised by the Republican Party. As Tim Dunkin writes, "one of the most consistent refrains heard within the Tea Party movement is that it should remain independent, that it should not allow itself to be co-opted. The entity against which this warning is sounded, the one that the Tea Partiers fear will subvert the purity and autonomy of their movement, is the Republican Party." Tim Dunkin, "Conservatives should Oppose the Hijacking of the Tea Party Movement," *Renew America*, January 5, 2010, available at: http://www.renewamerica.com/columns/dunkin/100105 (accessed May 28, 2011).

[7]With respect to party nominations, American political parties are much more inclusive than parties in other Western democracies.

[8]Michael Stickings, "Could a Tea Party Third Party Emerge to Divide the Right?" *The Moderate Voice*, May 12, 2011, available at: http://themoderatevoice.com/109774/could-a-tea-party-third-party-emerge-to-divide-the-right/ (accessed May 15, 2011).

[9]National Organization for Women Web site, www.now.org (accessed October 27, 2009).

[10]"Builders Urge Congress To Act On Home Buyer Tax Credit, Appraisal And Lending Issues," National Association of Home Builders Newsroom, October 7, 2009, available at: http://www.nahb.org/news_details.aspx?sectionID=148&newsID=9810.

[11]The NAACP continues to be active today promoting its stated mission: "to ensure the political, educational, social, and economic equality of rights of all persons and to eliminate racial hatred and racial discrimination," *NAACP*, available at: http://www.naacp.org/about/mission/ (accessed May 28, 2011).

[12]*National Socialist Party of America v. Village of Skokie*, 432 U.S. 43 (1977).

[13]Eric Weltman and Paul Lacherlier, "Growth in Independent Voters Challenges Our Democracy," *Asbury Park Press*, February 19, 2010, available at: http://www.app.com/article/CN/20100221/OPINION06/2210306/0/OPINION04/Growth-in-independent-voters-challenges-our-democracy (accessed April 18, 2011).

[14]Quoted in Leon D. Epstein, *Political Parties in the American Mold* (Madison, WI: University of Wisconsin Press, 1986), p. 32.

[15]E. E. Schattschneider, *Party Government* (New York: Farrar and Rinehart, 1942), p. 1. For further reading on the importance of political parties to political scientists, see, for instance, John K. White, "Responsible Party Government in America," *Perspectives on Political Science*, 21 (2, Spring 1992): 80–90. Also available online at: http://www.apsanet.org/~pop/APSA1950/White1992.html (accessed May 20, 2011).

[16]For additional reading on the call for a responsible party government in America, see Committee on Political Parties, *Toward a More Responsible Two-Party System* (New York: Rinehart and Company, Inc., 1950); Austin Ranney, *The Doctrine of Responsible Party Government: Its Origins and Present State* (Urbana, IL: The University of Illinois Press, 1954); Evron M. Kirkpatrick, "Toward a More Responsible Two-Party System: Political Science, Policy Science, or Psuedo Science?" (Paper presented at the Sixty-sixth Annual Meeting of the American Political Science Association, Los Angeles, 8–12 September 1970): 36. This paper was subsequently published in the *American Political Science Review* 65 (December 1971): 965–990.

[17]Wes Allison and Bill Adair, "Can Obama Keep Promise of Bipartisanship," *St. Petersburg Times*, November 6, 2008, available at: http://www.tampabay.com/news/politics/elections/article891974.ece (accessed May 10, 2011).

[18]Ibid.

[19]Ibid.

Chapter 10

POLITICAL PARTICIPATION, SOCIALIZATION, PUBLIC OPINION, AND THE MEDIA

Top Ten List

10 There are many ways to participate in politics.

9 More people are shunning traditional political activities but embracing new forms of participation.

8 Factors such as level of education and income play a key role in whether a person is likely to engage in the most basic form of democratic participation, voting.

7 Research shows swing and undecided voters are not always as persuadable as one might think.

6 New technology is changing the methods, modes, and patterns of participation.

5 Your political opinions are shaped by the people, institutions, and ideas to which you were exposed when you were young.

4 Public opinion polls measure the direction and intensity of public attitudes and opinions.

3 Americans' political opinions can be classified as liberal, conservative, libertarian, and populist.

2 The media's role is expanding, but its authority may be declining.

1 The media have contributed to the decline in meaningful political participation and knowledge.

The participation of Americans in their own governance has always been held up as a hallmark of American democracy. Concerns that Americans have withdrawn from meaningful political engagement in the last 30 to 40 years have produced a great deal of scholarship and media attention. Why do some groups participate more actively than others? How do the media impact civic engagement, knowledge, and participation? Increasingly, many Americans are turning to satirical news shows such as *The Daily Show* and the *Colbert Report* for their political information. Shown here, Jon Stewart and Stephen Colbert speak as thousands gather for the 2010 "Rally to Restore Sanity And/Or Fear" on the National Mall in Washington, DC.

YOUR LIST

Before you read this chapter, take a few moments to think about what you might include on a list of the Top 10 Most Important Things to Know About Political Participation, Socialization, Public Opinion, and the Media. At the end of the chapter you will be asked to compare and contrast your list with the one supplied in this chapter.

INTRODUCTION

Journalists, politicians, and people from all walks of life have long been dismayed by the decline in civic knowledge. This, compounded with concerns about low voter turnout in recent decades, has many worried. Are Americans not only ignorant but politically apathetic? And what does that mean for the health of our democratic system, which is based on informed individuals making the best choices for themselves and others?

It may be, however, a bit too early to pronounce the death of political participation in this country, particularly when we consider the vast changes that have taken place in the ways we become informed. In the 1960s, student demonstrations filled the streets of major cities throughout the Western world. In early 2011, Egypt was rocked with massive protests against the regime of Hosni Mubarak. While protesters certainly took to the streets with low-tech signs, banners, and slogans, these old-fashioned protest tactics were fueled and organized, in part at least, by social networking media sites like Facebook and Twitter. At one point, when the Mubarak regime blocked Internet access to Egyptians, Google took phone calls from protesters in the streets and converted them into tweets so that the prodemocracy protesters would not be silenced.

The Internet has become a way for citizens worldwide to take the sage advice of political scientist E. E. Shatscheider, whose work *The Semisovereign People* famously counsels political underdogs to widen the scope of a conflict in order to change the odds in their favor, something the Egyptian protesters in the streets clearly understood. But, while political scientists are increasingly interested in the forms political participation takes, they also continue to look at other aspects of participation. Why do some groups participate more actively than others? What factors impact how we develop and act politically? Can we, as citizens, believe what polls tell us about how the American public thinks about a variety of political issues? How do the media impact civic engagement, knowledge, and participation? Have the growth of new technology and 24-hour news media had a positive or negative impact on civic engagement? As we shall see in this chapter, these types of questions do not have clear answers.

10 There are many ways to participate in politics.

When you hear the term *political participation*, what do you think of? Most people would say "voting." They are right, of course. Voting is a basic, and the most widely recognized, form of political engagement, but political participation involves a number of other activities. You may not think of yourself as a political activist, but you are participating in politics when you . . .

- read or listen to the news,
- sign a petition,

- donate money to a cause,
- write a letter (or e-mail, text, or tweet) to the editor,
- serve on a jury,
- join or even just attend a demonstration,
- communicate with government officials about a matter of concern to you,
- attend a public meeting, such as a school board hearing, or
- campaign for a candidate.

Political participation Those activities of citizens that attempt to influence the structure of government, the selection of government officials, or the policies of government.

The term **political participation** or engagement refers to "those activities of citizens that attempt to influence the structure of government, the selection of government officials, or the policies of government."[1] Some scholars include the activity of merely paying attention to politics as a "passive" form of participation.[2] From this perspective, citizens who monitor the workings of government and politics with at least the potential of taking action can be seen as passive participants. Still others regard any contribution to community life by citizens as political, or at least as having political implications and consequences.

Some forms of political engagement are fairly benign, such as attending a school board meeting or writing a letter to an elected official. Other forms of engagement, however, are destructive. The boundaries of what is considered destructive have changed over the course of American history. Should burning the American flag in protest be illegal, or is it, as the Supreme Court has ruled, a permissible form of symbolic expression? In the 1960s, **civil disobedience**, a form of nonviolent political protest, became a common way for people to express dissent. Mohandas Gandhi initiated this form of participation in the early twentieth century when leading India in its fight for independence from Great Britain. In the 1960s, Dr. Martin Luther King, Jr. and the civil rights movement used civil disobedience to bring public attention to unjust laws. Students protesting against the Vietnam War held sit-ins, occupying a space and allowing themselves to be arrested. The peaceful violation of laws considered unjust, and the willingness to be arrested and convicted for doing so, while technically illegal, has since gained acceptance as a legitimate form of protest.

Civil disobedience A form of nonviolent political protest; became popular in the 1960s as a way to express dissent.

Though rarely included in discussions of political participation, terrorist acts, such as the bombing of the federal building in Oklahoma City in 1995 or the September 11 attacks in 2001, are often politically motivated actions. Although illegitimate, uncivilized, and unconventional, some scholars argue that these forms of political participation may be better understood by the study of individual motivations for participation in politics generally.[3]

Some types of participation are often left out of discussion of political engagement, such as volunteer work for nonprofit organizations like churches, charities, human service providers, as well as organizations that coordinate relief efforts in the wake of natural and unnatural disasters. Over the last 10 to 15 years, younger Americans have increased their involvement in these types of activities, which they see as nonpolitical. While not directly political, the motivation of many to take part in what constitutes civic engagement involves a sense of disgust and alienation from politics as they perceive it.

Many younger Americans in the so-called X, Y, and Z generations (the labels for the three post–baby boom generations) have negative impressions of political engagement and of those who engage in *politics*, which they perceive as a label for the selfish manipulation of public policy. These young Americans do want to be good citizens, but they want to devote their time and energy to activities that they think actually make a difference, a difference they can see. Volunteering to help the poor or organizing efforts to provide direct assistance to people in the wake of a natural disaster may be immediately gratifying, and it also cannot be mistaken for self-interested manipulation.[4] These younger Americans seem to have embraced the notions of civic obligation and self-sacrifice as the keys to good citizenship and to have assumed that political activity involves neither.

Generational effect Similar attitudes about politics among members of the same generation produced by shared national experiences.

It is possible that younger Americans turning away from politics but toward civic volunteerism are exhibiting what political scientists call a **generational effect**, which occurs when shared national experiences produce similar attitudes about politics among members of the same generation. The shared experience of the 9/11 terrorist attacks, Hurricane Katrina, and the very partisan politics of the last decade or so may be related to the political cynicism and frustration of Americans who have come of age in the last 10 years. The heroism of the 9/11 rescuers and the highly publicized efforts of Americans from all walks of life to pitch in and assist in the aftermath of subsequent natural disasters may well have provided young Americans with a more attractive model of participation.[5]

9 More people are shunning traditional political activities but embracing new forms of participation.

Though only a small fraction of Americans, young and old alike, regularly engage in organized politics as it has been traditionally defined and understood, there are signs that political engagement of a different sort is on the rise. The expansion of the Internet in the last 10 to 15 years has produced a whole new venue and set of activities that are increasingly regarded as political engagement.

Activities such as writing to government officials or to the editor of newspapers have been revolutionized by the Internet. Now, such efforts are mass-produced and distributed with incredible speed. The Internet has given a voice to everyone with access to an Internet connection, which, according to most estimates, includes more than 75 percent of adults in the United States. Where many would once have been unwilling to register support or opposition for a cause, candidate, or public policy, the ease of doing so has surely lured some who would otherwise be passive participants at best. Studies of traditional participation have long shown that once people get a taste of meaningful participation, the chances that they will continue to engage increase markedly. The question is: Will the Internet provide Americans with what they consider meaningful engagement?

Individuals can now enter the political fray in a very personal way, increasing the salience of cyberpolitics. Scholars and journalists have already begun to talk and write about the "YouTube effect." Since the site was created in 2005, videos shot by amateurs and attendees at political events have become powerful campaign tools, and weapons. In 2006, while running for reelection to the U.S. Senate, George Allen of Virginia became one of YouTube's first high-profile political victims when a video of remarks he made at a campaign event found its way to YouTube. Allen had used a derogatory term to refer to a supporter of his opponent who was videoing the event for that opponent's campaign. A thoughtless slip of the tongue was and is not unusual for politicians, especially in a competitive campaign, but Allen's slip was played thousands of times and viewed by millions of people. Allen, who was considered a serious contender for the 2008 Republican presidential nomination at the time, lost his bid for reelection and faded from the national political scene.[6]

Factors such as level of education and income play a key role in whether a person is likely to engage in the most basic form of democratic participation, voting.

Voting is one of the most basic and widely recognized ways in which Americans participate in public life. Voting is understood as both a fundamental right and a civic obligation by Americans. But if you ask around, you'll probably find that some of your friends, family members, and neighbors don't actually show up at the polls on Election Day. Do you vote? The study of voting behavior centers on a couple of key questions: Who votes and why? And, what separates or distinguishes people who vote from people who don't?

Research has long shown that there are some basic characteristics that help reveal the likelihood of whether or not an individual will vote. Three of the most useful predictive indicators are a person's age, income, and level of education. The older, wealthier, and more educated you are, the more likely that you will vote. Some other factors that correlate with voting might surprise you. Voter turnout rates, for example, also correlate with regular church attendance, marriage, and home ownership. Research suggests that men and women vote in roughly equal proportions. The correlation between race and voting, however, is a much different and more complex story. Throughout much of American history, for example, African American turnout rates were generally lower than white turnout rates. These differences may be attributed to a variety of complicated historical factors, including social barriers that kept African Americans from voting, such as the poll taxes and literacy tests. Scholars continue to try to understand the reasons for differences in turnout rates not only among racial and ethnic groups but others as well.[7]

So why does the likelihood of someone being a voter increase with age, income, education, marriage, and church attendance? Each of these categories correlates with varying degrees of establishment or settlement into lifelong habits, employment, and reduced geographic mobility. Each of these categories also correlates with the perception of a personal stake in governmental policy decisions, as well as knowledge of political processes. Furthermore, the more embedded a person is in his or her community, the more likely it is that he or she feels both an obligation to participate and a sense of **political efficacy**, or confidence in one's ability to participate meaningfully. Not surprisingly, demographic groups with lower voting rates tend to see themselves as having less of a material stake in their community, less involvement in and commitment to their community, less knowledge about politics, and less confidence in their own political efficacy.

Political efficacy Confidence in one's ability to participate meaningfully in politics.

Although political engagement can and does include many activities other than voting, the factors that make Americans more or less likely to vote are also correlated to civic knowledge and engagement outside of the voting booth. Citizens lacking knowledge, self-confidence, economic means or opportunities, education, life experience, and commitment to a community aren't just less likely to vote, they are also less likely to communicate effectively with neighbors, co-workers, and employers or to see any point in political activities. They may even view politics as a game of petty one-upmanship and greed. This sense of futility and helplessness directed toward politics has undoubtedly played a part in the increasing likelihood that younger Americans will choose nonpolitical civic activity, such as one-on-one mentoring, tutoring, and volunteering for churches and charities that provide services to the poor, elderly, and infirm. Many have argued that these activities fulfill people's desire to be helpful, without entangling them in group conflicts often characterized by pettiness and acrimony.[8]

One final point on voter turnout and political engagement statistics that is important to note is that while the data tell us a lot, they do not tell the whole story. Most importantly, they do not always help us predict accurately what will happen in the future, or when people who do not normally turn out to vote or participate may choose to do so. A good example of this is the 2008 presidential election. Despite what the data show us about participation rates by race and age, in the 2008 election there were sharp increases among both minority voters and young voters. Among African Americans, for example, turnout in 2008 rose 22 percent above its 2004 mark. Turnout among Latino voters went up 16 percent, and young voter turnout increased 9 percent.[9] Scholars continue to examine the reasons for this increase. Some findings suggest it was due to "the appearance of an African-American presidential candidate with a sympathetic message."[10] But it is unclear whether this trend will continue and lead to greater participation in politics.

Research shows swing and undecided voters are not always as persuadable as one might think.

Are American voters motivated by pure rational self-interest, by their pocketbooks, as the famous line from the 1992 Clinton campaign "it's the economy, stupid" implied? Are they driven by emotional reactions and cultural prejudgments? Or, are they faithful devotees of the ideologies of left and right? The data are mixed. Scholars have long debated the degree to which voters operate as economic rationalists, products of their surroundings, or on the basis of **political ideology**—a set of principles, beliefs, themes, or ideals that not only help explain how society operates but also provide a prescription for the future. At the end of the day, it turns out, it all depends on the context. Each election is unique in the degree to which external contextual factors weigh on the minds and choices of voters. Consensus among scholars on the weight of external factors across elections is not likely to emerge anytime soon.

Political ideology A set of principles, beliefs, themes, or ideals that not only help explain how society operates but also provide a prescription for the future.

The results of the 2008 election, for example, have been the subject of a debate along these lines. Political scientist David Campbell maintains that the election was a competitive one between Barack Obama and John McCain. He concludes that the financial crisis that emerged in mid-September was a "game changer," that without it, the election would have been much closer, and that McCain may well have won it. Political scientist Larry Sabato, on the other hand, argues that the election of Barack Obama was a virtual certainty and that political scientists had known this since the spring of 2008. For Sabato, there are three fundamental electoral conditions that provide clear evidence of which way presidential elections will go: presidential popularity, economic conditions, and war and peace. According to Sabato, "any mainstream Democratic candidate was destined to win in 2008" because of the combination of a very unpopular second-term Republican president, a slumping economy, and the most unpopular war since Vietnam. From this perspective, the financial situation that emerged in mid-September merely padded Obama's already considerable lead.[11]

Though the impact of contextual factors remains the subject of lively debate, there is a scholarly consensus on the factors that always play a role in voter choices: party loyalty, issue positions, and the characteristics of the candidates. Research shows, for instance, that most voters end up voting for the candidate of the political party with which they most identify—making partisanship the most important factor and the most reliable predictor of voter choices. Despite the popularity of political party bashing and the use of the term *partisan* as an epithet, 8 in 10 voters in 2000 and 2004 chose the candidate of their own party.[12] In 2008, over 70 percent of the electorate was made up of self-identified partisans. Both major-party candidates, Democrat Barack Obama and Republican John McCain, earned around 90 percent

Figure 10.1 **Votes Won by Two Major Parties versus Other Parties or Individuals in U.S. Presidential Elections, 1972–2008**

These graphs show the percentage of the popular vote and the number of Electoral College votes won by the two major political parties as compared with the percentage and number of votes won by other political parties or individuals.

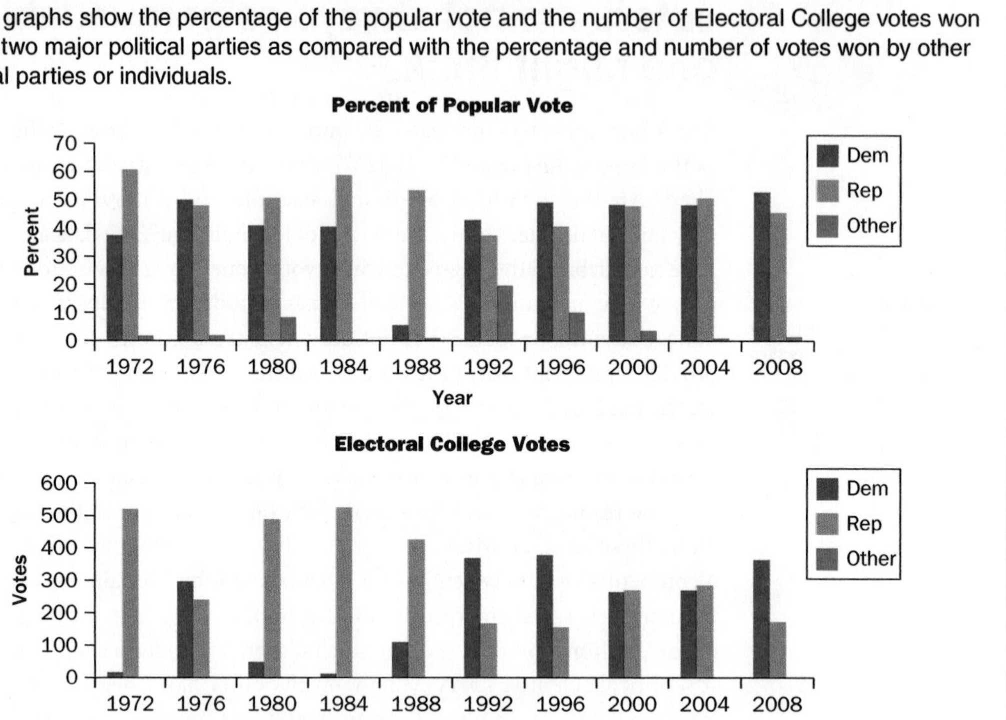

of their party's voters. Self-described independents gave 52 percent of their votes to the Democrat, 44 percent to the Republican, and 4 percent to other candidates.[13]

As Figure 10.1 shows, 2008 was not an anomaly in this regard. Presidential elections from 1972 through 2008 have been dominated by two political parties. In each of these elections, Democrats and Republicans have usually won all but a small fraction of the popular vote and almost all the Electoral College votes. In the more than thirty-five years covered in this table, only one third-party candidate—Ross Perot in 1992 and 1996—was able to get 10 percent of the popular vote. Despite this achievement, Perot failed to garner even one Electoral College vote.

Swing voters Those voters who are thought to be undecided, less partisan, and more receptive to persuasion by political campaigns.

The fact that most voters tend to vote along party lines seems to suggest that it is really a minority of voters in the middle, the so-called **swing voters** who are thought to be undecided, less partisan, and more receptive to persuasion by political campaigns, who choose our leaders. Although this conclusion has a lot of intuitive plausibility, the data do not support it. Voter preference data indicate that these voters don't really *swing* elections. They tend to either split fairly equally between the parties or to reinforce the candidate who won the majority of partisan voters. Furthermore, voters who claim to be "undecided" or "independent" are not as persuadable as one might think. Their early candidate preferences, though not commitments, are nearly as stable as that of party identifiers, meaning that campaigns that pour resources into persuading undecided voters as the campaign progresses are chasing a very small target that gets smaller very quickly.[14]

In addition, while partisan identification correlates with a number of demographic categories (e.g., African Americans are much more likely to be Democrats, and regular church goers are more likely to be Republicans), undecided or independent voters are a microcosm of the entire electorate. There are no demographic categories that correlate with nonparty identifiers, nor do they share issue positions as a group. The one factor that unites this group is attitudinal. Undecided or independent voters are less partisan and more moderate on issues generally. While they pay attention to politics more than nonvoters, they are not as attentive to or aware of politics as are partisan voters.[15] It may be that many self-professed independent or undecided voters are merely trying to avoid being labeled or stereotyped by identifying with a political party, or that their lack of attention to politics makes them incapable of declaring firm commitments.

6 New technology is changing the methods, modes, and patterns of participation.

Is worry over low voter turnout "much ado about nothing"? Many scholars believe that declining voter turnout endangers the integrity of the democratic system. Those who consider active and widespread citizen participation a fundamental symptom of civic health are particularly concerned with widespread perceptions of decline in voter turnout in American elections. Not all scholars, however, see declining voter turnout as problematic. Some argue that choosing not to exercise one's right to weigh in on the hiring and firing decisions of elected officials is a positive sign, indicating either satisfaction with the status quo or a sensible realization by a voter that he or she lacks the information needed to make a reasonable choice.

Scholars also disagree about whether there has been a significant change in voter turnout. The disagreement centers on how to count "eligible voters." Most measures of decline in the last few decades relied on U.S. Census data. Some scholars argue that such data include "ineligible voters," reducing the accuracy of the data.

Though the argument over measuring turnout is unsettled, the undisputed increases in turnout since 2002 seem to have pushed this disagreement into the background, replaced by investigations into the reasons for increased voting despite the persistence of many institutional, social, and economic barriers to meaningful political engagement. Thus transformed, the "turnout debate" becomes a debate about explaining correlations between increased turnout and the changing institutional, social, and behavioral patterns of twenty-first-century American politics.

But how can we explain this increase in voting in the 2004 and 2008 elections in light of the declines in civic knowledge, trust in government, and routine involvement in organized politics? Some people argue that the same forces we believed hurt political participation have instead begun to revitalize it. In the past, scholars viewed the explosion of communications and media technology over the last 20 years as harmful to participation. Now, some analysts studying the effects of things like television, the Internet, cell phones, and even video games are finding positive and transformative impacts on political engagement.[16] The ease and availability of access to government and politics through interactive media and communications technology has reduced the time and energy it takes for us to participate in politics. We can now monitor government actions on issues of particular concern more easily. We can also see the results of our efforts more quickly through online polls, the 24-hour news cycle, and other products of this media explosion.

Older methods of civic engagement seem to be giving way to newer modes. Though institutions like political parties cannot turn out people to events and rallies like they once did, campaigns using the Internet to organize both virtual and actual events have enjoyed tremendous success in this regard. Barack Obama's unprecedented use of the Internet to organize every aspect of his campaign quieted those who argued that the *virtual* campaigns would never realize the expectations of their proponents. By shattering fund-raising, event attendance, and voter turnout records with the help of the Internet, the Obama campaign showed the worth of this modern communications technology for increasing (at least quantitatively) political engagement in American politics.

5 Your political opinions are shaped by the people, institutions, and ideas to which you were exposed when you were young.

Many people have strong feelings about the political party they belong to and about politics in general. This raises a question: How did they get those strong feelings? How do individuals develop their political identities, opinions, and attitudes? Political scientists have long been interested in discovering the answers to these questions and the bases of **political socialization**, or the ways in which we learn about and develop our opinions and attitudes about politics and government.

Political socialization The ways in which we learn about and develop our opinions and attitudes about politics and government.

The answer lies in the people, social structures or institutions, and ideas to which we were exposed during the formative years of our psychological and intellectual development.[17] Research shows that the process of political socialization begins, like many things, in the home. As Herbert Hyman writes, "[f]oremost among agencies of socialization into politics is the family."[18] One of the key pieces of evidence to support the influence of parents and family on the development of political beliefs is the fact that the vast majority of children adopt the same political party identification as their parents. This finding was first developed most clearly in the groundbreaking *American Voter* and later confirmed in the *American Voter Revisited*, where the authors found that parents pass their party affiliation on to their

Table 10.1 Percent of Parents Who Voted for the Same Presidential Candidate as Their Children in the 2008 Election

	Obama Voters	McCain Voters
Same candidate	58%*	78%*
Different candidate	17%	5%
One parent voted the same; one parent voted different	20%	12%
Not voting	5%	3%

*Average of the responses from the four states (CO, NC, OH, and PA)

Source: October 6–18, 2008, CBS, UWIRE, and *The Chronicle of Education* poll of 25,000 students at four-year colleges in four key battleground states (Colorado, North Carolina, Ohio, and Pennsylvania).www.cbsnews.com/htdocs/pdf/081027_uwire.pdf (Page 7)

children 75 percent of the time.[19] The influence of family extends beyond party affiliation. In the 2008 election, for instance, pollsters found that a majority of college students supported the same presidential candidate as their parents. As Table 10.1 shows, there was a fairly sizeable correlation between the candidate favored by the students and by their parents.[20]

In addition to your parents, siblings, and extended family, other influential people in the process of political socialization include your classmates, teachers, and coaches. This is because during adolescence and into young adulthood, a person's school—whether elementary, secondary, or college—and the people who work in that system can play a powerful role in helping to develop and shape political opinions, attitudes, and beliefs. As James Simon and Bruce Merrill note:

> For more than 30 years, researchers have explored the role of the school as one of the locations where children develop the knowledge, attitudes and behaviors that shape their roles as future participants in a democracy. While family and home background are often viewed as the primary agents of socialization, schools are seen as a significant secondary agent.[21]

In addition to school, another important secondary agent in the socialization process is the mass media—including all the personalities and characters encountered on television, in books, and increasingly in cyberspace or other forms of new technology. According to Simon and Merrill, "[m]ass media exposure and the political context of the times also are seen as having an impact on political socialization. Exposure to campaign information from television and newspapers can have an important impact on cognitive processes."[22]

There is no question that as we get older and start work at a new job, interact with government agencies, listen to media reports, and travel in and out of the lives of many people along the way, ideas about right and wrong, good and bad, and how to live and how not to live are making impressions and helping to shape our world-views. Nevertheless, most research shows that socialization begins in childhood at home and in places where young people spend time—school, religious institutions, and so on. Since young people increasingly have access to new technology, the media have come to play an important role in this development process.

Public opinion polls measure the direction and intensity of public attitudes and opinions.

Political socialization research shows that the people, institutions, social structures, and ideas we are exposed to during our formative years play a key role in shaping our opinions about politics and government. But this raises another question—how do we know what Americans think? How can we measure the public's opinions? In fact, political scientists can learn quite a bit about Americans by analyzing public opinion. The primary tool for doing so is the **public opinion poll**, a survey of a representative sample of a population designed to measure the values, attitudes, and beliefs of the population on specific issues.

Public opinion poll A survey of a representative sample of a population designed to measure the values, attitudes, and beliefs of the population on specific issues.

By asking respondents a battery of questions designed to classify them by numerous demographic categories, political scientists can compare the voting rates and political preferences of Americans by race, age, gender, income, education level, occupation, religious affiliation, political party affiliation, marital status, and many other factors. This allows scholars, journalists, pundits, and political operatives to make reasonable inferences about how issue and candidate preferences correlate with citizens' demographic characteristics. Polls taken on Election Day as actual voters exit the polling place are called **exit polls**. This type of poll allows analysts to exclude nonvoters and isolate the opinions of those who matter most, voters.[23]

Exit polls Opinion surveys in which voters are questioned about their votes and preferences as they leave the polling place on Election Day.

Increasingly over the last half century, the science of measuring public opinion has become very important to political professionals and activists, mass media outlets, and business people eager to fully understand the demands of their customers. Dissecting every nuance of opinion and prejudice of American voters and consumers has become a very lucrative profession. In a political and commercial marketplace that is increasingly unmediated by institutions like political parties or local retailers, **pollsters** who conduct public opinion surveys for media, corporate, nonprofit, and political clients have become the most important advisors to presidents and corporate CEOs. Their job is to systematically describe what people believe, what motivates them, and what choices they are likely to make in a given situation. Because the methods of survey research require specialized knowledge, very few Americans

Pollsters Those who conduct public opinion surveys for media, corporate, nonprofit, and political clients.

understand how pollsters can confidently declare what people want and what they will do in a department store or a voting booth.

But how can polls be accurate when it is impossible to ask everyone what they think? The answer lies in **probability sampling**, a process in which participants are chosen randomly from the target population. Ideally, every member of the target population has the same chance of being polled. Noted pollster John Zogby explains:

Probability sampling A survey in which respondents are chosen randomly from the target population. Ideally, every member of the target population has the same chance of being polled.

> If there are a million marbles in a jar, some black and some white—how best do I determine the number of each color, short of counting every marble? If I draw 1,000 out at random, chances are I will get the same numbers of each 95 times out of 100 within a margin of error of + or −3%.[24]

Sample Opinion survey respondents who serve as a representative subgroup of a target population.

95% confidence level If a survey were repeated 100 times, the poll's results will be confirmed 95 out of the 100. No survey can achieve a higher level of confidence than 95 out of 100, or 95%.

Confidence level A pollster's way of saying how much confidence he or she has that the poll sample is reflective or representative of the population.

Margin of error or sampling error The range of the results that will be confirmed 95 out of 100 times. A typical margin of error is + or −3. If a poll found 50 percent of respondents answered a question the same way, then with a + or −3 margin of error, it means that between 47 and 53 percent will respond the same way 95 out of 100 times.

Zogby's example represents a random **sample** (representative subgroup of a target population) of 1,000 individuals the results of which are reported with a **95% confidence level** and a margin of error or sampling error of plus or minus 3 percent. The **confidence level** is simply a pollster's way of saying how much confidence he or she has that the poll sample is reflective or representative of the population. So if the results of a poll are reported with 95% confidence, this means if you did the same poll of the same population 100 times, 95 of those times you would get similar results. The **margin of error or sample error** is "not an 'error' in the sense of making a mistake. Rather, it is a measure of the possible range of approximation in the results because a sample was used."[25] You have probably heard, for instance, that a national poll has a "3 percentage point margin of error." What does this mean? "If the attempt were made to interview every adult in the nation with the same questions in the same way at the same time as the poll was taken, the poll's answers would fall within plus or minus 3 percentage points of the complete count's results 95% of the time."[26]

Converted into the language of politics, a random sample of 1,000 voters that yields 45 percent supporting candidate A and 55 percent supporting candidate B, within a margin of error of plus or minus 3 percentage points, means that candidate A's support is between 42 and 48 percent and candidate B's support is between 52 and 58 percent. Because the sample size was 1,000, the margin of error was just plus or minus 3 percent. Smaller samples have larger error margins, which means that sample size, as well as randomness, is important. A sample of 600 would have a margin of error of plus or minus 4 percent, while a sample of 400 would have a 5 percent margin of error. So this survey tells us that the race may be as close as four points or as lopsided as sixteen points.[27]

One of the biggest misconceptions about public opinion polling is that it can accurately predict future behavior. In fact, polling is really just a snapshot in time designed to describe how people feel or what they believe at the moment of the survey. Because the stakes of polling in politics and in business are so high, most pollsters, while admitting they do not have a crystal ball, do want their clients to believe they can accurately predict future behavior. This hope has spawned improved methods in

Tracking poll A survey that asks respondents a set of questions daily, reporting the averages of the latest three-day period.

polling, such as the **tracking poll**, which asks respondents a set of questions daily, reporting the averages of the latest three-day period. As each new day's results are factored in, results from an earlier day are dropped. The purpose of these rolling averages is to try to account for and track changes in opinion over time as quickly as possible.

The results of public opinion polls are hard to avoid in America today, especially during political campaign seasons. But the reliance on polling of business, government, and politicians both in office and on the campaign trail has made polls and reported poll results very familiar to Americans. In electoral politics the role of polls and pollsters has led many Americans to wonder if polls describe reality or shape it. The use of polls by mass media outlets in both reporting political news and in deciding what types of stories will generate viewer or listener interest has made it difficult for Americans to focus on policy debates instead of the daily ups and downs of candidates and their campaigns reported on in minute detail by media outlets that have to produce material 24/7. Cable news and Internet media outlets in particular that need to generate newsworthy stories constantly rely on polls as a source of news and analysis. Sometimes the polls and pollsters become the story. The good polls make great sages of their authors, and the bad ones generate hand-wringing about the value of polls in general.

Pollsters strongly defend their profession, saying that polls measure public opinion but do not shape it. That does not mean that polls do not have real-world consequences. Favorable polls provide candidates with something they can use to garner support, particularly financial support. Positive poll results help candidates convince donors that they are betting on a winner. Obviously, negative poll results have the opposite effect.[28] Donors are literally making a financial investment. To them, public opinion surveys are marketing surveys telling them whether or not a product, a candidate, or a cause is going to sell. Candidates also rely on polling data to craft and test their messages. Polls are valuable to voters in that they reveal a candidate's strengths and weaknesses and often highlight issues or ideas that the media have not picked up on and that would otherwise escape voters' attention. Sometimes the polls provide the media with a "reality check" and lead them to cover stories people care about.[29]

3 Americans' political opinions can be classified as liberal, conservative, libertarian, and populist.

American public opinion about politics has long been classified according to its place on a two-dimensional continuum from right to left. America's two major political parties philosophically occupy each side of the spectrum, with the Republicans on the right and the Democrats on the left. Increasingly, opinion researchers have sought to understand these divisions of opinion. This has led to the identification of

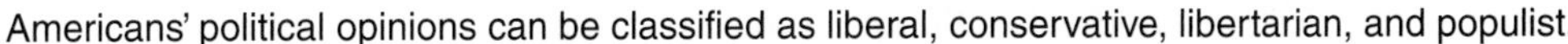

four distinct strands of public opinion on politics, each animated by distinct variations on the question of government activism in the protection of social order and individual freedom. To this extent, the four major political philosophies (American conservatism, American liberalism, libertarianism, and populism) each offer their own unique political ideology, views, principles, and beliefs that help explain not only how the society operates but also how it should operate.

Conservatives, for instance, disapprove of government interference in economic life, but not in the defense of traditional moral principles. **Liberals**, on the other hand, oppose government interference in the moral or societal values and choices of individuals, while supporting government efforts to regulate the economic marketplace. Both are distinct from **libertarians**, who oppose significant government involvement in both society and the economy alike, and **populists**, who have no problem with activist government, as long as it serves to protect social order and improve the material conditions of people's lives.

Conservatives Those who disapprove of government interference in economic life, but not in the defense of traditional moral principles.

Liberals Those who oppose government interference in the moral or societal values and choices of individuals, while supporting government efforts to regulate the economic marketplace.

Libertarians Those who oppose significant government involvement in both society and the economy alike.

Populists Voters who have no problem with activist government, as long as it serves to protect social order and improve the material conditions of people's lives.

While all Americans support government power in the preservation of physical security and private property, American conservatives are distinctive in their support of government power in the defense of social and economic morality. They believe that the maintenance of traditional Judeo-Christian social and economic values, norms, and institutions is crucial to government's core function of maintaining social order. They support laws against abortion, birth control, gay marriage, sodomy, prostitution, and sexually explicit publications and entertainment and oppose governmental tolerance of such activities. They support efforts to reduce government involvement in the free market and oppose public policies that alter the rational incentives of American consumers and producers, such as tax increases, minimum wage laws, collective bargaining laws, income support programs, publicly subsidized healthcare and housing, workplace safety regulations, and excessive environmental protection policies. Conservatives believe all of these things weaken the moral fiber of individuals and society by reducing the urgency of personal initiative and the individual's responsibility for his or her own fate.

American liberals, on the other hand, are much less supportive of government power exerted in the name of protecting social order and believe that government is obligated to provide a social safety net to individuals because of the inherent unequal distribution of opportunities in a free market society. They emphasize government's obligation to protect individuals from infringements on their personal freedom coming from both public and private sources. Liberals oppose undue restrictions on what they see as rights. They believe government is obliged to combat policies or practices, public or private, that unduly infringe on individuals' rights to things like due process, equal justice, privacy, education, economic opportunity, access to healthcare, affordable housing, and retirement security. This produces liberal support for policies that protect individuals from unfair competition in the marketplace as well as the unequal distribution of opportunities to pursue the so-called **American dream**, or the achievement of economic independence and personal and social fulfillment.

American dream The achievement of economic independence and personal and social fulfillment.

Social responsibility Governmental acts on behalf of the community that assist those in need.

Liberals emphasize **social responsibility**, wherein the government acts on behalf of the community to assist those in need.

For libertarians, the "best government is the government that governs least." Libertarians adhere to this Jeffersonian perspective without the Judeo-Christian moral overtones of conservatives. Libertarians share conservatism's confidence in the free market, but not its faith-based foundations. Libertarian voters, usually forced to choose between left and right, find themselves forced to prioritize constituent parts of their antigovernment perspective. When they are most fearful of too much governmental interference in the economy, they tend to support Republicans. When they are most worried about government dictates infringing on personal lifestyle or values choices, they tend to support Democrats.

The last category of public opinion in American politics finds its adherents torn in much the same manner as libertarians, though in opposite directions. American populists are distinguished from the other three strands of public opinion by their utter lack of ideological motivation. These are Americans whose interest in government is purely practical. They are socially conservative and economically liberal. While libertarians are driven by adherence to a distinct ideological variant of liberalism, populists support government actions based on their expectation that such actions can fix problems or improve people's lives. They tend to support conservative initiatives intended to bring social order to life as well as liberal government programs designed to improve the material conditions of people's lives.

That American public opinion about politics can be broken down into these four categories should not obscure the reality that the opinions of politics are hardly self-conscious expressions of political ideology. Social, cultural, and economic factors undoubtedly contribute significantly to the political opinions of Americans. Because our political conversation often focuses on right versus left, many people who researchers would classify as libertarians or populists understandably think of themselves as nonpartisan, or nonideological; yet, their opinions are no less consistent and no less political. The constant denigration of partisanship and even of ideology in American life further contributes to the popularity of Americans thinking of themselves as political independents.[30]

2 The media's role is expanding, but its authority may be declining.

Mass media All forms of mass communication, including television, radio, newspapers, magazines, Internet sites, films, and books.

One of the major factors shaping American public opinion is the mass media. Americans get virtually all of their political information from the **mass media**, which transmits information and entertainment electronically on radio and television, in print in newspapers, magazines, and books, and in cyberspace on the Internet. The line between informing and entertaining has been blurred by the increase of media formats designed to provide infotainment. One of the many questions researchers

Media literacy The ability to distinguish between reliable and unreliable information and/or analysis in the vastly expanded modern media environment.

ask today as it pertains to the role of the media and political participation concerns the extent to which people in the United States are "media literate." **Media literacy** is the ability to distinguish between reliable and unreliable information and/or analyze the vastly expanded modern media environment. As you think about the enormous role the media play in socialization, participation, and opinion formation, ask yourself how media savvy and literate you are? How competent are your friends and family when it comes to analyzing and evaluating the veracity of the messages we receive from an ever-expanding number of media outlets?

Media influence on Americans' political attitudes and participatory patterns is no longer limited to the so-called news media that explicitly cover politics. Politically relevant content in every form of mass media has increased dramatically in the last 30 to 40 years. Even before the Internet, television and radio had seen dramatic increases in political content. News magazine TV shows, like *60 Minutes*, *20/20*, *48 Hours*, and many more, were combining news and entertainment, and shows like *The West Wing* brought high-level politics into American living rooms and high ratings to NBC. Talk radio has been a source of contentious political communication in America for at least a quarter of a century now. Even reality television shows take advantage of the entertainment value of politics. The people on these shows routinely engage in political strategies, such as forming alliances, truces, strategic voting, and a number of other explicitly political tactics.

Talk shows designed as entertainment have been including politics more and more as well. One study that received a lot of publicity revealed that young Americans were getting a large percentage of their political information from late-night TV shows like *The Tonight Show* with Jay Leno or David Letterman.[31] The cable TV network *Comedy Central* pioneered an entertainment format that explicitly uses politics as a platform for entertainment. The so-called *fake news* shows, like *The Daily Show* with Jon Stewart and *The Colbert Report* with Stephen Colbert, bring their audiences sarcastic and politically charged commentary as entertainment. Politicians have increasingly acknowledged this crucial venue for communicating with young voters. Bill Clinton played the saxophone on late-night TV in 1992. Since then, every presidential nominee or candidate for a major party nomination has found his or her way to the late-night shows. Appearances on *Saturday Night Live* have even become standard for presidential aspirants as a way to connect with younger Americans.[32]

The line between informing and persuading has also become blurred in the wake of the 24/7 cable news networks and the Internet. The political battle lines are pretty clear in the print media where major newspapers' editorial perspectives are liberal or conservative, and readers are increasingly unable or unwilling to distinguish between editorial and news content. *The New York Times* and *The Washington Post*, for example, are considered reliably liberal in their editorial opinions, while conservatives look to *The Wall Street Journal* and *The Washington Times* for reliably conservative perspectives.

Magazines are also identifiable by their editorial viewpoints. *The New Yorker*, *The Nation*, *The New Republic*, and *Mother Jones* are among those with liberal perspectives, while the *National Review*, *Weekly Standard*, and *The American Spectator* provide outlets for conservative views. All of these publications and many more are also available on the Internet, where they compete with politically charged Web sites that have no print version at all. These sites provide politically partisan Web users with a portal through which to take in and participate in political debate and discussion. They also serve as clearing houses of sorts for those seeking to join others of the same political persuasion in mobilization efforts.

The massive expansion of competition in the political news business has transformed the perennial issue of bias in the media. Traditionally, media outlets were few enough that biases were more easily detected, and the real competition was about getting the story fast and getting it right. Today, the competition in the political news and commentary business has exploded in ways that have seriously blurred the line between conventional nonpartisan journalism and what some call **advocacy journalism**, wherein the news outlets' biases permeate news gathering, reporting, and analysis of political information. With the increasing speed of communications came a wave of sites purporting to be objective fact finders and analysts of politics. The reality is, however, that such outlets are virtually all one strand or another of politically biased journalism. Scholars Bill Kovach, chairman of the Committee of Concerned Journalists, and Tom Rosenstiel, director "of the Pew Research Center's Project for Excellence in Journalism," differentiate among three different types of advocacy journalism: the journalism of assertion, the journalism of affirmation, and interest-group journalism.[33]

Advocacy journalism
Journalism in which news outlets' biases permeate news gathering, reporting, and analysis of political information.

Because of the expansion of the news business and the lack of authoritative policing of media accuracy in the Information Age, news gatherers, old and new, have been hobbled in their efforts to practice the kind of journalism taught in journalism schools.[34] Instead, news consumers expect their news fast, preferably in real time, and without ambiguity, which incentivizes the rapid and compelling assertion of the important facts and what they mean. This *journalism of assertion* produces a sort of reversal of the bias problem in journalism. Instead of empowering the news media editors, who once could more easily shape and frame political news in carefully edited and prepackaged segments or reports, the need for instant analysis to keep up with competitors transfers the onus of editing and verification to the news consumer, whose own biases and preconceived notions are now a significant source of and reason for media bias.

The decline of carefully vetted news and analysis has facilitated the rise of news media outlets whose business plans call explicitly for a style of journalism (*journalism of affirmation*) intended to affirm the values and perspectives of a carefully chosen target demographic. In the cable news business, the Fox News Channel and MSNBC are vivid examples of journalism packaged to appeal to particular consumer biases. The appeal of this type of journalism "is in affirming the preconceptions of the audience, assuring them, gaining their loyalty, and then converting that loyalty into advertising revenue."[35]

The final category of advocacy journalism is *interest-group journalism*, wherein the middleman between advocates and the public has been completely eliminated. Though largely an Internet phenomenon, interest groups that produce advocacy claims packaged as objective news or expert analysis are often picked up by TV, radio, and even print journalists whose need for compelling stories frequently overpowers their obligation to verify the accuracy or credibility of sources.

The media have contributed to the decline in meaningful political participation and knowledge.

The dominant perspective among scholars, as it relates to the mass media's impact on political engagement, has been negative. While the dismal state of civic knowledge among Americans continues to be a dominant and compelling factor in explaining political behavior in America, the declines in voter turnout appear to have reversed themselves, with increased turnout rates in three straight presidential elections, in 2000, 2004, and 2008.[36] This increase in voter turnout seems to parallel the increasing influence of the Internet on political communication and mobilization, begging the question: Has the Internet played a part in restoring meaningful political engagement, or has it effectively diluted meaningful participation by expanding uncritical participation? Will the Internet's impact on political engagement in the future improve or reduce the quality of our democratic politics? In other words, will the Internet help reverse the persistent and indisputable decline of civic knowledge, or will it exacerbate it?

Some scholars fear that the Internet will exacerbate the fragmentation of political knowledge, interest, and meaningful engagement. Organizations such as political parties and other civic organizations that once served as reliable sources of information brought people together around shared values and helped structure political choices for their members. Mass media outlets, especially commercial ones, are sustained not by bringing people together, but by highlighting the divisions between people. The bottom line in commercial media is furthered by great clashes and conflicts of people, institutions, and ideas, which means that commercial viability requires media outlets to divide the electorate, something long associated by scholars and commentators with political cynicism, apathy, ignorance, and alienation.

Narrowcasting Tailoring media content to the preferences and prejudices of consumers in the target demographic.

Commercial mass media outlets not only have to live by the mantra "if it bleeds it leads," they must also cater to their target demographics in order to stay afloat. Maintaining the patronage of the type of media consumers an outlet attracts has a tendency to increase incentives for the use of **narrowcasting**, which involves the tailoring of media content to the preferences and prejudices of consumers in the target demographic—the journalism of assertion and affirmation discussed above. News media outlets trying to maintain journalistic neutrality are increasingly pressured to bring news reporting and news analysis closer together in order to compete with the increasing number of media outlets that do not separate the two. The blurred lines between news reporting, analysis, advocacy, and entertainment make the use of narrowcasting particularly counterproductive in the cultivation of political knowledge among media consumers.

If we are increasingly lured to media outlets whose content has been designed to cater to our present preferences and prejudices—cultural, social, and political—then the prospect for increasing civic knowledge seems dim. The test for the Internet, therefore, is whether it can help users to distinguish between legitimate and illegitimate, reasonable and unreasonable, sources of information and analysis. If so, then the Internet may well mitigate the harmful effects of commercial media competition on civic knowledge and engagement. Unfortunately, the present news media environment is driven by the subjective preferences of targeted users, which not only precludes the development of consensus on questions of accuracy and reasonableness of information, it actually amounts to a firm rejection of objective quality standards.

CONCLUSION

Alexis de Tocqueville called America "a nation of joiners." The participation of Americans in their own governance has always been held up as a hallmark of American democracy. Concerns that Americans have withdrawn from meaningful political engagement in the last 30 to 40 years have produced a great deal of scholarship, media attention, and calls for public action to restore the conditions that nurtured high levels of citizen participation in eras past.

This debate, joined by scholars, activists, journalists, and politicians, has been validated by public opinion surveys registering a persistent concern on the part of average Americans that something is going wrong. Declines in civic knowledge, trust in government, and participation in groups and associations that used to provide vital links between citizens and their government have fueled a consistent narrative of decline in the debate over the state of political engagement in America. When syndicated columnist E. J. Dionne published a book titled *Why Americans Hate Politics* in 1991, few questioned the implied premise.[37]

Although scholars disagree about the nature, causes, and extent of the decline in meaningful political engagement and whether it is primarily qualitative or quantitative, few have argued that participation patterns have not changed in alarming ways.[38] Yet in recent years, voter turnout has increased. The 2008 elections not only saw large numbers of young people and minorities voting but underscored

THEIR LIST

An Insider's View

JOHN ZOGBY

President, Zogby International

For nearly two decades John Zogby has been at the forefront of the public opinion polling business. Every major news media outlet reports Zogby's polling results during state and national elections in the United States. Zogby International does public affairs polling for corporate, nonprofit, and political organizations and candidates worldwide.

According to John Zogby, the key to understanding American public opinion is sound methodology and an appreciation of what really drives individual opinions across issue areas—"values." Reliable opinion research measures both the content and the "intensity" of people's opinions. The accuracy of opinion content is dependent on the wording of survey questions. If survey questions are not carefully worded to avoid bias, the results can be unintentionally skewed. There is no shortcut to identifying high-quality survey questions. According to Zogby, the best way to judge this element of polling is by looking at "the reputation and track record" of the pollster.

Large enough sample sizes, randomly selected respondents, and an accurate and precise population choice are all important elements of sound polling methodology as well. "Getting it right," for Zogby, involves polling the "opinions that matter—the voters." Making sure that polls reflect the attitudes and opinions of the people who will actually participate in the process makes polls more useful to candidates, media outlets, and voters alike. By focusing on "likely voters" a poll provides insights into the intensity of opinion among those most likely to follow up their opinions with action.

Zogby mentioned several times that the most important element of polling and public opinion in general is the underlying "values" being "tweaked" by an issue, candidate, or policy proposal. "Good polling is designed to get at the 'core values' of voters because it is this deeper commitment that governs, or frames, peoples' reactions to everything. Sometimes pollsters make the mistake of asking too many yes or no questions and then taking the answers at face value. Often, these superficial positive or negative responses disguise the real drivers of opinion lying beneath the surface. Values assumptions are far more telling of opinion direction and intensity than are specific responses to specific proposals."

the importance of new media technologies in inspiring political participation. Will new forms of participation lead to a resurgence of democratic involvement? Will the demographics of political participation change to better reflect the population of the country? Or was the 2008 election an aberration? These questions will no doubt be hotly debated in the months and years to come.

YOUR LIST REVISITED

At the beginning of the chapter you were asked to think about what you might include on your own list of the Top 10 Most Important Things to Know About Political Participation, Socialization, Public Opinion, and the Media. Now that you have read the chapter, take a moment to revisit your list. What, if anything, would you change about your list? Do you agree or disagree with the chapter list constructed by the author? What might you add or delete? Why?

KEY TERMS

95% confidence level 227
Advocacy journalism 232
American dream 229
Civil disobedience 217
Confidence level 227
Conservatives 229
Exit polls 226
Generational effect 218
Liberals 229
Libertarians 229
Margin of error or sampling error 227
Mass media 230
Media literacy 231
Narrowcasting 233
Political efficacy 220
Political ideology 221
Political participation 217
Political socialization 224
Pollsters 226
Populists 229
Probability sampling 227
Public opinion poll 226
Sample 227
Social responsibility 230
Swing voters 222
Tracking poll 228

CHAPTER REVIEW QUESTIONS

10 What is political participation? What are some common methods of participation?

9 How do you distinguish between old and new forms of participation?

8 Social scientists have found that certain types of people are more likely to participate than others. Provide some examples and discuss why this may be the case.

7 What are some of the common perceptions or myths about swing and undecided voters?

6 How has new technology impacted voter participation?

5 What is political socialization and what factors impact this process?

4 Can we trust political polls? How can a survey of 500–1,000 people accurately reflect the views of millions of Americans?

3 Compare and contrast the four categories of American public opinion: conservative, liberal, libertarian, and populist. On what questions are all four groups in agreement? Where does each group differ with the others?

2 Do you agree that the authority of the media is in decline?

1 How has the increase in media outlets impacted political engagement and participation in the United States?

SUGGESTED READINGS

- Bauerlein, Mark. *The Dumbest Generation: How the Digital Age Stupefies Young Americans and Jeopardizes our Future.* New York: Penguin Books, 2008.
- Dalton, Russell. *The Good Citizen: How a Younger Generation is Reshaping American Politics.* Washington, DC: Congressional Quarterly Press, 2009.
- Dionne, E. J. *Why Americans Hate Politics.* New York: Simon & Schuster, 1991.
- Kovach, Bill, and Tom Rosenstiel. *Blur: How to Know What's True in the Age of Information Overload.* New York: Bloomsbury, 2010.
- Lakoff, George. *Moral Politics: How Liberals and Conservatives Think.* Chicago: University of Chicago Press, 2002.
- Putnam, Robert. *Bowling Alone: The Collapse and Revival of American Community.* New York: Simon & Schuster, 2000.

- Skocpol, Theda, and Morris Fiorina, eds. *Civic Engagement in American Democracy.* Washington, DC: Brookings Institution Press, 1999.
- White, John K. *The Values Divide: American Politics and Culture in Transition.* New York: Chatham House Publishers, 2003.
- White, John K. *Barack Obama's America.* Ann Arbor, MI: University of Michigan Press, 2010.
- Zogby, John. *The Way We'll Be: The Zogby Report on the Transformation of the American Dream.* New York: Random House, 2008.

SUGGESTED FILMS

- *Citizen Kane* (1941)
- *The Autobiography of Miss Jane Pittman* (1974)
- *All the President's Men* (1976)
- *Network* (1976)
- *Being There* (1979)
- *Iron Jawed Angels* (2004)
- *Good Night and Good Luck* (2005)
- *Frost/Nixon* (2008)
- *Milk* (2008)
- *Recount* (2008)

SUGGESTED WEBSITES

- **CIRCLE: Center for Information and Research on Civic Learning and Engagement:** http://www.civicyouth.org/.
- **Gallup:** http://www.gallup.com/home.aspx.
- **GSS: General Social Survey:** http://www.norc.org/GSS+Website/.
- **Pew Research Project for Excellence in Journalism:** http://www.journalism.org/.
- **National Opinion Research Center:** http://norc.org/.
- **Pew Research Center:** http://pewresearch.org/.
- **Polling Report.com:** http://pollingreport.com/.
- **Roper Center for Public Opinion Research:** http://www.ropercenter.uconn.edu/.
- **Voting and Elections:** http://www.usa.gov/Citizen/Topics/Voting.shtml.
- **World Public Opinion.Org:** http://www.worldpublicopinion.org/.

ENDNOTES

[1]M. Margaret Conway, *Political Participation in the United States* (Washington, DC: CQ Press, 2000), p. 3.
[2]Ibid.
[3]Matej Makarovic, "The European Patterns of Political Participation: Towards the Issue of Convergence," llw.acs.si/ac/09/cd/full_papers_plenary/Makarovic.pdf (accessed May 27, 2011); David Hoffman, *The Oklahoma City Bombing and the Politics of Terror* (Venice, CA: Feral House, 1998); Martha Grenshaw, "The Psychology of Political Terrorism," Ch. 13 of Margaret G. Hermann's *Political Psychology*, www.law.syr.edu/Pdfs/0political_psychology.pdf (accessed May 27, 2011).
[4]See Russell Dalton, *The Good Citizen: How a Younger Generation is Reshaping American Politics* (Washington, DC: Congressional Quarterly Press, 2009).
[5]For a useful discussion of generational effects, see William Lyons and Robert Alexander, "A Tale of Two Electorates: Generational Replacement and the Decline in Voting in Presidential Elections," *The Journal of Politics*, 62 (4, Nov. 2000): 1014–1034.

[6]"The YouTube-ification of Politics: Candidates Losing Control," *CNN Politics*, available at: http://articles.cnn.com/2007-07-18/politics/youtube.effect_1_youtube-video-video-sharing-web-site-moments?_s=PM:POLITICS (accessed May 22, 2011).

[7]L. Sigelman, P. W. Roeder, M. E. Jewell, and M. A. Baer, "Voting and Nonvoting: A Multi-election Perspective," *American Journal of Political Science*, 29(4, 1985): 749–765; James H. Fowler, Laura A. Baker, and Christopher T. Dawes, "Genetic Variation in Political Participation," *American Political Science Review* 102 (2, May 2008): 233–248, available at: http://jhfowler.ucsd.edu/genetic_basis_of_political_cooperation.pdf (accessed May 25, 2011).

[8]See, for instance, "Why Incorporate Civic and Community Engagement, Student Benefits," http://focus.illinoisstate.edu/modules/whynot/student_benefits.shtml (accessed May 31, 2011).

[9]Jodie Herman and Lorraine Minnite, "The Demographics of Voters in America's 2008 General Election: A Preliminary Analysis. Project Vote," November 18, 2008.

[10]Steven Rosenfeld, "2008 Results: Fewer White Voters, While Minorities Set Records," *AlterNews*, November 18, 2008, available at: http://www.alternet.org/news/107472/2008_results:_fewer_white_voters,_while_minorities_set_records/ (accessed May 27, 2011).

[11]Professor Larry Sabato lays out the argument on his Web site, www.centerforpolitics.org/crystalball. It's an excerpt from his book, *The Year of Obama: How Barack Obama Won the White House*, being published by Pearson Longman.

[12]Karen M. Kaufmann, John R. Petrocik, and Daron R. Shaw, *Unconventional Wisdom: Facts and Myths About American Voters* (New York: Oxford University Press, 2008), p. 195. Based on exit polls reported on CNN.com

[13]Based on exit polls reported on CNN.com

[14]William Mayer, ed.,*The Swing Voter in American Politics* (Washington, DC: Brookings Institution Press, 2008).

[15]Ibid., p. 139.

[16]For examples, see "The Internet and the 2008 Election" and "Teens, Video Games, and Civics," and "Generation Online," all published by the Pew Center as part of its Pew Internet and American Life Project. See also Joseph Kahne, et al., "The Civic Potential of Video Games" (September 2008) published by the Civic Engagement Research Group at Mills College, available at www.civicsurvey.org.

[17]See David E. Campbell, *Why We Vote: How Schools and Communities Shape Our Civic Lives*, (Princeton, NJ: Princeton University Press, 2006).

[18]Herbert Hyman, *Political Socialization* (Glencoe, IL: Free Press, 1959).

[19]Angus Campbell, Philip E. Converse, Warren Miller, and Donald J. Stokes, *The American Voter* (New York: Wiley and Sons, 1960); Michael Lewis-Beck, William G. Jacoby, Helmut Norpoth, and Herbert Weisberg, *The American Voter Revisited* (Ann Arbor, MI: University of Michigan Press, 2008); Jennifer Wolak, "Political Context and the Development of Party Identification in Adolescence," available at: myweb.uiowa.edu/bhlai/voter/paper/wolak.pdf (accessed May 24, 2011).

[20]From October 6 to 18, 2008 CBS, UWIRE, and *The Chronicle of Education* surveyed 25,000 students at four-year colleges in four key battleground states (Colorado, North Carolina, Ohio, and Pennsylvania). Results of the survey can be accessed online at: http://www.cbsnews.com/htdocs/pdf/081027_uwire.pdf (accessed May 31, 2011).

[21]James Simon and Bruce Merrill, "Political Socialization in the Classroom Revisited: The Kids Voting Program," *The Social Science Journal* (January 1, 1998), available at: http://www.accessmylibrary.com/article-1G1-20567327/political-socialization-classroom-revisited.html (accessed May 10, 2011).

[22]Ibid.

[23]See Fritz J. Scheuren and Wendy Alvey, *Elections and Exit Polling* (Hoboken, NJ: John Wiley & Sons, 2008).

[24]See Frequently Asked Questions at http://www.zogby.com/about/faq.cfm.

[25]Sheldon R. Gawiser, Ph.D., and G. Evans Witt, "20 Questions a Journalist Should Ask About Poll Results," 3rd ed., *NCPP Council on Public Polls*, available at: http://www.ncpp.org/node/4/#11 (accessed May 22, 2011).

[26]Ibid.

[27]For more information on sampling error and how it is calculated, see "Fundamentals of Polling: Total Survey Error," *Roper Center*, available at: http://www.ropercenter.uconn.edu/education/polling_fundamentals_error.html (accessed May 21, 2011).

[28]Interview with John Zogby (January 16, 2009).

[29]Ibid.

[30]In his groundbreaking book *Moral Politics: How Liberals and Conservatives Think*, cognitive linguist George Lakoff discovered that the political preferences of Americans were discernable by eliciting their views on the ideal family structure and mores. In an age where politics is treated as a four-letter word, Lakoff discovered a way to understand what motivates citizens in their political expressions that avoids the messiness and biases of discussing politics directly. According to Lakoff, there are two competing notions of the ideal family in America: the *strong father model* of family, and the *nurturing parent* model of family. While Americans do enjoy a consensus on family values, there is a divide on the order in which these values should be prioritized. People who identify more with a *strong father model* of family, in which the values of discipline, obedience, courage, sobriety, and chastity are prioritized, are much more likely to prefer political conservatism and to support conservative candidates and causes. The *nurturing parent model* prioritizes compassion, social responsibility, inquisitiveness, and flexibility. Those more comfortable with this approach are significantly more likely to be liberal in their political expressions. Lakoff's work makes clear the importance of subconscious factors in the construction of political opinions and the difficulty of measuring public opinion that this reality implies. The primacy of values, rather than policy preferences, or other ostensibly rational cues is something pollster John Zogby has come to see as the key to understanding what people believe in every venue of their lives, from the voting booth to the grocery store, as citizens and as consumers.

[31]In the summary of the findings of the Pew Research Center Report on the media, the authors write, "young people, by far the

hardest to reach segment of the political news audience, are abandoning mainstream sources of election news and increasingly citing alternative outlets, including comedy shows such as the *Daily Show* and *Saturday Night Live*, as their source for election news." See the summary of findings or the full report, "Perceptions of Partisan Bias Seen as Growing—Especially by Democrats: Cable and Internet Loom Large in Fragmented Political News Universe," The Pew Research Center For the People and the Press, January 11, 2004, available online at: http://people-press.org/2004/01/11/cable-and-internet-loom-large-in-fragmented-political-news-universe/ (click on Complete Report) (accessed May 31, 2011). See also Lauren Feldman, "The News About Comedy: Young Audiences, The Daily Show, and Evolving Notions of Journalism," Paper presented at the annual meeting of the International Communication Association, Sheraton New York, New York City, May 25, 2009, available at: http://www.allacademic.com/meta/p13125_index.html; Michael Kalin, "Why Jon Stewart Isn't Funny," *The Boston Globe*/Boston.com, March 3, 2006, available at: http://www.boston.com/ae/movies/oscars/articles/2006/03/03/why_jon_stewart_isnt_funny/ (accessed May 31, 2011).

[32]Barry A. Hollander, "Late-night Learning: Do Entertainment Programs Increase Political Campaign Knowledge for Young Viewers?" *Journal of Broadcasting & Electronic Media* (December 2005).

[33]Bill Kovach and Tom Rosenstiel, *Blur: How to Know What's True in the Age of Information Overload* (New York: Bloomsbury, 2010).

[34]Ibid., p. 34.

[35]Ibid.

[36]A caveat that may impact the significance of the correlation between Internet use and voter turnout in the last three presidential election cycles involves the methodological dispute regarding the validity of measures used to identify declines in voter turnout in the 30 years prior to the 2000 election; discussed in the voter turnout section of this chapter.

[37]E. J. Dionne, *Why Americans Hate Politics* (New York: Simon & Schuster, 1991).

[38]An increasingly popular school of thought sees the transformation of political participation as a product of generational and technological change—as a transformation rather than a decline. An excellent example of this approach includes John Zogby, *The Way We'll Be: The Zogby Report on the Transformation of the American Dream* (New York: Random House, 2008).

Chapter 11

AMERICAN PUBLIC POLICY

Top Ten List

10. Public policy includes those things government chooses to do and *not* do.
9. Public policies are created to meet public needs and express public values.
8. Public policies come in three types depending on their function: distributive, redistributive, and regulatory.
7. Public policies are made by both official and unofficial actors.
6. The government employs four basic strategies to achieve its policy goals: establishing mandates, granting inducements, building capacity, and changing systems.
5. The policy process involves five stages: problem identification, agenda setting, formulation, implementation, and evaluation.
4. Tobacco policy provides a case study in policy change.
3. Economic policy imparts lessons on inaction, unintended consequences, and focusing events.
2. Environmental policy exemplifies the impact of a social movement, market failure, and the operation of public policy tools.
1. Healthcare policy demonstrates the emergence and force of public values.

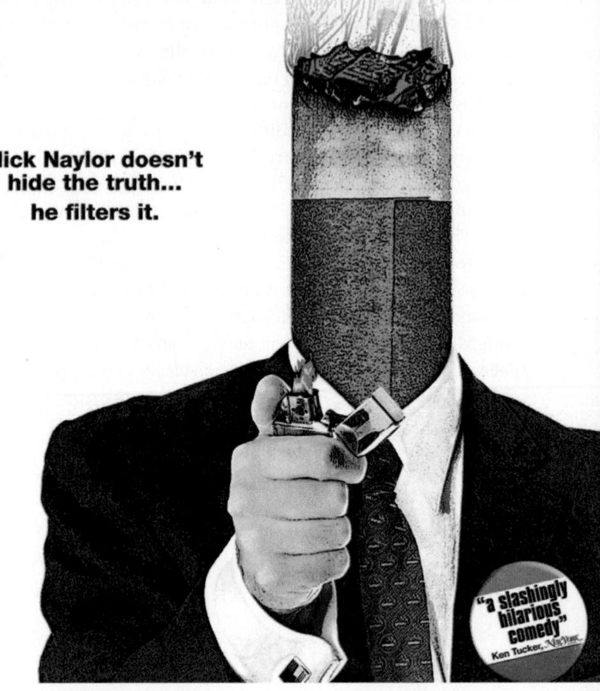

Nick Naylor doesn't hide the truth... he filters it.
"a slashingly hilarious comedy"
Ken Tucker,

Public policies are created to meet public needs and express public values, and public policy includes those things government chooses to both do and not do. The 2005 film *Thank You For Smoking* reveals some telling aspects about the American policy system, including the fact that it is common for regulated industries to resist regulation. However, while the policymaking process itself may be complicated and unpredictable, it is also a crucial function of American government.

YOUR LIST

Before you read this chapter, take a few moments to think about what you might include on a list of the Top 10 Most Important Things to Know About American Public Policy. At the end of the chapter you will be asked to compare and contrast your list with the one supplied in this chapter.

 Public policy includes those things government chooses to do and *not* do.

INTRODUCTION

In the 2005 film *Thank You for Smoking*, a fictitious tobacco spokesperson argues in a Congressional hearing that he doesn't see a reason for placing a warning label on something people already know is dangerous (cigarettes). A fictitious senator from Vermont counters that the label on the cigarette packages is a reminder of the dangers of smoking. The tobacco spokesperson responds that if we're going to put warnings on cigarettes, we should also put warning labels on cars and airplanes, since they are also dangerous; he even goes so far as to suggest that the state of Vermont put a warning label on its cheese, because he says cholesterol is the number one killer in America.

The scene recounted above is just one of the many hilarious moments throughout the film, but it reveals many telling aspects of the American policy system. First, it is common for regulated industries to often resist regulation since it is believed that regulation will increase production costs and hurt profit margins. Second, this policy resistance can take the form of trying to "game" the system with techniques designed to distract interest away from the real social and policy issue(s) (in this instance, the harm caused by smoking). Third, Americans often view the congressional committee hearing as a principal political vehicle to uncover information, highlight problems, or examine policy choices, but we often seem to view members of Congress as ineffective policy champions who are easily distracted or even led astray from the obvious.

We spend more time exploring tobacco policy later in this chapter, but our principal objectives are to provide you with fundamental ideas to better understand the dynamics of the American policymaking system and to more closely examine some key policy areas. In doing so, we also hope to challenge some common public perceptions about how and why policy is created. We do this by first explaining the most important concepts: definitions, catalysts for policy, types of policies, policy participants, policy strategies, and policy stages. We then turn our attention to exploring some specific policy areas: tobacco, economics, the environment, and healthcare.

Public policy includes those things government chooses to do and *not* do.

Public policy is not subject to one precise and widely accepted definition; instead, it is understood more as a collection of governmentally led responses to societal issues. However, public policy scholar Thomas Birkland surveyed the most popular policy textbooks and identified multiple definitions frequently used in the study of public policy, the salient elements of which are:

Public policy A collection of governmentally led responses to societal issues.

- Policy is made in the public's name, which reflects the fact that in a democratic society decisions must often reflect what is in the best interest of a majority of citizens, such as protecting the public's health from the use of cigarettes.

- Policy is made by government since the formal power to make, execute, interpret, and implement law rests with the formal institutions of government—the legislature makes law through the congressional bill process; the executive can issues executive orders directing an agency to perform a task; the courts issue judicial opinions in cases that flesh out the interpretations of laws; and administrative agencies promulgate regulations that provide greater specificity to laws created by the legislature.
- Policy is implemented by public/governmental agencies and sometimes private entities, such as nonprofit organizations, which are charged with the specific task of achieving policy goals specified by lawmakers. For instance, it is the Federal Food and Drug Administration, in accordance with the Family Smoking Prevention and Tobacco Control Act passed by Congress, that actually requires a Surgeon General's (another federal agency) health warning label on all cigarette packages sold within the United States.
- Policy can also mean what government intends to do, as expressed in the various competing political agendas of multiple policy "actors," such as Congress, the president, the media, lobbyists, and so on. For instance, the president may prioritize healthcare reform, while a faction of Congress may desire to prioritize economic stimulus instead. This will create a tug-of-war over which policy proposal will gain the greatest attention and move forward in the legislative process.
- Policy is also what government chooses not to do or what it actively blocks after determining that keeping things the same or unchanged is a better option.[1] For instance, a legislative body may choose not to take up and vote on a bill that would increase its salaries in a year leading up to an election for fear it would anger voters.

So, a broad view of public policy, in our estimate, includes both governmental action and inaction. Public policy as highlighted above includes governmental action to regulate private or public behavior (e.g., curfew laws); projects to build infrastructure (e.g., interstate highways, the Internet); and programs to produce services to achieve social, economic, public health, or other aims (e.g., laws requiring accessibility to public accommodations for persons with disabilities).

Public policy as inaction occurs primarily in the form of government institutions and decision-making bodies, such as Congress, choosing *not* to place an issue on the agenda or to block it. For example, during President Clinton's first term he tried aggressively to pass a healthcare reform bill that would have provided universal coverage, among other things. The policy idea and eventual proposal stirred up so much frenzy among insurance company lobbyists, the medical profession, conservatives, unions, and business owners that members of Congress could not figure out a viable political compromise. Consequently, the bill died in committee. The healthcare policy reforms enacted by Congress and signed by President Obama in many ways embodied a carryover of the policy discussion and ideas from Clinton's attempt to overcome congressional inaction on the topic.

Consequently, we should understand that the public policymaking process aims to address problems that confront our society, involves choice among a variety of responses, has lots of parts and pieces contributed to it from institutions of government to outside participants, and has several stages, from agenda formulation through actual implementation.

9 Public policies are created to meet public needs and express public values.

Why does government make public policy? The answer depends on whom you ask. Some would argue that government should exist only to provide (1) a minimal level of collective security—through maintaining a military to deal with foreign threats and localized police forces to keep basic social order at a community or regional level—and (2) a basic framework for economic activity that ensures some fundamental rules and allows citizens to freely pursue whatever they believe is in their own best interests. Others would agree with these two basic points but argue that society is far too complex today to limit governmental authority only to these two areas. They would insist that society needs a variety of policies to address new and unforeseen problems. The tension between these two sets of ideas about the scope of government authority often underlies most of the debate about current public policy issues. For instance, in the area of environmental regulation, the former view would argue that government should not be in the business of regulating private activity, even if the activity negatively affects the environment. The latter view would insist that any private or commercial activity resulting in pollution should be regulated to protect health and the environment.

However, it is also important to recognize that policies often serve to express the values, or changing values, held by the people. For example, in the mid- to late-twentieth century, the U.S. government issued laws and reinterpreted the Constitution to support the mass political calls for desegregation. Prior to this time, public institutions were segregated by race. In 1948, in response to public sentiments, President Truman issued an executive order desegregating the armed forces. Then, in 1954, the U.S. Supreme Court ruled in *Brown v. Board of Education* that segregation of schools based upon racial classification violated the basic value of equality as expressed in the Constitution.[2] Later, Congress enacted other civil rights legislation. These actions represent the federal government creating policy to reflect the changing values and corresponding views of the American public.

Other examples of policy decisions based primarily upon public values are not hard to find; think of state government policies addressing same-sex marriage, affirmative action, or sex offender registries. Recognizing the existence of underlying public values will help you better understand the origins and ultimate form of a given public policy.

Often, people in and out of government argue over the extent to which public policy should interfere in the private sector. Some believe government should interfere only when absolutely necessary. Others advocate for "bigger government" as a way to deal with social problems. Typical justifications for the creation of public policy are rooted in the concept of **market failure**, whereby the private sector produces conditions deemed unacceptable to society.[3] There are four forms of market failure: natural monopolies, negative externalities, information asymmetries, and public goods.

Market failure The production by the private sector of conditions deemed unacceptable by society.

Natural monopoly A type of market failure in which a product or service can be supplied to the consumer market more effectively and efficiently by one producer than many.

Negative externalities A type of market failure whereby the producer of a good or service fails to account for societal costs associated with its activity.

Information asymmetry A condition where consumers of goods or services are at an informational disadvantage relative to producers.

Public goods Goods or services that cannot be divided up and cannot be controlled by a single individual or organization.

Natural monopolies occur when a product or service can be supplied to the consumer market more effectively and efficiently by one producer than many. Natural gas and traditional landline phone service are two examples of natural monopolies. Government typically regulates natural monopolies to ensure that prices and service quality levels meet the needs of the people. **Negative externalities** are the undesirable consequences of the activities of public or private organizations or individuals, such as pollution caused by the processing of crude oil. Government addresses these negative consequences by regulating production processes and providing relief through the legal system.

Information asymmetry is a condition where consumers of goods or services are at an informational disadvantage relative to producers. Examples include the foods we eat and the skin care products we apply, the ingredients of which we rarely know or understand how they affect us. Government attempts to reduce information disparity by requiring the disclosure of information, such as warnings on product labels.

Public goods are goods or services that cannot be divided up and cannot be controlled by any single individual or organization. Everyone can benefit from them and none can be excluded. A few examples are national defense, clean air, and public parks. These goods are often controlled by government to ensure that their use reflects public values.

Public policies come in three types depending on their function: distributive, redistributive, and regulatory.

Overall, there are several approaches to drawing distinctions between types of policies, each of which captures an important dimension not incorporated or stressed in the others. The resulting categories are not necessarily mutually exclusive. We review three of the most common classifications: distributive, redistributive, and regulatory.[4]

 Public policies come in three types depending on their function . . .

Distributive policies Public policies that direct taxpayer monies to very specific groups or causes.

The classification of policies as distributive, redistributive, or regulatory focuses on their social and economic impacts. **Distributive policies** direct taxpayer dollars to very specific groups or causes.[5] They tend to be popular with elected politicians because the cost is widely distributed across all taxpayer groups and the benefit to the defined recipients is focused on a specific issue or area. Pork-barrel projects, such as building/funding local bridges or hospitals, typically fall into the distributive policy category. Other distributive actions would include monies for public land purchase, for research by universities, and for highway construction. Citizens often understand these policies as providing generalized benefits to society; they are, thus, typically less controversial.

Redistributive policies Government actions that transfer resources, usually in the form of taxation, from one area or group to another area or group.

The government exercises **redistributive policy** authority when it uses the power to tax and spend to transfer some form of wealth from one area or group to another area or group. An example would be the Social Security tax imposed on current workers to fund income benefits for retired workers. Another illustration would be in the area of social services where either federal or state government derives revenue from personal income taxes of citizens and then transfers a portion of those revenues to governmental and nonprofit agencies to pay for such services as job retraining for unemployed workers, shelter for homeless people, or support services to victims of violence. In the area of tobacco policy, the federal government uses excise taxes on the sale of cigarettes to, in turn, fund certain public health initiatives and campaigns designed to combat cigarette usage. Redistributive policies tend to be controversial because the funds are usually allocated to a specific class of individuals, such as unemployed people, while another class of individuals, such as workers, pays.[6] Often such redistributive policies produce conflicts that are predictably partisan, with Democrats more frequently favoring redistributive policies to ensure equity than Republicans.[7]

Regulatory policies Government actions that compel an individual or organization to perform or refrain from certain actions.

Regulatory policy is governmental action typically performed by administrative agencies that compels individuals and organizations to perform or refrain from performing specific actions. Government mandates to reduce the physical threat to worker safety by requiring that workers wear protective equipment in certain jobs is an example of regulatory policy. Another example is the bans many local governments place on smoking in public places like stadiums, restaurants, and parks, etc. However, such policies often impose substantial costs on those who must comply or enforce the regulations, such as factory or restaurant owners, thereby causing controversy and opposition.[8] Regulations that govern how prescription medications can be approved for public distribution, marketed or advertised, sold and used, or withdrawn from the market are regulatory policies. The authority of the government to recall and totally ban the sale of a medication (even if it has passed initial government screening) is an example of the government's direct regulatory authority. The central idea is that there is an important societal interest at stake behind the regulation, such as protection of the public's health, which provides a justification for government to act directly.

Public policies are made by both official and unofficial actors.

In a democratic political system, such as the United States, the policymaking process should be open to influence from many diverse types of participants, each with different resources and objectives but none with a monopoly on power. The framers of the U.S. Constitution believed in fragmenting the policymaking apparatus of government to ensure decentralized power and multiple access points for participants to influence the system. From a policy standpoint, these participants can be organized into two broad categories. The first set of participants is comprised of **official actors**, who operate on the "inside" of government and possess institutional authority to make formal decisions on policy. The second category includes **unofficial actors**, who are participants working on the "outside" that exert significant influence on the policymaking process.

Official actors Governmental policy participants who operate on the "inside" of government and possess institutional authority to make formal decisions on policy.

Unofficial actors Policy participants working "outside" the formal framework of government that exert significant influence on the policymaking process.

It is important to realize that each of the official, institutional actors can be divided into several smaller sets of participants who play their own role and bring their own resources to the table. For instance, the presidency consists of the president, Executive Office staff, department heads, and civil servants, all of whom possess expertise, networks, and funding that can be brought to bear on the policymaking process and gain influence. Congress is comprised of 535 elected representatives and senators, committee staff, and support organizations with similar resources and ability to direct resources toward different policy areas.

Overall, these official actors possess one or more of three primary policy resources. The first, possessed by every single actor, is information. This resource is important enough that the political system contains redundancies to cross-check the data produced by actors located in different parts of the policymaking system. Both the White House's Office of Management and Budget and the Congressional Budget Office, for example, produce budgetary analyses and predictions. The second resource is the power to participate in making formal, legally binding decisions. Congress enacts laws, the president signs or vetoes legislation, the judiciary rules on cases, and administrative agencies transmit rules and regulations. The third resource is the ability to set the policy agenda; no actor has a monopoly over the agenda, but some have an advantage relative to others. Among all the official actors in the policymaking process, the president appears to exercise the most influence because of his access to information, his high visibility, his formal powers, and his ability to influence the formal, institutional agenda.

Policy participation and influence in an open, democratic system does not necessarily need to be confined within the government's formal decision-making apparatus and to official actors. Many opportunities for access by "outsiders" exist. Unofficial actors (citizens, interest groups, political parties, think tanks, and the media) may advance their policy agendas in a variety of ways.

In the United States, citizen participation, especially through voting, is comparatively low, and individual citizens are typically disengaged from most aspects of the policymaking process. However, groups of citizens or individuals may mobilize to engage in direct political action and spread political messages through protests/rallies, letter-writing campaigns, voter registration drives, or social networking sites like Facebook or Twitter. If such activity gains enough momentum, it can cause shifts in overall public opinion and, in turn, influence official actors to take notice of the policy issue and policy alternatives.

For instance, political commentators often conclude that the sustained protests of the mid-to-late 1960s ushered in an age of civil rights consciousness that spawned a variety of major policy actions, from ending the war in Vietnam to eliminating officially sponsored segregation to creating environmental legislation. When Martin Luther King, Jr. led marches from Selma to Montgomery in Alabama to protest prohibitions on the right of African Americans to vote, he brought focused national media attention that was instrumental in gaining widespread public support for the signing of the 1965 Voting Rights Act.

Interest groups are comprised of individuals or organizations that share a common interest and desire to influence the policy system to benefit that interest. These groups can influence policymaking through the size of their memberships (members = potential votes), money (donations to campaigns and causes), and information and technical knowledge (opinion polls of their members or technical data on a given policy area). For example, the AARP (formerly the American Association of Retired Persons) has millions of members who vote with frequency and thereby exerts tremendous political influence over many policy areas, such as healthcare and Social Security. Some observers speculate that the potent lobbying effort of the AARP is one of the main reasons the financial solvency of the Social Security system has gone largely unaddressed as a policy matter. Other groups, such as the National Rifle Association (NRA), are very well funded and donate directly to campaigns. The NRA, through its Political Victory Fund, also keeps a yearly "grades and endorsements" list of the voting history of elected officials that can be accessed by all NRA members prior to each election.

Taxpayer or fiscal watchdog groups are examples of interest groups that wield influence because they perform sophisticated analyses of policy costs and other policy factors that are then shared with the public. For example, in New York State, the nonpartisan Citizens Budget Commission has been effective in influencing voters by highlighting the various fiscal implications of pursuing certain policy alternatives, such as pay raises for government workers.

Political parties are significant unofficial actors because they serve as a conduit for funding, political information, and influence between voters and elected officials. For instance, voters rely heavily on party endorsements in selecting a candidate to vote for, while officials seek the strong endorsement of their party to secure reelection. Furthermore, parties also help create specific policy platforms and language that officials are expected to follow, and they influence who is selected for key legislative committee posts.

Think tanks Unofficial policy actors who influence the policy system through research and dissemination of information.

Think tanks, or research organizations, exert influence through expertise and information. Often, these organizations will provide information in the form of technical reports and public opinion polls that support or discredit various policy positions. Some more widely known think tanks, such as The Brookings Institute or the American Heritage Foundation, are frequently consulted by the media and often cited by policymakers when offering or explaining policy positions. The media also have a role in policymaking primarily because they can increase the visibility of an issue or problem by focusing public attention on it for a sustained period of time.

6 The government employs four basic strategies to achieve its policy goals: establishing mandates, granting inducements, building capacity, and changing systems.

Policy tools The specific policy options available to government when trying to address societal issues. The most common forms are mandates, inducements, capacity building, and system change.

Mandates Legally enforceable requirements that direct a government agency or regulated field to specifically do or not do something.

Once public policy is created, typically by a legislative body, it must be implemented in order to meet its intended objectives. **Policy tools** are the specific options available to government in trying to address societal issues.[9] Viewing policy tools within a conceptual framework helps one understand how certain types of tools are more apt to be a better match with particular objectives.[10] There are four basic strategic tools: establishing mandates, granting inducements, building capacity, and changing systems. Each has certain costs and benefits.[11]

Mandates are legally enforceable requirements that direct a government agency or regulated field to do or not do something. The goal of mandates is to achieve compliance with some specific objective(s).[12] They come in several forms, such as legislation, administrative rules and regulations, and court orders. An example could be found in local health code laws that ban smoking in public places. Enforcement of these codes is usually necessary to promote compliance. Mandates tend to impose concentrated costs (for instance, on business owners or individual violators) and distribute diffuse benefits (in this case, to protect the public health from possible harm caused by second-hand smoke). Since mandates result in a direct cost, sometimes in the form of a fine, to certain individuals or businesses, these groups often lobby vigorously to try to persuade the public and elected officials not to apply the new policy, for fear it will violate some perceived individual right or will raise the cost of providing the good or service in question. As a result, the implementation of mandates is often controversial.

A particular subclass of mandates, widely known as "unfunded mandates," is derided in government circles. In this type of mandate, a higher-level government decision-making body orders a subordinate government to take some action that incurs costs, usually with limited, if any, reimbursement. For example, a state legislature may require local social service agencies to provide job training to benefit recipients but not provide the funds necessary to cover the substantial costs. Consequently, these mandates tend to cause tension between the federal government and the states and between the states and their constituent local governments.

Inducements Policy tools that use some form of financial value to motivate public or private organizations or individuals to take some action in the short-term in the absence of which they would not predictably perform.

Inducements are policy tools that use some form of financial incentive to motivate public or private organizations or individuals to take some action in the short-term that they would otherwise not predictably perform. Often, policymakers specifically intend that the inducement will motivate the individuals or organizations to mobilize and optimize by using their existing capacity. A typical form of inducement is a grant-in-aid program.[13] These programs provide money to local school districts, for example, to help teachers improve student scores on standardized tests.

Capacity building Policy tool with which government takes action to bridge the gap between current deficits in knowledge, skills, equipment, or other resources of a government agency and future capacity necessary to achieve policy aims.

Capacity building involves the government taking action to bridge the gap between current deficits in knowledge, skills, equipment, or other resources of a government agency and future capacity necessary to achieve policy aims.[14] It manifests in several forms. For example, a capacity-building initiative could come in the form of a grant-in-aid program to equip homeland security organizations with sophisticated surveillance tools or training. However, providing tools and training also captures one of the classic limitations of capacity building—there is no guarantee that providing tools or training now will result in improved governmental administration later.

Changing a system Policy tool that creates broad and sweeping change in the laws and rules that govern a particular area.

Changing a system is a policy tool used to create broad, sweeping change in the laws and rules that govern a particular area. The expectation is that the adjustment will significantly alter policy outcomes. Usually, doing so is very difficult because the system is populated by those who benefit from the existing arrangement.[15] There are many historical cases of system-changing initiatives. One example is the repeal in 1999 of the Depression-era banking legislation known as the Glass-Steagall Act of 1933, which separated the activities of investment banks and savings and loans lenders. The repeal of this legislation enabled local banks to make and sell "toxic" mortgages to far-away investors and free up cash to make more risky loans. Many believe this repeal contributed to the economic meltdown that began in 2008.

5 The policy process involves five stages: problem identification, agenda setting, formulation, implementation, and evaluation.

As Figure 11.1 shows, the policy process includes five major stages: problem identification, agenda setting, policy formulation, policy implementation, and evaluation.[16] These stages create a straightforward framework for understanding a complicated, overlapping process; we will examine each stage separately.

Figure 11.1 The Policy-Making Process

The major stages in the policy process are problem identification, agenda setting, policy formulation, policy implementation, and evaluation.

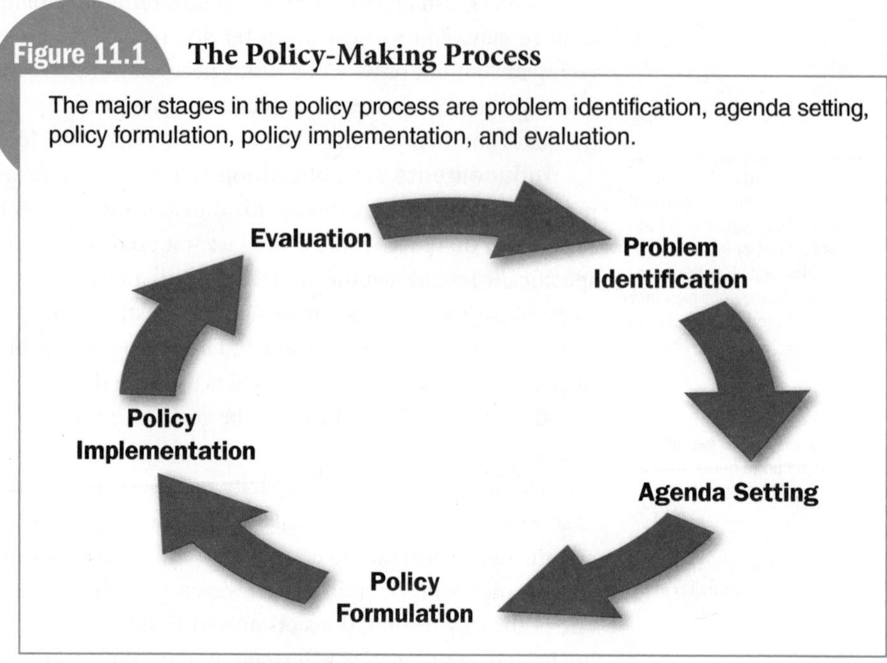

Problem identification The stage of the policymaking process in which a societal condition or problem is recognized by government as an issue worthy of political attention and possible policy action.

Problem identification is the beginning point of the policy process whereby a societal condition or problem is recognized by government as an issue worthy of political attention and possible policy action.[17] Problems may be long-standing conditions, such as racial discrimination or growing income disparity between rich and poor, that gain new attention or focus. Or problems may be newly recognized due to some innovation (e.g., the Internet and the problems of policing cyber crimes) or a dramatic event (e.g., the earthquake and subsequent tsunami in Japan in 2011, which led to concerns about the safety of nuclear energy in the United States). However, due to resource constraints, public opinion, political cultural forces, competition for attention, and information gaps, not all societal problems will get recognized as political issues.

Agenda setting The stage in the policymaking process whereby various political issues get prioritized for possible policy action.

Agenda setting is the process by which government entities, such as the legislature, decide which political issues get prioritized for possible policy action.[18] For instance, Congress can be faced with taking up any number of proposed bills on a variety of policy topics (environment, education, infrastructure, healthcare, national security, tax law, economic stimulus topics, etc.) but must choose to focus on those of paramount or immediate importance that can be addressed with available resources. Of course, mass public opinion and intense media coverage influence the degree to which policymakers will pay attention to particular issues. Moreover, interest groups often compete and, therefore, lobby to ensure their advocacy issues receive priority attention over others. In short, agenda setting involves intense competition among competing interests for policy action.

Focusing events Dramatic occurrences that direct public attention to a societal problem for a sustained period of time, thereby increasing the chance that the problem gets recognized as a political issue.

A leading policy scholar hypothesizes that rapid policy change occurs when windows of opportunity arise from dramatic, and usually unpredictable, **focusing events** that draw public attention for a sustained period of time to a major issue related to that occurrence.[19] For example, months after the September 11, 2001 terrorist attacks, the American public was immersed in the event and its aftermath by the constant imagery and discussion in all media outlets. The constant media and public focus created a broad and continued public discourse on a variety of policy issues related to terrorism and security. The focus and discourse, in turn, created a political "window of opportunity" for official and unofficial policy participants to promote numerous policy actions for such things as the creation of a new homeland security agency to integrate and centralize domestic security, the passage of the Patriot Act to give law enforcement agencies broader investigatory powers, and even to go to war with Afghanistan and Iraq to confront authoritarian leaders purportedly friendly to groups who might harm American interests. In sum, these far-reaching policies would likely not have been created but for the focusing event of the September 11 attacks.

Policy formulation The stage of the policymaking process in which a specific policy proposal is actually developed by an official entity in the form of legislative statutes, executive orders, or administrative regulations.

Policy formulation involves the development of proposals and the creation of actual policies, mostly in the form of legislative statutes but also as executive orders or administrative regulations. For instance, Congress may pass a provision within a financial "bailout" package requiring private companies to limit their compensation of executives; or the president may issue an executive order declaring illegal certain forms of detainment and interrogation of suspected terrorists; or the Social Security Administration, an administrative agency, may issue a regulation that reduces the benefits available for retirees. However, most attention at the policy formulation stage is on legislative enactments, as the legislature is the only government entity endowed with the legal authority to create totally new law.

Policy implementation The stage of the policymaking process at which a created policy gets executed by an administrative agency of government.

Policy implementation is a critical phase that deals with the execution of enacted policies through the executive and administrative apparatus of the government.[20] Administrative agencies typically produce regulations that have full binding authority and that provide precise details for achieving the goals of a broadly outlined policy initially created by the legislature. For instance, if Congress bans disposal of a certain type of chemical because it is potentially harmful to human health, it would be up to relevant agencies, such as the Environmental Protection Agency, to determine how the chemical can be stored, transported, and disposed of, in what quantity, and in what form, etc. In sum, the details of policy management are worked out in this phase, and administrative agencies wield significant authority since they determine the eventual reach of a policy.

Policy evaluation The stage of the policymaking process in which a policy is assessed to determine if it is reaching its stated objective(s).

Policy evaluation is the stage at which analysis is conducted, usually by administrators, outside experts, the media, think tanks, or interest groups, to determine if an implemented policy is achieving the goals identified in stage one (problem identification) of the policy process.[21] Ideally, such an evaluation would precisely identify a full range of impacts, including unintended consequences, and provide needed feedback to tweak or revise (or even reverse) certain policies to achieve greater effectiveness. For example, state and local governments frequently examine data about car accidents to determine the principal causes of injuries and fatalities, which often leads to a host of recommended and actual policy changes, such as reducing speed limits, changing the composition of roadways, raising the minimum age for obtaining a license, retesting drivers over a certain age, etc.—all in an attempt to reduce injuries and fatalities. These changes are then monitored to determine positive or negative impacts, which can, in turn, create new policy recommendations.

In sum, the stages approach (problem identification, agenda setting, formulation, implementation, and evaluation) provides an orderly analytical framework for understanding what is often a complicated, messy process involving many actors and sources of influence.

4 Tobacco policy provides a case study in policy change.

Tobacco usage is one of the most important public health policy issues in the United States: It claims approximately one-half million American lives annually and is responsible for the majority of heart disease and related illnesses. There is now agreement among policymakers and citizens over the dangers of tobacco and that policies should be designed to combat its usage as a result of a growing and more widely disseminated body of convincing scientific and medical information. But the current negative view of cigarette smoking and the tobacco industry did not always predominate. So, in terms of the policy framework explained above, most Americans did not even know that cigarette smoking was a policy problem until those with specific information began demonstrating the harmful effects.

Up until the 1950s, the tobacco industry was supported by a limited group of congressional members and other policymakers. Very few participants outside this limited, inside policy actor "clique" had control over tobacco policy, and the issue generated little attention from the media. Congressional insiders in the policy subsystem supported tobacco because it generated agricultural jobs, created highly profitable companies, and was an important export commodity that raised tax revenue for the Treasury.[22]

However, this clique, or subsystem, began breaking down in the 1950s because another set of inside policy actors, public health officials, successfully organized to raise critical questions about the effects of tobacco use on humans, thereby placing a policy problem on the political agenda for some form of action. They, in large part, effected a substantial increase in media coverage and a gradual shift away from the previously favorable assessment of the financial merits of tobacco to a more strongly unfavorable one based upon threats posed to human health. However, this change in perception occurred slowly (over decades) due to entrenched interests that benefited from an unregulated tobacco industry. So regulation of tobacco use and sales remained on the agenda for a long time.

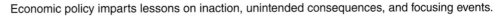

Over time, however, the original clique of congressional insiders was challenged by various congressional committees that began wresting control away from the clique and holding hearings in their own policy areas to debate such things as whether there should be warning labels on cigarette packaging (something for which public health experts were advocating). These newer participants (additional committees, public health officials, and the media) achieved a destabilization or break in the previous status quo mostly by changing who was paying attention to the issue, reframing the issues around tobacco use, and appealing to the broader public.[23] This allowed newer ideas and new policy formulations to emerge.

The result has been the creation of a more far-reaching policy framework around tobacco sales, marketing, taxation, and pubic usage. Today, tobacco sales, distribution, and use are carefully evaluated and monitored by congressional committees, public health advocates, the media, and administrative agencies, resulting in continually more restrictive tobacco control policies.

This story about tobacco policy in the United States is representative of the interaction of key elements in the national policymaking system that can lead to substantial change. For instance, public policy is a multifaceted dynamic with many possible participants (e.g., competing congressional subcommittees, health officials, and outside experts) with different agendas (financial versus public health) who compete for control over a policy domain; there are multiple access points and ways to influence policy (using the media to expose problems, for instance); and new ideas and information (scientific information that strongly links cigarette smoking to lung cancer and other diseases, for instance) can contribute to eventual policy change and disruption of an otherwise tightly held and closed policymaking clique.

3 Economic policy imparts lessons on inaction, unintended consequences, and focusing events.

Beginning in the last years of the nineteenth century, government began focusing on more complex policy problems, such as ensuring the stability of the economy. Many new institutions and tools were created for this purpose. Congress, for example, enacted legislation forming the federal banking system in 1913, in turn creating the **Federal Reserve Board (the Fed)** and empowering it with a set of policy tools to control the supply of money.

Federal Reserve Board (the Fed) A governmental agency that regulates many market activities, including the setting of prime interest rates.

During the early years of the Depression, and without any comparable occurrence against which to evaluate policy, the Fed failed to take action to reverse a significantly contracting money supply. Monetarists believe the level of the money supply is the central policy tool for directing the economy. Those like Milton Friedman believe that the Fed's failure to issue emergency bank loans as the number of bank failures increased in the late 1920s deepened what might have been a prolonged recession into the Great Depression. The Federal Reserve Board's decision can be viewed as an example of a public policy decision in the form of government inaction, or refusal to pursue a particular course of action, i.e., to provide emergency loans, which resulted, in this instance, in a severe negative outcome for American society.

Unintended consequences Policy outcomes not foreseen or intentionally desired during the initial creation or implementation of the original public policy.

Moreover, the negative outcome from the Fed inaction can be considered an unintended consequence of a policy decision. **Unintended consequences** are policy outcomes not foreseen or intentionally desired during the initial creation or implementation of the original public policy. In this instance, the Fed believed that the policy of issuing emergency loans would be too costly and would further weaken the value of the dollar, thereby increasing the damage to Americans' ability to afford basic items. So, although the Fed believed that tightening the monetary supply would actually improve economic conditions, the unintended consequence of this decision was to prevent the banks from recovering and offering more loans, which thwarted stimulus toward broader economic growth. As a result, the country fell into a prolonged economic depression.

As a result of the policy lessons learned from the Depression, the Fed now possesses stronger tools to ensure credit liquidity by acting as a lender of last resort to banks. Since, after 1973, American currency is no longer linked to gold reserves, the Fed can print money at will to expand the available supply. The policy change of moving away from gold as the basis for the currency is a solid example of how government can learn from past mistakes to direct future beneficial policies, a phenomenon that policy scholars label "policy learning."

The lesson of policy inaction just described became a vital rationale behind the Fed's approach to the economic crisis that began in 2008. In this instance, the Fed demonstrated a strong willingness to expand the money supply considerably and offer emergency or "bailout" loans to banks and many different industries. The idea was to keep financial institutions and major industries in a mode of active investing and business production that, in turn, would stimulate a variety of positive economic activities. Certain economists believe the level of Fed involvement lessened the severity and length of the recession and prevented another depression; others argue that it raised the national debt to unsustainable levels. The case demonstrates that consideration of past policy lessons and potential unintended consequences can result in better policy decisions during the planning, formulation, and implementation stages of policymaking.

Another way to think about the unprecedented bailout packages provided by the Obama administration to major companies in the banking/finance, automobile, and insurance industries in 2009 is to think about them in the context of focusing events. The 2008 bankruptcy of Lehman Brothers, one of the financial industry leaders, sent shock waves throughout the financial sector. Soon, many institutions failed or were near failure, which, in turn, had financial ripple effects on other large businesses. Throughout this time, these stories dominated the news media and focused public attention to the degree that public opinion polls consistently identified the economy as the number-one concern of voters (and bankers as the primary cause of the problem). As a result, the strong public opinion clearly indicated to official policymakers that political conditions were highly supportive of swift action to combat the growing economic crises. It is safe to say that multibillion-dollar bailouts of private industry and similar policy actions, such as restricting executive compensation, would not have been possible in an area traditionally governed by conservative policies without a triggering event that refocused public attention.

2 Environmental policy exemplifies the impact of a social movement, market failure, and the operation of public policy tools.

Today, protection of the environment is often understood to be an important policy priority, but that was not always the predominant view. The present extensive regulatory framework for environmental policy in the United States is largely a political product of a social movement that began in the early 1960s. In particular, it was the publication in 1962 of the book *Silent Spring*, by marine biologist Rachel Carson, that first drew large-scale public attention to the potential harmful effects of pesticide usage. The harsh criticism of the book and ensuing legal threats by the chemical industry sparked a sustained public outcry of support for the idea that pesticides should be viewed as dangerous chemicals. President John F. Kennedy responded by directing a full scientific investigation into pesticide use, which eventually resulted in a ban of many widely used pesticides.

It was this direct government response to growing public recognition of environmental hazards, identified by scientists and often coupled with focusing events such as major oil spills and contamination, that established the political dynamics necessary for the passage of groundbreaking environmental legislation in the early 1970s—the National Environmental Policy Act (1970), the Clean Air Act Amendments (1970), and the Federal Water Pollution Control Act (1972). In fact, the dynamic among the scientific community, its critics, the media, major events, public opinion, and ensuing political assessments of official policy actors still drives most of the movement in the field of environmental policy. It continues to generate numerous environmental policies in the United States over a broad range of issues, including clean air, clean water, wildlife protection, solid waste disposal, toxic substances and cleanup, pesticides, noise control, and forest and natural resource sustainability.

In all of these areas, typically complex federal, state, and sometimes local laws regulate activity in order to protect human health and the ecosystem from harm while balancing the needs of a technologically advanced society. The number of governmental agencies and official participants involved in environmental policy implementation is staggering. For example, at the federal level, it is common to involve many Cabinet-level and high executive offices like the Office of Management and Budget, the Environmental Protection Agency, the Council on Environmental Quality, and the White House—to name a few—in the passage, implementation, or evaluation of environmental policy. Moreover, Congress has no fewer than ten committees in each house that have jurisdiction in environmental matters. Therefore, it is important to realize that "environmental policy," like most other policy areas, actually refers to a fragmented patchwork of laws, regulations, and policymaking actors and bodies.

But, whatever the official source of environmental law or enforcement authority, environmental policy is typically a response to market failure—namely, negative externalities (recall that we examined the concept of market failure as an explanation of why public policies are created). In the environmental field, externalities are the central societal problem requiring a policy response. To illustrate, think of a rubber factory that makes tires. The company buys the raw material, equipment, and labor necessary to produce tires. In turn, it factors these costs into calculating its actual cost of production and then sets a price based on that cost to sell tires in the marketplace for a profit. However, the company has failed to factor in the cost associated with the harm caused to the environment by the production process that emits air pollution and the toxic chemicals that may harm the workers or surrounding community, if not stored and disposed of properly. It is precisely these additional costs to society (in the form of harm to human health or the environment) not factored into the market price of a good that constitute the negative externalities. From a market perspective, then, the company simply "passes on" the cost of addressing this harm to government and society. This type of analysis can be applied to almost any production process that creates by-products, such as cell phone manufacturing, plastic bottle production, and even the dry cleaning of clothes.

In an attempt to address negative externalities involving environmental harm, official policy actors often choose the policy tools of direct mandates (in the form of laws and administrative regulations) and inducements (mostly in the form of market-based incentives). An illustration of a mandate is air-quality emission standards, which require car manufacturers to build automobiles that generate only minimal amounts of certain pollutants, such as carbon monoxide. It is up to auto manufacturers, in turn, to engineer cars that meet the standards; otherwise, they can face enormous fines or risk having noncompliant cars forcibly recalled. In this way, government forces the cost of the negative externality (air pollution in this instance) back onto the producer of the problem (the auto manufacturer in this case), which, in turn, will factor the cost into the price it charges in the market. Mandates are often met with resistance by industries, which argue that their products will be made too costly for consumers. They are also met with resistance by conservative economists, who believe costs "forced" on industry violate the principles of a free market.

Inducements in the form of market-based financial rewards and punishments are growing in popularity in the area of environmental policy. The most common form of inducement includes emission taxes and permits. Emission taxes are punishments imposed on companies that exceed certain pollution standards. These taxes can be very high and therefore create an incentive for the company to figure out a less polluting means of production. Permits, on the other hand, are a form of legal permission given to companies to generate a certain level of pollutants. If a company exceeds the permitted allocation, it can be heavily fined or even shut down, although that is rare. In some other instances, if the company falls below the pollution allotment, the government allows the company to "sell" or trade its unused allotment to other companies producing the same kinds of pollutants in a given region or industry.

The policy rationale is that given the goal of limiting the total production of harmful pollutants to a specified maximum level, some reward to individual companies that are compliant with the policy is useful in obtaining "buy-in" to environmental standards. This is often referred to as a "cap and trade" system, which has gained some acceptance as a broad, market-based approach to curbing all sorts of pollution and correcting the misallocation of social costs due to externalities.

1 Healthcare policy demonstrates the emergence and force of public values.

Who has access to healthcare? Who pays for it now and in the future? How good is the healthcare we receive? These are all critical questions that surround healthcare policy discussions in the United States. Embedded within these debates, however, is a central philosophical question of whether or not healthcare is a fundamental legal right enforceable as a matter of public policy. By focusing on this latter question, we can understand the major policy dynamics at play—the public values present and the competition for influence by the multiple participants.

Those who advocated for universal health insurance coverage leading up to the passage of Patient Protection and Affordable Health Care Act of 2010 believe that access to healthcare is a basic human right worthy of protection under the law, similar to other fundamental legal rights, such as a right to free speech or a right to a public education. They also believe that insuring all Americans promotes greater market efficiency by covering the hidden costs of the uninsured, who access healthcare mostly through hospital emergency rooms and then cannot pay the bill.

On the other hand, there are many who advocate a free market approach; they believe healthcare, like any other private service, should be available on the basis of the ability to pay. Also, as an extension of this view, government should not be paying, or mandating others to pay, for this service. If you choose not to pay for the service, the reasoning goes, then you should not have the same access as a person who is willing to pay.

In addition to the philosophical debates that cut across healthcare policy issues, we also find a dizzying array of interest groups and think tanks, each with their own set of interests, attempting to influence policymakers. These groups range from well-known national interest groups, such as the AARP, to professional organizations, such as the National Physicians Alliance, to advocacy groups such as the Medicare Rights Center. Additionally, the insurance and health sector donated an estimated $170 million in political contributions to members of Congress leading up to the passage of the 2010 healthcare bill.

In terms of public opinion, just before passage of the 2010 healthcare reform bill Americans were roughly split on whether or not they viewed healthcare as a basic right, with somewhat more than half opposed to the bill. As the poll results in Table 11.1 indicate, Americans have remained generally split since the bill was

Table 11.1 **Percent of Public in Favor of and Opposed to the Healthcare Reform Bill***

"As you may know, a health reform bill was signed into law early last year. Given what you know about the health reform law, do you have a generally favorable or generally unfavorable opinion of it?"**

	Favorable	Unfavorable	Unsure/Refused
	%	%	%
5/11	42	44	14
4/11	41	41	18
3/11	42	46	13
2/11	43	48	8
1/11	41	50	9
12/10	42	41	18
11/10	42	40	18
10/10	42	44	15
9/10	49	40	11
8/10	43	45	12
7/10	50	35	14
6/10	48	41	10
5/10	41	44	14

*Kaiser Family Foundation Health Tracking Poll. Adults nationwide. Margin of error ±3.
**In 2010, the question was worded: "As you may know, a new health reform bill was signed into law earlier this year. Given what you know about the new health reform law, do you have a generally favorable or generally unfavorable opinion of it?"http://www.kff.org/kaiserpolls/trackingpoll.cfm

THEIR LIST

An Insider's View

VINCENT GIORDANO

Executive Director, New Jersey Education Association

Vincent Giordano is Executive Director of the New Jersey Education Association (NJEA), which is a democratic organization that prides itself on providing many opportunities for the voices of school employees to be heard on the issues of education policy in New Jersey. NJEA has more than 50 committees of members that review, analyze, and make recommendations to NJEA leadership and governance bodies for a final determination of NJEA's policy on education issues.

Mr. Giordano has been a member of the NJEA staff since 1970 and directed the statewide UniServ field operation for 15 years, serving members from 22 regional offices. Mr. Giordano also chairs the Labor-Management Committee at the Rutgers University School of Labor and Management. We asked Mr. Giordano what he thinks are the most important things students should know about how education policy is made in the United States generally and New Jersey specifically, and this is what he had to say:

"Our democracy provides our citizens many opportunities to influence public policy in education. Policy is determined by Congress and state legislatures through laws adopted by elected representatives. Regulatory bodies, such as the U.S. Department of Education and the N.J. Department of Education, adopt regulations to implement these laws, but ordinary citizens have many opportunities to influence education policy by electing candidates that support their positions, providing testimony before legislative committees or the state board of education, running for office, and joining organizations that represent their point of view."

"We are particularly proud that New Jersey provides many opportunities for citizens to engage with legislators and state board of education members about education issues, such as appearing before committee meetings, writing editorials or letters to the editor, contacting legislators, and attending town hall meetings. Our open public meetings act requires all government bodies to post advance notice of meetings so that the public can monitor and take part in discussions about policy issues."

passed. Given the lack of consensus, the multitude of participants, and the plurality of views, however, it is likely that healthcare reform and its implementation will continue to be a controversial public policy topic.

CONCLUSION

Public policy involves a variety of government actions and intentional nonactions that benefit some group(s) or segment(s) of society. Official actors are powerful and, therefore, have direct influence on policymaking through the use of mandates, inducements, capacity building, and reconfigurations, but unofficial actors also exert influence on policy through providing information, publicity, lobbying, and influencing public opinion.

Policies may be created to distribute resources in areas of priority, to redistribute an existing resource from one area of society to another, or to provide regulation of public or private behavior or conduct. Further, the government uses numerous tools to achieve its policy aims, such as mandates and inducements.

The policy process begins with the stages of issue identification and agenda setting and then moves to actual policy formulation and eventually to policy implementation and evaluation. Although in textbooks like this one the policymaking process looks neat and linear, in practice it is much more unpredictable, overlapping, and complicated.

Finally, through the examination of specific policy areas, we can see that policy change may occur (1) when there is alignment of public opinion against a particular industry, such as tobacco companies; (2) when the government learns from its past mistakes, such as the Fed's decision to increase the money supply during the economic crisis in 2008; (3) when scientific information reveals certain dangers, such as pesticide usage; or (4) when a public value begins to emerge, such as the one that emerged in 2010 around the idea of providing effective healthcare insurance coverage for more Americans.

YOUR LIST REVISITED

At the beginning of the chapter you were asked to think about what you might include on your own list of the Top 10 Most Important Things to Know About American Public Policy. Now that you have read the chapter, take a moment to revisit your list. What, if anything, would you change about your list? Do you agree or disagree with the chapter list constructed by the author? What might you add or delete? Why?

KEY TERMS

Agenda setting 250
Capacity building 249
Changing a system 249
Distributive policies 245
Federal Reserve Board (the Fed) 253
Focusing events 251
Inducements 249
Information asymmetry 244
Mandates 248
Market failure 244
Natural monopoly 244
Negative externalities 244
Official actors 246
Policy evaluation 251
Policy formulation 251
Policy implementation 251
Policy tools 248
Problem identification 250
Public goods 244
Public policy 241
Redistributive policies 245
Regulatory policies 245
Think tanks 248
Unintended consequences 254
Unofficial actors 246

CHAPTER REVIEW QUESTIONS

10 What are the key distinguishing elements of public policy?

9 Why are public policies created?

8 What are the differences among distributive, redistributive, and regulatory policies?

7 Who are the "official" and "unofficial" actors involved in public policymaking? And what are their respective policy resources?

6 Which policy tools can the government employ in creating and implementing policy?

5. Explain the various stages of the policymaking process.
4. What does the eventual policy shift towards closer regulation of tobacco companies reveal about the nature of American policymaking?
3. What lessons can be learned from studying the Fed's role in the economic crises of the 1920s and 1930s?
2. What forms of mandates and inducements are used in environmental policy?
1. What does the direction of public opinion in favor of universal health insurance coverage indicate about the idea that access to healthcare is a fundamental right?

SUGGESTED READINGS

- Bachrach, Peter, and Morton Baratz. "The Two Faces of Power," *American Political Science Review* 56 (1962): 947–952.
- Berry, Jeffrey M., and Clyde Wilcox. *The Interest Group Society*, 5th ed. New York: Longman Publishing Group, 2009.
- Cobb, Roger W., and Charles D. Elder. *Participation in American Politics: The Dynamics of Agenda-Building*, 2nd ed. Baltimore, MD: Johns Hopkins University Press, 1983.
- Dye, Thomas R. *Understanding Public Policy*, 13th ed. Englewood Cliffs, NJ: Longman, 2011.
- Heclo, Hugh. "Issue Networks and the Executive Establishment." In *The New American Political System*, ed. Anthony King. Washington DC: American Enterprise Institute, 1978.
- Iyengar, Shanto, and Donald Kinder. *News That Matters: Television and American Opinion.* Chicago: University of Chicago Press, 1989.
- Lindblom, Charles E. "The Science of Muddling Through." *Public Administration Review* 19 (1959): 79–88.
- Schattschneider, E. E. *The Semisoverign People.* Hinsdale, IL: Dryden Press, 1975.
- Theodoulou, Stella Z., and Matthew A. Cahn., eds. *Public Policy: The Essential Readings*. Englewood Cliffs, NJ: Prentice Hall, 1995.
- Wilson, James Q. *Bureaucracy*. New York: Basic Books, 1989.

SUGGESTED FILMS

- *Mr. Smith Goes to Washington* (1939)
- *Citizen Kane* (1941)
- *Wag the Dog* (1997)
- *A Civil Action* (1998)
- *Primary Colors* (1998)
- *The Insider* (1999)
- *Erin Brockovich* (2000)
- *Bowling for Columbine* (2002)
- *Thank You for Smoking* (2005)
- *Fast Food Nation* (2006)

SUGGESTED WEBSITES

- **Congressional Quarterly:** http://www.cqpolitics.com.
- **Government Accountability Office:** http://www.gao.gov.
- **International City/County Management Association:** http://www.icma.org.
- **Library of Congress/Thomas:** http://www.thomas.gov.
- **National Conference on State Legislatures:** http://www.ncsl.org.
- **National Governor's Association:** http://www.nga.org.
- **On the Issues:** http://www.ontheissues.org.
- **Policy Evaluation (Virtual Library):** http://www.policy-evaluation.org.
- **Policy Library:** http://www.policylibrary.com.
- **Roll Call:** http://www.rollcall.com.

ENDNOTES

[1]Thomas A. Birkland, *An Introduction to the Policy Process: Theories, Concepts, and Models of Public Policy Making,* 2nd ed. (New York: M.E. Sharpe, Inc., 2005), pp. 17–21.
[2]*Brown v. Board of Education of Topeka*, 347 U.S. 483 (1954).
[3]David Leo Wiemer and Aidan R. Vining, *Policy Analysis: Concepts and Practice*, 2nd ed. (Upper Saddle River, NJ: Prentice Hall, 1992).
[4]Theodore J. Lowi, *The End of Liberalism: The Second Republic of the United States*, 2nd ed. (New York: W.W. Norton, 1979); James E. Anderson, *Public Policymaking*, 5th ed. (Boston: Houghton Mifflin, 2002).
[5]Lowi, *The End of Liberalism.*
[6]Ibid.
[7]Anderson, *Public Policymaking.*
[8]Lowi, *The End of Liberalism.*
[9]Lester M. Salomon, *The Tools of Government: A Guide to the New Governance* (Oxford, UK: Oxford University Press, 2002).
[10]Richard F. Elmore, "Instruments and Strategy in Public Policy," *Review of Policy Research* 7 (1, 1987): 174 –186.
[11]Ibid.
[12]Ibid.
[13]Ibid.
[14]Ibid.
[15]Ibid.
[16]Birkland, *An Introduction to the Policy Process*, pp. 224–225.
[17]John W. Kingdon, *Agendas, Alternatives, and Public Policies*, 2nd ed. (New York: Harper Collins, 1995).
[18]Ibid.
[19]Ibid.
[20]Jeffrey Pressman and Aaron Wildavsky, *Implementation* (Berkley, CA: University of California Press, 1973).
[21]Eugene Bardach, *A Practical Guide for Policy Analysis: The Eightfold Path to Effective Problem Solving*, 2nd ed. (Washington DC: CQ Press, 2004).
[22]Frank Baumgartner and Bryan D. Jones, *Agendas and Instability in American Politics* (Chicago: University of Chicago Press, 1993).
[23]Ibid.

Chapter 12

FOREIGN POLICY

Top Ten List

10 The president establishes the foreign policy agenda.

9 Presidential attempts to shape foreign policy are limited by international and national context.

8 Only Congress can declare war, so presidents wage war "unofficially" to meet their foreign policy objectives.

7 The Senate can affect foreign policy by ratifying or failing to ratify treaties, but this influence is diminishing.

6 The executive branch often circumvents the need for Senate ratification of treaties by negotiating less formal international agreements.

5 The National Security Council plays an increasingly influential role in developing American foreign policy.

4 When foreign policy issues become important to the public, then public opinion can influence foreign policy.

3 The media educate and focus public attention on specific foreign policy issues.

2 The pursuit of national security can compromise civil liberties.

1 As a result of globalization, economic, environmental, and healthcare issues are increasingly moving into the realm of foreign policy.

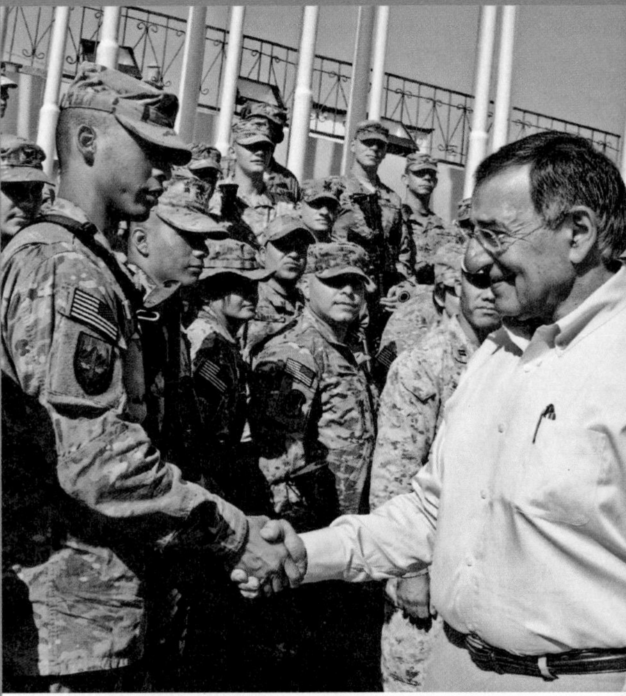

Many factors shape the goals and methods of U.S. foreign policy. Although many of these factors are domestic, many problems confronting the United States are not limited to its borders. Economic crises, immigration, environmental challenges, the spread of diseases, and security threats illustrate the need for the United States to partner with other actors to resolve its most pressing problems. Shown here, U.S. Secretary of Defense Leon E. Panetta meets with troops in Afghanistan in 2011. The involvement of the U.S. military around the world is often a contentious political issue.

YOUR LIST

Before you read this chapter, take a few moments to think about what you might include on a list of the Top 10 Most Important Things to Know About Foreign Policy. At the end of the chapter you will be asked to compare and contrast your list with the one supplied in this chapter.

INTRODUCTION

On May 25, 2009, North Korea exploded a nuclear device as powerful as the bomb the United States dropped on Hiroshima. The explosion triggered an earthquake measuring 4.5 on the Richter scale, which was felt as far as 130 miles away in the Chinese city of Yanji.[1] What message was North Korea sending to South Korea and its ally, the United States? Was the test a direct threat to security? Just a year earlier, in June 2008, North Korea had blown up a nuclear cooling tower to illustrate that it was ready to abandon its nuclear program for a package of international incentives that the United States and others had offered. The nuclear test in 2009 indicated not only that North Korea had reversed this policy but that it had, in the meantime, developed a much more powerful nuclear weapon than it had tested originally in 2006. Did this mean that negotiations and incentive packages had failed? If so, how can we stop nuclear proliferation? Should we try to stop it? Or should we disengage and disarm unilaterally?

The United States has one of the largest economies in the world and invests, buys, and sells goods and services to many different countries. As such, we—as citizens of this country—are some of the most powerful decision makers in the world. Should we spearhead a global effort to reverse global climate change? Should we establish democracies around the world in the hopes of establishing long-lasting peace and protecting human rights? And once we decide on the "right" policy, how do we influence the decision makers within our powerful country? Who makes these decisions? Although our Constitution clearly delegates powers to the president, Congress, and the people, the answer to this last question is changing in light of increased globalization and the evolving role of the media and the public in the political life of this country.

The president establishes the foreign policy agenda.

Foreign policy The goals identified and actions taken by a government to protect national interests.

National interests A country's goals and ambitions, whether economic, military, or cultural.

Foreign policy refers to the goals identified and actions taken by a government in the international arena to protect **national interests**, whether economic, military, or cultural.[2] There is no one foreign policy that a country such as the United States follows. Instead, foreign policy includes many goals that are sometimes in competition. These may include military and border security, economic prosperity, the promotion of democracy worldwide, and the protection of human rights.

According to Article II, sections 2 and 3, of the U.S. Constitution, the president is the commander-in-chief of the United States Armed Forces; he has the right to make treaties, grant powers, and nominate certain public officials and judges. Moreover, the president has the right to nominate and receive foreign ambassadors. Although the Constitution says nothing explicitly about the president's role in foreign policy and the instruments or means to accomplish it,[3] historically, U.S. presidents have been the actors in government who conceptualize and articulate what is in the national interest. This vision of the national interest stems from the context of international and economic security, domestic political and economic considerations, and a president's own understanding of international relations.

Containment A strategy pursued by the United States to stem the spread of Soviet influence and communism worldwide.

National Security Report (NSC)-68 A classified document written and adopted in 1950 by the Truman administration that made the case for the need of a massive arms buildup and an expansion of nuclear weapons research and development.

Cold War A period when the United States and the Soviet Union struggled for ideological dominance. While there was no official war between the two countries, they each supported political actors in the rest of the world that served their political and economic agendas.

For example, during his time in office, President Harry S. Truman identified the Soviet Union as the greatest threat to the United States and identified **containment** as the strategy to pursue in stemming the spread of Soviet influence worldwide. To this end, in 1950 the Truman administration adopted policies advocated by a classified document called the **National Security Report 68 (NSC-68)**, which created the foreign policy blueprint for the next several decades. Drawing upon the American Ambassador to the Soviet Union George Kennan's "Long Telegram," the document made the case for a massive arms buildup and an expansion of nuclear weapons research and development.[4] Truman's adoption of these goals laid the ground for a 40-year-long **Cold War**—a period when the United States and the Soviet Union struggled for ideological dominance (democracy and capitalism versus communism).

In his 1996 *National Security Strategy of Engagement and Enlargement*, President Bill Clinton outlined the need for the United States to assume a leadership position in a post–Cold War world and to attempt to "enlarge the world community of secure, democratic and free market nations."[5] President Clinton set the tone of U.S. foreign policy by looking to expand free trade arrangements, offer political assistance, and propose international institutional memberships for newly democratic or democratizing countries (or states, as they are known in international relations parlance) as a way to make the world a safer and more prosperous place, thereby decreasing the number of threats faced by the United States and the international community. One manifestation of this policy focus was Clinton's push to embrace the former Soviet satellite states in Central and Eastern Europe and to include them in **NATO**. The goal was not only to promote democracy but to make possible an arrangement of **collective security** whereby the states involved agreed to act together against any state that behaves aggressively.

NATO An intergovernmental military alliance based on the North Atlantic Treaty, which was signed on April 4, 1949.

Collective security An international arrangement whereby states agree to act together against any state that behaves aggressively.

Preemptive force A rationale for attacking other parties in response to an imminent threat.

Post 9/11, President George W. Bush established a different foreign policy vision. His decision to send troops into Afghanistan to topple the Taliban regime that had harbored al-Qaeda is one example. His National Security Strategy documents published in 2002 and 2006 further identified the war on terrorism as the number-one priority for U.S. foreign policy.[6] He indicated that **preemptive force**, or the use of force in response to an imminent threat, might be necessary to protect the United States. Better known as the Bush Doctrine, this rationale was used to launch the 2003 war in Iraq.

Following his election, President Obama reaffirmed the need to focus on terrorism as a threat to national security, but he also indicated that the United States should take a more active role in working with international organizations, such as the United Nations. He also emphasized that the United States should repair relationships with allies and avoid the use of torture and other coercive interrogation techniques.[7]

What these examples indicate is that the American president establishes the priorities for foreign policy. The president gives cues to Congress, the media, and the public about what is and should be important for the United States. This does not mean these other actors, such as Congress or the courts, have no input. They do. But the reality in American government is that presidents have the means to initiate diplomacy, work with international organizations, or use force to realize goals.[8]

Additionally, the president can reorganize the executive bureaucracy to achieve his desired ends. For example, just after the conclusion of World War II and in anticipation of the escalation of the Cold War, President Truman ordered the most widespread reorganization and expansion of the bureaucracy to date. He created the Department of Defense, which replaced the former Department of War, to coordinate and centralize decision making. A similar expansion and reorganization of the bureaucracy occurred in 2001 when President Bush created the **Department of Homeland Security (DHS)** to handle terrorist threats on American soil. Presidents have the means to create tools to serve foreign policy ends above any other institution or actor.

Department of Homeland Security (DHS) Created in the aftermath of 9/11 to reorganize and centralize the U.S. intelligence establishment.

9 Presidential attempts to shape foreign policy are limited by international and national context.

Every elected leader has goals and an agenda upon being elected or selected for office. A president may wish to emphasize the protection of human rights, as President Jimmy Carter did. Or, a president may wish to foster better trade relations with previous rivals, as President Bill Clinton and President Barack Obama have done with China. However, it is essential to understand that what may be the best of intentions are limited by the international and domestic context in which foreign policy must be conducted. Domestically, the political context sets public expectations for their governments in the international arena. Additionally, other countries and international organizations have their own goals. The United States must work within the constraints of these international frameworks to pursue its foreign policy goals. Thus, the timing and political climate in large part influence how and what political leaders are willing and able to accomplish.

The history of American foreign policy has been influenced by trends toward isolation or toward engagement with other nations, which have greatly impacted the U.S. president's ability to carry out his foreign policy agenda. During the first half of the twentieth century, public opinion in the United States strongly supported a foreign policy of isolationism, preferring to stay out of European affairs. The United States entered World War I in 1917 only after German attacks on merchant ships impacted the U.S. economy. In the period directly following the first World War, President Woodrow Wilson, a political scientist by training, tried to recast the way that international conflicts might be addressed and ideally resolved.

In his Fourteen Points speech, Wilson outlined the need for increased communication among states and a forum for dispute resolution other than the use of force. Part of this concept can be found in the **Treaty of Versailles**, the document that

Treaty of Versailles The treaty that officially ended World War I and created the first state-centered international organization, the League of Nations.

officially ended World War I and created the first state-centered international organization, the **League of Nations**. The League was a collective security organization designed to give states a place to voice grievances and allow for arbitration by other states. For example, if one state was invaded by another, all other states would rally to that state's aid and impose a series of punitive measures, such as economic sanctions, to alter the behavior of the aggressor. If those measures failed, the states would be obligated to intervene to remove the aggressor from the member state. In Wilson's mind, this would deter future conflict and make the world a safer place.

League of Nations A collective security organization of the post–World War I era designed to give states a place to voice grievances and allow for arbitration by other states. Despite efforts by President Wilson, the U.S. Senate rejected the Versailles Treaty and kept the United States out of the League.

The problem with this idea was that the American public and most other elected officials in Congress preferred a "return to normalcy," or isolation in foreign policy, rather than the more engaged approach Wilson embraced. Thus, the Senate voted to reject U.S. membership in the League. Despite Wilson's agenda, the postwar environment and the preference for focusing on American problems first, or perhaps exclusively, derailed his quest for further international collaboration.

Another example of how context shapes foreign policy may be seen in terms of the Cold War. At the conclusion of World War II, the international system was dominated by two countries who survived the war better than most—the United States and the Soviet Union. Instead of pooling their considerable political and economic resources to restructure the international system to avoid future conflicts, however, these two countries adopted a **zero-sum** approach in which one side's gain is the other side's loss. During the ensuing 50 years, these two opponents not only engaged in direct hostilities but became the most profound of enemies.

Zero-sum A situation in which one side's gain is the other side's loss.

During the Cold War, the United States and the Soviet Union struggled for ideological dominance—democracy and capitalism versus communism. The two countries never underwent face-to-face conflict. Instead, they engaged in "proxy wars" whereby they would support various political actors in the rest of the world who served their political and economic agendas. For example, in the 1960s, Latin America was an ideological battleground. In Guatemala, Argentina, and Brazil the United States funded, supported, and on occasion armed prodemocratic, or at least anticommunist, leaders, parties, and groups. The Soviet Union did the same for procommunist groups. This kind of battle took place in Southeast Asia, Africa, and Europe as well.

Another feature of the Cold War was the **nuclear arms race** that raged between the two superpowers. In order to gain international superiority, both the United States and the Soviet Union thought it necessary to secure military dominance. This included establishing the largest and best-trained militaries and the most sophisticated and deadly tools of warfare, nuclear weapons chief among them. During every administration from Truman to George H. W. Bush, the foreign policy priority was to outstrategize and offset the Soviet Union.

Nuclear arms race In order to gain international superiority, both the United States and the Soviet Union sought to secure military dominance by establishing the largest and best-trained militaries and the most sophisticated and deadly tools of warfare, nuclear weapons chief among them.

Some presidents may have preferred to pursue foreign policy goals aside from or outside of the Cold War calculus. For instance, President Jimmy Carter criticized the strategy and spending of the Cold War and wished to pursue the protection of human rights as the defining priority of U.S. foreign policy. While he had some success in this area and earned the respect of many activists in both the United States and other countries, the context in which he had to make decisions remained the same as for previous presidents. In 1979, the Soviet Union invaded Afghanistan. Regardless of his preference for relegating Cold War considerations to secondary status, in response Carter was forced to adopt the same zero-sum logic as his predecessors.

8 Only Congress can declare war, so presidents wage war "unofficially" to meet their foreign policy objectives.

Article I, section 8, of the Constitution grants Congress, and Congress alone, the power to declare war. As discussed earlier, the founders sought to create an executive who was decisive in times of crisis but not too strong or prone to the abuse of power. By requiring the president to consult with Congress, the founders were ensuring the implementation of the system of checks and balances they had designed. Getting a majority in both houses would ensure maximum deliberation rather than hasty action. And, in fact, there have been only five cases in which Congress has exercised this right: the War of 1812, the Mexican-American War, the Spanish-American War, World War I, and World War II. But, as Figure 12.1 shows, U.S. troops have been

Figure 12.1 U.S. Troops Overseas 1950–2005* by Region

This figure shows the number of U.S. troops engaged in conflict overseas by region from 1950–2005. Despite the number of troops deployed, the U.S. Congress has not declared war during this time period.

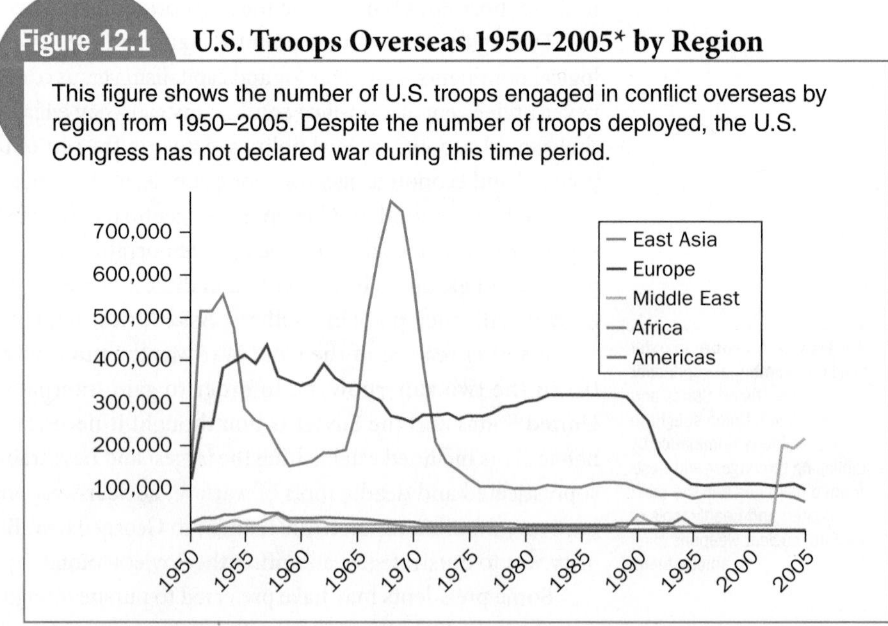

*Data for 1951 and 1952 are estimated.

Source: Calculations by Tim Kane, Ph.D., The Heritage Foundation, based on annual records from Department of Defense, DIOR.

involved in many more conflicts than these. In the late 1960s, for instance, more than 700,000 U.S. troops were deployed in East Asia, and yet Congress had not declared war. How is that possible?

As Article II, section 2, of the Constitution states, the "President shall be Commander in Chief of the Army and Navy of the United States, and of the Militia of the several States." What is implied here is that the president has the right to deploy troops even when there is no declaration of war. Korea, Vietnam, Lebanon, the Gulf War, Afghanistan, and the Iraq War were all military actions authorized by Congress, but without an outright declaration of war.

In September 2003, for example, President George W. Bush made the case to the United Nations that Iraq was pursuing an alleged nuclear weapons program and, therefore, was a threat to the United States and the international community. In October of 2002, persuaded by this argument and the evidence presented to them, members of the House and the Senate approved a joint resolution authorizing the president to use force against Iraq if the terms of United Nations Security Council resolutions and subsequent weapons inspections were not met. The House of Representatives vote was 297–133 in favor; the Senate voted 77–23 in favor.[9] It is important to note, however, that these were not formal declarations of war. Congress was approving an action initiated by the White House.

At times, however, the president uses his power to commit troops to override or circumvent the need for congressional approval, creating tensions between the two branches of government. Moreover, there have been instances where Congress may have approved the use of American military personnel but had little authority beyond that once troops were committed. One example of this was the Vietnam War. In 1964, Congress passed a joint resolution, the Gulf of Tonkin Resolution, authorizing President Lyndon Johnson to send American forces to respond to an alleged attack on the U.S. destroyer the U.S.S. *Maddox*. Once the troops were committed, even as the war was going poorly, Congress had no say in U.S. actions.

War Powers Resolution An attempt to exercise congressional power, restore some balance to congressional-executive roles in foreign policy, and limit the power of the presidency in troop commitments.

As a response to increasing casualties and mounting public opinion against the Vietnam War, Congress passed the 1973 **War Powers Resolution**. This law was an attempt to exercise congressional power, restore some balance to congressional-executive roles in foreign policy, and to limit the power of the presidency in troop commitments. In addition, Congress wished to prevent foreign entanglements with military forces without a clear objective. The War Powers Resolution attempts to define the circumstances under which the president can commit troops and specifies three such instances: "(1) a declaration of war by Congress, (2) Congressional legislative authorization, or (3) a national emergency created by attack upon the United States, its territories, or its armed forces." The resolution went further to specify that the president "in every possible instance shall consult with Congress" prior to committing U.S. forces and "shall consult regularly with Congress" until the troops are withdrawn. In addition, the War Powers Resolution requires that the president notify Congress within 48 hours of committing troops to military action and limits armed forces from remaining for more than 60 days without an authorization for the use of military force or a declaration of war.

The resolution introduced a reporting requirement for the president. He must inform Congress of the status of hostilities at least every six months if troops should be committed that long. Essentially, these requirements stipulated that Congress would be involved in every step of the process. The record of the War Powers Resolution and the effort to limit presidential commitment of troops is mixed. There has been an increase in reporting to Congress about troop commitments.[10] However, in many instances, including Nicaragua, Cuba, Grenada, Panama, Somalia, the former Yugoslavia, and Kosovo, the president committed American troops without congressional approval. For example, in September 1994, President Clinton committed 2,000 U.S. troops to Haiti to restore President Jean-Bertrand Aristide, contradicting a unanimous Senate vote that opposed this very action. More recently, in the spring of 2011, President Obama committed U.S. troops to help enforce the no-fly zone over Libya, and one member of Congress suggested publicly that President Obama may have committed an impeachable offense.[11] The struggle between the executive and legislative branches in this area of foreign policy continues.

The Senate can affect foreign policy by ratifying or failing to ratify treaties, but this influence is diminishing.

A **treaty** is a binding international agreement between two or more countries that can fundamentally affect the relationship between the countries. **Bilateral treaties** are treaties between two countries, parties, or "sides," and **multilateral treaties** are treaties among three or more countries. In 1977, for example, President Carter negotiated the bilateral **Torrijos-Carter Treaty**. This treaty guaranteed that Panama would gain control of the Panama Canal (which had been completed by Americans in 1914) after 1999, ending the control the United States had exercised in that area since 1903.

Treaty A binding international agreement between two or more countries.

Bilateral treaties Treaties between two countries, parties, or "sides."

Multilateral treaties Treaties among three or more countries.

Torrijos-Carter Treaty This treaty guaranteed that Panama would gain control of the Panama Canal after 1999, ending the control the United States had exercised in that area since 1903.

In the process of forging relationships with foreign countries and international organizations, the Senate plays a crucial role. Article II, section 2, of the Constitution states: "The President shall have Power, by and with the Advice and Consent of the Senate, to make Treaties, provided two thirds of the Senators present concur; and he shall nominate, and by and with the Advice and Consent of the Senate, shall appoint Ambassadors, other public Ministers and Consuls, Judges of the supreme Court, and all other Officers of the United States." In addition to approving the appointment of officials representing the United States to foreign countries, the Senate also must ratify treaties by a super-majority (two-thirds) vote. Moreover, the Constitution is clear that the Senate should assist in the drafting of treaties (advise).

 The Senate can affect foreign policy by ratifying or failing to ratify treaties . . .

Although the ideal of Senate involvement still exists, it is unusual for senators to be a part of the actual drafting of a treaty, especially multilateral treaties. Having fifty additional government officials voice opinions about international agreements would certainly complicate matters. Imagine President Obama along with the entire Senate trying to negotiate a nuclear nonproliferation treaty with North Korea. Logistics in part dictate that the Senate sees only the final product. However, this does not mean that the Senate waives the right to give input into a treaty. On the contrary, the Senate reserves the right to amend a treaty or make various changes, which may prompt other states to reconsider or renegotiate the treaty.

On the occasions when presidents have negotiated especially controversial or important treaties without consulting any individual senators, the treaties failed to be ratified. Two examples illustrate this point. At the conclusion of World War I, President Woodrow Wilson negotiated the terms of the Treaty of Versailles, which would end the war and establish the League of Nations. However, he neglected to include any senators as part of his delegation. When the treaty was presented to the Senate for a vote, it was defeated—twice. President Franklin Delano Roosevelt learned from this error and included U.S. senators in the negotiation of the United Nations Charter signed in 1945.

Comprehensive Test Ban Treaty A treaty designed to prohibit any type of nuclear weapons tests and to prevent testing by other states.

More recently, in October 1999, the Senate defeated the **Comprehensive Test Ban Treaty** negotiated by President Clinton. The CTBT was designed to prohibit any type of nuclear weapon tests and to prevent testing by other states.[12] Clinton assumed the Senate would sign on to the agreement. However, many senators feared that the United States might lose its military edge by adhering to such an agreement. Nonsignatory states would still be able to test weapons and perhaps supersede the United States. During his 2008 campaign, President Obama argued that he would work with the Senate to have the U.S. ratify the agreement. The Comprehensive Test Ban Treaty has been stalled for more than a decade now, but it is the exception. On balance, the Senate affirms most of the treaties presented to it. There have been only twenty-one instances in which treaties were voted down. There are other cases, however, where the Senate simply opts not to vote on a treaty, effectively tabling it indefinitely.

Anti-Ballistic Missile Treaty Treaty negotiated between the United States and the Soviet Union in 1972 to limit the proliferation of antiballistic missiles, which could be used offensively. The United States announced its withdrawal from the treaty in 2001.

Strategic Defense Initiative (Star Wars) Proposed by President Ronald Reagan in 1983 during the Cold War, this was a plan to use ground- and space-based systems to protect the United States from a nuclear attack.

In addition to these powers, the Senate can make its approval of treaties conditional upon common understanding or interpretation of a document. That is, if the Senate feels there is ambiguity or that a president might act in a manner contrary to what it feels the treaty is about, the Senate will write exactly what it takes the bill to mean. For example, President Reagan interpreted the **Anti-Ballistic Missile Treaty** of 1972 as a justification for the development of his **Strategic Defense Initiative (Star Wars)**. The so-called Star Wars project, proposed by Reagan in 1983, was a plan to use ground- and space-based systems to protect the United States from a nuclear attack. The Senate was quick to issue a condition to the treaty clarifying interpretation.[13]

Once a treaty is ratified, however, the Senate has no way to ensure that it is implemented in a manner that meets with Senate approval. In addition, the president does not need the Senate to terminate a treaty. For example, in 1971, President Richard Nixon made the decision to travel to the communist People's Republic of China to engage and reestablish ties with that nation. Until that time, the United States had strongly supported Taiwan over China and actually had a defense treaty with Taiwan, the Sino-American Mutual Defense Treaty, which was signed in 1954. Following Nixon's visit, the United States made the decision to seat the People's Republic of China rather than Taiwan in the United Nations. In 1978, President Carter, building upon Nixon's policy, established formal diplomatic relations with China. The decisions and actions by Presidents Nixon and Carter were a significant departure from past U.S. policy, and they in effect terminated the defense treaty with Taiwan that the Senate had approved, altering U.S. foreign policy without any input from the Senate.

With the growth of the number of multilateral agreements the United States has signed, the Senate's inability to affect the implementation of treaties is likely to be a long-term issue. According to a Congressional Research Service report, until the late 1800s, the United States had only bilateral treaties with individual countries. After 1900, the United States concluded many multilateral agreements on a wide array of subjects. Between 1980 and 1991, the United States was party to 259 multilateral agreements, 79 of which were treaties.[14] More multilateral agreements on foreign policy issues and a diminishing number of international commitments conducted via treaty may lessen the impact of the Senate on foreign relations in the future.

The executive branch often circumvents the need for Senate ratification of treaties by negotiating less formal international agreements.

Executive orders Unilateral directives issued by presidents on domestic and foreign policy matters. In some cases, these orders may serve to implement legislation passed by Congress.

Executive agreements International agreements entered into by the president with the chief executives of other countries. These agreements are legal, but they do not require the advice and consent of the Senate.

Apart from treaties, there are other ways that the executive branch can create and implement foreign policy. These are executive orders and executive agreements. **Executive orders** are presidential directives that serve to implement legislation carried out by Congress. In 2009, President Obama issued Executive Orders 13492 and 13493, both of which focused on closing detention camps at the U.S. Guantanamo base in Cuba.[15] In just his first two years in office, President Obama issued seventy-four executive orders (thirty-nine in 2009 and thirty-five in 2010) on a variety of topics (see Table 12.1).

Executive agreements are international agreements entered into by the president with the chief executives of other countries. These agreements are legal, but

Table 12.1 A Sample of Executive Orders Issued by President Barack Obama During His First Year in Office

Executive Order Number	Description
13489	Presidential Records Declassified
13490	Ethics Requirements for Executive Branch
13491	Lawful Interrogation Techniques
13492	Detainee Status and Closure of Guantanamo Bay, Cuba
13493	Review of Detention Policies
13494	Policies for Government Contracting
13495	Protections for Workers Under Service Contracts
13496	Employee Rights and Federal Labor Laws
13497	Repeal of Some Executive Orders on Regulatory Planning and Review
13498	President's Advisory Board for Faith-Based Initiatives and Neighborhood Partnerships
13499	Establishment of National Economic Council
13500	Establishment of Domestic Policy Council
13501	Establishment of President's Economic Recovery Advisory Board
13502	Use of Project Labor Agreements for Federal Construction Projects
13503	Establishment of the White House Office of Urban Affairs
13504	Amending Executive Order 13390
13505	Allowing Stem Cell Research
13506	Establishing a White House Council on Women and Girls
13507	Establishment of the White House Office of Health Reform

Source: National Archives, *Federal Register*. http://www.archives.gov/federal-register/executive-orders/2009-obama.html

they do not require the advice and consent of the Senate. There are no limits on the president's authority to make such agreements, as long as they do not violate or alter any existing laws or treaties. Tables 12.2 and 12.3 provide a visual comparison of the number of treaties and executive agreements entered into from the founding through the end of the twentieth century.

Table 12.2

Treaties and Executive Agreements Concluded by the United States, 1789–1989

Period	Treaties	Executive Agreements
1789–1839	60	27
1839–1889	215	238
1889–1939	524	917
1939–1989	702	11,698
Total	1,501	12,880

Source: Congressional Research Service, "Treaties and Other International Agreements," January 2001, p. 139.

Table 12.3

Treaties and Executive Agreements Concluded by the United States, 1989–1999

Period	Treaties	Executive Agreements
1989	15	363
1990	20	398
1991	11	286
1992	21	303
1993	17	257
1994	24	338
1995	17	300
1996	48	260
1997	40	257
1998	25	259
1999	26	199
Total	264	3,220

Source: Congressional Research Service, "Treaties and Other International Agreements," January 2001, p. 139.

The way the executive agreement process works is that the president or an official representing the executive branch, such as the Secretary of State, authorizes someone or a group of individuals to negotiate the terms of the agreement. Once the representative(s) work out the terms, it is then signed. At that point, the president is required to notify the Senate within 60 days. Congress then has the option of voting to cancel the executive agreement, refusing to pass the necessary legislation to implement the agreement, or refusing to fund its implementation. To be implemented, an executive agreement requires a simple majority vote of the House and Senate.

With the number of countries, international agencies, and issues the U.S. government must address, it is sometimes easier for the executive branch to negotiate directly with foreign governments to draft agreements rather than consulting the Senate on each one.[16] Although presidents use both executive agreements and orders frequently in conducting foreign policy, their constitutionality is criticized by some as an attempt to circumvent the Senate's power to advise and consent.[17] The president's authority to issue executive orders and to negotiate executive agreement stems from two sources: the power granted him in the Constitution as chief executive and/or specific powers delegated to him by an earlier act of Congress that the president "take care that Laws be faithfully executed." However, some argue that through the use of executive agreements and orders, presidents have expanded their powers considerably beyond the bounds envisioned by the founders.

Members of Congress have at various points tried to limit executive use of these arrangements. For example, in the 1950s, Senator John Bricker of Ohio, a conservative Republican, attempted to pass legislation that stated no treaty could be made by the United States that conflicted with the Constitution. This **Bricker Amendment** prohibited any treaty that was self-executing—that went into effect without the passage of separate legislation by Congress—or which granted Congress legislative powers beyond those specified in the Constitution. This amendment was also designed to limit the president's power to enter into executive agreements with foreign powers that might limit U.S. sovereignty. The amendment ultimately failed but lost by only one vote, suggesting that the Senate was serious about limiting executive use of agreements. Another example of attempts to limit executive use of agreements is the **Case Zablocki Act**. This was 1972 legislation that created a requirement for the executive branch, specifically the Secretary of State, to report to Congress any executive agreements negotiated and agreed to within 60 days after going into effect.[18] This amendment was in fact approved and is in effect today.

Bricker Amendment A series of amendments to the U.S. Constitution proposed in the 1950s that would have prohibited any treaty that was self-executing or which granted Congress legislative powers beyond those specified in the Constitution.

Case Zablocki Act 1972 legislation that created a requirement for the executive to report to Congress any executive agreements negotiated and agreed to within 60 days after the agreements go into effect.

5 The National Security Council plays an increasingly influential role in developing American foreign policy.

The American president leads foreign policy, but he does not create it on his own. The president has a team of advisors who make up his Cabinet, and each has specific areas of expertise, including the Secretary of State and the Secretary of Defense. The Secretary of State is head of the Department of State and in charge of implementing

National Security Adviser (NSA) Person responsible for advising the president and coordinating the NSC members.

National Security Council (NSC) Established by the National Security Act of 1947, the NSC is responsible for shaping and coordinating national security policy for the United States. The president chairs the committee.

foreign policies and programs. Likewise, the Secretary of Defense is the head of the Defense Department, which is in charge of U.S. national security and the armed forces. Both of these officials, as well as the **National Security Advisor (NSA)**, the Chairman of the Joint Chiefs of Staff of the military, and the Director of National Intelligence, are part of the president's team known as the **National Security Council (NSC)**. The National Security Council was established by the National Security Act of 1947 and is responsible for shaping and coordinating national security policy for the United States.[19] The NSA is responsible for advising the president and coordinating the NSC members. The NSC and NSA have had varying roles in presidential administrations since Truman. However, on balance, the NSC has increased in strength and influence.

During the Reagan administration, NSA Robert McFarlane and Deputy NSA John Poindexter increased the influence of the office tremendously. McFarlane was highly involved in foreign policy operations, a departure from past directors. But with this increased activity came some problems regarding boundaries and constitutional authority. For example, in 1982 the U.S. Congress passed the Boland Amendment prohibiting further U.S. funding or activity of political and military activities in Nicaragua. Disagreeing with this decision, McFarlane, Poindexter, and fellow NSC member Lt. Colonel Oliver North sought alternative funding for missions through the illegal sale of arms to the Iranian government in exchange for hostages. When news of this broke in 1985, the Iran-Contra scandal led to a widespread investigation of NSC activities by the Tower Board. As a result of the review and recommendations of this board, President Reagan implemented some changes in the NSC, including decreasing its size and appointing a legal counsel.

Since the NSA and some NSC members do not have to be confirmed by the Senate, they are beyond congressional oversight and so develop foreign policy initiatives independently. Frequently, prominent NSC members have considerable experience and well-formed opinions. President George W. Bush's first NSA was Condoleeza Rice, who would go on to become Secretary of State in his second term. Secretary Rice had served as a professor of political science at Stanford University and as a Soviet and Eastern Affairs advisor to President George H. W. Bush. As Secretary of State, Rice strongly advocated for the democratization of the Middle East, believing that stable democratic government would lead to peace and stability. Experienced NSC members, however, can disagree. For instance, Secretary of Defense Donald Rumsfeld frequently clashed with President Bush's first Secretary of State, Colin Powell, over important policy issues, such as how to conduct the war in Iraq.

General James Jones was the first NSA under President Obama. For almost two years he took a leading role in identifying threats and establishing priorities. Jones stressed the need to focus not only on traditional security threats such as terrorism and weapons of mass destruction but on the linkage between poverty and environment and security threats.[20] In addition, Jones announced a reorganization and merger of the National Security Council and Homeland Security Council staffs in the hopes of creating a broader and more efficient organization able to address the numerous issues affecting domestic and international security.[21] Jones retired in 2010 and was replaced by one of his former deputies, Tom Donilon.

When foreign policy issues become important to the public, then public opinion can influence foreign policy.

In a democracy, it is important that the citizens electing government officials have opinions on foreign policy. Moreover, what those citizens think ought to have some effect on what elected officials perceive to be important. However, many scholars are skeptical about how much the public really matters in shaping foreign policy.[22] They suggest not only that foreign policy does not matter to the public but also that the public does not matter to foreign policy. The public, they say, is disinterested in foreign policy decisions.[23]

More recently, some scholars have suggested the opposite—the public does care about foreign affairs and is actually quite "prudent" in assessing and critiquing foreign policy.[24] Still others argue that while the public matters, some groups matter more than others. That is, organized interest groups with fund-raising and mobilization capabilities and knowledge-based experts may have more impact than the average voter in influencing foreign policy. According to this view, there are, in fact, different publics. The mass public refers to those people who are not really very interested or informed about foreign policy and thus have no role in trying to influence opinion. The attentive public is the people who pay more attention to foreign policy issues and who may try to influence officials occasionally through letters, e-mails, phone calls, etc. The elite public refers to those people who are more heavily involved in foreign policy, either because they have financial means or access, occupy positions of power or authority, are active in private industry, or belong to significant interest groups.

In a study about who really influences foreign policy, Jacobs and Page suggest that "internationally oriented business leaders exercise strong, consistent, and perhaps lopsided influence on the makers of U.S. foreign policy."[25] They also find that experts such as scientists influence policy choices. Recent reevaluations of American environmental policy serve to support this claim. With more dire scientific evidence demonstrating climate change and its impact, U.S. policy is beginning to shift.

How do leaders know what the public is thinking, and why does public opinion matter? Polls conducted by newspapers, television stations, news services, private organizations, and other agencies give elected officials insight into public sentiments. The sentiments often change over time. For example, following the terrorist attacks of September 11, 2001, a 2002 public opinion poll about foreign policy indicated 68 percent of those surveyed felt that maintaining superior military power worldwide was very important.[26] More recent polling data reveals a shift in public opinion regarding what the most important priorities for the United States ought to be. In a series of New York Times/CBS News polls conducted from October 2006 up through February 2011, the most important problem confronting the country was the economy, up from 7 percent in 1996 to 48 percent in 2011.[27] The percentage of those who felt Iraq was the most important problem confronting the country decreased from 10 percent to 4 percent in that same time frame. Most surprising was that people who felt terrorism was the most important problem facing the country decreased from 12 percent to 2 percent. The trend indicates that the public opinion on foreign policy is volatile, shaped by the most recent crises.

Elected officials care about public opinion because when foreign policy becomes a significant concern to the mass public, electors can vote officials out of office if the government has been ineffective. A good example is the 2008 election. Although President George W. Bush was not running for reelection, many Republican members of the House and Senate were. In many ways, the election was a referendum on Bush's foreign policy, especially the war in Iraq. In New York Times/CBS News polls conducted over the course of Bush's two terms, respondents were asked the question "Do you approve or disapprove of the way George W. Bush is handling his job as president?" In February 2001, 53 percent of those surveyed approved of his performance.[28] In October 2001, this rose to 90 percent. However, by July 2003, Bush's approval rating dropped to 54 percent and continued to decline until he left office in January 2009, with a low of 22 percent of people approving of his conduct as president.[29]

3 The media educate and focus public attention on specific foreign policy issues.

Different forms of media—print, broadcast, and electronic—are now more easily accessible than ever before. Some of the information the media provides is factual; journalists report what is going on in Iraq, Afghanistan, and the Sudan. Other information is opinionated; op ed pieces, editorials, and blogs serve to influence people as well. Blog sites like CNN, NY Times, Fox News, rightwingnews.com, and MoveOn.org fill this function. The media's coverage helps to cue the public and policymakers about what is important and what foreign policy actions the United States should undertake.

Media coverage has a second important effect upon foreign policy and the public. Because most people get their information from the news, it has a tremendous impact on how much the public knows about politics, political attitudes, and political activity.[30] If the news covers a humanitarian crisis, the public might feel compelled to try to influence U.S. foreign policy. For example, just 9 weeks after the devastating earthquake hit Haiti in early 2010, American charities had raised more than $1 billion to support relief efforts. The money raised was in large part due to the extensive media coverage that followed the disaster. In response to a celebrity telethon broadcast on most major television stations, donors gave approximately $66 million.[31] While an impressive number, this is not nearly as large as the amount of funding generated by domestic and international coverage of the 2004 Asian tsunamis. As Table 12.4 shows, in that case donations topped $3.16 billion.

In addition to traditional news sources, "soft news" outlets are playing an even greater role in foreign policy. Increased coverage of foreign policy issues in mainstream entertainment media such as *Entertainment Tonight*, *The Daily Show*, and the *Colbert Report* make the public more aware of ongoing problems and crises.[32] The mass public is giving way to a somewhat more attentive public.

An additional role the media plays in foreign policy is in providing oversight of policy actions. Often the public is unaware of decisions undertaken by the government on individual foreign policy problems. However, the media are responsible for reporting whether or not the government behaves within the boundaries of what is constitutional and acceptable to the American people. For example, the media coverage beginning in the spring of 2005 of prisoner abuses at Abu Ghraib in Iraq and Guantanamo Bay, Cuba, led the public and Congress to question the tactics of

Table 12.4 **Money Donated by Various Organizations to Support Relief Efforts Following the 2004 Asian Tsunamis**

Organization	Donation Amount
American Red Cross	$194 million
U.S. Fund for UNICEF	$58 million
Catholic Relief Services	$41 million
Save the Children	$32 million
World Vision, USA	$24.1 million
CARE, USA	$23 million
Oxfam America	$20 million
Doctors Without Borders, USA	$20 million
Mercy Corps	$18 million
AmeriCares	$16 million

Source: Chronicle of Philanthropy, January 19, 2005, available at: http://philanthropy.com/free/update/2005/01/2005011901.htm (accessed May 31, 2009).

the American military and the role of the Bush administration in authorizing such techniques even in the name of the war on terror. The media prompted widespread investigations in Congress and the subsequent rescinding of executive orders by President Obama.

2 The pursuit of national security can compromise civil liberties.

National security The desire to keep a country's borders intact, to protect the population and the country's resources, and to ensure that a country's values and ideals are sacrosanct.

In the pursuit of American national interests in foreign policy, there have been and are always tensions among which goals ought to take priority. Perhaps the most important and obvious tension has been between national security and the protection of civil liberties.[33] **National security** is always a priority for any nation—the desire to keep a country's borders intact, to protect the population and the country's resources, and to ensure that a country's values and ideals are sacrosanct. However, oftentimes it is difficult to keep a land and people safe while also ensuring their ideals. Trying to discover individuals and uncover information that might compromise the safety of America is essential. But also important is how the government allows this to be done within the parameters of the Bill of Rights. Is it permissible to limit or infringe upon certain individuals' liberties in the name of national security? When? Under what conditions?

For the better part of the twentieth century, U.S. policy identified threats to national security that raised questions about civil liberties. During World War I, President Woodrow Wilson was concerned about creating public support for American involvement in the war and identifying domestic opposition or threats to this goal. To ensure national security, the United States passed two pieces of legislation. The first was the Espionage Act of 1917. This law prohibited anyone from assisting the enemy or interfering with the draft. The second law passed was the Sedition Act of 1918.[34] This law prevented Americans from speaking out against or criticizing the war. This latter law put significant limits on the right to free speech and received criticism from many citizens. In this case, the government felt that the right to free speech was less important than supporting American participation in the war.

During the Cold War, the government became concerned with identifying Communists or Communist sympathizers who might undermine U.S. national security. As was the case in World War I, the U.S. government took active measures to ensure that this would not occur. For example, the House of Representatives convened a special committee called the House Committee on Un-American Activities (HUAC) to investigate possible threats to national security. The director of the FBI, J. Edgar Hoover, kept a list of over 12,000 Americans whose political opinions might threaten the United States. He also created Operation Counterintelligence to identify and disrupt potential dissidents in the United States through illegal surveillance and wiretaps, tactics that raise questions about people's rights to political views and protection from invasion of privacy.

Patriot Act An act passed by Congress in 2001 that was designed to equip government and law enforcement agencies with tools to better protect the United States from terrorism.

Post-9/11, these same sorts of tensions exist. Perhaps the best example is the **Patriot Act**. Passed by Congress in October of 2001, the Patriot Act was designed to equip government and law enforcement agencies with tools to better protect the United States from terrorism. The specific provisions of the act are wide-ranging, but some of the key elements included allowing law enforcement agencies to search electronic and telephone communications and financial and medical records and to conduct surveillance on suspected terrorists, and to detain foreign and domestic suspects without typical protections. Some believe the provisions are essential to the protection of America; others have criticized the Patriot Act for going too far in sacrificing civil liberties in the name of national security.

Another example of this tension is the warrantless wiretapping controversy. Since 9/11, the National Security Agency (NSA) has engaged in the surveillance of individuals within the United States to collect intelligence about terrorist plots at home and abroad. By President Bush's executive order, the NSA was authorized to monitor, without warrants, telephone calls, e-mail, and other electronic communication that might involve any person believed to be associated with terrorist activities. To this end, the NSA was given total access to all fiber-optic communications going between some of the nation's major telecommunication companies, which include phone conversations, e-mail, Web browsing, and corporate private network traffic. As in the case of the Patriot Act, this activity has been criticized by many as unduly sacrificing civil liberties for security, while others feel it is absolutely necessary.

As a result of globalization, economic, environmental, and healthcare issues are increasingly moving into the realm of foreign policy.

Globalization A process through which countries of the world become further integrated via increased communication, technology, and exchange. This results in greater exposure and connections among economies, societies, and cultures.

Many factors shape the goals and methods of U.S. foreign policy. Although many of these factors are domestic, they are not the only forces at play. We live in a world of rapid **globalization**, and the problems confronting the United States are not limited to its borders. Economic crises, immigration, environmental challenges, and the spread of HIV/AIDS and other diseases illustrate the need for the United States to partner with other actors to resolve its most pressing problems. The stock market falls in one country and economic instability spreads across the world. Global climate change, caused by worldwide industrialization, affects all countries to one extent or another. Nations need to work together to solve these and other problems. As a result, economic policies, healthcare, and other political issues that once lay exclusively in the realm of domestic decision making are increasingly moving into the international realm.

Perhaps one of the most obvious indications of this trend is the rise of international organizations that deal with these issues. The economic sphere in particular has seen growth in trade blocks and other organizations. In 1994, the United States entered into the North American Free Trade Agreement (NAFTA) with Mexico and Canada, eliminating barriers to trade and investment among these three countries. NAFTA arose in the wake of the successful venture by European countries to establish a European trading block, now part of the European Union (EU). The EU has moved beyond lifting trade restrictions to establishing its own parliamentary system and its own currency. Other organizations, such as the G-8 and the World Trade Organization, attempt to establish international economic policies.

Noneconomic arenas have also witnessed the growth of international organizations to handle issues that a single country alone can no longer effectively address. In healthcare, the role of the World Health Organization (WHO) has been crucial in mitigating the threats caused by outbreaks of bird flu, swine flu, antibiotic-resistant tuberculosis, and other deadly diseases. By monitoring and issuing recommendations, the WHO has helped contain outbreaks that travel quickly across the world. In 2009, an outbreak of H1N1 flu led countries to work with international organizations and pharmaceutical companies to quickly get a sample of the virus, develop a vaccine, and distribute it. Countries could not simply close the door to international travel, so instead national and local governments had to decide how the vaccine should be distributed and who should get the vaccine first.

These examples underscore another trend. As health, environmental, and economic problems become more global in nature, the United States has less ability to protect its citizens from these types of crises and less choice over domestic policy.

CONCLUSION

The Constitution carefully defines the role of Congress and the executive branch in foreign policy. The Senate has the power to ratify or refuse to ratify treaties. Only Congress can declare war. But in a world in which wars are fought without formal declarations and international arrangements are less structured by formal treaties, the power of Congress is diminishing—and the power of the president, his appointed Cabinet, and the NSC is increasing. Moreover, as globalization intensifies and the world becomes smaller, more and more issues—economic stability, the environment, and health—move into the realm of foreign relations. Therefore, not only is the power of the president increasing but his jurisdiction is expanding as well.

Is this a good thing? As we have seen, public opinion and the media also play a role in setting the values and the issues that the federal government pursues through diplomacy and war. Is it more likely that the president and his appointed staff will take under additional advisement what the public has to say? Will the online media boom leave the public better informed? Many of these questions cannot yet be answered, but the trends are clear. Foreign policy is increasingly led by the president, and the challenges we face, including nuclear proliferation, worldwide epidemics, and major threats, cannot be controlled exclusively by one country—however powerful.

THEIR LIST

An Insider's View

DANIEL D.C. DON NANJIRA

Former Ambassador and Permanent Representative of Kenya to the UN Mission

Dr. Daniel D. C. Don Nanjira has spent more than 30 years in the Kenyan diplomatic service, rising to the rank of Ambassador Extraordinary and Plenipotentiary/Permanent Representative in bilateral and multilateral diplomacy. He is a former ambassador of Kenya to Italy, Greece, Poland, Turkey, and Cyprus and Malta and permanent representative of Kenya to the United Nations Mission. Dr. Don Nanjira spent more than ten years working as part of senior United Nations staff based in Geneva, Switzerland and New York, where he was the Director of the World Meteorological Organization for North America. He also serves as a representative of Kenya to the Food and Agriculture Organization of the United Nations, the International Fund for Agricultural Development, the World Food Programme, the World Food Council, and various other international organizations in Geneva.

When I asked Dr. Nanjira to reflect on the most important things he thinks people should know about American foreign policy from his perspective as a former ambassador to the UN, one of the first comments he made was the following: "American leadership of the free world has always been teeming with contradictions. This is my opinion. It is like wanting to eat your cake, and have it at the same time! It is true, I believe, that the United States has not taken advantage of her power in the world, as the richest and most powerful nation on earth. The United States could have led the free world even during the Cold War era, but handicaps have faced America during these years [the period is the post–WW II era: from 1945 to the present]."

When I asked Dr. Nanjira why this was, he said the main cause is an "arrogance of power" in the United States, which he said is "not helpful to the cause of American foreign policy."

Nanjira went on to explain that "An arrogance of power isolates and breeds hatred toward America, because any powerful nation that bullies, or that aims at demonstrating its might and big stick, will be hated by others. . . . At the UN, the behavior of some American delegations in drafting and adopting resolutions, and demanding that other nations 'support America or else,' isolates many U.S. stands on international issues. A good leader is one who listens attentively, and shows that he/she cares about the ideas and problems and interests and concerns of others. But if developing nations are accused of 'corruption and poor leadership,' and of violations of human rights, while in the United States corruption of the highest order happens, and rocks Wall Street, and poverty and exploitation of the poor consume most Americans in Harlem, etc., then it becomes very difficult to convince those who are preached to, of whatever ideas that American government representatives may preach. The poor often say they would prefer to be poor in dignity, rather than being lectured to on governance and government the 'American way.' These are serious paradoxes that have repercussions in American foreign policy practices."

YOUR LIST REVISITED

At the beginning of the chapter you were asked to think about what you might include on your own list of the Top 10 Most Important Things to Know About Foreign Policy. Now that you have read the chapter, take a moment to revisit your list. What, if anything, would you change about your list? Do you agree or disagree with the chapter list constructed by the author? What might you add or delete? Why?

KEY TERMS

Anti-Ballistic Missile Treaty 271
Bilateral treaties 270
Bricker Amendment 275
Case Zablocki Act 275
Cold War 265
Collective security 265
Comprehensive Test Ban Treaty 271
Containment 265
Department of Homeland Security (DHS) 266
Executive agreements 272
Executive orders 272
Foreign policy 264
Globalization 281
League of Nations 267
Multilateral treaties 270
National interests 264
National security 280
National Security Adviser (NSA) 276
National Security Council (NSC) 276
NATO 265
National Security Report (NSC)-68 265
Nuclear arms race 267
Patriot Act 281
Preemptive force 265
Strategic Defense Initiative (Star Wars) 271
Torrijos-Carter Treaty 270
Treaty 270
Treaty of Versailles 266
War Powers Resolution 269
Zero-sum 267

CHAPTER REVIEW QUESTIONS

10 What is foreign policy?

9 In what ways are the president's attempts to shape foreign policy limited by international and national contexts?

8 Why does Congress have the right to declare war? What limits exist on the president's right to commit troops?

7 How does the Senate affect foreign policy? Is the Senate's influence in foreign policy diminishing? Why or why not?

6 What are the differences between the two methods the executive can use for circumventing Senate ratification of treaties?

5 What role does the National Security Council play in U.S. foreign policy?

4 How does public opinion influence foreign policy?

3 What role do the media play in framing issues for the public and policymakers?

2 How can the pursuit of national security compromise civil liberties?

1 Can the United States create foreign policy without concern for other actors in the international community? Why or why not?

SUGGESTED READINGS

- Adler, David Gray, Larry N. George, and Arthur Meier Schlesinger, Jr. *The Constitution and the Conduct of American Foreign Policy.* Lawrence, KS: University of Kansas Press, 1996.
- Baum, Matthew. *Soft News Goes to War.* Princeton, NJ: Princeton University Press, 2003.
- Brzezinski, Zbigniew, and Brent Scowcroft. *America and the World: Conversations on the Future of American Foreign Policy.* New York: Basic Books, 2008.
- Friedman, Thomas. *Hot, Flat, and Crowded.* New York: Farrar, Straus and Giroux, 2008.

- Jervis, Robert. *American Foreign Policy in a New Era.* New York: Routledge, 2005.
- Kelly, Donald R., ed. *Divided Power: The Presidency, Congress, and the Formation of American Foreign Policy.* Fayetteville, AR: University of Arkansas Press, 2005.
- Peleg, Ilan. *The Legacy of George W. Bush's Foreign Policy: Moving Beyond Neoconservativism.* Boulder, CO: Westview Press, 2009.
- Sanger, David E. *The Inheritance: The World Obama Confronts and the Challenges to American Power.* New York: Three Rivers Press, 2009.
- U.S. Congress. *9/11 Commission Report.* Washington, DC: U.S. G.P.O, 2005.
- Zakaria, Fareed. *Post-American World.* New York: W.W. Norton, 2008.

SUGGESTED FILMS

- *The Ugly American* (1963)
- *Dr. Strangelove* (1964)
- *Seven Days in May* (1964)
- *Red Dawn* (1984)
- *Born on the Fourth of July* (1989)
- *The War Room* (1993)
- *Wag the Dog* (1997)
- *Black Hawk Down* (2001)
- *Fog of War* (2003)
- *Why We Fight* (2005)

SUGGESTED WEBSITES

- **Catholic Relief Services:** http://www.crs.org.
- **Council on Foreign Relations:** http://www.cfr.org.
- **PollingReport.com:** http://www.pollingreport.com.
- **The Economist:** http://www.economist.com/.
- ***The New York Times:*** http://www.nytimes.com.
- **The United States Senate:** http://www.senate.gov.
- **The United States House of Representatives:** http://www.house.gov.
- **The White House:** http://www.whitehouse.gov.
- **United Nations:** http://www.un.org.
- **U.S. Department of State:** http://www.state.gov.

ENDNOTES

[1]Justin McCurry and Tania Branigan, "North Korea Tests Nuclear Weapon 'as Powerful as Hiroshima Bomb,'" *The Guardian*, May 25, 2009, available at: http://www.guardian.co.uk/world/2009/may/25/north-korea-hiroshima-nuclear-test.

[2]For a general discussion of the concept of foreign policy, see Hans Morgenthau, *Politics Among Nations: The Struggle for Power and Peace* (New York: Knopf, 1973); James N. Rosenau, "The Study of Foreign Policy" in James N. Rosenau, Gavin Boyd, and Kenneth W. Thompson, eds., *World Politics* (New York: Free Press, 1976), pp. 15–35. For greater discussion of the national interest, see James N. Rosenau, "The National Interest," in James N. Rosenau, *The Scientific Study of Foreign Policy* (London: Frances Pinter, 1980), pp. 283–293; Hans J. Morgenthau, *Another "Great Debate": The National Interest of the United States,* in John A. Vasquez, ed., *Classics of International Relations*, 3rd ed. (Upper Saddle River, NJ: Prentice Hall, 1995); Arnold Wolfers, *"National Security" as an Ambiguous Symbol,"* in Vasquez, ed. *Classics of International Relations.*

[3]See, for example, James M. Scott and Ralph G. Carter, "Acting on the Hill: Congressional Assertiveness in U.S. Foreign Policy," *Congress and the Presidency*, 29 (2, Autumn 2002): 151–169.

[4]George Kennan, "The Sources of Soviet Conduct" *Foreign Affairs,* 65 (4, Spring 1987): 852–868. See also Michael J. Hogan, *A Cross of Iron: Harry S. Truman and the Origins of the National Security State, 1945–1954* (Cambridge, UK: Cambridge University Press, 1998); Ernest R. May, *American Cold War Strategy: Interpreting NSC 68* (Boston: Bedford/St. Martin's Press, 1993).

[5]William J. Clinton, "National Security Strategy of Engagement and Enlargement," White House, 1996.

[6]George W. Bush, "National Security Strategy of the United States," 2002, 2006. See also Robert Jervis, "Understanding the Bush Doctrine," *Political Science Quarterly,* 118 (September 2003): 365–388.
[7]Barack Obama, Office of the Press Secretary, May 21, 2009. "Remarks by the President on National Security" (National Archives, Washington, DC); Sheryl Gay Stolberg, "Obama Won't Bar Inquiry, or Penalty, on Interrogations," *New York Times,* April 22, 2009.
[8]Jeffrey E. Cohen, "Presidential Rhetoric and the Public Agenda" *American Journal of Political Science* 39 (February 1995): 87–107.
[9]United States House of Representatives Joint Resolution 114, October 16, 2002.
[10]See Richard F. Grimmett, *The War Powers Resolution: After Twenty-Eight Years* (Washington DC: Congressional Research Service, November 20, 2001); Grimmett, *War Powers Resolution: Presidential Compliance* (Washington, DC: Congressional Research Service, September 16, 2001).
[11]In response to President Obama's actions regarding Libya, Rep. Dennis Kucinich (D-OH) stated, "This president has assumed power that no president, not even President Bush, has assumed. I think that we need to focus on this, not as a matter of whether we like President Obama or not, not as a matter of whether we are Democrats or not, but whether or not we understand the basic constitutional principles of the separation of power." "Democracy Now: The War and Peace Report," available at: http://www.democracynow.org/2011/4/1/rep_kucinich_lack_of_congressional_approval (accessed May 20, 2011).
[12]Comprehensive Nuclear Test Ban Treaty, available at: http://www.state.gov/www/global/arms/treaties/ctbt/ctbt-art01.html (accessed May 3–5, 2009).
[13]Congressional Research Service, Treaties and Other International Agreements, available at: http://frwebgate.access.gpo.gov/cgi-bin/getdoc.cgi?dbname=106_cong_senate_print&docid=f:66922.wais. p. 21 (accessed May 30, 2009).
[14]Congressional Research Service, Treaties and Other International Agreements, available at: http://frwebgate.access.gpo.gov/cgi-bin/getdoc.cgi?dbname=106_cong_senate_print&docid=f:66922.wais, p. 17 (accessed May 30, 2009).
[15]http://www.whitehouse.gov/briefing_room/PresidentialActions/ (accessed May 30, 2009).
[16]Congressional Research Service, Treaties and Other International Agreements, available at: http://frwebgate.access.gpo.gov/cgi-bin/getdoc.cgi?dbname=106_cong_senate_print&docid=f:66922.wais (accessed May 30, 2009).
[17]See, for example, John R. Bolton and John Yoo, "Restore the Senate's Treaty Power," *The New York Times,* January 5, 2009, p. A21.
[18]http://www.state.gov/s/l/treaty/caseact/. "Reporting International Agreements to Congress Under the Case Act"
[19]Ivo H. Daalder and I. M. Destler, In the Shadow of the Oval Office: Profiles of the National Security Advisers and the Presidents They Served—From JFK to George W. Bush (New York: Simon & Schuster; 2009); David J. Rothkopf, *Running The World: The Inside Story of the National Security Council and the Architects of American Power* (New York: PublicAffairs (Publisher), 2006).
[20]"The National Security Council: Running the World," *The Economist,* February 12, 2009, available at: http://www.economist.com/node/13110064 (accessed October 20, 2011).
[21]*Voice of America News,* "National Security Adviser Helps Obama with Waves of Global Threats," May 28, 200, available at: http://www.voanews.com/english/2009-05-28-voa55.cfm (accessed May 31, 2009).
[22]See Lawrence R. Jacobs and Benjamin I. Page, "Who Influences U.S. Foreign Policy," *American Political Science Review,* 99 (1, February 2005): 107–123; Philip Powlick and Andrew Z. Katz, "Defining the American Public Opinion/Foreign Policy Nexus," *Mershon International Studies Review,* 42 (1998): 29–61; Philip Powlick, "The Sources of Public Opinion for American Foreign Policy Officials," *International Studies Quarterly,* 39 (1995): 427–451.
[23]Gabriel Almond, *The American People and Foreign Policy* (New York: Praeger, 1960); Bernard Coher, *The Public's Impact on Foreign Policy* (Boston: Little, Brown, 1973).
[24]See Thomas W. Graham, "Public Opinion and U.S. Foreign Policy Decision Making," in David A. Deese, ed., *The New Politics of American Foreign Policy* (New York: St. Martin's Press, 1994); Benjamin I. Page and Robert Y. Shapiro, *The Rational Public: Fifty Year of Trends in Americans' Policy Preferences* (Chicago: University of Chicago Press, 1992.); Bruce W. Jentleson, "The Pretty Prudent Public: Post-Vietnam American Opinion on the Use of Military Force," *International Studies Quarterly,* 36 (1992): 49–74.
[25]Jacobs and Page, "Who Influences U.S. Foreign Policy?" *American Political Science Review,* 99 (1, 2005): 120.
[26]Chicago Council on Foreign Relations, "Worldviews 2002: American Public Opinion and Foreign Policy," (2002), available at: http://www.worldviews.org/detailreports/usreport/index.htm (accessed May 31,2009).
[27]New York Times/CBS News, *New York Times/CBS News Poll: Obama's First 100 Days in Office,* April 22–26, 2009, available at: http://documents.nytimes.com/new-york-times-cbs-news-poll-obama-s-100th-day-in-office#p=5 (accessed May 31, 2009); CBS News, February 11–14, 2011, available at: http://www.pollingreport.com/prioriti.htm (accessed February 16, 2011).
[28]New York Times/CBS News, *New York Times/CBS News Poll,*, January 11–15, 2009, available at: http://graphics8.nytimes.com/packages/pdf/politics/20090117gwb_poll.pdf, p. 2 (accessed May 31, 2009).
[29]Ibid.
[30]John Zaller, Thomas J. Volgy, and John E. Schwarz, "On Television Viewing and Citizens' Political Attitudes, Activity, and Knowledge: Another Look at the Impact of Media on Politics," *Western Political Quarterly* (December 1978): 668–84
[31]See, for instance, http://philanthropy.com/article/American-Charities-Raise-Close/64684/ (accessed May 20, 2011).
[32]See, for example, Matthew Baum, *Soft News Goes to War: Public Opinion and Foreign Policy in the New Media Age* (Princeton, NJ: Princeton University Press, 2003).
[33]David B. Cohen and John W. Wells, eds., *American National Security and Civil Liberties in an Era of Terrorism* (New York: Palgrave, 2004); Daniel Farber, *Security versus Liberty: Conflicts Between Civil Liberties and National Security in American History* (New York: Russell Sage Foundation Publications, 2008); Laura K. Donohue, *The Cost of Counterterrorism: Power, Politics, and Libert,* (Cambridge, UK: Cambridge University Press, 2008).
[34]See, for example, John C. Miller, *Crisis in Freedom: The Alien and Sedition Acts* (Boston: Little Brown, 1951).

APPENDIX 1

The Declaration of Independence

***Note:** This text retains the spelling, capitalization, and punctuation of the original.*

IN CONGRESS, July 4, 1776.

The unanimous Declaration of the thirteen united States of America,

When in the Course of human events, it becomes necessary for one people to dissolve the political bands which have connected them with another, and to assume among the powers of the earth, the separate and equal station to which the Laws of Nature and of Nature's God entitle them, a decent respect to the opinions of mankind requires that they should declare the causes which impel them to the separation.

We hold these truths to be self-evident, that all men are created equal, that they are endowed by their Creator with certain unalienable Rights, that among these are Life, Liberty and the pursuit of Happiness.—That to secure these rights, Governments are instituted among Men, deriving their just powers from the consent of the governed,—That whenever any Form of Government becomes destructive of these ends, it is the Right of the People to alter or to abolish it, and to institute new Government, laying its foundation on such principles and organizing its powers in such form, as to them shall seem most likely to effect their Safety and Happiness. Prudence, indeed, will dictate that Governments long established should not be changed for light and transient causes; and accordingly all experience hath shewn, that mankind are more disposed to suffer, while evils are sufferable, than to right themselves by abolishing the forms to which they are accustomed. But when a long train of abuses and usurpations, pursuing invariably the same Object evinces a design to reduce them under absolute Despotism, it is their right, it is their duty, to throw off such Government, and to provide new Guards for their future security.—Such has been the patient sufferance of these Colonies; and such is now the necessity which constrains them to alter their former Systems of Government. The history of the present King of Great Britain is a history of repeated injuries and usurpations, all having in direct object the establishment of an absolute Tyranny over these States. To prove this, let Facts be submitted to a candid world.

He has refused his Assent to Laws, the most wholesome and necessary for the public good.

He has forbidden his Governors to pass Laws of immediate and pressing importance, unless suspended in their operation till his Assent should be obtained; and when so suspended, he has utterly neglected to attend to them.

He has refused to pass other Laws for the accommodation of large districts of people, unless those people would relinquish the right of Representation in the Legislature, a right inestimable to them and formidable to tyrants only.

He has called together legislative bodies at places unusual, uncomfortable, and distant from the depository of their public Records, for the sole purpose of fatiguing them into compliance with his measures.

He has dissolved Representative Houses repeatedly, for opposing with manly firmness his invasions on the rights of the people.

He has refused for a long time, after such dissolutions, to cause others to be elected; whereby the Legislative powers, incapable of Annihilation, have returned to the People at large for their exercise; the State remaining in the mean time exposed to all the dangers of invasion from without, and convulsions within.

He has endeavoured to prevent the population of these States; for that purpose obstructing the Laws for Naturalization of Foreigners; refusing to pass others to encourage their migrations hither, and raising the conditions of new Appropriations of Lands.

He has obstructed the Administration of Justice, by refusing his Assent to Laws for establishing Judiciary powers.

He has made Judges dependent on his Will alone, for the tenure of their offices, and the amount and payment of their salaries.

He has erected a multitude of New Offices, and sent hither swarms of Officers to harrass our people, and eat out their substance.

He has kept among us, in times of peace, Standing Armies without the Consent of our legislatures.

He has affected to render the Military independent of and superior to the Civil power.

He has combined with others to subject us to a jurisdiction foreign to our constitution, and unacknowledged by our laws; giving his Assent to their Acts of pretended Legislation:

For Quartering large bodies of armed troops among us:

For protecting them, by a mock Trial, from punishment for any Murders which they should commit on the Inhabitants of these States:

For cutting off our Trade with all parts of the world:

For imposing Taxes on us without our Consent:

For depriving us in many cases, of the benefits of Trial by Jury:

For transporting us beyond Seas to be tried for pretended offences:

For abolishing the free System of English Laws in a neighbouring Province, establishing therein an Arbitrary government, and enlarging its Boundaries so as to render it at once an example and fit instrument for introducing the same absolute rule into these Colonies:

For taking away our Charters, abolishing our most valuable Laws, and altering fundamentally the Forms of our Governments:

For suspending our own Legislatures, and declaring themselves invested with power to legislate for us in all cases whatsoever.

He has abdicated Government here, by declaring us out of his Protection and waging War against us.

He has plundered our seas, ravaged our Coasts, burnt our towns, and destroyed the lives of our people.

He is at this time transporting large Armies of foreign Mercenaries to compleat the works of death, desolation and tyranny, already begun with circumstances of Cruelty & perfidy scarcely paralleled in the most barbarous ages, and totally unworthy the Head of a civilized nation.

He has constrained our fellow Citizens taken Captive on the high Seas to bear Arms against their Country, to become the executioners of their friends and Brethren, or to fall themselves by their Hands.

He has excited domestic insurrections amongst us, and has endeavoured to bring on the inhabitants of our frontiers, the merciless Indian Savages, whose known rule of warfare, is an undistinguished destruction of all ages, sexes and conditions.

In every stage of these Oppressions We have Petitioned for Redress in the most humble terms: Our repeated Petitions have been answered only by repeated injury. A Prince whose character is thus marked by every act which may define a Tyrant, is unfit to be the ruler of a free people.

Nor have We been wanting in attentions to our Brittish brethren. We have warned them from time to time of attempts by their legislature to extend an unwarrantable jurisdiction over us. We have reminded them of the circumstances of our emigration and settlement here. We have appealed to their native justice and magnanimity, and we have conjured them by the ties of our common kindred to disavow these usurpations, which, would inevitably interrupt our connections and correspondence. They too have been deaf to the voice of justice and of consanguinity. We must, therefore, acquiesce in the necessity, which denounces our Separation, and hold them, as we hold the rest of mankind, Enemies in War, in Peace Friends.

We, therefore, the Representatives of the united States of America, in General Congress, Assembled, appealing to the Supreme Judge of the world for the rectitude of our intentions, do, in the Name, and by Authority of the good People of these Colonies, solemnly publish and declare, That these United Colonies are, and of Right ought to be Free and Independent States; that they are Absolved from all Allegiance to the British Crown, and that all political connection between them and the State of Great Britain, is and ought to be totally dissolved; and that as Free and Independent States, they have full Power to levy War, conclude Peace, contract Alliances, establish Commerce, and to do all other Acts and Things which Independent States may of right do. And for the support of this Declaration, with a firm reliance on the protection of divine Providence, we mutually pledge to each other our Lives, our Fortunes and our sacred Honor.

The 56 signatures on the Declaration were the following:

GEORGIA
Button Gwinnett
Lyman Hall
George Walton

NORTH CAROLINA
William Hooper
Joseph Hewes
John Penn

SOUTH CAROLINA
Edward Rutledge
Thomas Heyward, Jr.
Thomas Lynch, Jr.
Arthur Middleton

MARYLAND
Samuel Chase
William Paca
Thomas Stone
Charles Carroll of Carrollton

VIRGINIA
George Wythe
Richard Henry Lee
Thomas Jefferson
Benjamin Harrison
Thomas Nelson, Jr.
Francis Lightfoot Lee
Carter Braxton

PENNSYLVANIA
Robert Morris
Benjamin Rush
Benjamin Franklin
John Morton
George Clymer
James Smith
George Taylor
James Wilson
George Ross

DELAWARE
Caesar Rodney
George Read
Thomas McKean

NEW YORK
William Floyd
Philip Livingston
Francis Lewis
Lewis Morris

NEW JERSEY
Richard Stockton
John Witherspoon
Francis Hopkinson
John Hart
Abraham Clark

NEW HAMPSHIRE
Josiah Bartlett
William Whipple
Matthew Thornton

MASSACHUSETTS
Samuel Adams
John Adams
Robert Treat Paine
Elbridge Gerry
John Hancock

RHODE ISLAND
Stephen Hopkins
William Ellery

CONNECTICUT
Roger Sherman
Samuel Huntington
William Williams
Oliver Wolcott

APPENDIX 2

The Constitution of the United States of America

Note: This text retains the spelling, capitalization, and punctuation of the original. Brackets indicate passages that have been altered by amendments.

We the People of the United States, in Order to form a more perfect Union, establish Justice, insure domestic Tranquility, provide for the common defence, promote the general Welfare, and secure the Blessings of Liberty to ourselves and our Posterity, do ordain and establish this Constitution for the United States of America.

Article I

Section 1. All legislative Powers herein granted shall be vested in a Congress of the United States, which shall consist of a Senate and House of Representatives.

Section 2. The House of Representatives shall be composed of Members chosen every second Year by the People of the several States, and the Electors in each State shall have the Qualifications requisite for Electors of the most numerous Branch of the State Legislature.

No Person shall be a Representative who shall not have attained to the Age of twenty five Years, and been seven Years a Citizen of the United States, and who shall not, when elected, be an Inhabitant of that State in which he shall be chosen.

Representatives and direct [Taxes][1] shall be apportioned among the several States which may be included within this Union, according to their respective Numbers, [which shall be determined by adding to the whole Number of free Persons, including those bound to Service for a Term of Years, and excluding Indians not taxed, three fifths of all other Persons].[2] The actual Enumeration shall be made within three Years after the first Meeting of the Congress of the United States, and within every subsequent Term of ten Years, in such Manner as they shall by Law direct. The Number of Representatives shall not exceed one for every thirty Thousand, but each State shall have at Least one Representative; and until such enumeration shall be made, the State of New Hampshire shall be entitled to chuse three, Massachusetts eight, Rhode-Island and Providence Plantations one, Connecticut five, New-York six, New Jersey four, Pennsylvania eight, Delaware one, Maryland six, Virginia ten, North Carolina five, South Carolina five, and Georgia three.

When vacancies happen in the Representation from any State, the Executive Authority thereof shall issue Writs of Election to fill such Vacancies.

The House of Representatives shall chuse their Speaker and other Officers; and shall have the sole Power of Impeachment.

Section 3. The Senate of the United States shall be composed of two Senators from each State, [chosen by the Legislature thereof],[3] for six Years; and each Senator shall have one Vote.

Immediately after they shall be assembled in Consequence of the first Election, they shall be divided as equally as may be into three Classes. The Seats of the Senators of the first Class shall be vacated at the Expiration of the second Year, of the second Class at the Expiration of the fourth Year, and of the third Class at the Expiration of the sixth Year, so that one third may be chosen every second Year; [and if Vacancies happen by Resignation, or otherwise, during the Recess of the Legislature of any State, the Executive thereof may make temporary Appointments until the next Meeting of the Legislature, which shall then fill such Vacancies].[4]

No Person shall be a Senator who shall not have attained to the Age of thirty Years, and been nine Years a Citizen of the United States, and who shall not, when elected, be an Inhabitant of that State for which he shall be chosen.

The Vice President of the United States shall be President of the Senate, but shall have no Vote, unless they be equally divided.

The Senate shall chuse their other Officers, and also a President pro tempore, in the Absence of the Vice President, or when he shall exercise the Office of President of the United States.

The Senate shall have the sole Power to try all Impeachments. When sitting for that Purpose, they shall be on Oath or Affirmation. When the President of the United States is tried, the Chief Justice shall preside: And no Person shall be convicted without the Concurrence of two thirds of the Members present.

Judgment in Cases of Impeachment shall not extend further than to removal from Office, and disqualification to hold and enjoy any Office of honor, Trust or Profit under the United States: but the Party convicted shall nevertheless be liable and subject to Indictment, Trial, Judgment and Punishment, according to Law.

Section 4. The Times, Places and Manner of holding Elections for Senators and Representatives, shall be prescribed in each State by the Legislature thereof; but the Congress may at any time by Law make or alter such Regulations, except as to the Places of chusing Senators.

[The Congress shall assemble at least once in every Year, and such Meeting shall be on the first Monday in December, unless they shall by Law appoint a different Day.][5]

Section 5. Each House shall be the Judge of the Elections, Returns and Qualifications of its own Members, and a Majority of each shall constitute a Quorum to do Business; but a smaller Number may adjourn from day to day, and may be authorized to compel the Attendance of absent Members, in such Manner, and under such Penalties as each House may provide.

Each House may determine the Rules of its Proceedings, punish its Members for disorderly Behaviour, and, with the Concurrence of two thirds, expel a Member.

Each House shall keep a Journal of its Proceedings, and from time to time publish the same, excepting such Parts as may in their Judgment require Secrecy; and the Yeas and Nays of the Members of either House on any question shall, at the Desire of one fifth of those Present, be entered on the Journal.

Neither House, during the Session of Congress, shall, without the Consent of the other, adjourn for more than three days, nor to any other Place than that in which the two Houses shall be sitting.

Section 6. The Senators and Representatives shall receive a Compensation for their Services, to be ascertained by Law, and paid out of the Treasury of the United States. They shall in all Cases, except Treason, Felony and Breach of the Peace, be privileged from Arrest during their Attendance at the Session of their respective Houses, and in going to and returning from the same; and for any Speech or Debate in either House, they shall not be questioned in any other Place.

No Senator or Representative shall, during the Time for which he was elected, be appointed to any civil Office under the Authority of the United States, which shall have been created, or the Emoluments whereof shall have been encreased during such time; and no Person holding any Office under the United States, shall be a Member of either House during his Continuance in Office.

Section 7. All Bills for raising Revenue shall originate in the House of Representatives; but the Senate may propose or concur with Amendments as on other Bills.

Every Bill which shall have passed the House of Representatives and the Senate, shall, before it become a Law, be presented to the President of the United States: If he approve he shall sign it, but if not he shall return it, with his Objections to that House in which it shall have originated, who shall enter the Objections at large on their Journal, and proceed to reconsider it. If after such Reconsideration two thirds of that House shall agree to pass the Bill, it shall be sent, together with the Objections, to the other House, by which it shall likewise be reconsidered, and if approved by two thirds of that House, it shall become a Law. But in all such Cases the Votes of both Houses shall be determined by yeas and Nays, and the Names of the Persons voting for and against the Bill shall be entered on the Journal of each House respectively. If any Bill shall not be returned by the President within ten Days (Sundays excepted) after it shall have been presented to him, the Same shall be a Law, in like Manner as if he had signed it, unless the Congress by their Adjournment prevent its Return, in which Case it shall not bea Law.

Every Order, Resolution, or Vote to which the Concurrence of the Senate and House of Representatives may be necessary (except on a question of Adjournment) shall be presented to the President of the United States; and before the Same shall take Effect, shall be approved by him, or being disapproved by him, shall be repassed by two thirds of the Senate and House of Representatives, according to the Rules and Limitations prescribed in the Case of a Bill.

Section 8. The Congress shall have Power To lay and collect Taxes, Duties, Imposts and Excises, to pay the Debts and provide for the common Defence and general Welfare of the United States; but all Duties, Imposts and Excises shall be uniform throughout the United States;

To borrow Money on the credit of the United States;

To regulate Commerce with foreign Nations, and among the several States, and with the Indian Tribes;

To establish an uniform Rule of Naturalization, and uniform Laws on the subject of Bankruptcies throughout the United States;

To coin Money, regulate the Value thereof, and of foreign Coin, and fix the Standard of Weights and Measures;

To provide for the Punishment of counterfeiting the Securities and current Coin of the United States;

To establish Post Offices and post Roads;

To promote the Progress of Science and useful Arts, by securing for limited Times to Authors and Inventors the exclusive Right to their respective Writings and Discoveries;

To constitute Tribunals inferior to the supreme Court;

To define and punish Piracies and Felonies committed on the high Seas, and Offences against the Law of Nations;

To declare War, grant Letters of Marque and Reprisal, and make Rules concerning Captures on Land and Water;

To raise and support Armies, but no Appropriation of Money to that Use shall be for a longer Term than two Years;

To provide and maintain a Navy;

To make Rules for the Government and Regulation of the land and naval Forces;

To provide for calling forth the Militia to execute the Laws of the Union, suppress Insurrections and repel Invasions;

To provide for organizing, arming, and disciplining, the Militia, and for governing such Part of them as may be employed in the Service of the United States, reserving to the States respectively, the Appointment of the Officers, and the Authority of training the Militia according to the discipline prescribed by Congress;

To exercise exclusive Legislation in all Cases whatsoever, over such District (not exceeding ten Miles square) as may, by Cession of particular States, and the Acceptance of Congress, become the Seat of the Government of the United States, and to exercise like Authority over all Places purchased by the Consent of the Legislature of the State in which the Same shall be, for the Erection of Forts, Magazines, Arsenals, dock-Yards, and other needful Buildings;—And

To make all Laws which shall be necessary and proper for carrying into Execution the foregoing Powers, and all other Powers vested by this Constitution in the Government of the United States, or in any Department or Officer thereof.

Section 9. The Migration or Importation of such Persons as any of the States now existing shall think proper to admit, shall not be prohibited by the Congress prior to the Year one thousand eight hundred and eight, but a Tax or duty may be imposed on such Importation, not exceeding ten dollars for each Person.

The Privilege of the Writ of Habeas Corpus shall not be suspended, unless when in Cases of Rebellion or Invasion the public Safety may require it.

No Bill of Attainder or ex post facto Law shall be passed.

[No Capitation, or other direct, Tax shall be laid, unless in Proportion to the Census or enumeration herein before directed to be taken.][6]

No Tax or Duty shall be laid on Articles exported from any State.

No Preference shall be given by any Regulation of Commerce or Revenue to the Ports of one State over those of another; nor shall Vessels bound to, or from, one State, be obliged to enter, clear, or pay Duties in another.

No Money shall be drawn from the Treasury, but in Consequence of Appropriations made by Law; and a regular Statement and Account of the Receipts and Expenditures of all public Money shall be published from time to time.

No Title of Nobility shall be granted by the United States: And no Person holding any Office of Profit or Trust under them, shall, without the Consent of the Congress, accept of any present, Emolument, Office, or Title, of any kind whatever, from any King, Prince, or foreign State.

Section 10. No State shall enter into any Treaty, Alliance, or Confederation; grant Letters of Marque and Reprisal; coin Money; emit Bills of Credit; make any Thing but gold and silver Coin a Tender in Payment of Debts; pass any Bill of Attainder, ex post facto Law, or Law impairing the Obligation of Contracts, or grant any Title of Nobility.

No State shall, without the Consent of the Congress, lay any Imposts or Duties on Imports or Exports, except what may be absolutely necessary for executing it's inspection Laws: and the net Produce of all Duties and Imposts, laid by any State on Imports or Exports, shall be for the Use of the Treasury of the United States; and all such Laws shall be subject to the Revision and Controul of the Congress.

No State shall, without the Consent of Congress, lay any Duty of Tonnage, keep Troops, or Ships of War in time of Peace, enter into any Agreement or Compact with another State, or with a foreign Power, or engage in War, unless actually invaded, or in such imminent Danger as will not admit of delay.

Article II

Section 1. The executive Power shall be vested in a President of the United States of America. He shall hold his Office during the Term of four Years, and, together with the Vice President, chosen for the same Term, be elected, as follows:

Each State shall appoint, in such Manner as the Legislature thereof may direct, a Number of Electors, equal to the whole Number of Senators and Representatives to which the State may be entitled in the Congress: but no Senator or Representative, or Person holding an Office of Trust or Profit under the United States, shall be appointed an Elector.

[The Electors shall meet in their respective States, and vote by Ballot for two Persons, of whom one at least shall not be an Inhabitant of the same State with themselves. And they shall make a List of all the Persons voted for, and of the Number of Votes for each; which List they shall sign and certify, and transmit sealed to the Seat of the Government of the United States, directed to the President of the Senate. The President of the Senate shall, in the Presence of the Senate and House of Representatives, open all the Certificates, and the Votes shall then be counted. The Person having the greatest Number of Votes shall be the President, if such Number be a Majority of the whole Number of Electors appointed; and if there be more than one who have such Majority, and have an equal Number of Votes, then the House of Representatives shall immediately chuse by Ballot one of them for President; and if no Person have a Majority, then from the five highest on the List the said House shall in like Manner chuse the President. But in chusing the President, the Votes shall be taken by States, the Representation from each State having one Vote; A quorum for this purpose shall consist of a Member or Members from two thirds of the States, and a Majority of all the States shall be necessary to a Choice. In every Case, after the Choice of the President, the Person having the greatest Number of Votes of the Electors shall be the Vice President. But if there should remain two or more who have equal Votes, the Senate shall chuse from them by Ballot the Vice President.][7]

The Congress may determine the Time of chusing the Electors, and the Day on which they shall give their Votes; which Day shall be the same throughout the United States.

No Person except a natural born Citizen, or a Citizen of the United States, at the time of the Adoption of this Constitution, shall be eligible to the Office of President; neither shall any Person be eligible to that Office who shall not have attained to the Age of thirty five Years, and been fourteen Years a Resident within the United States.

[In Case of the Removal of the President from Office, or of his Death, Resignation, or Inability to discharge the Powers and Duties of the said Office, the Same shall devolve on the Vice President, and the Congress may by Law provide for the Case of Removal, Death, Resignation or Inability, both of the President and Vice President, declaring what Officer shall then act as President, and such Officer shall act accordingly, until the Disability be removed, or a President shall be elected.][8]

The President shall, at stated Times, receive for his Services, a Compensation, which shall neither be increased nor diminished during the Period for which he shall have been elected, and he shall not receive within that Period any other Emolument from the United States, or any of them.

Before he enter on the Execution of his Office, he shall take the following Oath or Affirmation:—"I do solemnly swear (or affirm) that I will faithfully execute the Office of President of the United States, and will to the best of my Ability, preserve, protect and defend the Constitution of the United States."

Section 2. The President shall be Commander in Chief of the Army and Navy of the United States, and of the Militia of the several States, when called into the actual Service of the United States; he may require the Opinion, in writing, of the principal Officer in each of the executive Departments, upon any Subject relating to the Duties of their respective Offices, and he shall have Power to grant Reprieves and Pardons for Offences against the United States, except in Cases of Impeachment.

He shall have Power, by and with the Advice and Consent of the Senate, to make Treaties, provided two thirds of the Senators present concur; and he shall nominate, and by and with the Advice and Consent of the Senate, shall appoint Ambassadors, other public Ministers and Consuls, Judges of the supreme Court, and all other Officers of the United States, whose Appointments are not herein otherwise provided for, and which shall be established by Law: but the Congress may by Law vest the Appointment of such inferior Officers, as they think proper, in the President alone, in the Courts of Law, or in the Heads of Departments.

The President shall have Power to fill up all Vacancies that may happen during the Recess of the Senate, by granting Commissions which shall expire at the End of their next Session.

Section 3. He shall from time to time give to the Congress Information of the State of the Union, and recommend to their Consideration such Measures as he shall judge necessary and expedient; he may, on extraordinary Occasions, convene both Houses, or either of them, and in Case of Disagreement between them, with Respect to the Time of Adjournment, he may adjourn them to such Time as he shall think proper; he shall receive Ambassadors and other public Ministers; he shall take Care that the Laws be faithfully executed, and shall Commission all the Officers of the United States.

Section 4. The President, Vice President and all civil Officers of the United States, shall be removed from Office on Impeachment for, and Conviction of, Treason, Bribery, or other high Crimes and Misdemeanors.

Article III

Section 1. The judicial Power of the United States shall be vested in one supreme Court, and in such inferior Courts as the Congress may from time to time ordain and establish. The Judges, both of the supreme and inferior Courts, shall hold their Offices during good Behaviour, and shall, at stated Times, receive for their Services a Compensation, which shall not be diminished during their Continuance in Office.

Section 2. The judicial Power shall extend to all Cases, in Law and Equity, arising under this Constitution, the Laws of the United States, and Treaties made, or which shall be made, under their Authority;—to all Cases affecting Ambassadors, other public Ministers and Consuls;—to all Cases of admiralty and maritime Jurisdiction;—to Controversies to which the United States shall be a Party;—to Controversies between two or more States; [— between a State and Citizens of another State,—][9] between Citizens of different States,—between Citizens of the same State claiming Lands under Grants of different States, [and between a State, or the Citizens thereof, and foreign States, Citizens or Subjects.][10]

In all Cases affecting Ambassadors, other public Ministers and Consuls, and those in which a State shall be Party, the supreme Court shall have original Jurisdiction. In all the other Cases before mentioned, the supreme Court shall have appellate Jurisdiction, both as to Law and Fact, with such Exceptions, and under such Regulations as the Congress shall make.

The Trial of all Crimes, except in Cases of Impeachment, shall be by Jury; and such Trial shall be held in the State where the said Crimes shall have been committed; but when not committed within any State, the Trial shall be at such Place or Places as the Congress may by Law have directed.

Section 3. Treason against the United States, shall consist only in levying War against them, or in adhering to their Enemies, giving them Aid and Comfort. No Person shall be convicted of Treason unless on the Testimony of two Witnesses to the same overt Act, or on Confession in open Court.

The Congress shall have Power to declare the Punishment of Treason, but no Attainder of Treason shall work Corruption of Blood, or Forfeiture except during the Life of the Person attainted.

Article IV

Section 1. Full Faith and Credit shall be given in each State to the public Acts, Records, and judicial Proceedings of every other State. And the Congress may by general Laws prescribe the Manner in which such Acts, Records and Proceedings shall be proved, and the Effect thereof.

Section 2. The Citizens of each State shall be entitled to all Privileges and Immunities of Citizens in the several States.

A Person charged in any State with Treason, Felony, or other Crime, who shall flee from Justice, and be found in another State, shall on Demand of the executive Authority of the State from which he fled, be delivered up, to be removed to the State having Jurisdiction of the Crime.

[No Person held to Service or Labour in one State, under the Laws thereof, escaping into another, shall, in Consequence of any Law or Regulation therein, be discharged from such Service or Labour, but shall be delivered up on Claim of the Party to whom such Service or Labour may be due.][11]

Section 3. New States may be admitted by the Congress into this Union; but no new State shall be formed or erected within the Jurisdiction of any other State; nor any State be formed by the Junction of two or more States, or Parts of States, without the Consent of the Legislatures of the States concerned as well as of the Congress.

The Congress shall have Power to dispose of and make all needful Rules and Regulations respecting the Territory or other Property belonging to the United States; and nothing in this Constitution shall be so construed as to Prejudice any Claims of the United States, or of any particular State.

Section 4. The United States shall guarantee to every State in this Union a Republican Form of Government, and shall protect each of them against Invasion; and on Application of the Legislature, or of the Executive (when the Legislature cannot be convened), against domestic Violence.

Article V

The Congress, whenever two thirds of both Houses shall deem it necessary, shall propose Amendments to this Constitution, or, on the Application of the Legislatures of two thirds of the several States, shall call a Convention for proposing Amendments, which, in either Case, shall be valid to all Intents and Purposes, as Part of this Constitution, when ratified by the Legislatures of three fourths of the several States, or by Conventions in three fourths thereof, as the one or the other Mode of Ratification may be proposed by the Congress; Provided that no Amendment which may be made prior to the Year One thousand eight hundred and eight shall in any Manner affect the first and fourth Clauses in the Ninth Section of the first Article; and that no State, without its Consent, shall be deprived of its equal Suffrage in the Senate.

Article VI

All Debts contracted and Engagements entered into, before the Adoption of this Constitution, shall be as valid against the United States under this Constitution, as under the Confederation.

This Constitution, and the Laws of the United States which shall be made in Pursuance thereof; and all Treaties made, or which shall be made, under the Authority of the United States, shall be the supreme Law of the Land; and the Judges in every State shall be bound thereby, any Thing in the Constitution or Laws of any State to the Contrary notwithstanding.

The Senators and Representatives before mentioned, and the Members of the several State Legislatures, and all executive and judicial Officers, both of the United States and of the several States, shall be bound by Oath or Affirmation, to support this Constitution; but no religious Test shall ever be required as a Qualification to any Office or public Trust under the United States.

Article VII

The Ratification of the Conventions of nine States, shall be sufficient for the Establishment of this Constitution between the States so ratifying the Same.

Done in Convention by the Unanimous Consent of the States present the Seventeenth Day of September in the Year of our Lord one thousand seven hundred and Eighty seven and of the Independance of the United States of America the Twelfth In witness whereof We have hereunto subscribed our Names.

G. WASHINGTON,
Presid't. and deputy from Virginia

Attest
WILLIAM JACKSON,
Secretary

DELAWARE
George Read
Gunning Bedford Jr.
John Dickinson
Richard Bassett
Jacob Broom

MASSACHUSETTS BAY
Nathaniel Gorham
Rufus King

CONNECTICUT
William Samuel Johnson
Roger Sherman

NEW YORK
Alexander Hamilton

NEW JERSEY
William Livingston
David Brearley
William Paterson
Jonathan Dayton

PENNSYLVANIA
Benjamin Franklin
Thomas Mifflin
Robert Morris
George Clymer
Thomas FitzSimons
Jared Ingersoll
James Wilson
Gouverneur Morris

NEW HAMPSHIRE
John Langdon
Nicholas Gilman

MARYLAND
James McHenry
Daniel of St. Thomas Jenifer
Daniel Carroll

VIRGINIA
John Blair
James Madison, Jr.

NORTH CAROLINA
William Blount
Richard Dobbs Spaight
Hugh Williamson

SOUTH CAROLINA
John Rutledge
Charles Cotesworth Pinckney
Charles Pinckney
Pierce Butler

GEORGIA
William Few
Abraham Baldwin

Articles in addition to, and amendment of the Constitution of the United States of America, proposed by Congress and ratified by the Legislatures of the several states, pursuant to the Fifth Article of the original Constitution.

(The first ten amendments were passed by Congress on September 25, 1789, and were ratified on December 15, 1791.)

Amendment I

Congress shall make no law respecting an establishment of religion, or prohibiting the free exercise thereof; or abridging the freedom of speech, or of the press; or the right of the people peaceably to assemble, and to petition the Government for a redress of grievances.

Amendment II

A well regulated Militia, being necessary to the security of a free State, the right of the people to keep and bear Arms, shall not be infringed.

Amendment III

No Soldier shall, in time of peace be quartered in any house, without the consent of the Owner, nor in time of war, but in a manner to be prescribed by law.

Amendment IV

The right of the people to be secure in their persons, houses, papers, and effects, against unreasonable searches and seizures, shall not be violated, and no warrants shall issue, but upon probable cause, supported by Oath or affirmation, and particularly describing the place to be searched, and the persons or things to be seized.

Amendment V

No person shall be held to answer for a capital, or otherwise infamous crime, unless on a presentment or indictment of a Grand Jury, except in cases arising in the land or naval forces, or in the Militia, when in actual service in time of War or public danger; nor shall any person be subject for the same offence to be twice put in jeopardy of life or limb; nor shall be compelled in any criminal case to be a witness against himself, nor be deprived of life, liberty, or property, without due process of law; nor shall private property be taken for public use, without just compensation.

Amendment VI

In all criminal prosecutions, the accused shall enjoy the right to a speedy and public trial, by an impartial jury of the State and district wherein the crime shall have been committed, which district shall have been previously ascertained by law, and to be informed of the nature and cause of the accusation; to be confronted with the witnesses against him; to have compulsory process for obtaining witnesses in his favor, and to have the assistance of counsel for his defence.

Amendment VII

In Suits at common law, where the value in controversy shall exceed twenty dollars, the right of trial by jury shall be preserved, and no fact tried by a jury, shall be otherwise re-examined in any Court of the United States, than according to the rules of the common law.

Amendment VIII

Excessive bail shall not be required, nor excessive fines imposed, nor cruel and unusual punishments inflicted.

Amendment IX

The enumeration in the Constitution, of certain rights, shall not be construed to deny or disparage others retained by the people.

Amendment X

The powers not delegated to the United States by the Constitution, nor prohibited by it to the States, are reserved to the States respectively, or to the people.

Amendment XI *(Ratified on February 7, 1795)*

The Judicial power of the United States shall not be construed to extend to any suit in law or equity, commenced or prosecuted against one of the United States by Citizens of another State, or by Citizens or Subjects of any Foreign State.

Amendment XII *(Ratified on June 15, 1804)*

The Electors shall meet in their respective states, and vote by ballot for President and Vice-President, one of whom, at least, shall not be an inhabitant of the same state with themselves; they shall name in their ballots the person voted for as President, and in distinct ballots the person voted for as Vice-President, and they shall make distinct lists of all persons voted for as President, and of all persons voted for as Vice-President, and of the number of votes for each, which lists they shall sign and certify, and transmit sealed to the seat of the government of the United States, directed to the President of the Senate;—The President of the Senate shall, in the presence of the Senate and House of Representatives, open all the certificates and the votes shall then be counted;—The person having the greatest number of votes for President, shall be the President, if such number be a majority of the whole number of Electors appointed; and if no person have such majority; then from the persons having the highest numbers not exceeding three on the list of those voted for as President, the House of Representatives shall choose immediately, by ballot, the President. But in choosing the President, the votes shall be taken by states, the representation from each state having one vote; a quorum for this purpose shall consist of a member or members from two-thirds of the states, and a majority of all the states shall be necessary to a choice. [And if the House of Representatives shall not choose a President whenever the right of choice shall devolve upon them, before the fourth day of March next following, then the Vice-President shall act as President, as in the case of the death or other constitutional disability of the President.][12]—The person having the greatest number of votes as Vice-President, shall be the Vice-President, if such number be a majority of the whole number of Electors appointed, and if no person have a majority, then from the two highest numbers on the list, the Senate shall choose the Vice-President; a quorum for the purpose shall consist of two-thirds of the whole number of Senators, and a majority of the whole number shall be necessary to a choice. But no person constitutionally ineligible to the office of President shall be eligible to that of Vice-President of the United States.

Amendment XIII
(Ratified on December 6, 1865)

Section 1. Neither slavery nor involuntary servitude, except as a punishment for crime where of the party shall have been duly convicted, shall exist within the United States, or any place subject to their jurisdiction.

Section 2. Congress shall have power to enforce this article by appropriate legislation.

Amendment XIV
(Ratified on July 9, 1868)

Section 1. All persons born or naturalized in the United States, and subject to the jurisdiction thereof, are citizens of the United States and of the State wherein they reside. No State shall make or enforce any law which shall abridge the privileges or immunities of citizens of the United States; nor shall any State deprive any person of life, liberty, or property, without due process of law; nor deny to any person within its jurisdiction the equal protection of the laws.

Section 2. Representatives shall be apportioned among the several States according to their respective numbers, counting the whole number of persons in each State, excluding Indians not taxed. But when the right to vote at any election for the choice of electors for President and Vice President of the United States, Representatives in Congress, the Executive and Judicial officers of a State, or the members of the Legislature thereof, is denied to any of the male inhabitants of such State, being twenty-one years of age, and citizens of the United States, or in any way abridged, except for participation in rebellion, or other crime, the basis of representation therein shall be reduced in the proportion which the number of such male citizens shall bear to the whole number of male citizens twenty-one years of age in such State.

Section 3. No person shall be a Senator or Representative in Congress, or elector of President and Vice President, or hold any office, civil or military, under the United States, or under any State, who, having previously taken an oath, as a member of Congress, or as an officer of the United States, or as a member of any State legislature, or as an executive or judicial officer of any State, to support the Constitution of the United States, shall have engaged in insurrection or rebellion against the same, or given aid or comfort to the enemies thereof. But Congress may by a vote of two-thirds of each House, remove such disability.

Section 4. The validity of the public debt of the United States, authorized by law, including debts incurred for payment of pensions and bounties for services in suppressing insurrection or rebellion, shall not be questioned. But neither the United States nor any State shall assume or pay any debt or obligation incurred in aid of insurrection or rebellion against the United States, or any claim for the loss or emancipation of any slave, but all such debts, obligations and claims shall be held illegal and void.

Section 5. The Congress shall have power to enforce, by appropriate legislation, the provisions of this article.

Amendment XV
(Ratified on February 3, 1870)

Section 1. The right of citizens of the United States to vote shall not be denied or abridged by the United States or by any State on account of race, color, or previous condition of servitude.

Section 2. The Congress shall have power to enforce this article by appropriate legislation.

Amendment XVI
(Ratified on February 3, 1913)

The Congress shall have power to lay and collect taxes on incomes, from whatever source derived, without apportionment among the several States, and without regard to any census or enumeration.

Amendment XVII
(Ratified on April 8, 1913)

The Senate of the United States shall be composed of two Senators from each State, elected by the people thereof, for six years; and each Senator shall have one vote. The electors in each State shall have the qualifications requisite for electors of the most numerous branch of the State legislatures.

When vacancies happen in the representation of any State in the Senate, the executive authority of such State shall issue writs of election to fill such vacancies: Provided, That the legislature of any State may empower the executive thereof to make temporary appointments until the people fill the vacancies by election as the legislature may direct.

This amendment shall not be so construed as to affect the election or term of any Senator chosen before it becomes valid as part of the Constitution.

Amendment XVIII
(Ratified on January 16, 1919)

Section 1. After one year from the ratification of this article the manufacture, sale, or transportation of intoxicating liquors within, the importation thereof into, or the exportation thereof from the United States and all territory subject to the jurisdiction thereof for beverage purposes is hereby prohibited.

Section 2. The Congress and the several States shall have concurrent power to enforce this article by appropriate legislation.

Section 3. This article shall be inoperative unless it shall have been ratified as an amendment to the Constitution by the legislatures of the several States, as provided in the Constitution, within seven years from the date of the submission hereof to the States by the Congress.

Amendment XIX
(Ratified on August 18, 1920)

The right of citizens of the United States to vote shall not be denied or abridged by the United States or by any State on account of sex.

Congress shall have power to enforce this article by appropriate legislation.

Amendment XX
(Ratified on February 6, 1933)

Section 1. The terms of the President and Vice President shall end at noon on the 20th day of January, and the terms of Senators and Representatives at noon on the 3d day of January, of the years in which such terms would have ended if this article had not been ratified; and the terms of their successors shall then begin.

Section 2. The Congress shall assemble at least once in every year, and such meeting shall begin at noon on the 3d day of January, unless they shall by law appoint a different day.

Section 3. If, at the time fixed for the beginning of the term of the President, the President elect shall have died, the Vice President elect shall become President. If a President shall not have been chosen before the time fixed for the beginning of his term, or if the President elect shall have failed to qualify, then the Vice President elect shall act as President until a President shall have qualified; and the Congress may by law provide for the case wherein neither a President elect nor a Vice President elect shall have qualified, declaring who shall then act as President, or the manner in which one who is to act shall be selected, and such person shall act accordingly until a President or Vice President shall have qualified.

Section 4. The Congress may by law provide for the case of the death of any of the persons from whom the House of Representatives may choose a President whenever the rights of choice shall have devolved upon them, and for the case of the death of any of the persons from whom the Senate may choose a Vice President whenever the right of choice shall have devolved upon them.

Section 5. Sections 1 and 2 shall take effect on the 15th day of October following the ratification of this article.

Section 6. This article shall be inoperative unless it shall have been ratified as an amendment to the Constitution by the legislatures of three-fourths of the several States within seven years from the date of its submission.

Amendment XXI
(Ratified on December 5, 1933)

Section 1. The eighteenth article of amendment to the Constitution of the United States is hereby repealed.

Section 2. The transportation or importation into any State, Territory, or possession of the United States for delivery or use therein of intoxicating liquors, in violation of the laws thereof, is hereby prohibited.

Section 3. This article shall be inoperative unless it shall have been ratified as an amendment to the Constitution by conventions in the several States, as provided in the Constitution, within seven years from the date of the submission hereof to the States by the Congress.

Amendment XXII
(Ratified on February 27, 1951)

Section 1. No person shall be elected to the office of the President more than twice, and no person who has held the office of President, or acted as President, for more than two years of a term to which some other person was elected President shall be elected to the office of the President more than once. But this Article shall not apply to any person holding the office of President when this Article was proposed by the Congress, and shall not prevent any person who may be holding the office of President, or acting as President, during the term within which this Article becomes operative from holding the office of President or acting as President during the remainder of such term.

Section 2. This article shall be inoperative unless it shall have been ratified as an amendment to the Constitution by the legislatures of three-fourths of the several States within seven years from the date of its submission to the States by the Congress.

Amendment XXIII
(Ratified on March 29, 1961)

Section 1. The District constituting the seat of Government of the United States shall appoint in such manner as the Congress may direct:

A number of electors of President and Vice President equal to the whole number of Senators and Representatives in Congress to which the District would be entitled if it were a State, but in no event more than the least populous State; they shall be in addition to those appointed by the States, but they shall be considered, for the purposes of the election of President and Vice President, to be electors appointed by a State; and they shall meet in the District and perform such duties as provided by the twelfth article of amendment.

Section 2. The Congress shall have power to enforce this article by appropriate legislation.

Amendment XXIV
(Ratified on January 23, 1964)

Section 1. The right of citizens of the United States to vote in any primary or other election for President or Vice President, for electors for President or Vice President, or for Senator or Representative in Congress, shall not be denied or abridged by the United States or any State by reason of failure to pay any poll tax or other tax.

Section 2. The Congress shall have power to enforce this article by appropriate legislation.

Amendment XXV
(Ratified on February 10, 1967)

Section 1. In case of the removal of the President from office or of his death or resignation, the Vice President shall become President.

Section 2. Whenever there is a vacancy in the office of the Vice President, the President shall nominate a Vice President who shall take office upon confirmation by a majority vote of both Houses of Congress.

Section 3. Whenever the President transmits to the President pro tempore of the Senate and the Speaker of the House of Representatives his written declaration that he is unable to discharge the powers and duties of his office, and until he transmits to them a written declaration to the contrary, such powers and duties shall be discharged by the Vice President as Acting President.

Section 4. Whenever the Vice President and a majority of either the principal officers of the executive departments or of such other body as Congress may by law provide, transmit to the President pro tempore of the Senate and the Speaker of the House of Representatives their written declaration that the President is unable to discharge the powers and duties of his office, the Vice President shall immediately assume the powers and duties of the office as Acting President.

Thereafter, when the President transmits to the President pro tempore of the Senate and the Speaker of the House of Representatives his written declaration that no inability exists, he shall resume the powers and duties of his office unless the Vice President and a majority of either the principal officers of the executive department or of such other body as Congress may by law provide, transmit within four days to the President pro tempore of the Senate and the Speaker of the House of Representatives their written declaration that the President is unable to discharge the powers and duties of his office. Thereupon Congress shall decide the issue, assembling within forty-eight hours for that purpose if not in session. If the Congress, within twenty-one days after receipt of the latter written declaration, or, if Congress is not in session, within twenty-one days after Congress is required to assemble, determines by two-thirds vote of both Houses that the President is unable to discharge the powers and duties of his office, the Vice President shall continue to discharge the same as Acting President; otherwise, the President shall resume the powers and duties of his office.

Amendment XXVI
(Ratified on July 1, 1971)

Section 1. The right of citizens of the United States, who are eighteen years of age or older, to vote shall not be denied or abridged by the United States or by any State on account of age.

Section 2. The Congress shall have power to enforce this article by appropriate legislation.

Amendment XXVII
(Ratified on May 7, 1992)

No law, varying the compensation for the services of the Senators and Representatives shall take effect until an election of Representatives shall have intervened.

Endnotes

1. See Amendment XVI.
2. See Amendment XIV.
3. See Amendment XVII.
4. See Amendment XVII.
5. See Amendment XX.
6. See Amendment XVI.
7. See Amendment XII.
8. See Amendment XXV.
9. See Amendment XI.
10. See Amendment XI.
11. See Amendment XIII.
12. See Amendment XIV.

Glossary

95% confidence level If a survey were repeated 100 times, the poll's results will be confirmed 95 out of the 100. No survey can achieve a higher level of confidence than 95 out of 100, or 95%.

1996 Welfare Reform Act Signed by President Clinton, this program placed limits on how many years a person can receive welfare.

Actual malice In order for a public official to prove libel, he or she must prove a statement was made with knowledge that it was false or with reckless disregard of the statement's truth or falsity.

Adversarial process In this system, each side in a conflict argues its position before a neutral third party who makes the final decision.

Advocacy journalism Journalism in which news outlets' biases permeate news gathering, reporting, and analysis of political information.

Affirmative action Positive steps taken to make up for past discrimination against minorities and/or women.

Agenda setting The stage in the policymaking process, whereby various political issues get prioritized for possible policy action.

American dream The achievement of economic independence and personal and social fulfillment.

American Recovery and Reinvestment Act Signed in 2009 by President Barack Obama, this was a nearly $1 trillion stimulus package to help get the economy moving again after the recession that began in 2008.

Amicus curiae (friend of the court) brief Brief filed with an appellate court by a person or organization that is not a party to the case but that wishes to bring information on the conflict to the court's attention.

Anarchism A situation in which government is not involved in any way with maintaining order or providing public services. Anarchy has generally only existed for short periods of time after the fall of a state.

Anti-Ballistic Missile Treaty Treaty negotiated between the United States and the Soviet Union in 1972 to limit the proliferation of antiballistic missiles, which could be used offensively. The United States announced its withdrawal from the treaty in 2001.

Anti-Federalists Those who opposed the Constitution and favored a decentralized national government that left more power to the state governments.

Appellate courts Courts in the middle tier of the federal court system. These courts have jurisdiction to hear any case appealed from the lower federal (or district) courts.

Appellate jurisdiction Refers to the authority of a court to hear a case on appeal from a lower court.

Articles of Confederation Adopted in 1777, this governing document reflected the founders' fears of a powerful national government. The thirteen states retained supreme powers within their borders, while the national government was given very little power.

Associate Justices These eight justices are appointed by the president and confirmed by the Senate. They have the same responsibilities as the Chief Justice as it pertains to cases, but different administrative responsibilities.

Autocracy A form of government in which power is concentrated in the hands of one person, such as a monarch.

Bad tendency test A standard used by the Supreme Court that allows restrictions on speech that would probably lead to the performance of criminal acts.

Bicameral legislature A legislative body made up of two chambers. In the United States, Congress is divided into a House of Representatives and a Senate

Bilateral treaties Treaties between two countries, parties, or "sides."

Bill of Rights The first ten amendments to the Constitution.

Bills Proposed laws

Bipartisan Campaign Reform Act (BCRA) Passed in 2002, this piece of legislation regulates the financing of political campaigns.

Block grants Money given by the national government to state or local governments to address general policy needs and goals; these grants allow spending flexibility in meeting general goals.

Bricker Amendment A series of amendments to the U.S. Constitution proposed in the 1950s that would have prohibited any treaty that was self-executing or which granted Congress legislative powers beyond those specified in the Constitution.

Briefs Documents filed with the Supreme Court that outline the facts of the case, the law to be applied, and the legal argument that each side is making.

Brownlow Committee Formally known as The President's Committee on Administrative Management, this committee recommended sweeping organizational changes for the executive branch in 1937.

Brown v. Board of Education of Topeka, Kansas Landmark Supreme Court decision in 1954 declaring that segregation in public education is unconstitutional. This decision overturned *Plessy v. Ferguson* (1896).

Bureaucracy A complex system of organization that employs standardized rules, procedures, communication, and organizational controls for achieving public good.

Cabinet agencies The various administrative departments of the federal government.

Cabinet The informal designation of the group who are the heads of the major departments in the federal government

Campaign An attempt by a candidate to gain the support of backers and voters to help win election to political office.

Campaign finance reform Efforts to limit or otherwise regulate the amount of money spent on election campaigns.

Capacity building Policy tool with which government takes action to bridge the gap between current deficits in knowledge, skills, equipment, or other resources of a government agency and future capacity necessary to achieve policy aims.

Capitalism Economic system based upon the free exchange of privately owned property between individuals.

Case Zablocki Act 1972 legislation that created a requirement for the executive to report to Congress any executive agreements negotiated and agreed to within 60 days after the agreements go into effect.

Caucuses Meetings in which members of a party gather to choose their party's nominee.

Caucus The House Democrat's party conference.

Centralized federalism The period of time between 1964 and 1980 when the relationship between the national government and the state and local governments transitioned from being supportive to being more direct and sometimes coercive.

Cert pool Each participating Supreme Court justice assigns one or more clerks to review each petition and to make recommendations to the justices about which cases to hear.

Changing a system Policy tool that creates broad and sweeping change in the laws and rules that govern a particular area.

Charter schools Public schools that are freed from some bureaucratic requirements and that encourage innovation in curriculum and spending.

Checks and balances Principle reflected in the Constitution that grants each of the three branches (legislative, executive, and judicial) some control and scrutiny over one another.

Chief diplomat The president is the chief representative and spokesperson for the United States in foreign affairs.

Chief executive The president controls and directs the executive branch and its various agencies.

Chief Justice The presiding justice on the Supreme Court appointed by the president and confirmed by the Senate.

Chief legislator The president's role in proposing a set of legislative initiatives to Congress on the major issues of the day.

Circuits Refers to the thirteen courts of appeal located within one of eleven numbered geographic boundaries. Most of these appellate courts hear cases on appeal from district courts.

Citizens United v. Federal Election Commission A 2010 Supreme Court case in which in a 5–4 ruling the Court ruled that key portions of the BCRA were unconstitutional.

Civil disobedience A form of nonviolent political protest; became popular in the 1960s as a way to express dissent.

Civil law Involves conflicts of a noncriminal nature; in federal court, these are likely to include cases involving contracts, personal injury, and bankruptcy.

Civil law regime Conflicts that come before the courts are decided according to an extensive code or set of laws; less attention is paid to past court decisions.

Civil liberties Constitutional and legal guarantees of people's freedom.

Civil Rights Act of 1964 The first effective civil rights legislation. With passage of this law, discrimination in stores, hotels, and restaurants became illegal, as did racist practices in hiring and promotion.

Civil service A system of governmental employment based on merit in which employees cannot be fired without legitimate cause related to job performance. Also, government employees (except those in the military).

Clear and present danger test A standard used by the Supreme Court that allows restrictions on speech, if the speech will lead directly to criminal acts.

Clientele agency An agency that serves a particular industry, group, or constituency.

Closed primaries Elections in which only party members can participate.

Cloture A vote in the Senate that brings an end to debate. Senate rules require three-fifths of the Senate (60 members) to invoke cloture.

Cold War A period when the United States and the Soviet Union struggled for ideological dominance. While there was no official war between the two countries, they each supported political actors in the rest of the world that served their political and economic agendas.

Collective action problems Situations in which individually rational behavior leads to a collectively irrational outcome.

Collective security An international arrangement, whereby states agree to act together against any state that behaves aggressively.

Commander in chief The president is the ultimate civilian commander of all the U.S. armed forces, and thus he is able to authorize use and deployment of military forces in combat or peacemaking roles.

Commerce clause This clause in the Constitution grants Congress the power "to regulate commerce with foreign nations, and among the several states, and with the Indian Tribes."

Common law system Conflicts that come before a court are decided based largely on previous judicial decisions.

Compensatory (or actual) damages Money awarded in a civil suit to compensate an injured party for direct losses or injuries sustained.

Comprehensive Test Ban Treaty A treaty designed to prohibit any type of nuclear weapons tests and to prevent testing by other states.

Concurring opinion An opinion written by a justice that agrees with the outcome but whose reasoning differs.

Confederation An alliance of sovereign states united for common objectives, in which ultimate authority is vested in subnational governments, and the national government has virtually no power.

Conference committees Ad hoc committees created to reconcile differing versions of a single piece of legislation that has been passed on the floor of each chamber.

Confidence level A pollster's way of saying how much confidence he or she has that the poll sample is reflective or representative of the population.

Congressional Budget Office (CBO) Congressional agency established in 1974 to provide members of Congress with budgetary and economic analyses independent of those offered by the executive branch.

Conservatives Those who disapprove of government interference in economic life, but not in the defense of traditional moral principles.

Constituents The people whom elected officials represent.

Constitutional Convention Meeting of delegates from twelve of the thirteen states in 1787 to encourage uncensored debate and discussion about changing the structure of government created by the Articles of Confederation.

Constitutional democracies Types of governments that arose largely in the eighteenth and nineteenth centuries and that were inspired by the liberal philosophies of great theorists such as John Locke and Jean-Jacques Rousseau.

Constitution A set of rules and principles that establish a system of government.

Containment A strategy pursued by the United States to stem the spread of Soviet influence and communism worldwide.

Cooperative federalism An era in which the national government assisted the states in addressing the nation's economic and social crises.

Counties Divisions of American states. There are 3,000 counties in the United States that carry out state and federal programs, particularly in areas of health and welfare.

Courts Formal organs of government that resolve disputes using rules of law.

Creative federalism President Johnson's vision of federalism in which the national government would take on new responsibilities in assisting state and local governments as well as private organizations and individuals in overcoming social and economic inequality.

Criminal law Reflects the collective will of the citizenry; when an individual violates a criminal law, lawyers representing society at large bring the suit.

Declaration of Independence Drafted in 1776 by Thomas Jefferson of Virginia, this document summarized the purpose of government and the political rights of citizens.

***De facto* discrimination** Discrimination that exists in fact, regardless of the law.

De jure discrimination Discrimination that is mandated by law.

Delegates Individuals who are selected to represent the party at state or national party conventions and who cast votes

Delegate The role members of Congress serve in representing the interests and policy preferences of their constituents.

Democracy A form of government that allows for the people to rule, either directly or indirectly.

Department of Homeland Security (DHS) Created in the aftermath of 9/11 to reorganize and centralize the U.S. intelligence establishment.

Departments The largest units of bureaucratic organization.

Dillon's Rule A theory of state and local relations, which holds that state constitutions breathe life into all local governments, and that theoretically states can abolish all of their local governments.

Discharge petition The power to pull a bill from a recalcitrant committee; this is not used frequently in practice.

Dissenting opinion An opinion written by a judge who differs with his or her colleagues on the outcome.

Distributive policies Public policies that direct taxpayer monies to very specific groups or causes.

District courts Courts at the base or the lowest tier of the three-tiered U.S. federal court system. These courts hear cases that involve original jurisdiction.

Diversity of jurisdiction These cases make up a substantial portion of federal suits. They are cases that involve litigants of different states and/or countries.

Divided government A situation in which different parties control at least one branch of the national government: either the executive or one house of the legislature.

Dual federalism Legal theory in operation in the United States until 1900 that promoted the idea of separate spheres of authority for national and state governments.

Elastic clause The alternate name given to the necessary and proper clause because Congress has stretched the clause's interpretation over the years.

Elections The process by which voters select people to represent them in office.

Electoral College A slate of electors within each of the 50 states and the District of Columbia that cast the ultimate vote for president on behalf of voters.

Equal protection clause Fourteenth Amendment provision that requires the states not to discriminate against groups of people.

Equitable remedy A plaintiff asks the court to take a specific action, such as issuing an injunction or a restraining order, to correct a problem.

Establishment clause First Amendment provision that requires separation of church and state.

Exclusionary rule Evidence obtained by law enforcement authorities illegally cannot be used in a criminal case.

Executive agreements International agreements entered into by the president with the chief executives of other countries. These agreements are legal, but they do not require the advice and consent of the Senate.

Executive clause This clause in the Constitution states that "executive powers shall be vested in a president."

Executive Office of the President A conglomeration of offices meant to directly assist the president in managing the executive branch.

Executive orders Administrative directives drawn from the president's formal discretionary powers, which have the force of law and can direct the actions of executive branch officials. In some cases, these orders may serve to implement legislation passed by Congress.

Exit polls Opinion surveys in which voters are questioned about their votes and preferences as they leave the polling place on Election Day.

Factions Narrowly self-interested political organizations, or a small group of people who share a common belief, interest, or opinion.

Federalism A political structure that divides political power between a national government and one or more subnational governments that must share power and responsibilities with one another.

Federalist Papers Written by three influential authors and proponents of stronger national government, they were published as a series of 84 newspaper articles and critical in persuading Americans to adopt a system of federalism.

Federalists Those who supported the Constitution and the strong government it created.

Federal question A lawsuit related to federal law, the U.S. Constitution, or treaties.

Federal Reserve Board (the Fed) A governmental agency that regulates many market activities, including the setting of prime interest rates.

Filibuster A delaying tactic employed to tie up the Senate until the majority decides to pull a bill from consideration on the Senate floor.

First Amendment rights Freedom of religion, speech, press, and peaceful assembly.

First Continental Congress In 1774, delegates from twelve of the thirteen American colonies (Georgia was absent) met in Philadelphia with the goal of reconciling with Britain.

Focusing events Dramatic occurrences that direct public attention to a societal problem for a sustained period of time, thereby increasing the chance that the problem gets recognized as a political issue.

Foreign policy The goals identified and actions taken by a government to protect national interests.

Fourteenth Amendment Guarantees citizenship to all born or naturalized in the United States; mandates equal protection of the laws.

Freedom of expression First Amendment protection of all forms of communication.

Free exercise clause First Amendment protection of the right to practice the religion of one's choice.

General election The contest between candidates who have either succeeded in winning the nomination of their party or who are running independently.

Generational effect Similar attitudes about politics among members of the same generation produced by shared national experiences.

Gerrymandered Refers to the way House districts across the country are drawn in such a way that a disproportionate number of voters in the district are registered voters in the incumbent's party.

Globalization A process through which countries of the world become further integrated via increased communication, technology, and exchange. This results in greater exposure and connections among economies, societies, and cultures.

"Going native" A process by which Cabinet appointees' sympathies and identification over time flow more to the agency they manage than to the president who appointed them.

Government An organization with the authority to exercise control over human behavior.

Government corporation An organization that provides "market-oriented public service" and that generates roughly enough revenue to cover its expenses.

Grants-in-aid Money given by the national government to state or local governments to address specific policy goals; assistance often comes with specific requirements for how the money is to be spent.

Great Compromise Compromise at the Constitutional Convention that involved incorporating equal and proportional representation into a two-chamber legislature.

Great Society President Johnson's program during the 1960s that expanded the reach of the national government into private social and economic relations.

Hate speech Expression that urges violence or oppressive behavior toward a group.

Hierarchy of needs theory Developed by psychologist Abraham Maslow, this theory suggests that people are motivated by their desire to satisfy specific needs; physiological needs (e.g., food and water) are the most primary, followed by safety needs, social belonging needs, esteem needs, and, at the top, self-actualization needs.

Home-rule charter A municipal "constitution" that allows cities to carve out autonomy from state requirements.

Hoover Commission In the late 1940s, this commission was established to reduce the number of government agencies created during World War II. However, it actually recommended an increase in the capacity of the Executive Office of the President.

Hoover Commission II In 1955, this commission recommended eliminating nonessential government services and activities and made the case that the federal government should not be in competition with private enterprise.

Impeachment Article II, section 4, gives this power to the House of Representatives. The power to impeach is analogous to the power of indictment exercised by a grand jury. In order to be removed from office, the president must be convicted by the Senate.

Impeach The power to charge an executive or judicial officer with misconduct or wrongdoing.

Incorporation The process of creating a new municipality out of county territory. Or, the fact that states are bound to respect rights guaranteed by the U.S. Constitution.

Incumbent A candidate for office who currently holds the seat.

Incumbent Elected government official currently holding an office.

Independent agencies Agencies or bureaus that exist independently of a full department and are usually supervised by a single director who is appointed by the president and confirmed by the Senate.

Independent commissions and boards Organizations that are structured so as to be sealed off, to some extent, from political influence by legislators and executives.

Inducements Policy tools that use some form of financial value to motivate public or private organizations or individuals to take some action in the short-term, in the absence of which they would not predictably perform.

Information asymmetry A condition where consumers of goods or services are at an informational disadvantage relative to producers.

Initiatives In nearly every election cycle, voters in almost half the states are asked to indicate their support or opposition to particular measures at the voting booth.

Interest groups Organizations formed around narrow and specific economic or social interests to protect and advance the cause of their members.

Intermediate scrutiny Standard used by the Supreme Court that allows gender/sex discrimination only if it is needed to achieve an important government objective.

Invidious discrimination Harmful, irrational discrimination.

Iron triangles Cozy policymaking relationships among small numbers of players that are not at all representative of the wider variety of stakeholders who might want to influence policymaking.

Jim Crow laws Laws that required racial segregation.

Joint committees Committees made up of members of both chambers that usually perform some specialized function.

Judicial activism Role adopted by a judge who is willing to use his or her authority to influence public policy, especially to protect rights established in the U.S. Constitution.

Judicial restraint Role adopted by a judge who sees his or her job as limited to making only those decisions that are essential to a resolution of the conflict before the court.

Judicial review The authority of a court to invalidate actions of other governmental actors, if these actions are in violation of the nation's constitution.

Jurisdiction The authority of a court to hear and decide a case.

LAPS test Sexually explicit material is not considered obscene if it contains literary, artistic, political, or scientific value.

Layer cake A metaphor for American federalism as three more or less independent spheres of policymaking among national, state, and local governments.

League of Nations A collective security organization of the post–World War I era designed to give states a place to voice grievances and allow for arbitration by other states. Despite efforts by President Wilson, the U.S. Senate rejected the Versailles Treaty and kept the United States out of the League.

Legislative supremacy Fearful of a monarchy, the founders of the Constitution sought to establish a government in which the legislative branch was more powerful than the executive.

Libel False and damaging publication.

Liberalism A philosophy reflected in many constitutional democracies that every individual has natural rights that the government should respect and protect. This philosophy is rooted in the strong belief in individual freedom.

Liberals Those who oppose government interference in the moral or societal values and choices of individuals, while supporting government efforts to regulate the economic marketplace.

Libertarians Those who oppose significant government involvement in both society and the economy alike.

Line agencies Organizations that directly deliver a service to citizens, such as the U.S. Postal Service or each state's Department of Motor Vehicles.

Logrolling A bargaining strategy in which one member of Congress agrees to support another member's bill in exchange for their support on some other piece of legislation.

Majority Leader In the Senate, this person has the formal power to bring bills to the floor (or not).

Majority opinion Judicial findings that reflect the view of the majority of the justices on the outcome of the appeal.

Mandates Legally enforceable requirements that direct a government agency or regulated field to specifically do or not do something.

Marble cake View of federalism, which holds that policies are made and implemented by multiple levels of government simultaneously rather than independently.

Margin of error or sampling error The range of the results that will be confirmed 95 out of 100 times. A typical margin of error is + or −3. If a poll found 50 percent of respondents answered a question the same way, then with a + or −3 margin of error, it means that between 47 and 53 percent will respond the same way 95 out of 100 times.

Market failure The production by the private sector of conditions deemed unacceptable by society.

Markup The process of amending or changing a bill.

Mass media All forms of mass communication, including television, radio, newspapers, magazines, Internet sites, films, and books.

Media literacy The ability to distinguish between reliable and unreliable information and/or analysis in the vastly expanded modern media environment.

Merit pay system A system in which compensation is based, at least in part, on performance and in which performance bonuses are handed out to those performing better on the basis of some set of measurable indicators.

Merit system A system in which an individual must show competence to be hired and under which they can only be fired for cause (not political party affiliation).

Midterm elections Elections that occur midway through a president's term (nonpresidential election years).

Minority Leader Represents the minority party in the House of Representatives; also refers to the person who represents the minority party in the Senate.

Monarchy A form of government in which all political power rests with a single individual; it is usually passed down through heredity.

Multilateral treaties Treaties among three or more countries.

Multiparty system A political system in which getting a majority in government requires coalitions of two or more parties.

Municipalities Cities that are created out of county territory. They provide land-use planning and other important services.

Narrowcasting Tailoring media content to the preferences and prejudices of consumers in the target demographic.

National interests A country's goals and ambitions, whether economic, military, or cultural.

National nominating convention An assembly of party delegates where the formal nomination of a candidate takes place.

National party conventions An assembly with delegates chosen from all of the states whose function is to nominate candidates for president and vice president and to oversee the governance of the party.

National Security Adviser (NSA) Person responsible for advising the president and coordinating the NSC members.

National Security Council (NSC) Established by the National Security Act of 1947, the NSC is responsible for shaping and coordinating national security policy for the United States. The president chairs the committee.

National Security Report (NSC)-68 A classified document written and adopted in 1950 by the Truman administration that made the case for the need of a massive arms buildup and an expansion of nuclear weapons research and development.

National security The desire to keep a country's borders intact, to protect the population and the country's resources, and to ensure that a country's values and ideals are sacrosanct.

NATO An intergovernmental military alliance based on the North Atlantic Treaty, which was signed on April 4, 1949.

Natural monopoly A type of market failure in which a product or service can be supplied to the consumer market more effectively and efficiently by one producer than many.

Necessary and proper clause The clause in Article I, section 8, of the Constitution, also known as the elastic clause, which provides Congress with broad latitude to expand its powers beyond the powers already explicitly granted to it in the Constitution.

Necessary and proper clause This clause in the Constitution grants Congress the power "to make all laws which shall be necessary and proper for carrying into execution the foregoing powers."

Negative externalities A type of market failure, whereby the producer of a good or service fails to account for societal costs associated with its activity.

New Deal The name given to the programs laid out by President Franklin Delano Roosevelt to create a social safety net as well as ensure federal oversight of financial markets.

New England town meetings A common practice in many small New England towns, whereby residents gather together to decide issues of policy.

New federalism A process of deregulation in which the national government reduced aid grants to state and local governments.

New Jersey Plan Proposal introduced at the Constitutional Convention that would have amended rather than replaced the Articles of Confederation.

No Child Left Behind Act (NCLB) Signed by President Bush in 2002, this law mandates annual standardized testing for students in grades 3 through 8 and greater accountability for teachers, among other reforms.

Nuclear arms race In order to gain international superiority, both the United States and the Soviet Union sought to secure military dominance by establishing the largest and best-trained militaries and the most sophisticated and deadly tools of warfare, nuclear weapons chief among them.

Obscene expression Sexually explicit speech or publication that has as its prime or only purpose sexual arousal.

Official actors Governmental policy participants who operate on the "inside" of government and possess institutional authority to make formal decisions on policy.

Off-year elections Elections held in the United States that occur in odd-number years. These elections are generally for the selection of local and municipal offices rather than major state or federal offices.

Oligarchy A form of government in which power is concentrated in the hands of a few members from an elite segment of society, such as the military.

Oligopolies Economic markets or sectors that are controlled by a small number of owners.

Open primaries Elections in which all registered voters can decide on the day of the election in which party's election they will participate.

Original jurisdiction Granted to a court to hear a case for the first time.

Party conferences Every member of Congress is a member of either the Democratic or Republican conference in their chamber. House Democrats call theirs a caucus.

Party platform A formal written statement of a political party's position on those key issues that it deems most important.

Patriot Act An act passed by Congress in 2001 that was designed to equip government and law enforcement agencies with tools to better protect the United States from terrorism.

Patronage The practice of handing out government jobs on the basis of political loyalty rather than objective measures of expertise or experience.

Pendleton Act Enacted in 1883, it declared officially that government jobs should be handed out on the basis of merit.

Permanent campaign This phrase refers to the notion that in order to govern successfully, modern presidents must campaign continually while in office.

Plaintiff The person who initiates or files a lawsuit.

Plessy v. Ferguson An infamous 1896 ruling in which the Supreme Court upheld racial segregation in private businesses, especially railroad cars.

Plurality elections An electoral system, such as the one we have in the United States, where the person who gets the most votes wins; also known as the "first past the gate."

Police-patrol versus fire-alarm oversight A distinction between two forms of congressional oversight of the bureaucracy. In police-patrol oversight, Congress patrols for violations of congressional preferences in settings like hearings. In fire-alarm oversight, legislators respond to complaints from groups and individuals about agency actions.

Policy evaluation The stage of the policymaking process in which a policy is assessed to determine if it is reaching its stated objective(s).

Policy formulation The stage of the policymaking process in which a specific policy proposal is actually developed by an official entity in the form of legislative statutes, executive orders, or administrative regulations.

Policy implementation The stage of the policymaking process at which a created policy gets executed by an administrative agency of government.

Policy tools The specific policy options available to government when trying to address societal issues. The most common forms are mandates, inducements, capacity building, and system change.

Political efficacy Confidence in one's ability to participate meaningfully in politics.

Political ideology A set of principles, beliefs, themes, or ideals that not only help explain how society operates but also provide a prescription for the future.

Political participation Those activities of citizens that attempt to influence the structure of government, the selection of government officials, or the policies of government.

Political parties Organizations of ordinary citizens, popularly chosen, who come together around a common program of their design with the aim of electing individuals who will support that program in government.

Political socialization The ways in which we learn about and develop our opinions and attitudes about politics and government.

Pollsters Those who conduct public opinion surveys for media, corporate, nonprofit, and political clients.

Populists Voters who have no problem with activist government, as long as it serves to protect social order and improve the material conditions of people's lives.

Pork-barrel spending The incentive each individual member of Congress has to fight for federal dollars that will lead to projects and create jobs in their state.

Precedents Past judicial decisions of courts used to resolve current conflicts.

Preemptive force A rationale for attacking other parties in response to an imminent threat.

Preferred freedoms doctrine First Amendment rights are fundamental to a free society and receive heightened protection from the courts.

President's Private Sector Survey on Cost Control (PPSSCC) Also known as the Grace Commission, it concluded in its 1984 report that the U.S. government was wasting billions of dollars every year on bureaucratic inefficiencies.

Primary elections Elections in which voters go to the polls to choose the nominee for a political party.

Prior restraint Censorship of expression before it reaches the public.

Probability sampling A survey in which respondents are chosen randomly from the target population. Ideally, every member of the target population has the same chance of being polled.

Probable cause Reason to think that it is likely that someone is guilty or in possession of evidence.

Problem identification The stage of the policymaking process in which a societal condition or problem is recognized by government as an issue worthy of political attention and possible policy action.

Progressive movement (or Progressivism) A U.S. political movement in the late nineteenth and early twentieth centuries that called for greater governmental intervention in economic and social relations.

Public goods Goods or services that cannot be divided up and cannot be controlled by a single individual or organization.

Public opinion poll A survey of a representative sample of a population designed to measure the values, attitudes, and beliefs of the population on specific issues.

Public policy A collection of governmentally led responses to societal issues.

Punitive damages Money awarded to punish or deter the wrongdoer from behaving in the same way again.

Ratification An act that gives official sanction or approval to a formal document such as a treaty or constitution.

Redistributive policies Government actions that transfer resources, usually in the form of taxation, from one area or group to another area or group.

Regulatory agencies Agencies established to issue regulations or rules that have the force of law.

Regulatory policies Government actions that compel an individual or organization to perform or refrain from certain actions.

Reinventing government A sweeping set of reforms employed during the Clinton administration aimed at streamlining governmental processes, making the federal bureaucracy more efficient, and focusing bureaucratic efforts on clients and outcomes rather than processes.

Representative democracy A form of democratic government in which the people elect representatives to act on their behalf; also known as a republic.

Republic A form of democratic government in which the people elect representatives to act on their behalf; also known as a representative government.

Right to privacy The right to conduct one's life without government interference. It is one of the implied rights protected by the Ninth Amendment.

Rulemaking The process by which agencies create regulations that have the force of law.

Rule of Four If four or more Supreme Court justices want to hear a case, it is put on the court's docket.

Rules Committee The committee in the House of Representatives that helps determine the conditions under which bills will come to the floor. The committee is headed by the Speaker of the House.

Sample Opinion survey respondents who serve as a representative subgroup of a target population.

School districts More than 13,000 local districts run public schools in many parts of the country.

Second Continental Congress A meeting of delegates in May 1775, some of whom wanted to work toward reestablishing harmony between Britain and the American colonies, and others who wanted to break all ties with the Crown and form an independent nation.

Select committees Ad hoc bodies created to deal with a particular issue or even a single piece of legislation.

Selective incorporation The process by which parts of the Bill of Rights were applied to the states through the Fourteenth Amendment.

Senatorial courtesy A practice that sometimes occurs in the U.S. Senate when a federal district court nominee is appointed by the president. Once the name is submitted to the Senate Judiciary Committee, senators from the nominee's state are notified. If one of the senators disapproves of the nominee, no hearing is held.

Seniority An important criterion in selecting committee leadership; the longer members of Congress have been in office, the more senior they are, and the greater likelihood that they will be selected to chair a committee.

Separate but equal A rule that segregation would be constitutional so long as both races had some access to public services.

Separation of powers The Constitution established a legislative branch with the power to make laws, an executive branch with the power to enforce laws, and a judicial branch with the power to interpret laws.

Sex discrimination The practice of treating females and males differently.

Shays' Rebellion In 1786, Daniel Shays, a Revolutionary War veteran, led a group of discontented farmers in Western Massachusetts in uprisings over debt. The national government was unable to muster the power needed to put down the uprisings, reflecting the weaknesses of the Articles of Confederation.

Single-member districts A system, such as the one we have in the United States, where there can be only one winner in an election for president or a seat in Congress.

Slander A false and harmful spoken statement.

Social responsibility Governmental acts on behalf of the community that assist those in need.

Social Security New Deal-era program created to provide direct financial assistance to elderly and disabled persons.

Solicitor General Senior staff person in the Department of Justice; when the U.S. government is a party to a case, he or she plays a key role in determining which cases to appeal and how to shape appellate arguments.

Sovereignty Supreme power or authority, especially over a political or governmental body.

Speaker of the House The leader of the majority party in the House of Representatives. He or she is the most recognized and most powerful member of the House.

Special districts Local governmental units that typically provide a single service, ranging from flood control, cemeteries, transportation, fire, and air quality.

Staff agencies Agencies that indirectly serve the public by providing support and advice to line agencies.

Staggered elections Only one-third of the U.S. Senate is up for election every two years. Staggered elections help ensure stability and maintain a more deliberative legislative body that is less subject to the whims of opinion.

Standing committees Semipermanent bodies made up of members from both parties; each committee has its own policy jurisdiction.

Stare decisis Latin for "let the decision stand"; the process of deciding cases based largely on previous judicial decisions.

Strategic Defense Initiative (Star Wars) Proposed by President Ronald Reagan in 1983 during the Cold War, this was a plan to use ground- and space-based systems to protect the United States from a nuclear attack.

Strict scrutiny A presumption that laws infringing on fundamental rights or treating historically oppressed groups differently are unconstitutional, unless there are compelling reasons for upholding them.

Super Duper Tuesday The Tuesday in February during a presidential election year when an unprecedented twenty-three states hold their primaries simultaneously.

Swing voters Those voters who are thought to be undecided, less partisan, and more receptive to persuasion by political campaigns.

Tea Party movement A movement that first emerged in 2009 in opposition to the national healthcare reform proposal and that has chartered an alternate path for the nation along the core tenants of American conservatism: low taxes, small government, and less regulation.

Theocracy A form of government in which power resides in the hands of the religious leadership.

Think tanks Unofficial policy actors who influence the policy system through research and dissemination of information.

Third party Any political party that is not one of the two major parties.

Three-Fifths Compromise A compromise at the Constitutional Convention that determined, for the purpose of apportioning seats in the House of Representatives, each state's population was to be calculated using a formula that counted five slaves as three people.

Tillman Act Enacted in 1907, this was the first piece of legislation in the United States to prohibit monetary contributions to national campaigns by corporations.

Torrijos-Carter Treaty This treaty guaranteed that Panama would gain control of the Panama Canal after 1999, ending the control the United States had exercised in that area since 1903.

Totalitarianism A form of government in which the government exercises total power and is involved in nearly every facet of people's lives.

Tracking poll A survey that asks respondents a set of questions daily, reporting the averages of the latest three-day period.

Treaty A binding international agreement between two or more countries.

Treaty of Versailles The treaty that officially ended World War I and created the first state-centered international organization, the League of Nations.

Trial courts Most often the courts of original jurisdiction.

Trickle-down economics The idea that freeing up capital for the nation's wealthy would spur investment and ultimately create jobs for everyone.

Troubled Asset Relief Fund (TARP) A program that passed in 2008 in the waning months of President George W. Bush's administration, which injected roughly $700 billion into the American financial system to address the unfolding subprime mortgage crisis.

Trustee The role members of Congress serve in acting on behalf of the interests of the home constituents and nation regardless of whether constituents would immediately approve of the members' decisions.

Trusts A nineteenth-century name for monopolies; power and wealth are concentrated in corporations.

Two-party system A political system in which successful candidates for public office are nominees of one of two major parties.

Unanimous consent agreements Agreements that guide operation of the floor of the Senate. Floor leaders ask for consent, and if any Senator objects, action in the Senate can grind to a halt.

Unified government A situation in which the same party controls all popularly elected branches of the national government.

Unintended consequences Policy outcomes not foreseen or intentionally desired during the initial creation or implementation of the original public policy.

Unitary executive theory A theory that argues the president's wartime constitutional power as commander-in-chief supersedes the authority of other branches of government.

Unitary government Ultimate power is vested in a single national government.

Universal suffrage The right of all adult citizens to vote.

Unofficial actors Policy participants working "outside" the formal framework of government that exert significant influence on the policymaking process.

U.S. Court of Appeals for the Federal Circuit One of the thirteen courts of appeal in the United States. Unlike the other twelve, this appellate court has nationwide jurisdiction based on subject.

U.S. Courts of Appeal Courts at the middle tier of the three-tiered U.S. federal court system. These courts hear cases on appeal from the lower courts.

U.S. Supreme Court This court is the most powerful court in the nation. It hears appeals in less than 1 percent of the cases it is asked to review.

Veto (presidential veto) The power of a president to prevent a bill passed by both houses of Congress from becoming law. Presidential vetoes can only be overridden by a two-thirds vote of both chambers, which is rare.

Virginia Plan Proposal introduced at the Constitutional Convention that recommended a more powerful government to replace the Articles of Confederation.

Voter turnout The percentage of eligible voters who cast a ballot in a given election.

War Powers Act of 1973 (or War Powers Resolution) Law passed by Congress in the wake of the Vietnam War designed to curb the power of the president to unilaterally commit American troops and resources to international conflict.

Warrant A document issued by a court authorizing a search or arrest.

Ways and Means Committee One of the most powerful committees in the House of Representatives that deals with tax and entitlement laws.

Winner-take-all system The candidate who wins a particular state receives all of the state's Electoral College votes.

Writ of certiorari Latin term meaning "to be informed"; is issued by the U.S. Supreme Court to a lower court when agreeing to review the case coming from that lower court.

Zero-sum A situation in which one side's gain is the other side's loss.

Photo Credits

Chapter 1: National Archives and Records Administration

Chapter 2: Pattie Steib/Shutterstock

Chapter 3: Ron Sachs/CNP-PHOTOlink./Newscom

Chapter 4: Official White House Photo by Pete Souza

Chapter 5: ERIK S. LESSER/epa/Corbis

Chapter 6: Evan Vucci/AP Images

Chapter 7: Newscom

Chapter 8: ROBYN BECK/AFP/Getty Images/Newscom

Chapter 9: AP Photo/Charles Dharapak

Chapter 10: SAUL LOEB/AFP/Getty Images/Newscom

Chapter 11: ROOM 9 ENTERTAINMENT/TYFS PRODUCTIONS LLC/CONTENTFILM/Album/Newscom

Chapter 12: U.S. Air Force/AFLO/Newscom

Text Credits

Figure 3.2, pg. 65: House and Senate Party Means on Liberal-Conservative Dimension
By permission of Keith Poole.

Table 6.2, pg. 126: 2008 Caseload Comparison of Filings in Federal and State Courts
Reprinted by permission of the National Center for State Courts.

Table 6.3, pg. 137: U.S. District Court Appointees by Administration
Reprinted from Judicature, the journal of the American Judicature Society. Goldman, Sheldon, Sara Schlavoni, Elliot Slotnick, © 2009.

Figure 8.1, pg. 179: U.S. House and Senate Reelection Rates, 1998–2010
By permission of the Center for Responsive Politics (opensecrets.org).

Figure 8.2, pg. 180: Structure of a Modern Campaign
By permission of Rowman & Littlefield Publishers.

Table 8.2, pg. 178: Incumbent Advantage
By permission of the Center for Responsive Politics (opensecrets.org).

Table 10.1, pg. 227: Percent of Parents who Voted for the Same Presidential Candidate as Their Children Supported in the 2008 Election
By permission of CBS News Archives.

Figure 12.1, pg. 268: U.S. Troops Overseas 1950–2005 by Region
Kane, Tim, "Global U.S. Troop Deployment, 1950–2005," by permission of the Heritage Foundation, Center for Data Analysis Report 06-02, May 24, 2006.

Table 12.4, pg. 279: Amount of Money Donated by Various Organizations to Support Relief Efforts Following the 2004 Asian Tsunamis
By permission of the Chronicle of Philanthropy.

Index